Mastering Ethereum

Implement advanced blockchain applications using
Ethereum-supported tools, services, and protocols

Merunas Grincalaitis

BIRMINGHAM - MUMBAI

Mastering Ethereum

Commissioning Editor: Sunith Shetty
Acquisition Editor: Winston Christopher
Content Development Editor: Nathanya Dias
Technical Editor: Joseph Sunil
Copy Editor: Safis Editing
Project Coordinator: Kirti Pisat
Proofreader: Safis Editing
Indexer: Rekha Nair
Graphics: Jisha Chirayil
Production Coordinator: Aparna Bhagat

First published: April 2019

Production reference: 1250419

Published by Packt Publishing Ltd.
Livery Place
35 Livery Street
Birmingham
B3 2PB, UK.

ISBN 978-1-78953-137-4

www.packtpub.com

`mapt.io`

Mapt is an online digital library that gives you full access to over 5,000 books and videos, as well as industry leading tools to help you plan your personal development and advance your career. For more information, please visit our website.

Why subscribe?

- Spend less time learning and more time coding with practical eBooks and Videos from over 4,000 industry professionals

- Improve your learning with Skill Plans built especially for you

- Get a free eBook or video every month

- Mapt is fully searchable

- Copy and paste, print, and bookmark content

Packt.com

Did you know that Packt offers eBook versions of every book published, with PDF and ePub files available? You can upgrade to the eBook version at `www.packt.com` and as a print book customer, you are entitled to a discount on the eBook copy. Get in touch with us at `customercare@packtpub.com` for more details.

At `www.packt.com`, you can also read a collection of free technical articles, sign up for a range of free newsletters, and receive exclusive discounts and offers on Packt books and eBooks.

Contributors

About the author

Merunas Grincalaitis, born in Lithuania and based in Spain since he was 4, has worked with blockchain companies all around the world, helping them create ICOs, dApps, MVPs, technical whitepapers, web apps, and audits so that they improve the Ethereum ecosystem with decentralized solutions that return people's trust in themselves.

He created one of the first books about Ethereum development, named Ethereum Developer - Learn Solidity From Scratch, which sold a lot of copies worldwide, as a quick guide to provide a bridge for programmers interested in the world of Ethereum and smart contract programming.

Currently, he's working on providing free learning resources through his Medium blog to all developers looking for expert guidance.

About the reviewers

Narendranath Reddy is an experienced full-stack software engineer and Hyperledger Fabric expert with a proven track record of helping enterprises to build production-ready, blockchain-backed applications. He is an experienced innovator and a creative thinker. He has won four hackathons on blockchain and is a keynote speaker, regularly speaking about blockchain and distributed ledgers. He is currently working as a Hyperledger Fabric engineer at Consensys, Dubai, and previously worked as a blockchain developer at Blockgemini, Dubai, and a software developer at UST Global, Trivandrum, and Spain, Madrid.

Iqbal Singh is the CEO and founder of Immanent Solutions, a management consulting and blockchain solutions firm based in Chandigarh, India. He is also the chief blockchain architect for the Blockchain Solutions Asia 2018 conference. Iqbal possesses 15 years' extensive hands-on experience in blockchain, IT, IoT, AI, automation, and the RIA industry. Iqbal has provided business solutions for Bitcoin, Ethereum, Ripple, and R3's Corda blockchain platform. He heads 30 professional teams working in the fields of data science, algorithms, cryptography (SHA256, X11, and Script), blockchain, ICOs, Coin, ERC20, Exchange, BTC, and ETH Expert Architect.

Packt is searching for authors like you

If you're interested in becoming an author for Packt, please visit `authors.packtpub.com` and apply today. We have worked with thousands of developers and tech professionals, just like you, to help them share their insight with the global tech community. You can make a general application, apply for a specific hot topic that we are recruiting an author for, or submit your own idea.

Table of Contents

Preface

Ethereum is one of the most commonly used platforms for building blockchain applications. It's a decentralized platform for applications that can run exactly as programmed without being affected by fraud, censorship, or third-party interference.

This book will give you a deep understanding of how blockchains work so that you can discover the entire ecosystem, core components, and implementations. You will get started by learning how to configure and work with various Ethereum protocols for developing dApps. Next, you will learn how to code and create powerful smart contracts that scale with Solidity and Vyper. You will then explore the building blocks of dApps architecture and gain insights into creating your own dApp through a variety of real-world examples. The book will even explain how to deploy your apps on multiple Ethereum instances with the required best practices and techniques. The next few chapters will delve into advanced topics such as building advanced smart contracts and multi-page frontends using Ethereum. You will also learn how to implement machine learning techniques to build decentralized autonomous applications, in addition to several use cases across a variety of domains such as social media and e-commerce.

By the end of this book, you will have the expertise you need to build decentralized autonomous applications confidently.

Who this book is for

This book is for anyone who wants to build fast, highly secure, and transactional decentralized applications. If you are an Ethereum developer looking to perfect your existing skills in building powerful blockchain applications, then this book is for you. Basic knowledge of Ethereum and blockchain is necessary to understand the concepts covered in this book.

What this book covers

Chapter 1, *Blockchain Architecture*, covers basic blockchain knowledge, which is essential before starting to make sure we understand the requirements that will be used across the book. We will cover the history of Ethereum from the beginning and end up in more complicated topics regarding development.

Chapter 2, *Ethereum Ecosystems*, shows us the infrastructure and setup of a blockchain. We will conduct a deeper analysis on how blockchains work so that we understand the entire ecosystem. We will also learn about the Ethereum components and their various implementations.

Chapter 3, *Ethereum Assets*, shows us how to configure and work with various implementations of the Ethereum protocol before developing applications in it. There are several flavors, which can be used interchangeably for development, testing, and deployment. Later, we will look at the Modified Ghost implementation, computation, and Turing completeness to understand the Ethereum workflow better. It is also important to understand and use the tools and services in the Ethereum ecosystem.

Chapter 4, *Mastering Smart Contracts*, teaches us advanced smart contracts that go beyond normal use cases. It is useful because it will help us understand advanced techniques, methods, and tools to improve our Solidity and Vyper coding skills in order to create powerful smart contracts that scale.

Chapter 5, *Mastering dApps*, introduces you to the decentralized app (dApp) architecture and its building blocks. Then we will create one dApp step by step from scratch, from a blank application to writing smart contracts, creating crypto wallets, and unit testing them. We will show you how to create specialized UIs for these apps. We will also show you how to use other testing services, such as Truffle, to build seamless dApps. We will then show you how to deploy your apps on multiple Ethereum instances, such as testrpc, private chain, test chain, and main net.

Chapter 6, *Tools, Frameworks, Components, and Services*, introduces us to several important tools available for Ethereum developers to create powerful dApps and smart contracts that scale and that are secure enough to serve millions of potential users.

Chapter 7, *Deployment on Testnet*, shows us how to deploy our blockchain applications on testnet. Ethereum blockchain applications can be deployed on Rinkeby-testnet. Testnet provides test gathers, with which developers can test all smart contracts and the behavior of dApps. Gas calculation and other factors can be tested on testnet.

Chapter 8, *Various dApps Integrations*, moves ahead and shows you how to create more efficient dApps with workflows that will help us to develop code more quickly and safely. We will understand all the aspects related to decentralized web app development including web client code using React; backend code with Node.js, Solidity, or Vyper; and using web3.js for dApp communication.

Chapter 9, *Decentralized Exchanges Workflow*, shows you how to create complex **decentralized exchanges** (**DAXs**) by understanding the intricacies of such complex systems in an easy-to-assimilate language that covers each section in great detail.

Chapter 10, *Machine Learning on the Ethereum Blockchain*, uses the smart contract in blockchains to automatically validate the solution, so there will be no debate about whether the solution was correct or not. Users who submit the solutions won't have counterparty risk that they won't get paid for their work. Contracts can be created easily by anyone with a dataset, even programmatically by software agents.

Chapter 11, *Creating a Blockchain-Based Social Media Platform*, goes through the steps required to create a solid decentralized social media platform that uses Swarm for distributed storage of resources, such as videos, while leveraging the trustless nature of the blockchain to guarantee the privacy of each individual.

Chapter 12, *Creating a Blockchain-Based E-Commerce Marketplace*, goes through the steps required to set up a decentralized marketplace for buying, selling, renting, and exchanging goods, similar to OpenBazaar. We will be build a unique marketplace with scalability in mind.

Chapter 13, *Creating a Decentralized Bank and Lending Platform*, creates a decentralized bank that uses Ethereum for managing and storing crypto in a safe environment. We will use cold storage for added security and lending systems with collateral default protections in place. This is an online chapter and can be found at the following link: `https://www.packtpub.com/sites/default/files/downloads/Creating_a_Decentralized_Bank_and_Lending_Platform.pdf`.

To get the most out of this book

You need to have basic knowledge of what blockchains and Ethereum are.

Download the example code files

You can download the example code files for this book from your account at `www.packt.com`. If you purchased this book elsewhere, you can visit `www.packt.com/support` and register to have the files emailed directly to you.

You can download the code files by following these steps:

1. Log in or register at `www.packt.com`.
2. Select the **SUPPORT** tab.
3. Click on **Code Downloads & Errata**.
4. Enter the name of the book in the **Search** box and follow the onscreen instructions.

Once the file is downloaded, please make sure that you unzip or extract the folder using the latest version of:

- WinRAR/7-Zip for Windows
- Zipeg/iZip/UnRarX for Mac
- 7-Zip/PeaZip for Linux

The code bundle for the book is also hosted on GitHub at `https://github.com/PacktPublishing/Mastering-Ethereum`. In case there's an update to the code, it will be updated on the existing GitHub repository.

We also have other code bundles from our rich catalog of books and videos available at `https://github.com/PacktPublishing/`. Check them out!

Download the color images

We also provide a PDF file that has color images of the screenshots/diagrams used in this book. You can download it here: `http://www.packtpub.com/sites/default/files/downloads/9781789531374_ColorImages.pdf`.

Conventions used

There are a number of text conventions used throughout this book.

`CodeInText`: Indicates code words in text, database table names, folder names, filenames, file extensions, pathnames, dummy URLs, user input, and Twitter handles. Here is an example: "They use a library called `0x.js` that allows you to interact with relayers with a high-level, clean interface that feels great to use."

A block of code is set as follows:

```
pragma solidity 0.5.0;
contract Example {
    uint256 myStateVariable;
    string myOtherStateVariable;
    function example(){
        uint256 thisIsNotAStateVariable;
    }
}
```

When we wish to draw your attention to a particular part of a code block, the relevant lines or items are set in bold:

```
function example(string memory myText) public {
    require(bytes(myText)[0] != 0);
}
```

Any command-line input or output is written as follows:

```
$ git clone https://github.com/merlox/dapp
```

Bold: Indicates a new term, an important word, or words that you see onscreen. For example, words in menus or dialog boxes appear in the text like this. Here is an example: "Go to the **Droplets** sections and click on **Create Droplet**."

Warnings or important notes appear like this.

Tips and tricks appear like this.

Get in touch

Feedback from our readers is always welcome.

General feedback: If you have questions about any aspect of this book, mention the book title in the subject of your message and email us at customercare@packtpub.com.

Errata: Although we have taken every care to ensure the accuracy of our content, mistakes do happen. If you have found a mistake in this book, we would be grateful if you would report this to us. Please visit www.packt.com/submit-errata, selecting your book, clicking on the Errata Submission Form link, and entering the details.

Piracy: If you come across any illegal copies of our works in any form on the Internet, we would be grateful if you would provide us with the location address or website name. Please contact us at copyright@packt.com with a link to the material.

If you are interested in becoming an author: If there is a topic that you have expertise in and you are interested in either writing or contributing to a book, please visit authors.packtpub.com.

Reviews

Please leave a review. Once you have read and used this book, why not leave a review on the site that you purchased it from? Potential readers can then see and use your unbiased opinion to make purchase decisions, we at Packt can understand what you think about our products, and our authors can see your feedback on their book. Thank you!

For more information about Packt, please visit packt.com.

1
Section 1: Blockchain - Ethereum Refresher

In this section, you'll develop a solid understanding of how to program better smart contracts and dApps while reviewing assumptions to improve the psychology behind code.

The following chapters are included in this section:

- Chapter 1, *Blockchain Architecture*
- Chapter 2, *Ethereum Ecosystem*
- Chapter 3, *Ethereum Assets*

Blockchain Architecture 1

Blockchain architecture covers the fundamentals when it comes to understanding how the blockchain works internally. It is essential to be able to work on different projects that use different areas of Ethereum, because once you have a solid understanding about how everything works together, your mind will begin to see things differently. You will get a high-level overview of what happens in the blockchain when you use it and when you program for it. The moving parts of this complex ecosystem will begin to make so much sense once you go through this chapter, because you'll receive a high-level overview of how smart contracts work and how they are related to the underlying structure.

In this chapter, we will cover the following topics:

- Beyond Ethereum
- The EEA
- Understanding the Ethereum blockchain
- A high-level overview of how smart contracts work
- Essential smart contract programming

Beyond Ethereum

You probably understand what Ethereum is, but just to make sure that we are on the same page, it's important that you have some background knowledge about what Ethereum really is in order to progress further without too many distractions.

Explaining Ethereum

Ethereum is, first and foremost, a blockchain. Ethereum is a technology that runs on many computers and provides its consumers with a guarantee that they are trusting a solid system that will work as expected.

> *"Ethereum is the world computer."*
>
> *-Vitalik Buterin*

 To learn more about the core Ethereum ideas, check their official website: `https://ethereum.org`.

A web of thousands of computers connected all over the world are called **nodes** and they allow others to get the information they need while trusting the code with the goal of decentralizing the internet as we know it.

Why is decentralization so important for the internet? Because we have come to a point where a few big companies control the information that you and I can produce or consume.

Governments have so much power that they are getting out of control with their rules. They are biased toward what benefits them and their governors. And it's understandable—whenever some entity is at the top of the food chain, it is inevitable that they end up controlling the entire system below it sooner or later.

Ethereum's goal is to create a censorship-resistant and open platform that allows people to trust smart contracts that enforce rules that cannot be controlled by third-party entities.

When you publish a smart contract, you have a 100% guarantee that the code will run at any point and nobody will be able to interfere with it, unless the rules of it say so.

Ethereum's history

Ethereum was described in Vitalik Buterin's 2013 whitepaper, which can be found at: `https://github.com/ethereum/wiki/wiki/White-Paper`. He talked about the need of a scripting language that would run on top of Bitcoin, since he was involved in *Bitcoin Magazine* and he understood the limitations of the Bitcoin blockchain.

He saw an opportunity to create a platform that would run on decentralized technology to create new types of applications.

Not many believed in his vision, so he decided to create an entire new blockchain by himself with a small team that saw the potential in Vitalik's ideas. He founded the Ethereum Switzerland group and decided to run an **Initial Coin Offering** (**ICO**) in July 2014, where he sold Ether in exchange for Bitcoin, raising a total of about $18 million dollars.

He created the smart contracts technology, which is basically programs that run by themselves without requiring a trusted entity to execute them. They are always available, and they run without failure.

The fact that Ethereum provided a system that allows people to create their own applications on top of a blockchain is what made it successful. Before Ethereum, there was no simple way to create **decentralized applications** (**dApps**) in a decentralized platform. Bitcoin has a protocol to create simple applications using opcodes with a programming language called Script, but it's not capable of much since it is very low level and it's limited by the block size.

Ethereum's development

The development of Ethereum was planned to be done in four different stages, with major changes in each one:

- Frontier
- Homestead
- Metropolis
- Serenity

It was used to deliver and research innovative solutions as they were required, with a hard fork for functionality that is not backward compatible. In 2015, Frontier was launched as the first version of Ethereum. A year later, Homestead was launched, which included many improvements and made Ethereum a capable system with enough power to process smart contracts.

One of the biggest ICOs conducted on top of Ethereum was the decentralized autonomous organization ICO, also known as **the DAO,** which raised $150 million dollars with contributions from more than 11,000 people. The problem is that it got hacked by an unknown group of individuals that moved the funds to a different DAO. Interestingly enough, a group of programmers known as **the White Hat Group** saw the hack happening and extracted as many funds as possible into a separate decentralized organization known as the **White Hat DAO**, where they stored people's money to distribute them later.

This event originated a heated debate in the community that caused Ethereum to be divided in two groups, where some believed in the fact that Ethereum must be immutable and shouldn't be modified, while others believed in a hard fork to revert the damage done.

That was the beginning of Ethereum Classic and Ethereum as we know it. Ethereum Classic has a noticeable smaller user base, but it preserves the initial immutability ideals that they consider essential for a blockchain. In March 2017, several companies joined efforts to create the **Ethereum Enterprise Alliance** (**EEA**), which is currently a non-profit organization made of more than 500 members whose goal is as follows:

"To create open-source, standards-based blockchain specifications."

-Ethereum Enterprise Alliance

In other words, they created a group of people collaborating on solutions for future blockchains to come, so that they are better, faster, and more capable.

It suffered from several hacks, where millions of dollars were stolen. They had to do a hard fork to save people's funds and have a notorious price volatility, but the future looks bright and it continues, improve as demand increases.

The EEA

The **EEA** (entethalliance.org) is one of the most exciting projects being developed by the core Ethereum team, because they intend to help companies from all over the world to benefit from decentralized technology. By learning about this project, you'll be well positioned when it comes to working as an EEA expert.

In this section, we will cover the following topics:

- The EEA's vision
- The EEA membership
- The EEA architecture

Vitalik funded the organization because he received a huge demand from executives to create software that could be used in big companies to handle demanding dApps. Those companies now want to build a private version of Ethereum to fulfill their research and development needs.

What's interesting about this initiative is that they work with hundreds of companies to research and develop solutions that are shared across them. For instance, if a company member of the EEA creates a new implementation protocol for better and faster dApps, they will share it with the other members so that they can also benefit from this cutting-edge research, while together growing the Ethereum ecosystem.

The EEA's vision

The EEA's four big public goals that they envision they will achieve in the longer term are as follows:

- **Be an open source standard, not a product**:

  They only work with open source code that can be shared with anybody publicly without restrictions in order to spread development advances that may or may not help others improve their blockchain products. You see, they are a non-profit organization that wants to move blockchain (as we know it) further by combining the efforts of many companies interested in private blockchain solutions.

- **Address enterprise development requirements**:

  The EEA helps companies incorporate the new innovations that are being discovered by others for free, so that they can enjoy the benefits of the latest requirements.

- **Share improvements between public and private Ethereum**:

  They want to improve what they are building by taking improvements from the public blockchain so that they can evolve faster while keeping a great product in mind.

- **Leverage existing standards**:

  When it comes to the blockchain technology, much is left to research and discover. Many problems regarding scalability, security, and transparency are being studied, since this type of decentralized structure is new to modern computing. So, the idea is to learn from existing standards, such as **proof-of-stake (PoS)**, to improve faster than anyone else.

In essence, they are trying to fulfill the demands that many companies are making regarding private enterprise and fast blockchains for their personal applications.

The EEA membership

What's interesting about the EEA is that any company is free to join by just filling a form on their website to become a member of the group for a yearly cost. This openness helps many individuals stay relevant with the new improvements on the Ethereum blockchain.

Here's the breakdown in yearly costs to become a member:

- Less than 50 employees: $3,000 per year
- Between 51 and 500 employees: $10,000 per year
- Between 501 and 5,000 employees: $15,000 per year
- More than 5,000 employees: $25,000 per year

Non-profit organizations only pay $3,000 dollars per year, regardless of company size. By becoming a member of the Alliance, you can enjoy a series of general benefits, such as being able to participate in discussions, voting, open source code, meetups, and the prestige that you get from having the EEA logo in your website. As a big blockchain company, it makes sense to become a member just for the reputation that you'll get by becoming a member with the EEA logo on your website.

The benefits depend on the type of company you are in, and you can see them in the following section:

- Class A members are the directors that run the companies associated with the Alliance. They have priorities when reaching decisions and have access to all the benefits.
- Class B members are those that have a normal company, so they get standard benefits without exclusiveness.

- Class C members are lawyers and legal firms that are in charge of the legal challenges when it comes to the research done in the EEA.
- Class D members are non-profit companies and academic institutions. They get basic benefits for the lowest price without voting rights.

The EEA has a powerful pool of about 500 companies, including giants such as Intel, Microsoft, and J.P. Morgan. If you run a decent-sized company, you may be interested in becoming a member of the EEA just to be a part of this revolution when it comes to enterprise blockchains.

The EEA architecture

The enterprise grade applications built with EEA's tools have a very interesting structure that builds on top of the existing Ethereum structure. They developed the **Enterprise Ethereum Architecture Stack** (**EEAS**), which is a design that specifies how this new type of Ethereum blockchain should work in a private setting, with features designed for privacy. The team working on the Ethereum Enterprise project details functions of this type of private blockchain without regard to the underlying technology below it, such as software code, APIs, and communication protocols. What the EEA intends to do is focus on creating what's described in their specification so that people can enjoy private blockchains for their companies.

The tooling will benefit from innovative solutions exclusive to the Enterprise Ethereum blockchain, such as the following:

- **Hardware security module** (**HSM**): This is a physical computing device that safely stores digital keys, such as your private cryptocurrency keys, with maximum security features. For instance, Ledger and Trezor are hardware wallets that are also called HSMs, because they provide security in a physical device for your blockchain private keys.
- **Permissioning and authentication**: This is useful in order to give users specific roles with limited access to certain areas in a more structured fashion.
- **Enterprise management systems**: This is used to help companies control their private blockchain internal workings.
- **Oracles**: These are helpful for communicating with external services for custom smart contracts written on top of the enterprise private blockchain. They are essential to exchange key information with the outer world.

Regarding privacy and scaling, we know that many different teams are working on creating unique solutions that could benefit the entire community. However, we know that, initially, the blockchain will use two main systems to scale the capacity of existing dApps:

- **Off-chain transactions with trusted execution**: Protocols such as plasma and state channels are being developed to leverage off-chain transactions that can be executed locally by users' computers to reduce the computing load of the main blockchain.
- **Private transactions**: Transactions that use zero-knowledge proofs, ring signatures, and many other famous protocols to guarantee the privacy of the data being exchanged with the public blockchain. This is an important aspect that companies demand because they have private data and internal processes that can't be shared publicly. We cannot know which solution they will choose, so it's up to them to decide. They will also implement private code execution that will allow companies to execute certain smart contract transactions in a secure environment, where the users will see an encoded hash.

The EEA is building three additional elements on top of the existing core blockchain:

- **On-chain private state**: This is a separate storage compartment where they will store private states of smart contracts. It will provide us, the developers, truly private variables and store functions that we'll be able to use for keeping information secure and unseen by the public. It's very powerful for enterprise-grade dApps.
- **Trusted execution**: These are systems that will provide a trusted execution environment where the code will be executed without interfering with public processes.
- **Private consensus**: Companies will have the ability to reach agreements using their own private blockchain for their own systems, similar to voting systems that we can see in the *Decentralized autonomous organizations* section in: `Chapter 3`, *Ethereum Assets*.

Lastly, the blockchain network layer will benefit from Enterprise P2P, which will be used to exchange transactions in smaller networks of nodes that are set up by the company, so that they enjoy the benefits of faster processing speeds and confirmation times. Enterprise blockchains will be able to interact with other networks, including the public blockchain to exchange information.

Understanding the Ethereum blockchain

The Ethereum blockchain is a complex system made of several important components that work together to achieve an impressive platform that everybody can use to create unstoppable applications. You'll learn the intricacies of the internal workings of the blockchain to gain a greater understanding about how it's made.

The reasoning behind a decentralized blockchain

At the most basic level, the Ethereum blockchain is a set of connected blocks that contain information that many nodes share so that there's an unchangeable data structure to keep information permanently. The goal of any blockchain is to preserve information without the possibility of changing it or deleting it to avoid censorship or manipulation by external entities.

As such, the Ethereum blockchain builds upon that concept by implementing several well-known tools, thanks to Bitcoin and previous research to create programs that run on top of those blocks.

To understand how the Ethereum blockchain works internally, we have to understand each component that makes up a blockchain. First, I'll give you a high-level overview of the blockchain as a set of nodes, and then we'll go through each component from higher to lower levels in the pyramid that makes the blockchain.

The blockchain as a set of nodes

Ethereum is a decentralized platform, which means that two or more nodes work together in a coordinated fashion to achieve a common outcome in a way that the end user sees as a single operation. A node performs various types of functions depending on the role it decides to take. It can propose and validate transactions with mining software to achieve consensus while securing the blockchain using the **proof-of-work** (**PoW**) protocol or be a light-weight node that performs payment verification and many other tasks that can be done with limited resources.

The Ethereum blockchain is based on Bitcoin, since the system created by Satoshi Nakamoto is a very robust decentralized solution. In fact, it uses a system to execute decentralized code using opcodes that can process basic instructions on top of a network of hundreds of thousands of computers in a safe manner. They must be simple to preserve security above all.

Although both blockchains are quite similar in their systems, they have noticeable differences, such as the following:

- Bitcoin and Ethereum use PoW to generate blocks, while Ethereum intends to move to PoS as the block generation system in the future to avoid wasting computational power.
- Ethereum uses the Ethash algorithm, while Bitcoin uses SHA256 for processing transactions and generating blocks.
- Ethereum's block time is about 15 seconds, which is about 100 times faster than Bitcoin's. This gives people better confirmation times.

The Ethereum blockchain is decentralized and distributed, which means that the connected nodes have several relationships with each other independently, while running the same software at different locations. This is very important to guarantee the unstoppable aspect of the blockchain. Here what each term means:

- **Decentralized network**: This is a network of computers running without a single point of control, no entity controls the entire system, and each node is connected to other nodes directly in a **peer-to-peer** (**P2P**) relationship. If the blockchain wasn't decentralized, some government or entity could locate the main controller node and stop the entire system immediately.
- **Distributed network**: This is a network where many different computers run on different locations with the same software. If the blockchain wasn't distributed, some entity could go to where all the nodes are located and stop the entire operation because they are all in the same place, so none are safe from such an attack.

You can see in the following diagram how the structure of these types of technologies connect nodes together so that they can communicate with complete security, in their own way, since it's often a confusing point when trying to understand the differences between distributed and decentralized systems:

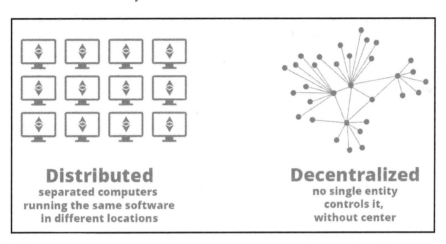

Distributed
separated computers
running the same software
in different locations

Decentralized
no single entity
controls it,
without center

Those two characteristics give the Ethereum network the capacity to work without having to rely on anybody, because thousands of nodes are able to communicate between each other in a secured and independent fashion. Notice that Ethereum is a completely open blockchain, meaning that anybody is free to join and participate in the decisions that take place, such as block creation and transaction processing. It allows people to join the network of nodes as a participant without any requirements, since the entire structure is secured by cryptographically-safe algorithms.

Nodes can work together or become malicious by executing unexpected code. Those that exhibit arbitrary behavior are known as **Byzantine nodes**. The main goal is to create a system where nodes cooperate even in the worst situations, with fault-tolerance protections in place to avoid breaking the entire structure. But how do they work together if the nodes making the blockchain can behave randomly because they are Byzantine nodes?

At the end of the day, it's a group of computers working voluntarily toward the same objective. Nothing stops them from doing unexpected actions. That's where one of the most interesting problems that blockchain is facing lies. There are several solutions, but research is still being done to obtain a perfect balance between performance and security in a decentralized system.

The CAP theorem

The CAP theorem, introduced originally by Eric Brewer in 1998, states that any distributed system cannot have all three of these properties simultaneously:

- **Consistency**: This is a capability of the network of nodes to keep a consistent copy of the blockchain data in their computers at the same time.
- **Availability**: This means that the system of connected nodes is online and available at all times while being accessible by all users to respond to requests without failure when required to do so.
- **Partition tolerance**: If a group of nodes of the entire network stops working or loses connection for any reason, the system should not be affected, and it should continue working properly as if nothing happened.

It has been proven that a distributed or decentralized system cannot have all three of these properties at the same time, which is interesting because Ethereum, just like Bitcoin, achieves all of them at what appears to be the same time. The truth is that consistency is not achieved at the same time as partition tolerance and availability, but at a later time. You see, in order to have order in such a diverse variety of computers, we can only hope to achieve the same level of data over time whenever the blockchain grows at an established pace. It lags behind the others. This is called **eventual consistency**, where the goal is achieved as a result of validating multiple nodes over time. For this reason, the concept of mining was introduced in Bitcoin and Ethereum to agree on a consensus with the PoW protocol.

Eventually, Ethereum plans to move to PoS, which consists of the idea that a node or user maintains a stake, a certain number of Ether or any type of valuable investment in the system, so that the negative consequences of any malicious activity would outweigh the benefits of attacking the network.

For instance, if I want to become a miner to earn some Ether in exchange for my time and resources, I have to lock 100 Ether in a smart contract that runs the PoS protocol. If I decide to validate invalid blocks or transactions, and someone notices my malicious behavior via several security mechanisms, I would lose all those 100 Ether and wouldn't be able to attack again. The reward for processing a block successfully would be a percentage of the resources invested, for example, 0.1 ETH. This forces nodes to cooperate and act responsibly to avoid losing a big stake, even if they agree to attack the system.

Alternatively, **delegated proof-of-stake** (**DPoS**) could be used in later versions of Ethereum. It consists of delegating the validation of a transaction to other nodes by voting. It is used in the BitShares blockchain.

Introducing the Ethereum Virtual Machine

The **Ethereum Virtual Machine** (EVM) is a virtual machine that allows code to be executed with limitations regarding gas costs and price, where each individual interacting with it must pay a fee to protect the network from spamming attacks, so that many decentralized nodes can interact with each other using the same software. It processes bytecode that gets generated with assembly code, which, in turn, uses instruction called **operational codes** (**opcodes**). It's a **Turing complete** computer.

When I say Turing complete, I mean that the smart contract programming languages running on top of Ethereum have the following properties:

- They have unlimited access to **random access memory** (**RAM**)
- They can make decisions based on the information available in memory
- They can run forever with the help of `while`, `for`, and `recursive` loops
- They can use functions

What this means, is that smart contracts are capable of executing any operation that you give them, given enough time and resources. This is important to understand to avoid confusions when someone says that Ethereum is a Turing complete blockchain.

Introducing the state machine

The state machine is a mechanism that keeps track of the state changes that occur on the blockchain. For instance, a normal day has two simple states, either day or night. A state machine would record the situation of each day at every moment so that when the sun goes down, the state of the day changes to night. It is the same thing with the days of the week. Each day can be one out of seven different states, such as Monday or Friday. Whenever it changes at 12 am, the state that keeps track of the day of the week gets updated in the state machine.

The state machine enforces consensus rules to make sure that users are processing valid transactions in a Byzantine resistant system:

- **A P2P network**: It connects the participants and propagates the transactions and blocks of verified transactions. This is the network used by the nodes of the blockchain to propagate information between them to achieve consensus.

- **An incentivization scheme**: In the case of Ethereum, that scheme is PoW for creating an economically secure state machine. Ethereum developers plan to move to a PoS system where the users will process transactions using a passive system of transaction verification based on the number of ETH that the miner locks at that moment.
- **An open source client**: This client is the one used by the nodes to interact with the blockchain. In Ethereum, we have Geth, Parity, and many others that allow you to connect to the blockchain for mining and processing transactions and all sorts of tasks after downloading the blockchain.

> You can download a light version of the blockchain by downloading the client Geth and running `geth --fast`, which only keeps track of the reference numbers of each block to limit the download size of the blockchain, since it can reach several hundreds of gigabytes. The purpose of the light client is to make the Ethereum blockchain available for low-spec computers with limited storage and computing power.

The P2P network

The blockchain runs on top of a P2P network, where nodes are connected to each other to exchange data and state updates. Because of this technology, we are able to interact directly with other computers in order to process orders so that we all agree on the block generation system. It allows miners to be rewarded for completing PoW challenges.

Consensus rules

When we say consensus, we talk about a group of techniques used in systems with many participants to agree on decisions that benefit the whole underlying system. While voting gives the power to decide to a few selected individuals that fulfill a set of requirements, consensus takes in consideration each and every one of the participants to agree on the global way of thinking.

Each algorithm that implements any form of consensus when it comes to blockchain technology must provide the following features:

- **To agree on decisions that benefit the whole system**: The idea is to take choices that not only benefit the individual, but the entire network, so that everybody has a better platform.

- **To allow open participation**: Every person should be completely free to join and make decisions that they believe will be positive.
- **To be secure enough so that malicious actors can't prejudice the system**: All the consensus agreements have to be toward the betterment of the systems, where malicious users can't have enough power to decide for many others.

The problem with reaching consensus started with what's known as the **Byzantine Generals Problem**, a problem that consists on the fact that many computers can't easily agree on a predetermined order. Some computers will receive the order late, others will ignore it because they don't benefit from fulfilling it, while others will follow the order as best as they can.

In essence, consensus rules are mandatory to achieve a global state that all agree with, while being rewarded for participating in a beneficial manner in the decision-making process.

Proof-of-work

This is a method to guarantee that the result of a task was hard to achieve. Why do we want to make processing tasks difficult? To reward those that are best at completing it. In a blockchain, it costs processing power, which is just hardware, energy, and time, to process transactions made by individuals using the network. It is used to generate blocks in a simple process:

- The miner proposes a new block that contains a hash number made of the header of the most recent block and the nonce counter.
- Then, the miner compares the hash to the target value which is determined by the mining difficulty.
- If the hash is of the target difficulty, the user gets rewarded with the solution by getting ETH. If not, the nonce gets incremented until a hash is generated with the desired solution.

Since the miner will be competing with many others, there must be a system to make sure that the block times are consistent, because we want to keep generating blocks with the same periodicity even when new nodes join the mining network. To guarantee similar block times, the mining difficulty was created.

Proof-of-stake

PoS is a new algorithm to reach consensus between nodes in a decentralized blockchain that focuses on removing the high computing performance requirements from PoW while still keeping the network safe from attacks and malicious behavior. The way it works is based on locking Ether as a stake and validating blocks with the risk of losing your stake if you misbehave. Here's the process:

- People that want to participate in the PoS process are called **validators**. They start by locking a specific number of coins as their stake (for instance, 100 Ether) that they can't touch while they are mining. It should be expensive enough to guarantee that groups of people don't agree on attacking the system with the risk of losing their stake if they're unsuccessful.
- Then, they start receiving transactions from people using the Ethereum blockchain. Validators run programs to validate that the transactions they are receiving are valid so that they can create new blocks by grouping transactions in order. When they have enough transactions to cover the gas limit per block, they place bets on those blocks – for instance, 20 Ether from the initial 100 Ether staked.
- The block with the most bets is selected as the winner.
- When the winning block is selected from the pool of generated blocks, the miners that bet on that valid block get a percentage of the total gas used in that block based on their bets. They are not paid in block rewards but in transaction fees. For instance, if the block selected has 100 transactions accumulating a total of 0.5 Ether in transaction costs, that 0.5 Ether will have to be distributed between all the validators that bet on that block. If that block has a sum bet of 1,000 Ether from 10 users and you bet 20 ether, you'd get a 2% of 0.5 Ether, since that's how much you bet for that block. In total, you'd earn 0.01 Ether.

You don't lose any money when betting for blocks, it's just an indicator of how much you trust the validity of that block. It may seem a small reward considering that there aren't block rewards, just fees, but you must consider that these blocks are being generated in a matter of seconds. Maybe even one second per block, which ends up generating a lot of money over the day.

It looks great in theory, but there's a major roadblock that's stopping PoS from being completely viable. It's called the **Nothing at Stake** problem and is shown in the following scenario, where there is a main chain and a new chain being created with PoS:

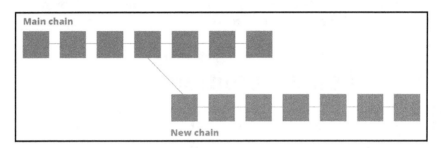

When it comes to PoW, you can mine on any fork that you desire without any risk, since you can place bets on every block that looks good to you. What's stopping you from deciding to put all your eggs in a new chain, thus generating a hard fork?

If we were using PoW, you couldn't move to a new chain without having to spend lots of processing power and time generating new blocks for as long as people decide to accept it as a new blockchain. You'd be mining for many months with a very slim chance of creating a new chain that could be accepted as a new coin, worth much less money because of its reduced use.

But with PoS, you can simply diversify your portfolio and bet on all the blocks that look appealing without consequences, since you won't be losing your stake as long as you're validating good transactions. You'd be generating blocks on several different blockchains without risks. This kind of possibility could end up creating hundreds of different blockchains, since people could be mining on all of them simultaneously. That's why it's called the **Nothing at Stake** problem, because you don't lose anything when participating in the mining process.

This is one of the main reasons why Ethereum has been unable to switch fully to PoS in recent times.

Researchers at Ethereum have been working on solving this problem for a long time. One of the proposals, known as **Casper**, intends to solve it by punishing users that mine on new chains mindlessly by taking their stake out of them, so that users focus on betting for the longest chain. Casper also punishes nodes that don't actively participate on the network so that they don't start consuming resources without providing value.

At the end of the day, PoW has to improve or change completely to become sustainable, given that many large mining pools are starting to gain too much power. We are at a point where four mining companies can achieve about 60% of the total transaction power, giving them the choice to run a 51% attack and force all users to mine on their own terms with their own corrupted blockchains. PoS is here to stay and bring balance back once again.

Workings of smart contracts

Smart contracts are blockchain applications that can execute code and do a diverse variety of tasks. These are programs that the miners execute when mining blocks. They are secure and unstoppable agreements that are automatically executed and enforced. You are probably familiar with them, since this book is aimed at Ethereum developers; however, if you don't know how to use them or if you want to learn more about them, you can rest assured that you'll understand everything because of detailed explanations that you'll be given at the appropriate times.

Unlike traditional paper contracts, smart contracts don't have real-world legal consequences on Ethereum, and they can't be enforced by a legal entity when they break. Instead, they rely on the principle that code is law, which means that the code is the one governing the behaviors of the contract. You can't execute functions that are not defined in the smart contract and you must respect each function's requirements.

What's interesting about smart contracts is that they allow the creation of unstoppable applications that will keep the data and functionalities running on top of the blockchain regardless of whether the underlying web interface is not available or is censured for whatever reasons. Smart contracts open the world to a new type of application that you can deploy and forget, knowing that it will work under any circumstances.

There's an ongoing debate about whether the code is acceptable as a real contract in a court of law. One side thinks that smart contracts have to go further and be enforced legally for a more general view of applications, while the other side thinks that the code as law is enough to guarantee the security and enforcement of the agreements.

Smart contracts are programs that run on top of the blockchain in the software layer. They allow developers to create decentralized trustless programs that have certain functions for managing transactions between individuals. Instead of relying on a centralized server, they are the database and the server in decentralized applications.

Inherently, smart contracts must be limited in their capacity given that we are executing code that will stay as a transaction on the blockchain permanently, meaning that every function you execute gets registered in the blockchain without having the option to undo what's been done. This imposes some natural limitations, since you can't just modify the public database that every node of the Ethereum will have to download without some restrictions. Every change has to be downloaded by all the peers of the network.

The purpose of them is to solve the trust problem that many companies are facing when dealing with voting, banking, and situations where people are expected to blindly trust companies without disclosing what they do with your data and money. They also provide accessibility, since anybody with an internet connection will be able to access them and retrieve the data stored inside.

However, smart contracts are limited in what they can do. They are not a great solution for many cases, such as the following:

- Applications that require a performing backend that is able to process information at a rapid pace, such as creating users and interacting with an application. They are slow by nature, since they depend on the block times of Ethereum and they cannot work in real-time situations.
- Applications that store large amounts of data on a database. Smart contracts work like a database, since they allow anybody to store certain information on top of the blockchain, but they are limited and it's costly to do so.

Gas is another concept that is important to understand properly. It was created because smart contracts are Turing complete, which means that they can execute loops such as `while` or `for` endlessly until a task is done. It could happen that developers create endless loops that are stuck in the same state forever. To avoid a situation where thousands of nodes are stuck processing one transaction with no limit, each transaction has a gas cost that depends on the processing power required to execute it.

So, they created a system where you have to pay for every action you take using the blockchain. You can store information on the blockchain, but you'll have to pay an important cost, because every single node using it will have to download your changes. The way it calculates the gas cost is simple:

1. You pay a certain maximum gas that you're willing to spend for your transaction.
2. Your local Ethereum node calculates how much it will cost to execute your transaction by checking the opcodes used to generate a precise approximation of the computing power needed. You see, every small operation using the blockchain can be measured because we use a sort of assembly language that tells us when this super computer is being used and how.
3. The right amount of gas is used, and the rest is refunded to you.

You also have to determine a gas price ranging from 1 to usually 100 or more to tell miners which transactions to process first, since they get paid more the more expensive each gas is.

Smart contract deployment process

Smart contracts run on top of the Ethereum blockchain in a similar way to how a server-side web application works. However, the process of deploying a smart contract to it is vastly different. In order to be an expert Ethereum developer, you must understand how the smart contract code is processed and stored in the blockchain blocks for you to be able to use them, because it will give you an understanding of why and how things can go wrong when pushing your newly written smart contract code.

It's not uncommon to receive errors when trying to deploy your code to the blockchain, so to be able to debug it successfully, you need to understand what happens under the hood.

Ethereum transactions

To understand how smart contracts are deployed on the network, it's important to understand first how transactions work, since when you deploy a smart contract, what you're actually doing is generating a transaction with the bytecode of the application that you just built.

The message that makes up a transaction on Ethereum is made up of the following encoded components:

- **Recipient**: This is the receiver Ethereum address that will get the transaction.
- **Value**: This represents the amount of ether to transfer to the recipient address. This value can be zero, and you can access it in Solidity with the global `msg.value` variable. The value is always in **wei**, the smallest unit in Ethereum.
- **Data**: This is a hexadecimal bytecode string that is mostly used to call a specific function with the required parameters. This is specific information that you need your smart contract to execute. When smart contracts communicate with each other, they need a way to tell when to execute a specific function with a given set of variables. Thanks to this data parameter, we can encode the functions that we want to call in the contract when the transaction is processed. On the other hand, when the smart contract is deployed to the blockchain for the first time, the data parameter contains the smart contract converted to bytecode so that machines can understand it. In general, it contains the smart contract functions to be executed in the next block by the miners.
- **Gas limit**: This represents the gas limit, which is how much gas you're willing to spend to process your function transactions. The gas limit is represented in wei, and it's mandatory to give miners as much gas as possible to process your code.
- **Gas price**: The gas price determines how much each gas you provide will cost. If your gas cost is one, you'll pay one wei per gas. If it's 20, you'll pay 20 wei per 1 gas. It's used to help miners process the transactions, since they will be rewarded partially with the transaction fees.
- **Nonce**: The nonce is a unique counter number that is used to identify transactions. This unique counter is used to identify each block, and it helps miners to identify invalid blocks, since the nonce must always be one number bigger than the previous block.
- **Signature**: This is a parameter made of three independent variables known as v, r, and s. These variables are used to sign transactions with your unique Ethereum address data so that people can confirm that you're the one that created it.

When a user makes a transaction to a smart contract, it's called a **message** instead of a transaction. This difference between transaction and message exists, because messages don't have signature data since they don't have to be signed by the other party. The nonce is required to prevent replay attacks where an external user could take the same transaction data and execute it again for his own benefit.

When you deploy a smart contract, you're actually sending a transaction to the address 0x0 with a special bytecode identifier, so that miners understand that you're creating a new smart contract. The data parameter in this case contains all the smart contract logic, including function names and parameters.

In summary, creating and working with smart contracts is a transparent process, where you tell miners to process your data. They will then understand the bytecode behind it and make the required changes to the blockchain with the needed parameters.

Essential smart contract programming

After understanding how smart contracts are created and where they integrate in the blockchain system, you will now get a more practical insight about how to create smart contracts using the two most popular languages for it—**Solidity** and **Vyper**.

Solidity

Solidity is the most advanced programming language created for developing smart contracts on the Ethereum network. Its syntax is similar to JavaScript, but with statically typed variables and functions. It provides simple features, such as functions, loops, and several types of variables, as well as complex functions, such as assembly, encryption functions, and signature verification systems.

It's been used in many projects, especially ICOs, with great success, so it's mature enough to be used by any kind of developer interested in developing decentralized applications and secure smart contracts.

The main drawback of it is that it's harder to secure, given that it provides a more complete set of features that could lead to security issues if not audited.

File structure

We'll use the 0.5.0 version of Solidity for all the examples in this book. A smart contract in Solidity always starts with the version that is used in the file to ensure that the contract is not compatible with newer versions that could break the contract because of newly added functionalities.

Let's look at the structure of a contract in Solidity using the following steps:

1. You define the version at the beginning of the file with the `pragma` statement:

```
pragma solidity 0.5.0;
```

2. Then you can start writing your contracts. All statements in Solidity must end with a semicolon (;) to be valid. After defining the version used in the file, you have to create the contracts, as shown here:

```
pragma solidity 0.5.0;
contract Example {}
```

3. You can define multiple contracts in one single file:

```
pragma solidity 0.5.0;
contract Example {}
contract Another {}
contract Token {}
contract ICO {}
```

4. Inside the contract, you'll have state variables, functions, modifiers, and a single constructor. I'll explain later how they are used in detail:

```
pragma solidity 0.5.0;
contract Example {
    uint256 counter;
    modifier onlyOwner {}
    constructor() {}
    function doSomething() {}
}
```

5. The variables that are defined directly in the contract, meaning that they are outside functions, are called **state variables**. These are special variables that store their value even after executing the contract. Think of them as special permanent variables that you can always read and modify:

```
pragma solidity 0.5.0;
contract Example {
    uint256 myStateVariable;
    string myOtherStateVariable;
    function example(){
        uint256 thisIsNotAStateVariable;
    }
}
```

As you can see, they are outside functions but inside the contract, and they are defined at the top of the file, right when the contract begins. As I said, they keep their value forever, even after making changes to your contract. So, if your `myStateVariable` has a value of `5`, you'll be able to read the value of that variable days or months after it has been modified, as long as you don't modify it.

They store their value directly on the blockchain storage, not in memory. In-memory variables, as you'll learn later, lose their value and are reset after the contract execution.

Finally, Solidity files use the `.sol` extension, for instance, `example.sol`. You will learn how to deploy them with the **Remix IDE** and `Truffle` in `Chapter 3`, *Mastering Smart Contracts*, and `Chapter 9`, *Decentralized Exchanged Workflow*.

Variables

Solidity is a statically typed language, which means that you have to define the type of every variable that you create.

Let's define the types of variables available in this programming language to later understand how to use them, but before that, you need to understand the visibility of variables.

Visibility of variables

Every variable and function in Solidity has a specific visibility. The visibility is a keyword you use after the variable type to define who should have access to it:

- **Public**: This means that the variable can be read or written by any contract, including external ones, as long as there's a function to update them.
- **Private**: Private variables can't be accessed by a derived smart contract, those that implement your contract with the `is` keyword; for example, `contract Example is Another {}`, where `Another` is a smart contract with private variables that can't be accessed by `Example`.
- **External**: These variables and functions are not accessible by the contract containing them. Only external contracts and users can use them.
- **Internal**: These are variables and functions that can't be read or written by external entities, only by the contract itself or by inherited contracts, as you saw in the example for the private variable.

To keep things simple, I recommend you to always write `public` for your variables unless it's a special variable, which doesn't happen that often. If you don't define any visibility, the variable will be `public` by default, although it's better to just write the `public` keyword in every variable to make sure that you understand the visibility of the variable and it's not a mistake.

Uints

Uints are unsigned integers, which means that they are numbers starting from zero that can't be negative.

You define them as follows:

```
uint public myNumber;
```

As you can see, you first define the type of the variable, then the visibility, and then the name of the variable. Remember that if you don't define the visibility of the variable, the variable will be `public`.

Uints can be of the following types:

- `uint8`
- `uint16`
- `uint24`
- `uint32`
- `uint64`
- `uint128`
- `uint256`

The number for each variable means the size of the `uint`. A `uint8` type of variable will be able to store up to 256. So, the maximum variable of a `uint8` variable is `256`. If you want to store the number 255, the variable will work properly, but, if you want to store the number `256` as follows, then the variable will overflow, and it will reset to zero instead of `256`, because it exceeds the capacity of that type of variable:

```
uint8 public myNumber = 256;
```

When you try to store a value `256`, the variable resets because it starts at zero, so the capacity is the calculated number minus one.

What happens when you try to store another number that exceeds the capacity of the variable, such as `300`? Then, the value of the variable will be `44`. So, input the following:

```
uint8 public myNumber = 300;
```

It will become the following:

```
uint8 public myNumber = 44;
```

Note that you can't assign a value that is bigger than the variable's capacity, because you'll get a compilation error in some cases when trying to deploy your contract. The overflow problem can happen when you have a function that receives a `uint8`, but the user inputs a value bigger than 255.

This is the same thing with `uint16`, which has a maximum value of *65536-1*. Likewise, `uint24` has a maximum value of *16777216-1*. The `uint32` variable has a maximum value of *4294967296-1*. The `uint64` variable has a maximum value of *1844674407370955e19-1*. The `uint128` variable has a maximum value of *3402823669209385e38-1*. The `uint256` variable has a maximum value of *1157920892373163e77-1*.

As you can see, the maximum number grows pretty quickly. This is great to avoid overflows when you are dealing with big numbers.

On the other hand, you have the problem of underflows. These happen when you try to store a negative number into a `uint`. For instance, try to do this:

```
uint8 public myNumber = -5;
```

You'll get the following:

```
uint8 public myNumber = 251;
```

This happens for the same reason as overflows; you are going from zero to the biggest number possible that that variable can hold.

Those problems can result in heavy vulnerabilities. That's why it's important that you check that the values that the user inputs in your functions are within the range of acceptable numbers. You'll later see how to verify inputs from functions with a global function called `require()`.

Addresses

In Solidity 0.4.0, there was only one type of address. Now, we have two types to define whether an Ethereum address should be payable or not.

An **address** contains the account number of each user in Ethereum. It's a 42-character piece of hexadecimal text, such as this one:

```
0xeF5781A2c04113e29bE5724ae6E30bC287610007
```

To create an `address` variable in your contract, you have to define it as follows:

```
pragma solidity 0.5.0;
contract Example {
    address public myAddress = 0xeF5781A2c04113e29bE5724ae6E30bC287610007;
}
```

Addresses don't have quotes because they are not strings of text. In this version of Solidity, you must define the type of address, which could be one of the following:

- **Address** `payable`: A payable address is a new type of variable introduced in Solidity `0.5` that allows the address to receive and store Ether inside. Previously, all addresses were `payable`, now only those explicitly marked as `payable` will be able to receive or send Ether and use functions that deal with Ether, such as `.transfer()` or `.send()`.
- **Address:** A normal address that can't receive or send Ether to prevent users from doing so.

You define the `payable` addresses as follows:

```
address payable public myAddress;
```

It's useful to have payable addresses when you want to send Ether to that address. For instance, let's say that user A wants to receive 10 ether from the balance stored in the smart contract. They would do something like the following:

```
pragma solidity 0.5.0;
contract TransferExample {
    address payable public userAAddress;
    function transferFunds() public {
        userAAddress.transfer(10 ether);
    }
}
```

So, user A would receive 10 ether from the funds stored in this smart contract.

Another important aspect of the addresses is that you sometimes need to access the address of the current smart contract, because, as you know, smart contracts can hold Ether inside.

To get the address of your smart contract, use the following code:

```
address public myContractAddress = address(this);
```

Here, `this` is the special keyword used to reference the active smart contract being used at that moment. But because it is an instance of a smart contract, you need to convert that instance to an address with the type conversion function, which essentially gets the address of this smart contract.

You can also access the balance of this smart contract with the `.balance` function as follows:

```
uint256 public myContractBalance = address(this).balance;
```

That will return the number of wei in the smart contract, useful for making transfers with the `transfer()` function:

```
myUserAddress.transfer(address(this).balance);
```

That will send `myUserAddress` all the Ether stored inside this contract.

You can convert payable addresses to normal addresses, but not the other way around, based on the fact that payable addresses are an augmented version with additional functions that can't be passed easily.

Strings and bytes

Strings and bytes hold pieces of text in single or double quotes, as follows:

```
string public myText = "This is a long text";
bytes public myTextTwo = "This is another text";
```

They allow you to store about 1,000 words and they are essentially the same. You can have smaller variations of bytes, such as `bytes1`, `bytes2`, and `bytes3`, up to `bytes32`.

Now, `bytes32` is an interesting type of variable, because it allows you to store about 32 characters of text in a very compact and efficient way. They are used in many cases where short text is required:

```
bytes32 public shortText = "Short text.";
```

They are used in many other advanced uses cases, such as checking if a string or byte's text is empty. For instance, if you have a function that receives text, you may want to make sure that the text is not empty. Here's how you'd do it:

```
function example(string memory myText) public {
  require(bytes(myText)[0] != 0);
}
```

Don't worry about the technicalities of the function. If you don't know or remember them yet, to check if a string is empty, you must do the following:

```
require(bytes(yourString)[0] != 0);
```

This tells the contract to make sure that the first letter of the string is not empty. That's the right way to check for empty strings. We do the same thing with bytes, but without the conversion to bytes.

Use them whenever you need to add special characters to your strings in Ethereum.

Structs

If you are familiar with JavaScript, you can think of structs as objects with properties and values. A `struct` looks similar to the following:

```
struct Example {
    propertyOne;
};
```

Enums

Enums are fixed size lists with unique names that you define. You can use them as custom modifiers for specific objects, or to hold a specific state in your smart contract. This is ideal for controlling the state of ICOs.

You declare them as follows:

```
enum Trees { RedTree, BlueTree, GreenTree, YellowTree }
```

Then, you create the `enum` variable:

```
Trees public myFavoriteTree = Trees.RedTree;
```

Note that you don't have to add a semicolon at the end of the `enum` declaration, but you do have to add it for the variable with the `enum` type that you just created.

Booleans

A Boolean variable can either be `true` or `false`:

```
bool public isValid = true;
```

Arrays

Arrays allow you to store large amounts of the same type of variable in one place. They are used as lists that contain a specific type of information for your smart contracts so that you can store your data in an orderly manner. They can be accessed with a simple `for` loop by getting the length of them.

You can create arrays of uints, strings, structs, addresses, and pretty much any other type:

```
uint256[] public myNumbers;
string[] public myTexts;
```

You can also delete elements from an array with the following keyword:

```
delete myTexts[2];
```

You can also use `.push()` and `.pop()` to add or remove elements from the array in dynamically-sized arrays.

Mappings

Mappings are a special type of variable in the sense that they can hold an endless amount of data. It's like a combination of an array and a struct. You can add elements to it for a set of types:

```
mapping(string => bool) public validStrings;
```

Mappings store information as an unlimited array. They work similar to objects in JavaScript, where each key has a value associated and they can be accessed randomly. They don't have a fixed length, nor can you get the length of them, as with arrays, for looping their values. What you must do instead is save the latest updated key of your mapping and go from there.

You can set values for mappings as follows:

```
validStrings['example'] = true;
```

In our example, all values of `validStrings` will be `false` until you set them to `true`.

Data location

In Solidity, you have the option to define where your variables will be stored. You can decide to store them in the following places:

- **Storage**: This is a permanent place that gets written on the blockchain, therefore it's expensive to use
- **Memory**: This is a non-permanent place where variables are held for only as long as the smart contract is running
- **Calldata**: This is where the `msg` object data information is stored, a place dedicated to global variables

An example of this is in the following code:

```
uint256 memory myNumber;
string storage myText;
```

Events

Events are a special type of function. Their purpose is to log data on the blockchain and actions that you want to retrieve at a later date. They can be **subscribed to** to receive an update whenever a new event is generated, almost in real time.

Essentially, you want them to keep a registry of the things that are happening inside your smart contract to later analyze them in order to fix bugs and to understand what happened if you need to read the past in an easy way.

Here's how you declare events inside your smart contract in Solidity:

```
pragma solidity 0.5.0
contract EventsExample {
    event LogUserAddress(address userAddress);
    function registerUser() public {
        emit LogUserAddress(msg.sender);
    }
}
```

In this example, you can see how an event is declared and emitted. When you declare your event, you have to decide the parameters that it will be able to receive; all of them are always optional, so you can omit them.

When you emit the event inside a function, you must make sure that they are of the right type. In the declaration, you can add a name for each parameter, or you can leave it with just the type, as follows:

```
event LogUserAddress(address);
```

It's good practice to name the parameters inside the event, to help others understand the purpose of each of those parameters.

You can also add an optional keyword called `indexed`. It's a modifier to the parameter of the event that allows you to search past events for that specific event. Think of `indexed` parameters as searchable entries in a database:

```
event LogUserAddress(address indexed userAddress);
```

Note that you must name the parameters that are `indexed`. Later you'll see how to retrieve those events and search for specific ones with web3.js.

Modifiers

Modifiers are a special type of function that are used to verify data or execute something before the current function execution as a middleware. They are mostly used to verify that the user executing the function has the required permissions and to verify the parameters:

```
address public owner;
modifier onlyOwner() {
    require(msg.sender == owner, 'You must be the owner');
    _;
}

function doSomething() public onlyOwner {}
```

As you can see, the `onlyOwner` modifier is used to check if the `doSomething` function is being executed by the owner of the contract or by another user. If the caller is the owner, the functions gets executed, and if it's an external address, the contract will revert, and an exception will be thrown.

Note that the `require()` function is a global assert function to verify that the condition inside it it's true or not. If not, it will throw, and it will stop executing the smart contract.

The underscore statement inside the _ modifier is used to indicate where the code of the function will be executed. Sometimes, you want to execute the function before the modifier's checks. The underscore statement is mandatory in modifiers. Also note that the modifier can have parameters optionally. If none are required, you can remove the brackets as follows:

```
modifier onlyOwner { ... }
```

Modifiers are very powerful tools that you'll often use whenever you see repetitive code doing the same verifications for several functions.

In the next section, you'll see the types of special modifiers that functions can take for visibility and payments.

Functions

Functions in Solidity are pretty similar in syntax to those in JavaScript, but they have some key differences that you must understand, such as the fact that you must specify return types, the visibility of the function, and the modifiers that apply to each particular function, if any. The syntax is the following:

```
function example() public returns(uint256) { }
```

Functions have visibility just as variables do, where public functions can be executed by external users, contracts, and in the contract itself. External functions can only be by external entities, not by the contract itself. Internal functions can only be executed by the containing contract. Private functions can be executed only inside the current contract, or by inherited contracts.

Now, a function can have special modifiers that determine the type of function it is. This includes modifiers such as the following:

- **View**: A view function is one that doesn't modify state variables but can read them. Remember that state variables are declared at the beginning of the contract, and they are used to store information directly on the blockchain. So, if your function doesn't modify any state variable, you have to mark it as `view`.
- **Pure**: A pure function is even more restrictive. It applies to those functions that don't even read state variables. Pure functions are normally functions that make some type of calculation inside them without relying on external data. This usually includes mathematical functions or formatting functions.

- **Payable**: A `payable` function is able to receive Ether when it is executed. It will store that Ether inside the contract, so it's very important that you create systems to extract the Ether that gets sent to the smart contract, otherwise the money will be stuck inside there forever. If your function is not marked as `payable`, when you send Ether alongside the function execution, you'll receive an error and the transaction will revert.

Here's how it looks:

```
string public myStateString = 'Hi';
function exampleOfView() public view returns(string memory) {
    return myStateString;
}
```

In that function, we are simply reading and returning the `myStateString` state variable, so we can mark it as `view`. Note that we must use the `memory` keyword for string types, since they are a type of array internally like an array of each individual character.

Another example is as follows:

```
function sumTwoNumbers(uint256 numberA, uint256 numberB) public pure
returns(uint256) {
    uint256 result = numberA + numberB;
    return result;
}
```

This `pure` function is simply adding two numbers and returning the result to the caller. It doesn't modify the state and it doesn't read the state variables.

Here's a `payable` function:

```
function receiveDonation() public payable {}
```

The `receiveDonation` function is empty because we only need to receive the Ether. We don't have to do anything with it.

The fallback function

This is a special type of function that doesn't have a name. It is executed whenever someone uses the `.send()` or `.transfer()` function to this contract address, similar to a default function. It is often used in ICOs to receive Ether and return the specified number of tokens for the Ether received. This allows anybody to buy tokens without having to understand and deploy the contract instance, with just the address of the contract.

Here's how it looks:

```
function () external payable {}
```

Fallback functions must be marked `external` to help people understand that it shouldn't be executed inside this contract by mistake. If you don't add the `payable` modifier, it will reject all the transactions sending it Ether.

I recommend that you should write and try different functions using the `remix.ethereum.org` IDE, which will show you errors and notifications about things that must be verified. That way, you'll be able to write your own contract securely.

Vyper

Vyper is a new programming language for smart contracts that has a syntax similar to Python. It was created by Vitalik himself and it's one of the most interesting choices for new decentralized applications, given that it provides a different approach to traditional Solidity smart contracts.

Its goal is to be a simple programming language that has increased security based on simplicity, where the code should be easily understandable, even by non-developers. That's why the syntax is so minimalistic. They also wanted it to be a programming language where it's increasingly hard to write buggy or vulnerable code, so that developers don't spend countless hours analyzing the security of every single application while avoiding unexpected vulnerabilities by default.

That's the main reason Vyper added several interesting features, such as the following:

- **Knowing how much gas each function call will cost every time**: Having a precise indication of gas costs is important, because you want users to be able to calculate precisely how much Ether they will invest per transaction. It saves people's money while making the program predictable.
- **Automatic vulnerability checking**: Overflows, underflows, reentrancy attacks, and many other well-known vulnerabilities are automatically fixed in Vyper, without having to manually pay attention to every single function of your smart contracts.

On the other hand, they removed important characteristics found in other smart contract programming languages, such as Solidity:

- **No more modifiers:** Modifiers are not allowed in Vyper, because they make code confusing to read, given that you have to jump back and forth between the modifier definition and its use. Also, they can be used maliciously by executing code unexpectedly; for instance, creating a modifier called `onlyOwner` but then executing a `transfer()` function totally unrelated to what's expected from its name.
- **No more assembly:** Assembly code is hard to understand, even to experienced developers, because you're dealing with very low-level functions that can be misleading. This means that you won't be able to create smart contracts that use signatures, state channels, and similar applications relying on assembly.
- **No more recursive functions:** To avoid reentrancy attacks while guaranteeing a precise calculation of gas costs, they removed recursive functionality where functions can call themselves an uncertain amount of times.

In general, Vyper is a powerful language that's great for smaller projects and won't require advanced functionality, such as assembly. You can quickly create an easy-to-maintain smart contract that your users will be able to understand within a few minutes for its light syntax and minimalistic code.

Vyper by example

To get up to speed with this new exciting language, we'll go through a simple smart contract so that you can see the full complexity of Vyper. We'll see all the types of variables and functions in one single smart contract.

Go ahead and create a new `example.vy` file. As you can see, Vyper smart contracts have the `.vy` termination. Inside it, type down the following code; we'll later explain what every variable means and how they are used. This is just a quick exercise to get your programming hands familiar with how Vyper is written. This code will be your go-to guide to familiarize yourself with Vyper's syntax:

```
# Events
LogTransfer: event({from: indexed(address), to: indexed(address), amount:
uint256})

# Custom units
units: {
    kg: "kilogram"
}
```

```
# Numbers
myPositiveInteger: uint256
myDecimalNumber: decimal
myInteger: int256

# Addresses
owner: address

# Strings
myName: bytes32
myLongArticle: bytes[1000]

# Booleans
isThisTrue: bool

# Mappings
todoList: map(uint256, bytes32)

# Structs
struct Client:
    name: bytes32
    age: uint256

myClients: Client[100]

# Timestamps
myBirthday: timestamp
expirationTime: timedelta

# Wei value
etherToSpend: wei_value

# Custom unit types
myKilo: uint256(kg)

# Public functions
@public
def subNumbers(first: int128, second: int128) -> int128:
    return first - second
# Payable functions
@public
@payable
def transferFunds(_from: address, to: address, amount: uint256):
    log.LogTransfer(_from, to, amount)
# Functions that update state
@public
def updateBoolean(result: bool):
    self.isThisTrue = result
```

```
# Constructor
@public
def __init__():
    self.owner = msg.sender
# Fallback function
@public
@payable
def __default__():
    self.myBirthday = now
```

These are some clarifications to help you understand what is going on:

- Events must be declared at the top of the Vyper file, and they have to come inside curly brackets, like these: ({}).
- Unsigned integers can only be positive, and their maximum value is 2**256. You can't have uint8 or equivalent; all uints must be uint256.
- Signed integers, normal integers, can be positive or negative with a maximum value of 2**128 from both sides. They can only be int128, so you can't have smaller sizes.
- Decimals have a precision of 10 decimal places, meaning that you can have up to 10 characters after the dot, for instance, 1.2394837662.
- Strings can either be bytes32 or byte arrays with a custom size, such as bytes[2000]. Note that you don't have the string type of variable, so your strings will be stored as hexadecimal texts after you upload them. Also, you can't have variable-size bytes, such as bytes[], because they create uncertainty when calculating gas costs.
- Mappings must be declared with the map() function and they can be accessed with brackets, for instance, todoList[3] = "Start something".
- Timestamp is a fixed date for events such as your birthday, or a specific time in the future. This is mostly used as date containers. timedelta is more like a counter without a precise date in the calendar. For instance, timedelta could store 2 months, while timestamp could store January 1 2019, all in numerical format.
- The wei value is the type used for storing Ether in wei.
- Custom unit types are personalized types that you define at the top of the file and you can then use for your variables. They must be casted as uints, ints, or decimals.
- Functions can be public or private. Public functions must have the @public decorator on top of them. The return value of functions is specified with the arrow sign, ->.

- Payable functions must use the `@payable` decorator and they can access the Ether sent (if any) with `msg.value`.
- To update state variables inside functions, you must use the `self.` keyword in front of them to update them as state variables. In Vyper, you don't need to add the underscore `_` in front of parameter names, because you can easily reference the variable with the same name in state, while in Solidity you can't, so you had to use underscores to differentiate them.
- The constructor is called `__init__()`, while the fallback function is called `__default__()`.

That's it! The fastest way you can master Vyper in a few pages. Make sure that you keep this guide in a special place for whenever you write Vyper contracts to save you hours of headaches and uncomfortable moments.

Summary

In this chapter, we started by getting a high-level overview of Ethereum's history to understand where it came from and where it's headed. Then, we moved to specific topics, such as the EEA, since it's great to know how the Ethereum technology is being applied in different real-world scenarios. After that, we covered many different topics regarding the specifics of the Ethereum blockchain to understand it more on a technical level that makes sense as a developer, since we'll be dealing with all aspects related to its blockchain. Next, we moved to more technical topics regarding smart contracts, since they are at the core of what an Ethereum developer does, so that you get a clear vision of how they are implemented in the grand scheme of things. Finally, we moved to essential smart contract programming with Solidity and Vyper to kick-start your understanding of how the most popular languages are used in the real world, setting up a solid foundation for future projects to start your journey to become a master Ethereum developer.

If you weren't familiar with Vyper, you should now be able to program simple contracts using the online compiler, which can be found at: `https://vyper.online/`. Make sure that you practice the functions described in this chapter by yourself and continue reading once you have an intuitive understanding on the concepts explained.

In the next chapter, we're going to explore the Ethereum architecture in depth to understand how each component works at a fundamental level and the main driving forces behind blockchain technology.

Ethereum Ecosystems

2

In this chapter, we'll be covering several important aspects of the blockchain. For example, among other interesting topics, we will look at the technology inventions that made an organized, decentralized network of computers possible, and we will explore the economics behind it all to help you solve the important question, *why is this technology worth real money?* This will help you to become an expert in this field of decentralized applications. You'll be able to explain, better than ever, how it all works together so that you're able to direct your future clients in the right direction, because you'll understand exactly what's going on in the Ethereum blockchain behind all those layers of protocols, technology, and cryptography, and you'll subconsciously solve the burning questions that concern you about this invention.

In this chapter, we're going to cover the following topics:

- Introducing the Ethereum chain specification
- Blockchain technology
- Blockchain consensus
- Blockchain economics
- Blockchain metrics

Introducing the Ethereum chain specification

The Ethereum chain specification is a format used to describe how the Ethereum blockchain should look. It describes what parameters, components, and elements it should have to actually be considered an Ethereum blockchain, so that you can create your own private Ethereum blockchains with different properties for testing your applications or forking a new version of Ethereum. The spec defines what you need to create your own blockchain. For instance, WhaleCoin used the Ethereum specification to create a new blockchain with the same core technology, but with their own modifications, thanks to the Ethereum chain spec.

It is important to have a clear specification that tells us how to create our own Ethereum-like blockchain, because hard forks are an elemental part of every blockchain, and because advanced developers may feel that they want more control for testing their applications on private blockchains. Ethereum gives people the choice to create their own system based on Ethereum; in my opinion, this is really good as a developer or miner that processes transactions because, for instance, you can change the consensus algorithm, the gas costs per transaction, the block times, and so on, while still having a valid Ethereum blockchain.

With the Ethereum chain spec, you can create forks or your own private Ethereum blockchain as a testing tool to see how your smart contract code would interact in the real world.

The genesis object

The chain spec states that the Ethereum blockchain must be generated from a single block, called the **genesis block**. This is a special one, because it doesn't have information from previous blocks, and it contains the configuration of the entire blockchain.

It's based on a `genesis.json` file, and it has the following parameters:

- `name`: This is the chain name. For instance, **Homestead**, **Constantinople**, and **Morden**.
- `forkName`: This is an optional secondary name for this chain.
- `engine`: This is an enum that specifies the consensus engine, which can be **Ethash** or **Null**.

- `params`: This is an object with several attributes of the consensus engine if you specified **Ethash** only. The different parameters are as follows:
  - `minimumDifficulty`: This is a number specifying the minimum difficulty a block may have.
  - `gasLimitBoundDivisor`: This is a separator string. It is usually 0x400 which is the character @ when converted to an utf8 string.
  - `difficultyBoundDivisor`: This is an integer specifying the difficulty per block, which must be divisible by two. For instance, 2084.
  - `durationLimit`: This is the point at which difficulty is increased.
  - `blockReward`: This is the reward for discovering an Ethereum block.
  - `registrar`: This is the Ethereum address of the registrar contract on this chain.

Different consensus engines may allow different keys in the `params` object, however there are a few common to all:

- `accountStartNonce`: This integer specifies what nonce all newly created accounts should have.
- `frontierCompatibilityModeLimit`: This integer specifies the number of the block that frontier-compatibility mode finishes, and homestead mode begins.
- `maximumExtraDataSize`: This integer specifies the maximum size in bytes of the `extra_data` field of the header.
- `minGasLimit`: This integer specifies the minimum amount of gas a block may be limited at.
- `networkID`: This integer specifies the index of this chain on the network.
- `genesis`: An object with the header of the genesis block as you saw in Chapter 1, *Blockchain Architecture*. The header contains specific information about the contents of the block, such as the gas used, the timestamp, and the nonce.

The `genesis` object contains a series of mandatory parameters for the first block created, namely the following:

- `seal`
- `difficulty`
- `author`

- `timestamp`
- `parentHash`
- `extraData`
- `gasLimit`

- `nodes`: An array of strings containing the initial nodes of the blockchain in the enode format. We'll later see how it's structured.
- `accounts`: An object with the accounts of the `genesis` block. Each account must have several keys about each address:
  - `balance`: How much Ether this account has specified in wei.
  - `nonce`: The nonce of the account at `genesis`, which will usually be zero.
  - `code`: The address of the contract associated with this account or any other.
  - `storage`: The object mapping hex-encoded integers for the account's storage at `genesis`.
  - `builtin`: An alternative to code used to specify that the account's code is natively implemented. Value is an object with further fields:
    - `name`: The name of the built-in code to execute as a string such as **identity** or **ecrecover**.
    - `pricing`: An enum to specify the cost of calling this contract.
    - `linear`: This specifies a linear cost to calling this contract. Value is an object with two fields: base, which is the basic cost in Wei and is always paid; and word, which is the cost per word of input, rounded up.

Now that you know which parameters go into the `genesis.json` file, you can start creating your own private blockchain with custom parameters for your own personal applications. In Chapter 3, *Ethereum Assets*, you'll learn the exact process for creating a custom Ethereum blockchain.

Now, you possess the fundamental understanding about how Ethereum blockchains are kick-started, how they operate, and a solid perception about how to create your own personalized blockchain for testing purposes.

Blockchain technology

The technology that makes blockchain a reality is a complex set of inventions working together to achieve the common goal of a global source of agreements. To understand how they all tie together, it's good to break the technology down into four main pieces so that we can see the layers where all the decentralized applications run:

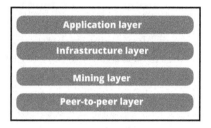

What makes Ethereum possible is a set of tools and protocols that are widely used in the community. You'll be able to use those tools for personal projects whenever you want to implement advanced mechanisms that would be very hard to recreate from scratch.

Application layer

The application layer is the one where external programs interact with the blockchain. It also includes smart contract languages, such as Solidity and Vyper. This layer is the most important one, because it gives people the option to use the Ethereum blockchain for something more than just sending and storing cryptocurrencies, it's the next step regarding decentralized technology use cases. The following diagram shows the application layer:

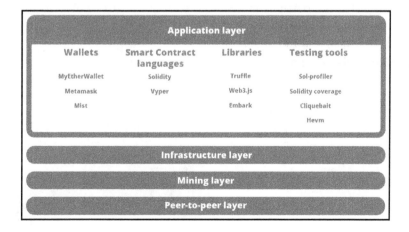

First off, we have **wallets** that allow everyday users to manage private keys in order to be able to interact with **decentralized applications (dApps)** and make transfers.

The main ones are **Mist**, **MetaMask** and **MyEtherWallet**:

- **Mist** is a work-in-progress browser that is always connected to Ethereum. It allows you to use dApps directly from it without having to worry about managing your account or using external plugins.
- **MetaMask** is a plugin available on most browsers that give you the superpower to connect to the Ethereum blockchain without having to have a local copy of the blockchain, since it connects to a network of computers known as INFURA, where you can create transactions freely.
- **MyEtherWallet** is a famous Ethereum wallet manager where you can store your funds, connect to your accounts, and interact with smart contracts online. You can also download an offline version for increased security and reliability.

Then, we have **smart contract languages**, such as **Solidity** and **Vyper**. They are the ones used to create smart contracts that interact with the blockchain with bytecode instructions. These work thanks to the miners that execute the code when blocks are mined. Solidity is the most used in ICOs, decentralized applications, and tokens, where users are able to interact with the blockchain in a trustless environment.

Next, we have **libraries**, such as **Truffle**, **Embark** and **web3.js.** They give you the tools to create better dApps while being able to interact with smart contracts:

- **Truffle**: This library is well-known for being used in **minimum viable products (MVPs)**, dApps, ICOs, and token contracts, since it provides a secure and tested environment for developers that want to go further.
- **Embark**: This is a dApp framework made by the guys in Status that gives you utilities such as the capacity to automatically deploy contracts from the `.js` code, watch changes, and manage a variety of chains.
- **Web3.js**: This is the most used library to interact with existing smart contracts on you web apps via JavaScript. It provides you with a simple interface that is intuitive and easy to learn.

Finally, you have **testing tools** to verify the security of your smart contracts. Keep in mind that these tools are not perfect, because they only provide you with extended options to test your code without forcing you to fully test all aspects of a decentralized application:

- **Sol-profiler**: This is a simple profiler to generate a beautiful table that displays all your contracts and functions in an easy to understand manner. This is great for larger projects, where it starts to become hard to understand the relationship between all the components so that you're able to test them more efficiently.

- **Solidity coverage**: This is a great testing tool written in JavaScript to ensure that your tests are actually checking every single line of code to at least guarantee that it is being fully tested without regards to quality testing. Truffle is a great tool to write tests, since it provides you with a testing framework that helps you execute unit tests.

- **Cliquebait**: This provides you with a clean Docker image with the Ethereum blockchain using proof-of-authority with extremely fast block times so that you can deploy and check every feature of your decentralized applications without dependencies.

- **Hevm**: With hevm, you have a customized implementation of the **Ethereum Virtual Machine** (**EVM**) that shows you exactly what's going on in your smart contracts, including opcodes and a debugger where you can interact with the deployed smart contract directly.

Infrastructure layer

Below the application layer, there is the infrastructure layer that provides a set of lower-level utilities to interact more closely with the blockchain. Things such as decentralized storage, **peer-to-peer** (**P2P**) real-time messaging, and Ethereum clients.

The following diagram shows what the infrastructure layer contains:

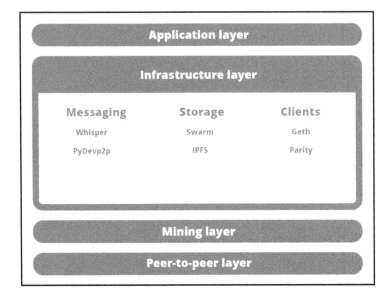

Because the blockchain is built on top of a P2P network where nodes interact with each other directly, we can take advantage of **messaging** utilities such as **Whisper** and **PyDevp2p**:

- **Whisper**: This is a protocol maintained by the core Ethereum developers that you can use on your own dApps to send almost instant messages between apps. It's great for encrypted chat-like application, since you only exchange hashes.
- **PyDevp2p**: This is a similar tool that works directly with the DEVP2P protocol to exchange messages without waiting for blocks to confirm transactions. It's fully written in Python, so it's great for personal projects connecting to Ethereum directly.

In this layer, you also have access to **decentralized storage**, which essentially allows you to keep your data on the blockchain without restrictions. This protocol is pretty similar to torrent, where large files are exchanged directly between peers.

The most popular storages that work with Ethereum are **IPFS** and **Swarm**:

- **Swarm**: This is a decentralized storage built on top of Ethereum that is maintained by the core developers. With it, you can create decentralized applications that have the capacity to upload specific types of data while getting a hash with your content. The way it works is simple; a user uploads some files to swarm while keeping them online for other users and whenever someone else wants to get some of those files, he simply has to download it directly from the uploader without having to ask for permission. It provides a fault-tolerant system that is similar to the way the internet works, but without the centralization. This fact forces users to keep their content alive by themselves, which could become a problem when this technology starts gaining massive traction by general internet users.
- **InterPlanetary File System** (**IPFS**): This, on the other hand, is almost identical to Swarm when it comes to having a decentralized protocol to store large amounts of data, including files, between users, with some notable differences. First of all, IPFS is focusing on removing redundancy from their network. You see, one of the problems with decentralized storage is the fact that you will have a great deal of identical copies from different nodes.

When you have the same file on different computers with different processing times, you have no choice but to choose the one that's fastest every time. You also don't know for sure whether the file that you're downloading from the network is actually what is says it is or not. It could contain malicious software full of malware. To solve that, IPFS provides a GitHub-like system where each specific file has a unique identifier. If two files have the exact same content, meaning that they are identical, they will have the exact same hash.

That is great, because it gives people a guarantee that they are getting the valid content without any modifications. It also increases the availability of the network so that you can reliably get the right file from many different providers. IPFS is still a work in progress and it's developing a coin that will be used to reward users for keeping files alive on the network.

Finally, we have the **clients** that work on top of Ethereum. This is the software that is directly used to mine and download the public Ethereum chain. The core Ethereum developers made sure that they provided a wide variety of similar clients so that people can choose which one fits their best interest openly, so that there isn't a monopoly of software that is forced onto people with all the centralization that it entails.

These are the main clients, although there are many more written in different languages and maintained by different organizations:

- **Geth**: This is the most popular client written in Go language, popular because of its simplicity. You can use it to download the main blockchain, mine with your CPU, deploy contracts, and interact with them, create Ethereum accounts, and many more functions that are interesting to the general Ethereum developer. It provides a command line interface where you can quickly have access to all the functions.
- **Parity**: This is a bigger client created by one of the co-founders of Ethereum and written in Rust, which is similar to C++ in syntax while leaning toward security in every aspect of it. Parity provides you with a command line and web interface that you can use to create accounts, download the blockchain, and deploy smart contracts, among many other tasks. Parity is famous for creating the multi-signature wallet, which is a smart contract that helps organizations reach decisions when dealing with funds and voting since all of the members have to agree on each decision being made.

Alternatively, you have clients written in Python, C++, and other languages that you can use for your personal projects. The choice is yours, so make sure that you check all of them for a better understanding of what each client can do for you.

Mining layer

Below the infrastructure, you have the mining layer, where you have a different set of utilities available to mine Ethereum using your graphics card or your CPU. As you probably know, the only somewhat profitable way to generate Ethereum is with cheap electricity and GPU cards. Realistically, you can mine on your own, or join pools that pay a fraction of the block reward.

The following diagram shows what the mining layer contains:

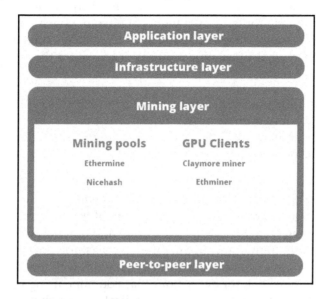

Mining is the process that increases the size of the blockchain by adding blocks that contain valid transactions, thanks to a group of computers participating in mining that reach consensus via the proof-of-work scheme. This is fundamental in order to make cryptocurrency transfers and to be able to run smart contracts using the combined power of the mining network.

The mining network is huge in Ethereum and it's the one in charge of processing all the transactions that take place, including smart contract executions and deployment. It's the foundation of any strong blockchain. The more miners you have processing transactions, the more censorship-resistant and secure the entire system is.

When it comes to mining, you have **mining pools** and mining clients that use all the available graphic cards for solving **proof-of-work (PoW)** challenges. The mining pools give all the participants a portion of the block reward they'd get from mining alone because of the simple fact that mining has become exponentially difficult and only the combined efforts of many computers can generate blocks consistently. They are great for getting consistent rewards without spending days mining on your own, not knowing whether you'd ever find a block or not:

- **Ethermine**: Among many other similar pools, Ethermine is well-known for its great payouts and consistent returns. One of the biggest that you'll find, you have a great guarantee that you will receive your mined Ether after reaching a minimum of 0.05 ETH.

- **Nicehash**: This is a special pool in the sense that it works with a much bigger variety of cryptocurrencies. It's more like a marketplace for selling hashing power in exchange for larger payments in Bitcoin, which you can easily convert to ETH. The payment threshold is 0.001 BTC, which is considerably more expensive than what Ethermine requires. It's great for those that are in it for the longer-term benefits.

After choosing your mining pool, you'll need to get a mining software that will take care of using your computer resources in the most efficient way possible for the biggest payouts. The most popular **GPU** miners are Claymore and Ethminer, although many others, such as Geth and Parity, can be used for the same purpose using your CPU with a much lower hash output:

- **Claymore**: This is a fantastic tool to use your Nvidia and AMD GPUs to their full capacity, since it's optimized for each variety of those cards. Including support for dual mining, you are able to mine Ether and other cryptocurrency of your choice with minimum affect to the Ethereum hashing power, since they use similar and complementary algorithms that work well together. The only catch with this miner is that, for every hour that you mine using it, 36 seconds will be used to mine for the developer of the application, which is understandable and fair for such an efficient tool that provides a much better performance that other miners.
- **Ethminer**: Ethminer, written in C++ is dedicated exclusively to mine any cryptocurrency that uses the hashing algorithm Ethash, which includes Ethereum, Ethereum Classic, and Musicoin, among many others. It's not as efficient as Claymore, but it has a strong open source community behind it that works endlessly to provide the best support and programming possible from a small team of enthusiastic developers.

Ideally, you should test both miners to see which one is generating the best performance, because every setup and computer is slightly different. Make sure that you adjust the settings they provide if you're getting sub-optimal performance.

Peer-to-peer layer

This is the lowest layer that Ethereum has to function properly. The P2P layer is in charge of communicating nodes with each other in a real-time fashion without middlemen via messages.

The following diagram shows what the P2P layer contains:

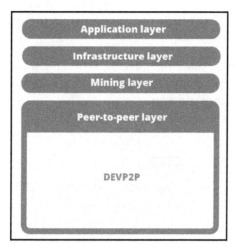

Every node in the P2P network is discoverable because of a unique IP identifier and a hash table that contains data about every node that you are connected to. For instance, when you connect to node 123.456.123, you can send a request to see which nodes it is connected to, thus giving you the option to extend your range of known nodes that you can connect in the future. This is important for being able to discover nodes and connect to new peers when required. The more nodes you are connected to, the stronger your communication will be for getting the important messages faster.

Understanding DEVP2P

DEVP2P is a networking protocol in charge of managing the negotiations between nodes when they want to interact by sending messages. Each message is encrypted using a protocol named **RLPx**, which allows nodes to exchange encrypted data over the network with a secure guarantee that nobody but the recipient will be able to decode the message.

For nodes to connect to each other, they expose any TCP port they would like to use, which, by default, is 30303. So, if you want to connect to a specific node, you must know exactly which port it is using, which protocol it is using, and the IP address or unique identifier of it. For instance, Whisper, the messaging protocol that we discussed earlier, uses the shh protocol, while Ethereum uses the eth protocol. This is just a simple distinction that becomes apparent when you use web3.js, because it shows each function in each corresponding protocol.

In summary, you've seen which components make up the Ethereum architecture, so you are able to discern which parts you're actually using when developing your smart contracts. You should be able to identify different protocols used in the network and understand which tools you have available.

You have just developed an increased awareness when it comes to the tools that are at your disposal, which is essential for all kinds of Ethereum developers that want to implement time-tested solutions to common problems.

Blockchain consensus

The Ethereum blockchain is working on a network of thousands of computers connected with each other exchanging information. Now, in order to guarantee that they all are processing the same transactions and working for the same goals as a combined group of efforts, we need something to reach agreements, which is called consensus, so that they all agree on the result. It's the best way to combine the efforts to benefit the whole.

In the following diagram, you can see how all the computers are running the same mining software while agreeing on a single protocol that provides them with a reward for their computing power:

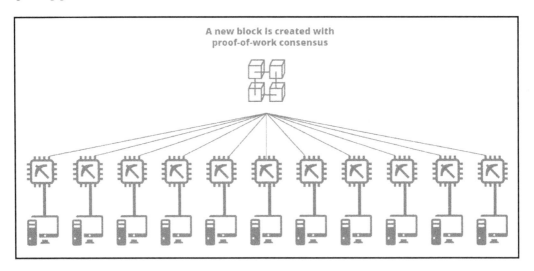

Introducing blockchain consensus

Compared to a standard voting process, where all individuals decide independently what they want to achieve, **consensus** in blockchain goes a step further and aims toward making decisions that help in reaching the ultimate goal in the most efficient manner. For instance, the decisions that managers of a bridge construction project make are based on consensus to agree on the best solution to build the bridge in the most efficient time and cost manner. When it comes to blockchain, consensus is the combined group of actions that miners take to generate the best blocks possible in the most efficient manner, so that block times are reduced while miners are awarded a profitable amount of Ether.

PoW is the scheme used to process transactions and generate blocks that include those valid transactions in exchange for a difficult task, so that only the most capable computers get rewarded with the block generation. What the miners are doing when generating transactions is simply generating random hashes until they find the one that is required for the next block. Each computer is doing this independently. When a miner finds the right hash, they distribute the ingredients that generated that hash to all of their connected nodes so that they can do the same and eventually add this new block to the network while getting a reward for his efforts.

Why do all of the miners agree on the fact that the finder is the one that should get a reward for discovering the right hash for the next block? Because, when they mine, they are agreeing on a set of rules.

These rules are as follows:

- The user that finds the block gets a reward.
- As a miner, you must distribute this new block to all of your connected peers to synchronize the entire network with new transactions contained in that block.
- You must only add valid transactions to the block.

At this point, you may be asking yourself *what happens when an invalid transaction is added into a block?* The answer is that whenever a miner adds invalid transactions to the block, solves the proof-of-work challenge, and tries to distribute it to others in order to update the main chain, the other miners will notice those invalid transactions and will stop distributing that block so it won't get any further, since each one of them is a validator for what goes inside each block.

The miner that solved the PoW challenge for the block that contains those invalid transactions has wasted his computing power, since it won't propagate further. That's the punishment for acting maliciously, it's a waste of energy and time.

This is a very powerful and simple checking mechanism that protects the blockchain from malicious intentions so that it only approves valid transactions that have been successfully verified.

Envisioning the future

Ethereum core developers are working on the next version of Ethereum's consensus with the scheme **proof-of-stake** (**PoS**), which will be released in the hard fork named **Serenity** somewhere in the near future, in about one or two years. Instead of using Ethash as the algorithm for achieving and processing consensus with PoW, Ethereum will use something called **Casper** as the protocol for achieving consensus with a combination of PoS and PoW.

Why are they changing the protocol for generating blocks and reaching consensus? Because PoW is not sustainable resource-wise, since it forces miners to waste insupportable amounts of energy and resources. There's no real need to waste all that energy in cryptographic challenges. We can reach the same goal with simpler protocols that don't require much energy. Also, the biggest crypto-organizations are able to afford large amounts of computing power, making a few companies the owners of almost the entire mining network. This is a serious problem, since it destroys decentralization principals. If they can control the entire network, then the system can be considered centralized, so they attain a stronger position to decide how the cryptocurrency develops.

Theoretically, they can combine efforts and launch a 51% attack to manipulate transactions as they please.

Casper plans to solve those issues that the unexpected growth of PoW created by using a PoS algorithm. Miners then lock a specific amount of Ether on the network to be able to validate transactions while getting paid in transaction fees, since new block creations will stop being rewarded. Each miner bets whatever number of Ether they want on the blocks they think are valid and they get paid a portion of their bet if they are right. This makes the entire network more decentralized, because many more computers are able to participate in the consensus process for speeding up and freeing resources from the hands of a few big players.

In the following diagram, you can see a visual representation of how validations generate blocks by proposing bets on randomly generated blocks:

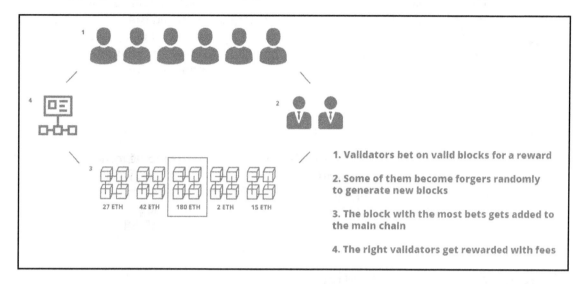

1. **Validators bet on valid blocks for a reward**
2. **Some of them become forgers randomly to generate new blocks**
3. **The block with the most bets gets added to the main chain**
4. **The right validators get rewarded with fees**

In Casper, there will be a special type of miner, called **forgers**, who will generate blocks by combining transactions and adding their public key in the process to demonstrate that they were the ones that created that block. They will also get rewarded with fees if they end up adding the right block to the blockchain. Those that bet on the right block will be known as **validators**. Whenever a block has enough bets in it and if it's in the right time, meaning that it was generated within the standard block time of the blockchain, the block will be added. Forgers will be randomly selected from all the validators so that a few are able to create the blocks.

The nothing-at-stake problem

When Casper with PoS is implemented, participants will be able to push blocks forward by placing a bet on them if they believe they are valid while getting rewarded if they choose the valid one. But, what happens if they decide to vote on a malicious block? Nothing stops them for doing so, since they don't lose anything when betting on a malicious block. This is known as the **nothing-at-stake** problem.

These miners will be able to bet on every block they see for a possible reward.

 One possible solution to this issue is to punish those that are constantly betting on the wrong block. So, if a miner makes 10 bad calls, he will lose a portion of his stake. However, this only happens if the majority of the network decides to vote for the wrong blocks, if the miners are distributed enough it would be very hard to agree on the wrong choice.

Blockchain economics

The interesting thing about cryptocurrencies is the fact that they combine technology with real assets that have value in the real world. For the first time in history, we are able to create digital money that runs completely on its own. Historically speaking, money was always backed by a centralized government where they controlled the supply and demand. They were the only ones capable of printing money in order to control inflation.

Understanding inflation

In simple terms, inflation is the increase in price that all assets in the economy suffer. For instance, a house in 1890 would normally cost about $10,000 dollars, but the same house now costs about $350,000 dollars, even though it got older – that's the result of a high inflation. It could be caused by the increases in material costs because of reduced supply when natural resources are scarce. Maybe it is because there's a shortage of jobs, so people request better wages since the requirements are increasing. It could also be because land costs are increasing, caused by the fact that not enough houses are being sold. All of these, and many other factors, force businesses to increase prices, which forces people to earn more money while increasing inflation.

Cryptocurrencies such as Ethereum are able to increase in price, because adoption is rising since the technology is constantly improving and more use cases are being developed, that makes them somewhat resistant to external inflation. The fact that supply is increasing more slowly every year keeps the value relatively stable compared to fiat money, where governments and agencies are able to print on demand, which makes Ethereum and many others a great store of value.

Evaluating cryptocurrency economics

Asking why cryptocurrencies have value is equivalent to asking why anything has value. We put a numerical value on things because it gives us something – a house that provides us with a secure place to sleep, a car that gives us the capacity to travel to distant places, or food for survival. Generally speaking, blockchains have utilitarian value as a tool to store money, to make almost instant digital coin transfers, and to use a specific type of applications that wouldn't work without blockchain.

Exchanges play a big part when it comes to converting cryptocurrencies. You can go to any exchange that accepts Ether and convert it to any other currency, since they agreed that it's something valuable. Money is based on agreements. We all agree that an apple has a specific dollar value that could vary slightly, as long as people want to consume that apple and accept dollars in exchange, they will buy it. It's the same thing with Ether—as long as people want Ether for whatever they can do with it and accept dollars in exchange, they will buy it.

Before money existed, people exchanged things by agreement, for instance, a table for a potato sack. Then, they decided to use an abstraction, a number, that could be used for understanding the value of things in a more precise manner.

 Note that price is never fixed. It's not like the metric system, where 1 kilogram is the same for the entire planet. Fiat and cryptocurrencies derive their price by comparing themselves with other currencies. $1 dollar is $1 dollar compared to 0.8 euros. 1 Ether is 1 Ether compared to 200 dollars. The global exchange of fiat currencies in the world is called Forex (foreign exchange). For cryptocurrencies, there are individual exchanges that deal with prices on their own.

The moment that someone is willing to exchange a coin for another, both coins attain a price. For instance, imagine the following scenario:

1. Think about a new virtual coin called RED that someone just created. It doesn't have any value, because nobody wants to buy it since it's not well-known yet.
2. Now, John reads about this new RED coin and decides that it will help him purchase apples at a lower price, because they have reached agreements with local producers. The RED coin has a utility value.

3. He goes to the exchange and negotiates with the owner of the coin. John wants to buy 100 RED coins, so they talk until they decide that 100 RED coins are worth $300 dollars based on the utility of the coin.

4. At that moment, the RED coin gains a value of $3 dollars until the creator of the coin decides to reduce the price to increase buyers or vice versa.

The market decides the prices of all currencies that depend on the people's willingness to buy them.

Determining the value of cryptocurrencies

The value of anything is dependent on supply and demand. The more people want it, the more expensive it will become as long as supply stays consistent.

In the following diagram, you can see how supply and demand affects the price of a specific cryptocurrency in relation to a stable fiat counterpart:

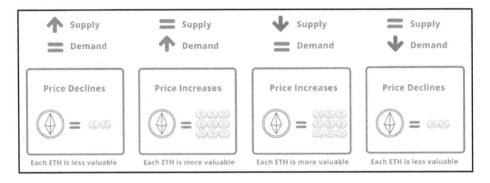

There are many exchanges that have their own liquidity pool where ETH has a different value, since people use different exchanges based on preference. So, how do they all synchronize to have a standard price across all of them? The truth is that they still have slightly different prices. Arbitrageurs work on keeping prices consistent; since they get paid based on the difference in price from exchange to exchange, that's the reason behind the overall stability in prices for each cryptocurrency, especially big cryptocurrencies, such as Ethereum, where the volume of daily exchanges in big enough to be worth the investment.

The result of price movements over time can be seen in the charts in the next section, where you can quickly analyze the value of the cryptocurrency at specific relevant historical events. Charts provide a great understanding of blockchain adoption.

Ethereum-based tokens

One of the reasons the Ethereum blockchain is so well-known is because of the simplicity it provides for creating tokens. Each token that has a significant following will invariably affect the price, since the technology behind is still the same. In the upcoming chapters, you'll learn how ERC20 tokens are created. For now, it's enough that you understand that whenever someone invests in buying a token, the price of the token increases, while also increasing the overall value of Ethereum.

The more tokens there are on Ethereum, the more valuable the blockchain becomes, so the price of it increases. If you go to `https://coinmarketcap.com/`, where you can see the price of all the big Ethereum-based tokens, you'll realize that most tokens have the same price pattern as Ethereum, for the simple reason that anyone buying a token is actually investing in the underlying technology, which is Ethereum.

 The total amount of money invested into Ethereum is called the market cap, because Ethereum's market cap is so big that only large purchases of Ether can move the price noticeably. So, whenever you see huge spikes in price it is probably because of a big corporation investing in the technology for their own motives.

Blockchain metrics

Blockchain metrics are important measurable features of the blockchain that can help you understand its state, so that you are able to determine how good the Ethereum blockchain is doing and what the adoption rate is, so that you're able to predict the future when it comes to pricing, developments, and adoption rates.

Number of transactions

The number of transactions in a blockchain is the most important metric, since it shows the usage of the technology in everyday situations. Transactions represent activity. The more transactions, the more people actively using the blockchain for investing in projects, running dApps and using smart contracts.

It doesn't make sense to have billions of users if no one is using the technology; the more transactions there are, the more useful the technology is. You'll also see in the next heading that Ethereum is experiencing growing pains and is not being used as much as it should. People are joining it, but they are not using it enough. This is a huge concern in the community that must be surpassed to become mainstream.

When Ethereum started, there were 8,893 transactions, which then became 448,168 daily transactions on January 1st, 2019. The record was 1,349,890 on January 4th, 2018.

Here's a visual of the number of transactions since Ethereum was launched in 2015 for your reference:

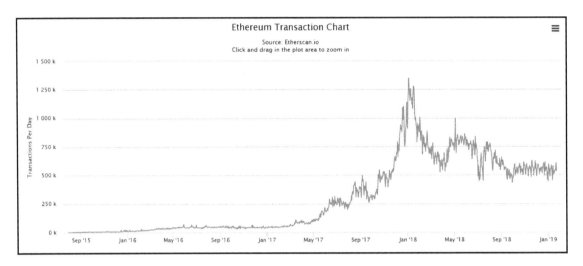

The preceding screenshot tells us that 448 thousand daily transactions are coming from daily transfers, people using dApps, investors participating in ICOs, and people playing with smart contracts. In contrast, PayPal is handling 7.6 billion transactions per year as of December 2017, which is about 633 million transactions per day. PayPal is a mainstream technology used all over the world, so, for Ethereum to reach such level of mass adoption, it has to grow about 1,413 times its current level of transactions. This clearly indicates to us that Ethereum is still in its infancy and it will take several years, with the current usage, to become relevant at such a scale.

The chart reveals that Ethereum is not increasing the number of daily transactions since last year. This is usual in the blockchain space and is expected to continue growing after a while because of the many improvements that the technology is yet to experience.

 You can explore the data on your own by checking the graph of Ethereum transactions at `https://etherscan.io/chart/tx`.

Address growth

Addresses in Ethereum are similar to accounts in real life, although they are easier to generate, so it's not unusual for people to manage 10 addresses at any given point. When Ethereum was founded, a total of 9,205 addresses were created. Since then, Ethereum hasn't stopped growing and by January 1st, 2019 there were 54,281,633 addresses created with a daily growth of about 51,139. Those are 50 million addresses that we can approximate to 5 million users, since we can assume that normal users have about 10 addresses given the easiness to create them.

Here's how the total of Ethereum addresses has been growing over the years:

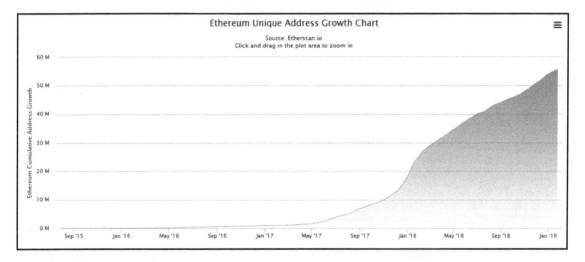

 If you want to explore more past historical data regarding Ethereum addresses, you can check the graph at `https://etherscan.io/chart/address`.

The 54 million addresses indicates to us that Ethereum is still in the adoption phase while growing consistently. People are discovering this technology for the first time, they are joining, and they are bringing more people in. Whenever we reach 1 billion addresses, we can say with confidence that the technology is mainstream, and that people have integrated it into their daily lives.

Ether market capitalization

The price per Ether indicates to us how much people believe in the technology. There's a saying that goes *put your money where your mouth is* that fits this statistic perfectly. The more money people invest in the technology, the more they believe in it, which indicates expansion. Funds raised in ICOs, TGEs, and STOs are also great sources of Ether price increases, since many projects are using the technology successfully. People are putting money in useful projects based on Ethereum.

In the following diagram, you can see how the price of Ethereum has been moving over time with several sudden spikes caused by people's interest in the technology:

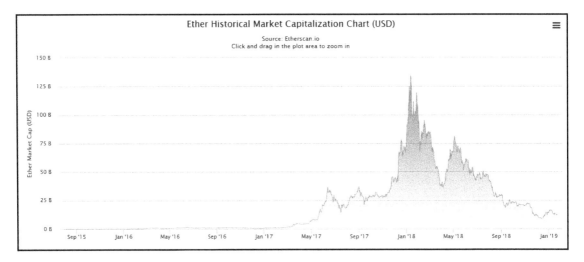

Ethereum was born four years ago in 2015, where one ETH was worth $0.31 USD. After two years it was worth more than $1,000 dollars by the end of December 2017. Recently, the price is falling and it's about $142 as of January 1st, 2019. This indicates to us that people are running away from it because they got scammed, because they don't have a use for it, or simply because the hype ran out. The real reasons are uncertain, but what's for sure is that the price is in decline because the technology needs to provide innovative solutions to real-world problems that could only be solved with the blockchain.

 Check the graph on Etherscan if you want to know more about how the price changed over time at `https://etherscan.io/chart/marketcap`.

Developer adoption

A project is nothing without people behind it improving it and growing it to new frontiers. The quality and number of developers behind Ethereum are an indicator of how it will look in the future. The more great people work on it, the sooner it will be able to face new challenges that could solve people's problems for increased utility. We can measure developer adoption by the number of dApps published using Ethereum and the number of ERC20 tokens in circulation.

Etherscan, a block explorer, says that there is a total of 164,188 token contracts published on the Ethereum blockchain as of January 24th, 2019. You must consider the fact that many of those are scams. About 1,000 are actually the real ones, considering that, per each good token, there are 10 fake or abandoned tokens. This number indicates to us that Ethereum is the dominant blockchain when it comes to developer adoption, since the others hardly reach a few hundred tokens. People are joining the network and learning more about it for useful purposes because tokens have useful applications behind them.

State of the dApps is the most popular website that congregates most of the applications built on Ethereum. It says that there are 2,432 dApps for this blockchain. This is way more that any other blockchain. However, we must compare it to a real-world scenario where applications are being deployed, since Ethereum is mainly a protocol for building unstoppable applications. Google Play, for instance, lists about 2.6 million active applications, which is more than 1,000 times the size of apps deployed on Ethereum.

We can conclude, based on this data, that Ethereum is, again, in its growing phase, and adoption is just starting, so we must continue building on it until people decide to participate to solve decentralized problems.

 To know more about this you can look at `https://etherscan.io/tokens` and `https://www.statista.com/statistics/266210/number-of-available-applications-in-the-google-play-store/`.

Miner activity

Finally, miner activity is a great measure of the power behind the technology. The more miners join the network, the stronger it becomes, which, in turn, increases its decentralization reaching record high hashrates.

Ethereum started in 2015 with just 11 GH/s in hashrate. That is extremely low, and it's expected from any new blockchain. However, that number hasn't stopped growing and now we have about 180,000 GH/s as of January 1st, 2019.

Take a look at this screenshot of how the Ethereum's network hashrate has been increasing consistently to clearly appreciate the relation between price and adoption:

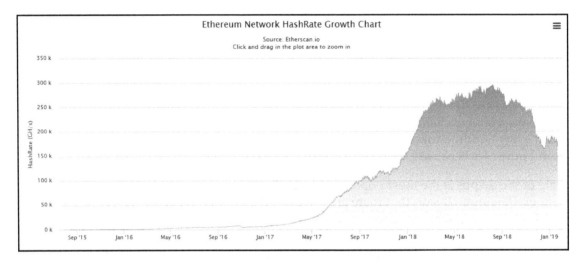

You can see in the preceding chart that the growth has been consistent until September 2018, where it fell drastically while it recovers slowly. By interpreting this data, we can come to the conclusion that it's slowly being accepted by miners that believe in the technology, especially in recent times, where the difficulty has increased while rewards have been reduced. This type of crypto winter is still going surprisingly strong, supported by people that will mine it even at a loss. It's a great indicator of how much people believe in the underlying system.

 Be sure to check the official graph to analyze by yourself the hashrate of this interesting blockchain to discover interesting points in time where people decided to participate in the mining process at `https://etherscan.io/chart/hashrate`.

Summary

In this chapter, we've learned a great deal of things related the mechanisms that integrate blockchain technology with real-world scenarios, such as exchanges and adoption rates. You are now capable of using powerful tools to improve the quality of your decentralized applications and smart contracts, while also being able to predict future price movements based on the most important metrics about Ethereum. In the first section, you saw how the Ethereum blockchain is defined using a specific set of rules known as the chain spec, then you learned about the different parts that make such impressive technology possible, including the many applications built on each layer. Finally, you saw how Ethereum consensus, economics, and metrics work to help you understand why Ethereum is such a valuable coin, while also seeing the way many nodes cooperate toward a singular objective using what's known as consensus.

In the next chapter, we'll cover different implementations of the Ethereum protocol to become capable of exploiting the full potential of Ethereum in your own projects.

3
Ethereum Assets

In this chapter, you will be introduced to different Ethereum protocol implementations so that you can better understand how the blockchain can be integrated in many different ways. After learning about protocol implementations, we will continue with INFURA, wallets, and **decentralized autonomous organizations**—also known as **DAOs**—so that you will learn how to create business networks that live on the blockchain without being limited by centralized governments. We will discuss several block explorers to learn how to examine your transactions so that you can analyze what happens when you upload smart contracts on the blockchain. Finally, you'll learn about some of the important issues regarding blockchain implementation to help you solve common problems that you will most likely face at one point or another.

In this chapter, we'll cover the following topics:

- Ethereum protocol implementations
- INFURA essentials
- Decentralized autonomous organizations
- Miscellanea and concerns
- Creating your own private Ethereum network
- Choosing a wallet for Ethereum
- Using Etherscan for transactions
- Creating accounts

Ethereum protocol implementations

Ethereum is an open source system that can be implemented in different languages to provide people with the option to interact using their preferred tool. Some of those full-node implementations are Geth and Parity. We will explore how they differ and what the best scenario to use them is in this section.

Protocol implementations

As you read in the preceding paragraph, the Ethereum implementations that we will cover are Geth, Parity, Mist, and Embark. Why these four only? It's because they are the most popular implementations, which give you the power to fully execute all the capabilities of the blockchain. Things like mining, making transactions, downloading the entire blockchain, interacting with your deployed contracts, and creating accounts are possible with all of them.

Understanding Geth

Geth, also known as Go Ethereum, is the most popular Ethereum implementation that allows you to do a wide variety of tasks. We will go through how to do most of them in the following sections to help you understand how to execute each of the commands that are required for every task.

You can install Geth easily with the following commands on macOS:

```
brew update
brew install ethereum
brew upgrade ethereum
```

Alternatively, if you're using Windows or Linux, you can go to `geth.ethereum.org/downloads/` and get an executable for your system. In either case, the `geth` command will be available in your Terminal or command line after installation.

Creating accounts

You can create unlimited accounts with Geth, as they are generated from an algorithm known as **Rivest Shamir Adleman (RSA)** that creates the public and private keys off-chain. The number of possible combinations is so big that it is nearly impossible to generate the exact same account as another user. To generate an account with Geth, run the following command:

```
$ geth account new
```

This will ask you for a password to keep your credentials safe. You can then manage your accounts with the following code:

```
$ geth account list
$ geth account update <your-accounts-address>
```

The `update` command is used to change the password of a specific account so that you can unlock it easily if you decide to do so. You can use this command to remove your existing password.

You can also unlock your Geth account using the following command:

```
$ geth --unlock <your-accounts-address> --password <your-password>
```

This essentially unlocks your Geth account so that you can send transactions via the console directly.

Note that you can also create accounts without a password by pressing *Enter* when asked, without typing anything.

Downloading the blockchain

The main function of Geth is to download the blockchain, so that you can have a full node on your device for whatever purpose you may need. To do so, execute this command on your Terminal:

```
$ geth
```

Running `geth` without parameters starts to automatically download the latest version of the blockchain in the default directory with a RAM default of about 1 MB. You can change the location where the blockchain will be downloaded with this flag:

```
$ geth --datadir "<your-location>"
```

To change the portion of RAM used to download the blockchain, use this flag:

```
$ geth --cache=1024
```

The number in this flag is how much RAM you want to dedicate exclusively to this process. The more you give it, the faster it will download each component of the main Ethereum chain. Nonetheless, it will take several hours to get the complete chain of data since it has massive amounts of information made of past transactions. Remember that the chain stores every single transaction permanently without the option to delete the past.

You can then visualize node metrics after downloading the chain with the following command:

```
$ geth monitor
```

Mining with your CPU

Geth is also capable of mining Ether on its own using your CPU, which is not an efficient process compared to alternatives such as mining with your graphic cards or with **Application-specific integrated circuits** (**ASICs**). Nevertheless, its addition to this tool may be useful in different situations where low-resource mining is required, such as with IoT devices.

To mine with Geth, execute the following command:

```
$ geth --mine
```

It will start downloading and synchronizing your chain if it's not synchronized already. You'll be able to receive funds after you set up your `etherbase`, which can be easily done as follows:

```
$ geth --etherbase 0
```

The last number indicates which account will be used from your list. You can see your accounts with the `geth account list` command.

Parity

Parity is one of the most developed Ethereum protocol implementations, since it provides you with a stunning interface from which you can use all the functions, including deploying contracts and interacting with the blockchain.

To install Parity, run this command on Linux or Mac:

```
bash <(curl https://get.parity.io -L)
```

It will automatically download the latest version, compile it, and get the required components to work right away. For Windows, though, you'll have to acquire the executable from their official website, here: `www.parity.io/ethereum/`.

Downloading the blockchain

Before being able to interact with Parity, you'll have to download the blockchain, which can be done simply by executing the following command:

```
$ parity
```

After installing it, you'll then be able to access the web interface on the `localhost:8080` website, which will show you all the options at your disposal.

Creating accounts

To create accounts with Parity, you simply have to click on the **ACCOUNTS** tab and select **+ ACCOUNT**, right below the main tab, to generate a new account, as shown in the following screenshot:

Mining with your CPU

Parity can be used in coordination with other GPU miners that will provide you with better hashrates so that you can become profitable from the beginning, compared to mining with your CPU. Nevertheless, you can mine with your processor by running the following command:

```
$ parity --author <your-ethereum-address-without-0x>
```

You'll then start generating a minuscule amount of ether to that address.

Best scenario for each protocol

Geth and Parity are both great tools that can do the same job for all kinds of decentralized application and smart contract development frameworks. However, there are specific use cases where one could be better than the other.

Smart contract development

and both offer a simple way of deploying and interacting with your smart contracts after downloading the full Ethereum main chain. Nevertheless, Parity is the better choice given the fact that it provides you with a dedicated tab to write your smart contract code in an easy-to-use IDE. You can compile smart contracts to a specific version, save them, and deploy them to the network. What's better is that it will automatically highlight your code, which it quite uncommon with most Solidity and Vyper editors.

Geth, on the other hand, uses a command-line interface that makes smart contract development harder.

Personally, I find Parity's interface a fantastic tool for any kind of Ethereum developer. It's fast, looks great, you have full control of your own node, it feels good, and it's easy to use.

Managing accounts

When it comes to managing several Ethereum accounts, you can either use the web interface that Parity provides or use the command-line tools from Geth. In this situation, both are great options for different purposes:

- Use Parity if you are managing multi-signature wallets because it has a built-in section to administer those types of complex wallets, which is missing from Geth.

- Use Geth if you need a simpler system based on a command-line interface that provides you with fewer headaches for faster operations given that you don't need to open the web interface to interact with them. You won't have to wait for the small but noticeable load times that such a UI exposes.

Other use cases

When it comes to different situations such as mining, downloading the blockchain, transferring funds, and exploring your local blockchain's history, deciding which is the better option is up to you. Both are equivalent to one another and will give you the same results with small differences.

You've learned about the main features that these Ethereum implementations can do for you. We saw how Geth and Parity are used, how they interact with the blockchain, and some real-world commands that you can directly apply for your own personal projects. Remember to take a look at Parity's fantastic smart contract code editor: you'll love it.

INFURA essentials

INFURA is a popular technology for connecting to the blockchain without having to download the several hundred gigabytes that it contains, because it freely provides you with full nodes.

Understanding INFURA

INFURA helps millions of users get connected to the blockchain by providing them with ready-to-use Ethereum instances. It's one of the biggest projects that aims to revolutionize Ethereum's adoption, since everybody is able to connect to Ethereum immediately to process transactions and interact with the blockchain.

It powers popular applications such as MetaMask to make transactions from your browser. That's one of the reasons ICOs became so popular—because people found a simple way to interact with the blockchain to make transactions that are easy to execute with MetaMask and INFURA's infrastructure. You are free to use INFURA in your own applications by simply using a link to the right network for your project:

- For the main network, use this link: `https://mainnet.infura.io`
- For test networks, use the test net's name, for instance: `https://ropsten.infura.io`, `https://rinkeby.infura.io` and `https://kovan.infura.io`

Now, those are free URLs, but they are limited in the number of requests that you can make. If you want unrestricted access to the blockchain, you'll have to create an account on `https://infura.io` and you'll get a unique token ID that you will be able to use for your own needs without restrictions.

INFURA also works with IPFS, which is a protocol for decentralized storage, similar to torrent, so that you can upload content in a decentralized network without centralization.

Inner workings of INFURA

INFURA, on the surface, provides a clean API that many blockchain developers can use freely for their decentralized applications to improve Ethereum adoption.

Behind the scenes, they have a set of computers with the latest version of the Ethereum blockchain downloaded and synchronized to dynamically scale the resource requirements whenever users are generating larger amounts of transactions. The following diagram shows how it works:

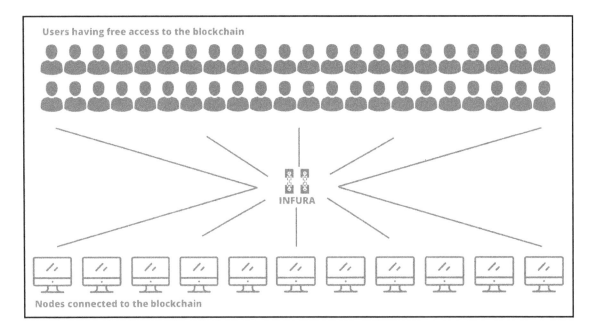

Instead of having to download the blockchain on your own while spending countless gigabytes and hours downloading the latest chain, you can simply connect to INFURA, where you'll have immediate access to the various Ethereum chains without restrictions.

Using INFURA's dashboard

When you register as a new user on INFURA, you'll have access to the dashboard, where you can create projects to see statistics and detailed information about your project's ID:

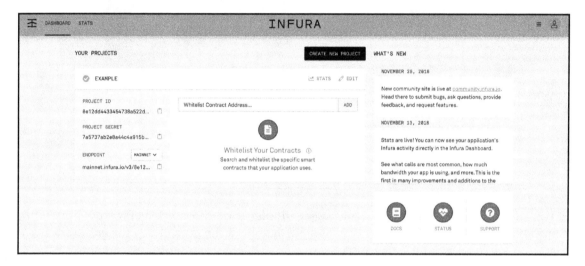

The first thing that you'll want to do is create a new project by clicking on the **Create New Project** button so that you get an endpoint that's usable by your dApps to connect to the right blockchain, whether it's Ropsten, mainnet, Rinkeby, or Kovan. Once you click that button, you'll be asked to name it and a project will be created:

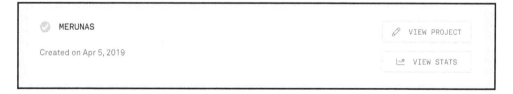

If you click on **View Project**, you'll see a page with settings to modify the security of that endpoint and the name of it, and the option to delete it:

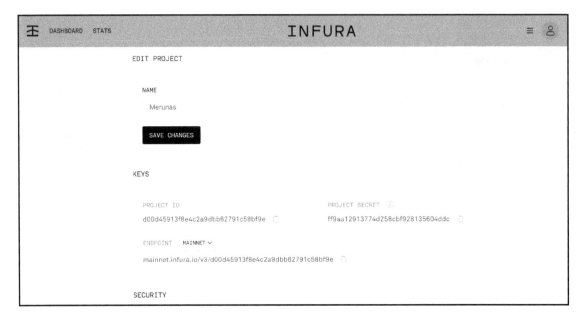

If you click on **View Stats**, you'll see a page with plenty of information about the number of requests and bandwidth usage, as well as statistics about the time of day the endpoint is used, among other valuable information:

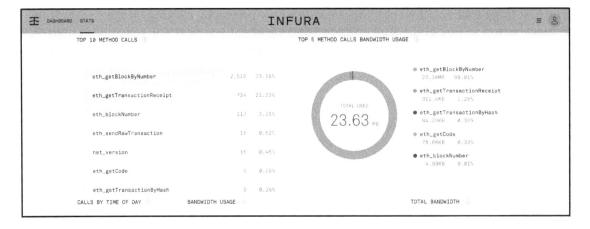

Besides those buttons, you have a few clickable links where you can quickly access the docs and the status of INFURA, and receive support in case you need it:

The infrastructure that powers INFURA is truly an interesting proposition, made by the guys at ConsenSys, who created a gigantic network of connected users wanting to participate in the blockchain revolution without the excessive demands in time and storage that downloading such a large blockchain would require.

It's one of the best ways to provide open access to all the new users that will soon take advantage of this exciting technology. It's also perfectly aligned with blockchain core concepts of open technology. However, it could become a problem in the future if too many applications and users end up depending on it, making it a centralized point of failure that could disable thousands of dApps if the service fails. To avoid such a tragic scenario, remember to set up your own Ethereum nodes for production applications to increase decentralization.

Decentralized autonomous organizations

Decentralized autonomous organizations, also known as **DAOs**, are some of the best use cases of the blockchain since they're the perfect link between trust and old systems that should be updated for modern times.

Explaining DAOs

A **DAO** aims to be the main place where businesses make decisions. They are the decentralized version of traditional companies that reach decisions by discussing with stakeholders and key components of each DAO. Simply, they use the trustless nature of the Ethereum blockchain to form a legal company with all of its possibilities.

They rely on smart contracts to provide hardcoded functionalities where users can make decisions and reach agreements with multi-signature wallets. Multi-signature wallets are similar to Ethereum accounts in the sense that they store ETH and are capable of making transfers; however, the underlying technology is made up of smart contracts that force members to agree on each decision by signing it with their own address.

They are called **autonomous** because they run by themselves on top of the blockchain without requiring anybody to maintain them, compared to traditional companies where the evolution of every component must be studied to avoid legal consequences and structural problems.

Operating within a DAO

The idea of creating unstoppable organizations that aren't controlled by governments or external entities is simpler to understand than it may appear at first. That's why I've prepared a simple diagram showing the process that DAOs partake in on a normal, day-by-day basis:

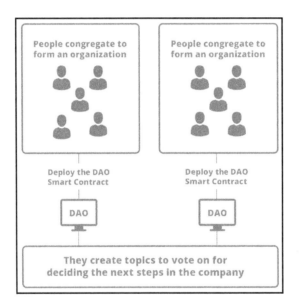

Each DAO works independently, and each user is able to create topics to vote on for reaching decisions. Each token holder has the option to vote with a weight that depends on how many tokens he or she has. The larger percentage of the total tokens you have, the more decision power you get in your organization.

Initially, this shouldn't be a problem, since it's expected that people will vote on the best outcome for the company, but later on it could cause centralization issues where a few hands end up controlling most of the tokens, thus being able to collaborate for personal benefits. This is similar to a 51% attack where a portion of the entire company makes all the decisions.

Tooling for DAOs

You could code your own DAO smart contracts to give organization members functions to create proposals with voting mechanisms, but there are already existing solutions that will help you simplify the process to speed the setup times.

AragonOS is one of the most used development frameworks for creating decentralized autonomous organizations, which gives you the following options:

- Update your DAO smart contract to the latest version with all the improvements
- Limit access to specific users with permission control
- Add additional voting apps on top of it for extended functionalities

The idea is to simply create the DAO, configure permissions, and start building the components of the organization for reaching governance decisions. You can also use the AragonUI for interacting with your organization in a beautiful and simple manner. The famous ICO that was later hacked known as **The DAO** is not available after such impactful consequences, so you can't benefit from the options they gave for creating new decentralized organizations.

Miscellanea and concerns

Ethereum is a complex system of tools working together to achieve a grant solution that helps thousands of users make decentralized transactions where they don't have to trust external entities with their private data and abusive rules. That's why it's completely normal to have questions regarding the way those internal sections communicate with one another. Here, we'll provide you with answers to some of the most common questions any user faces during development and use of the blockchain so that you can tie this new knowledge together with a strong foundation.

Understanding Ethereum improvement proposals

Ethereum is a breathing technology that is continuously improving with new research being generated by all kinds of experts so that they move decentralized technology forward. The way new changes are included in this blockchain is via **Ethereum Improvement Proposals**, better known as **EIPs**.

Standards such as ERC20 and ERC721 were born from EIPs, and were identified by the numbers 20 and 721, respectively. Those EIPs are being created in the official Ethereum GitHub repository under the name EIPs, located at `https://github.com/ethereum/EIPs/issues`, where you can see people contributing to the core Ethereum innovations with improvements that benefit the system as a whole. In fact, the ERC20 standard was created from the need to generate unique cryptocurrencies based on Ethereum.

They are an essential part of Ethereum's evolution and provide very interesting features that make this blockchain one of the best for real-world use cases to solve people's problems through technology.

Differentiating the usage of Truffle and IDEs

You are probably familiar with the framework known as **Truffle**, which allows you to write, deploy, and test contracts in a sustainable manner with minimal configurations once set up. It's one of the best tools for deploying advanced and simple projects; however, you may not want to use it for specific use cases.

For instance, you may be working on a simple 50-line smart contract that runs a few basic functions for an application that you're building. In those situations where you know the smart contract code will be small, you are better off using an IDE that lets you develop your code without having to spend some precious time setting up a project with Truffle. Sometimes, you only need to write a smart contract once because you don't intend on upgrading it with new features. It's in those cases where you should choose an IDE such as Remix to save time and for simplicity.

Truffle, on the other hand, should be chosen when you are working on complex dApps with larger smart contracts that require testing and maintainability so that they are secure.

Understanding smart contract limitations

When you intend to work on a new blockchain-based project, you must take into account the limitations that current smart contract languages face, because they will determine how far you can go complexity-wise in your development. Remember, your dApp is only as good as the smart contracts behind it, so it makes sense to consider what can and cannot be done in a smart contract.

Some of the problems that you'll face as a smart contract developer will come from the fact that your programs are constantly being reduced in size because you can't create an infinitely large smart contract. There's a fixed limitation to how big your contracts can be, so you have to work within those limits.

Pay attention to what compilers tell you when creating complex smart contracts to understand when you hit a roadblock and how to solve it. You will face cases where programs simply can't be done the way you thought possible. It's in those cases that you have to understand loop limitations, function costs, and smart contract interoperability to successfully create larger code.

Creating your own private Ethereum network

At some point or another as a blockchain developer, you'll have to create an Ethereum blockchain with custom properties. This is now more relevant considering that side-chains are starting to emerge with the famous scaling technology **plasma**.

Setting up a private blockchain on Mac

So, how do we create a custom Ethereum blockchain? These are the instructions for Mac. I've tried them and they should work for you:

1. First, install the Ethereum packet with homebrew by executing the following command:

   ```
   brew install Ethereum
   ```

   It will take some time to process, especially if it's your first time executing brew. In my case, it said Updating Homebrew... and after some time, it was installed.

2. Now, you should have access to the geth and puppeth commands. Geth is the main command-line interface that's used to interact with the Ethereum blockchain to download the main chain among other tasks. Puppeth is a tool for setting up your own private blockchain.

3. You'll need an Ethereum address before setting up your `genesis.json` file. Create an account with the following command:

```
geth --datadir .ethereum/ account new
```

4. It will ask you for a password. Just type in the password and you'll see your account's address. Make sure to copy it somewhere safe.

5. After that, execute the following command:

```
puppeth
```

This results in the following output:

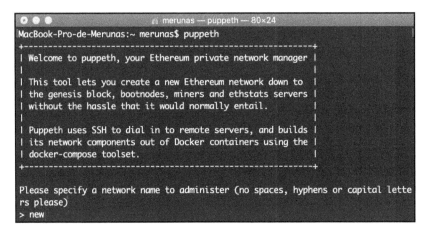

6. It may ask you for a network to administer. In that case, just type a random name for the new network that you want to create:

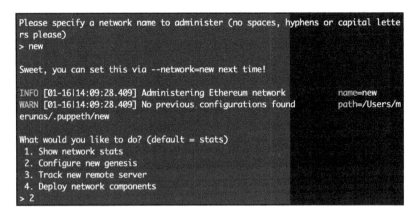

7. Then, choose the second option to create a new `genesis` file:

```
What would you like to do? (default = stats)
 1. Show network stats
 2. Configure new genesis
 3. Track new remote server
 4. Deploy network components
> 2

What would you like to do? (default = create)
 1. Create new genesis from scratch
 2. Import already existing genesis
> 1

Which consensus engine to use? (default = clique)
 1. Ethash - proof-of-work
 2. Clique - proof-of-authority
> 1
```

8. Create a new `genesis` file from scratch and choose the first consensus engine, `proof-of-work`.

9. Now, it will ask you which accounts should be pre-funded. Here's where you'll paste the account address that you copied after generating a new address with the `geth` command previously:

```
Which accounts should be pre-funded? (advisable at least one)
> 0x35e5615fce373ecf40251071fe2cb5cc1554213b
> 0x
```

10. Then, it will ask you if the precompile-addresses should be pre-funded with 1 wei. Say `yes` to that. It is basically a bunch of addresses that will be required for compiling the blockchain. After that, specify a random network ID: in my case, I chose `77` as the ID. The main Ethereum public network has an ID of `1`, so you have to choose a different number to differentiate your blockchain from theirs. This is important to avoid replay attacks where a malicious user could take a transaction from one blockchain and execute it again in another blockchain for their own benefit. This ID number avoids precisely that vulnerability:

```
Should the precompile-addresses (0x1 .. 0xff) be pre-funded with 1 wei? (advisable yes)
> yes

Specify your chain/network ID if you want an explicit one (default = random)
> 77
[32mINFO [0m[04-12|12:51:11.103] Configured new genesis block
```

11. You've configured and created the `genesis.json` file that will be used to start your own private blockchain at any time. Now, you have to export it to be able to use it. To do so, select the second option of the already executing `puppeth` command – `Manage existing genesis` – then select `Export genesis configurations`:

```
What would you like to do? (default = stats)
  1. Show network stats
  2. Manage existing genesis
  3. Track new remote server
  4. Deploy network components
> 2

  1. Modify existing fork rules
  2. Export genesis configurations
  3. Remove genesis configuration
> 2
```

12. Then, it will ask you where you want to export the genesis files to:

```
Which folder to save the genesis specs into? (default = current)
  Will create new.json, new-aleth.json, new-harmony.json, new-parity.json
> desktop/node/
INFO [01-16|14:29:31.241] Saved native genesis chain spec          path=desktop/
node/new.json
INFO [01-16|14:29:31.242] Saved genesis chain spec                 client=aleth
path=desktop/node/new-aleth.json
INFO [01-16|14:29:31.243] Saved genesis chain spec                 client=parity
 path=desktop/node/new-parity.json
INFO [01-16|14:29:31.244] Saved genesis chain spec                 client=harmon
y path=desktop/node/new-harmony.json
```

13. You'll see your files in the selected folder. If you didn't choose one, the files will be created in your user folder or wherever your Terminal's location is at that moment. These are the files that you'll find:

- `genesis.json`: Or whatever name you've chosen for your genesis network. This file contains the general chain specification that we saw earlier.
- `genesis-aleth.json`: This is the genesis file for the Aleth Ethereum client. Aleth is just an Ethereum client written in C++. It was previously known as cpp-ethereum.

- `genesis-harmony.json`: Harmony is another independent client written in JavaScript and Java. This is the genesis file compatible with their specification.
- `genesis-parity.json`: Parity is a well-known Ethereum client written in the programming language Rust. This is the genesis file that's compatible with Parity.

14. Great! You have now exported the genesis file for your private Ethereum blockchain. To initialize your blockchain, execute the following command:

```
geth --datadir .ethereum/ init <your-genesis-file-location>.json
```

That will load the genesis blockchain state and start your private Ethereum blockchain. Make sure to add the `0x` prefix in front of your Ethereum address if you haven't already done so. Remember that the address is the one you created with the `geth` command earlier. It will ask you for your account's password, which you set up when you created it. Type it in and press *Enter* to unlock it. If you don't remember your password or your account, you'll have to go back to create a new account with the `geth` command and create a new genesis file with that address when asked.

That's about it! You now have a working private Ethereum blockchain with your own configuration parameters. What's interesting about this private blockchain is that you can connect it to the Remix IDE. This will allow you to deploy and test contracts at extreme speeds. To be able to connect your private blockchain with the remix IDE, you have to allow the remix domain in your list of allowed domains. Simply execute this modified command to start the blockchain:

```
geth --nodiscover --datadir .ethereum/ --unlock 0x<YOUR-ETHEREUM-ADDRESS> -
-mine --rpc --rpcapi eth,net,web3 --rpccorsdomain
https://remix.ethereum.org
```

With my Ethereum address, it looks like this:

```
geth --nodiscover --networkid 77 --datadir .ethereum/ --unlock
0xf30c37b1e5ed82eebd1a7cf4c66cb9497faa4799 --mine --rpc --rpcapi
eth,net,web3 --rpccorsdomain https://remix.ethereum.org
```

Now, go to `https://remix.ethereum.org`. Note that the domain must start with `https` with an s at the end for added security. Once there, select the **Run** tab and change the **Environment** to **Web3 Provider**:

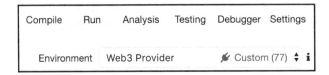

It will ask you if you're sure that you want to connect to an Ethereum node. Click on **OK** and **OK** again when asked to confirm the **Web3 Provider Endpoint** without modifying it:

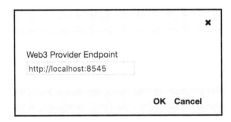

That will give you access to your accounts running on your private Ethereum instance so that you can deploy and test your smart contracts freely.

Setting up a private blockchain on Windows

I decided to ignore Linux and other operating systems for the simple fact that Windows and Mac are the most used platforms for development by a large margin. So, in this section, you'll learn how to create a private blockchain on Windows. The steps are almost the same, but there are some subtle differences that need to be addressed so that you have a clear guide for what to do if you want to build this kind of custom private blockchain.

You already understand that building a private Ethereum blockchain is useful because you can speed up your development times, you can configure the blockchain to your own preferences with faster block times, and you can attain the required knowledge to spin up your own Ethereum instance whenever you need. Via the following steps, you'll learn how to set up a private blockchain on Windows, that's a skill necessary for larger projects that you need to master:

1. The first step is to download Geth. Geth is the main Ethereum client that contains the logic needed to run a custom blockchain. You can download it by going to `geth.ethereum.org/downloads`:

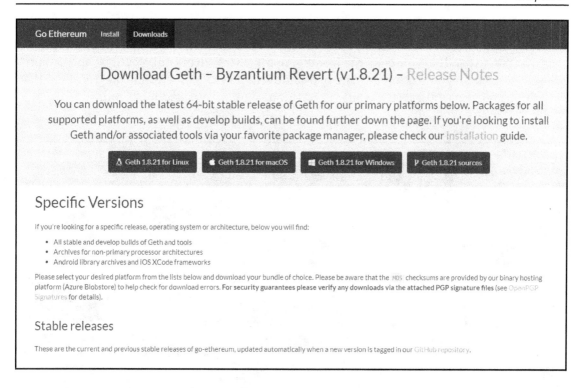

2. Click on the **Geth for Windows** button to start the download. When you run the installer, you'll be asked if you want to install the development tools:

3. Be sure to activate it. Select the preceding option because you will use the required tools for setting up your custom blockchain. Then, just click on **Next** and **Install** to complete the installation. If it was successful, you'll be able to run `geth` on your command line or Windows PowerShell, which is the Terminal that I recommend, since it contains additional commands and looks more professional:

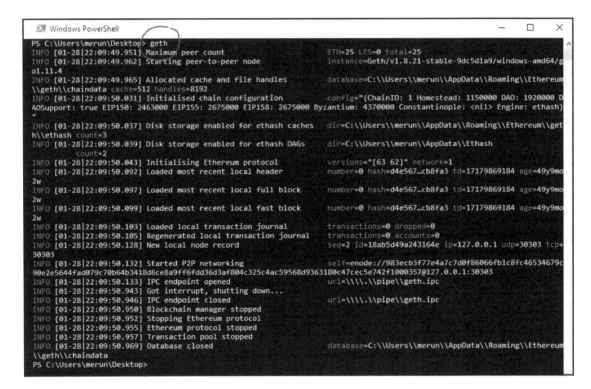

4. Make sure to *Ctrl* + *C* if you run the `geth` command to avoid downloading hundreds of gigabytes of blockchain data from the main Ethereum network. The next steps are practically the same as the ones that you read in the previous section, but we'll go through them just in case to avoid potential confusion.

5. You now need to create an Ethereum account locally, which you'll use later for your blockchain. To do so, run the following command:

```
$ geth account new
```

6. You'll have to write down a password twice, so be sure to remember it. After that, run the `puppeth` command:

```
$ puppeth
```

This results in the following output:

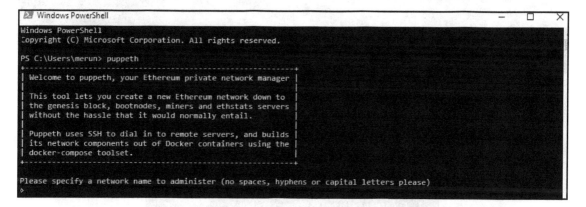

```
Windows PowerShell                                              —   □   ×
Windows PowerShell
Copyright (C) Microsoft Corporation. All rights reserved.

PS C:\Users\merun> puppeth
+--------------------------------------------------------+
| Welcome to puppeth, your Ethereum private network manager |
|                                                        |
| This tool lets you create a new Ethereum network down to |
| the genesis block, bootnodes, miners and ethstats servers |
| without the hassle that it would normally entail.      |
|                                                        |
| Puppeth uses SSH to dial in to remote servers, and builds |
| its network components out of Docker containers using the |
| docker-compose toolset.                                |
+--------------------------------------------------------+

Please specify a network name to administer (no spaces, hyphens or capital letters please)
>
```

If you can't execute `puppeth` or you get an error when trying to do so, it is because it wasn't installed when you installed `geth`. Make sure to open the Geth installer again and check the developer tools when asked, since that's where `puppeth` will be included in your system. Then, reopen your command line or Terminal to see the changes.

7. You will see that it asks you for a network to administer. Create a random name that you'll later use to identify your own custom blockchain. In my case, I used `merunas` as the network name.

8. Right after that, it will ask you for additional instructions. Select the second
   option – `Configure new genesis` – since what we want to do is create a
   private blockchain and for that, we need to create a genesis file, which is the first
   block of it:

```
Please specify a network name to administer (no spaces, hyphens or capital letters please)
> merunas

Sweet, you can set this via --network=merunas next time!

[32mINFO [0m[01-28|22:25:42.621] Administering Ethereum network          [32mname[0m=merunas
[33mWARN [0m[01-28|22:25:42.622] No previous configurations found         [33mpath[0m=.puppeth\\merunas

What would you like to do? (default = stats)
 1. Show network stats
 2. Configure new genesis
 3. Track new remote server
 4. Deploy network components
> 2
```

9. Then, select the first option: `Create new genesis from scratch`. It will ask
   you for the consensus engine that you want to use. In this case, I decided to use
   `Ethash`, since it is the one used by the real Mainnet, although `Clique` is a good
   option to experiment with `proof-of-authority`:

```
What would you like to do? (default = create)
 1. Create new genesis from scratch
 2. Import already existing genesis
> 1

Which consensus engine to use? (default = clique)
 1. Ethash - proof-of-work
 2. Clique - proof-of-authority
>
```

10. Next, you'll have to provide your Geth account that you just created since it
    needs a pre-funded account for initialization. Just copy and paste the address
    that you received. If you don't remember it, open another terminal and type `geth`
    `account new` for generating a new account before continuing.

11. Then, it will ask you if the precompile-addresses should be pre-funded with 1
    wei. Say `no` because you don't need those accounts, and they will fill your genesis
    files with unnecessary configurations. Finally, specify a network ID for the
    blockchain that you just set up. I recommend a number bigger than 10 because
    the lower numbers are being used by the main network and testnets, so you want
    to use a unique identifier to avoid replay attacks:

```
Which accounts should be pre-funded? (advisable at least one)
> 0x9d7917b7f7d3d0ec317397677ce7190337812a03
> 0x

Should the precompile-addresses (0x1 .. 0xff) be pre-funded with 1 wei? (advisable yes)
> no

Specify your chain/network ID if you want an explicit one (default = random)
> 100
```

12. Congratulations! You just configured your genesis file, which is the building block of you own private Ethereum blockchain. Now, what you have to do is export it. Do this by selecting the second option – Manage existing genesis – and then the second option again: Export genesis configurations:

```
[32mINFO [0m[01-28|22:32:31.592] Configured new genesis block

What would you like to do? (default = stats)
 1. Show network stats
 2. Manage existing genesis
 3. Track new remote server
 4. Deploy network components
> 2

 1. Modify existing fork rules
 2. Export genesis configurations
 3. Remove genesis configuration
> 2

Which folder to save the genesis specs into? (default = current)
 Will create merunas.json, merunas-aleth.json, merunas-harmony.json, merunas-parity.json
> C:\Users\merun\Desktop\puppeth blockchains
[32mINFO [0m[01-28|22:37:05.896] Saved native genesis chain spec          [32mpath[0m="C:\\Users\\merun\\Desktop\
ppeth blockchains\\merunas.json"
[32mINFO [0m[01-28|22:37:05.899] Saved genesis chain spec                 [32mclient[0m=aleth [32mpath[0m="C:\
rs\\merun\\Desktop\\puppeth blockchains\\merunas-aleth.json"
[32mINFO [0m[01-28|22:37:05.910] Saved genesis chain spec                 [32mclient[0m=parity [32mpath[0m="C:\
ers\\merun\\Desktop\\puppeth blockchains\\merunas-parity.json"
[32mINFO [0m[01-28|22:37:05.913] Saved genesis chain spec                 [32mclient[0m=harmony [32mpath[0m="C:
sers\\merun\\Desktop\\puppeth blockchains\\merunas-harmony.json"
```

13. Now, you should have your configuration files in the selected folder. To load your custom blockchain on Geth, use this command with the location of your custom genesis file that you just exported:

```
$ geth init <your-genesis-file-location>.json
```

For example, in my case, it's as follows:

```
$ geth init 'C:\Users\merun\Desktop\puppeth
blockchains\merunas.json'
```

I have used quotes so that I can include a whitespace between the folder names, since the folder that I created is called `puppeth blockchains` and it was giving me an error when I was running the command without quotes:

```
INFO [01-28|22:40:51.745] Maximum peer count                       ETH=25 LES=0 total=25
INFO [01-28|22:40:51.756] Allocated cache and file handles         database=C:\\Users\\merun\\AppData\\Roaming\\Ethereum
\\geth\\chaindata cache=16 handles=16
INFO [01-28|22:40:51.772] Writing custom genesis block
INFO [01-28|22:40:51.774] Persisted trie from memory database      nodes=1 size=172.00B time=0s gcnodes=0 gcsize=0.00B
ctime=0s livenodes=1 livesize=0.00B
INFO [01-28|22:40:51.778] Successfully wrote genesis state         database=chaindata
           hash=00594f..3908b7
INFO [01-28|22:40:51.783] Allocated cache and file handles         database=C:\\Users\\merun\\AppData\\Roaming\\Ethereum
\\geth\\lightchaindata cache=16 handles=16
INFO [01-28|22:40:51.798] Writing custom genesis block
INFO [01-28|22:40:51.800] Persisted trie from memory database      nodes=1 size=172.00B time=0s gcnodes=0 gcsize=0.00B
ctime=0s livenodes=1 livesize=0.00B
INFO [01-28|22:40:51.805] Successfully wrote genesis state         database=lightchaindata
           hash=00594f..3908b7
```

14. If you get an error saying `Failed to write genesis block: database already contains an incompatible genesis block`, simply execute the following:

    ```
    $ geth removedb
    ```

    When you run `geth removedb`, you're deleting the downloaded blockchain, which solves the problem of incompatible genesis blocks. It's mainly caused because you've started to download the blockchain with a genesis file while at some point you decided to use a different genesis file, which is invalid because the configuration gets permanently stored in the first block, also known as the genesis block. You can't change the blockchain settings after mining the genesis block without deleting the previous blockchain first.

15. Finally, to run this blockchain of yours, execute the following command:

    ```
    $ geth --networkid 100 --unlock 0x<YOUR-ETHEREUM-ADDRESS> --mine
    ```

16. It will ask you for your account's password. Just type it and you'll see the blockchain ready to mine blocks. Now, you can use it for whatever projects you desire, including connecting it to the Remix IDE, as you saw previously. You can do so with the exact same command:

    ```
    $ geth --nodiscover --networkid 77 --datadir .ethereum/ --unlock
    0xf30c37b1e5ed82eebd1a7cf4c66cb9497faa4799 --mine --rpc --rpcapi
    eth,net,web3 --rpccorsdomain https://remix.ethereum.org
    ```

Now, you can finally connect the node on the Remix IDE so that you can deploy your contracts on your own blockchain.

Choosing a wallet for Ethereum

Ethereum wallets are as diverse as you can imagine. From software wallets, to hardware and even paper wallets, the choice of selecting the best wallet for your needs is increasingly difficult if you don't understand the differences. That's why in this section we'll explore the options when it comes to wallets so that you choose the best one for every project.

Understanding the concept of an Ethereum wallet

It seems intuitive – a wallet is a place where you store your crypto funds – but in reality, wallets are much more complex than they appear. Wallets connect to the Ethereum blockchain to find your latest balance, which is accessible via smart contracts, dApps, or via the blockchain client itself. Ethereum clients download the entire chain data, and they are able to search for the transactions associated with your account. Some of them will be transfers, while others can be smart contract executions where you pay gas. At the end, it's possible to obtain your current balance just by reading the transactions contained in the latest block with your address, as shown in the following diagram where balances are being updated after several transactions:

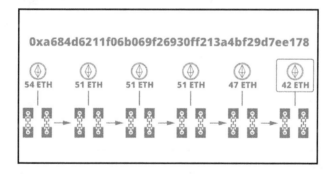

Since security is a big issue when dealing with money, wallets have to protect every vulnerable area in which your credentials may be used. Your private keys, your seed, and your address shouldn't be easily accessible by anyone. That's the reason why there are different wallet implementations. They can be online or offline, and you can go a step further by using offline hardware wallets made specifically to store cryptocurrencies.

Explaining online wallets

These are wallets that you can access only when you have an internet connection, since they are web-based and allow you to interact with your wallets from almost anywhere as long as you're connected. Note that they don't always keep your private keys in their servers: some do, but most require you to provide your private keys to them every time you want to access your wallet. Let's take a look at some of them to understand how they work.

Choosing MyEtherWallet

MyEtherWallet is the most popular Ethereum wallet app, which you can use to access your wallet. It will ask you for your private keys whenever you want to log in; since it doesn't store your credentials online, it's just a platform to interact with your funds:

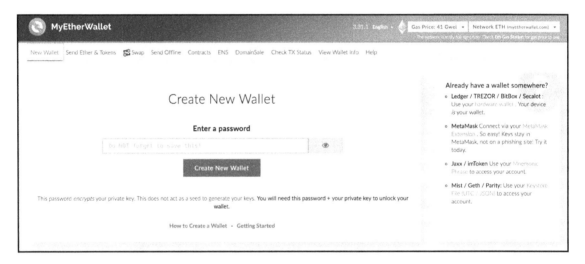

When you open myetherwallet.com, you'll see a clear box, indicating that you can create a new wallet. If you already have one, just click on the **Send Ether & Tokens** tab, which will ask you to upload your private key in different format options.

If you don't have a wallet yet, click on **Create New Wallet** to generate a new account after typing your password. Then, it will ask you to save your private key and store it somewhere safe. Remember that your private key is the main element of your wallet: if you lose it, you won't be able to access it and your funds will be forever lost.

Using MetaMask

MetaMask is another famous wallet that is mainly used as an intermediary wallet where people send ether to interact with decentralized applications and smart contracts. MetaMask uses INFURA in the backend, so the connection to the blockchain is immediate and you don't have to download hundreds of blocks.

What's interesting about this wallet is that it injects `web3.js` into whatever page you're examining, meaning that you can use any dApp as long as you have logged into MetaMask:

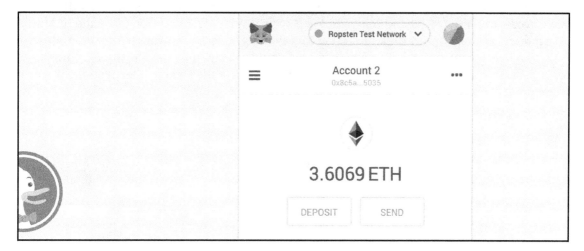

Whenever you want to interact with the blockchain by making a transaction on a decentralized application, MetaMask will open a pop-up window, asking you how much it will cost you, with gas price included. Then, you'll be able to make the transaction straight from the browser.

What's also great about this wallet is that you can change your blockchain network at any point with a few clicks. This is great for developing since you can deploy your smart contracts to Ropsten and then to Mainnet if everything looks right. Overall, this is a fantastic wallet for developers and users alike who want to interact with decentralized applications, including ICOs.

Understanding hardware wallets

These are wallets that keep your funds offline in a small device that stores your cryptocurrencies safely. The interesting thing about these devices is that they don't interact using your private keys; they have a system to log you into wallets without putting your private keys at risk, since they store them internally and are encrypted for increased safety.

The most popular ones are Ledger and Trezor. Those companies build different devices that you set up with a seed and then use with your cryptocurrencies for as long as they work. Note that they are only as good as a printed private key, meaning that nobody will have access to them online and they will keep your funds safe if you don't lose them. Think about them as keys. If they break or if you lose them, you lose your funds forever. That's why I always recommend that you buy several copies of the same device, three or more with the same private key and seed, so that you can access the same wallet even if one of them breaks.

Using Ledger

Ledger and the popular Ledger Nano look like a traditional pen drive with an OLED screen and two buttons on top:

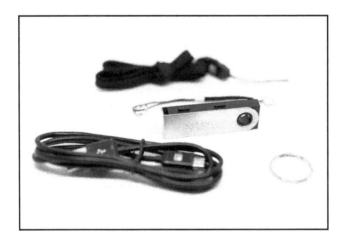

You use it by connecting it to your computer with a USB cable and opening a custom wallet application. You can use MetaMask and MyEtherWallet, among others, with this hardware device. It keeps your funds safely by using a 4-digit pin, just like a credit card, and a password if you have set up one when you created your wallet. You can store thousands of different cryptocurrencies, including Ethereum, that will stay in the same device.

Using Trezor

Trezor is another popular hardware wallet with a distinct flat design, also with two buttons, and a high quality black and white display. This device comes in a sealed package that must be completely broken to access the wallet to ensure that nobody touches your Trezor before you get it in your hands for the first time, due to the massive damage that it could cause when used by a hacker.

You'll also get several small pieces of cardboard to write down your unique seed for recovering your account in case you lose access to the wallet. Make sure you don't lose those paper wallets since they will be required whenever Trezor's firmware updates:

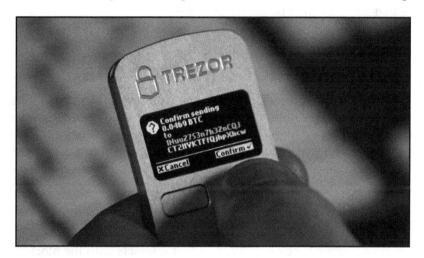

The two buttons are used to confirm transactions after you've checked that they correspond to the ones shown on your computer. This is an additional security layer to prevent people from sending funds to the wrong addresses. It also supports hundreds of cryptocurrencies and has the same security features of the Ledger Nano. In the end, it comes down to personal preference, since most of these hardware wallets function the same way and are secure enough.

Learning to use multi-signature wallets

Multi-signature wallets are a special type of wallet, in the sense that they are actually smart contracts that implement multi-signature functions so that a group of members can sign transactions when they all agree on the result. The only way to interact with these wallets is by using the smart contract directly or through Parity's application, since Parity created the biggest multi-signature wallet of all applications.

To interact with this type of wallet, simply open Parity's web interface and deploy a new multi-signature wallet from the accounts section with the addresses of the members that will participate in it. The way these wallets work is that each member can create a proposal to move a specific amount of ether out of the wallet to a given address. If they all agree, the funds will be transferred; otherwise, the transfer will be cancelled. It's a simple way for crypto startups to keep their funds in a group treasury.

You've just obtained a high-level overview of all the Ethereum wallet types that are available out there. Now, you can choose which one fits your requirements and you can start storing ETH safely for as long as you need. Remember that a wallet is as good as long as it gives you access to your funds, so be sure to choose a wallet that doesn't restrict your access and one that has proven to be secure over the years.

Using Etherscan for transactions

Etherscan, just like all block explorers, provides vast amounts of valuable information during your smart contract development journey whenever you need to understand how smart contracts operate on a deeper level. Knowing how to use a block explorer such as Etherscan is a precious skill that's required for any kind of Ethereum developer to be able to debug and understand real-world events in the form of blockchain transactions.

Understanding block explorers

Block explorers are a specific type of application that interacts with the blockchain by searching for specific information that may be relevant to the user. They are the bots of the blockchain that help you understand what is going on behind the code. They were created because people wanted a simpler way to understand transactions as they happen, since most of the transactions are messy and it's really hard to discover the things that matter when all you get are hexadecimal pieces of information.

The most popular ones are Etherscan, Etherchain, and Ethplorer. All of these block explorers are web-based, so you can use them from any internet-connected device with ease.

Using Etherscan for analyzing transactions

Etherscan is by far the biggest block explorer out there, for the simple reason that it provides you with a concise and clean interface for interacting with your transactions. Etherscan is mainly a place to see what your transactions are actually doing after you deploy them. For instance, when you send 10 ETH to another address, you can't really know if it was successful or if there was some kind of mistake in the addresses that you used. Etherscan will show you exactly what happened and the reason why:

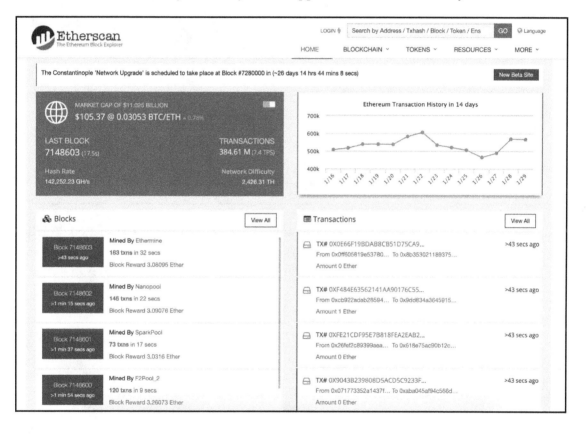

Let's say that someone stole 1 ETH from you because they got access to your Ethereum account. How would you track such information? Well, you can paste your Ethereum address in the search box of Etherscan and see where it went:

Just click on **TxHash** to see expanded information about that particular transaction. You'll see the following:

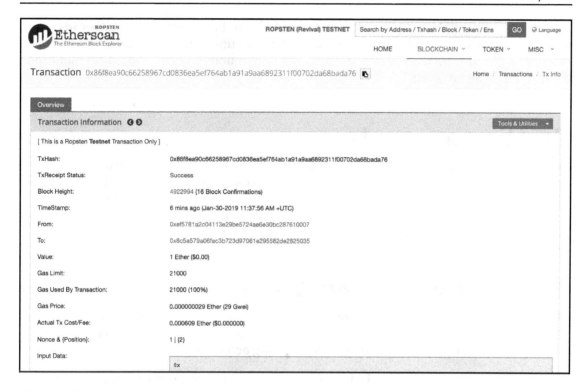

This is telling you the following things:

- The transaction was successful
- It was a simple transfer for 1 Ether to the address **0x8c5a579a06fac3b723d97061e295582de2825035** from your own address
- It was made on January 30, 2019

With that information, you can begin researching who's behind that address, and you may be able to find who stole your funds if that's the case. In the **Input Data** section, you'll see the code that was executed if this were a contract transaction. You can also use Etherscan to examine tokens, smart contracts, graphs, and much more, since they are dedicated to providing you with the best information possible regarding blockchain transactions.

 You can also create your own blockchain explorer using web3.js and Truffle contracts!

You now know that block explorers are great tools for an Ethereum developer because they provide you with invaluable information in a simple-to-understand format, which is essential when dealing with permanent Mainnet transactions where hundreds of thousands of dollars may be involved.

Creating accounts

Accounts are the main components of every Ethereum application. If you want to participate in the network, you need an Ethereum account with your private key and address. There are many ways in which you can create Ethereum accounts, which is why it's good for you to be familiar with the different tools so that you can become proficient in the process of creating accounts: you'll need accounts for all the projects that you'll build.

Creating accounts with MetaMask

MetaMask, as you already know, is one of the most popular Ethereum wallets. It allows you to create unlimited accounts for different Ethereum chains without restrictions, using the same seed word. Here's how to use it for creating accounts:

1. First, download MetaMask for Chrome or Firefox by going to `metamask.io`:

2. Then, you can click on the fox icon that you just installed to start MetaMask, which will open this page:

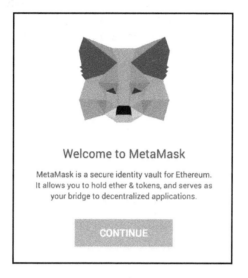

3. Click on **CONTINUE** and set up a password for your wallet, and then scroll down to accept the terms of use:

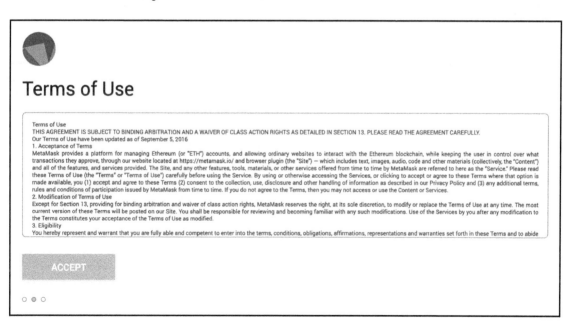

4. After that, it will show you different windows, warning you about the risks of using beta software like this and that you must never give them your recovery seeds unless you are completely secure about the process. Then, you'll have to click and store your seed phrase somewhere safe. This is a unique set of words that will help you recover your account if you lose it. It is your main private key that you can't lose, or your wallet will be inaccessible:

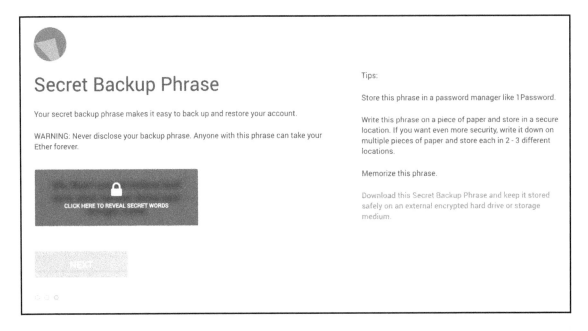

5. Finally, it will ask you to deposit Ether using Coinbase or ShapeShift, or directly:

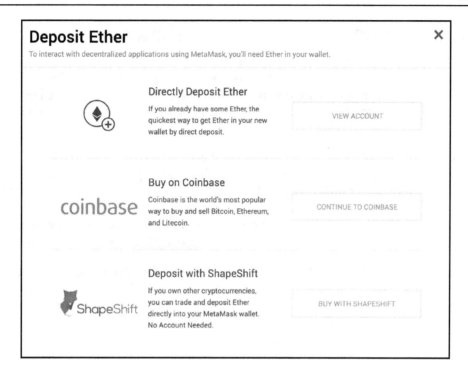

6. You can simply ignore this and add funds later. That's about it—you should now be able to use MetaMask by clicking the little orange fox on your extensions bar:

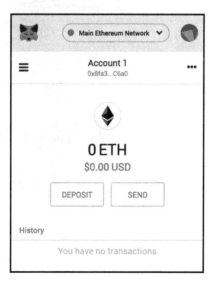

Creating an account with Coinbase

Now that you saw how to create your own private wallet, let's create a wallet hosted in an exchange such as Coinbase where you can buy and sell cryptocurrencies directly. Note that these types of wallets are not secure because the exchange keeps your private keys and seed phrases to themselves, so you can't have total control of your wallet, nor secure it by yourself.

One of the advantages of these type of wallets is that you can exchange your cryptocurrency for money almost immediately without having to wait for transfers. This is ideal for traders that need quick access to their funds. The major problem with this is the lack of control, given that you provide them with your keys and you're dependent on the fact that they keep them secure – which is not always the case. Always review the history of an exchange to see if they are trustworthy or if your money is at risk of possible hacks.

Coinbase is the biggest cryptocurrency exchange and is well-received because of the simplicity it provides when it comes to exchanging fiat currencies for crypto using your bank or credit card. In the following steps, you'll learn what needs to be done to create an Ethereum account that's linked to Coinbase:

1. First, open their website at `coinbase.com`:

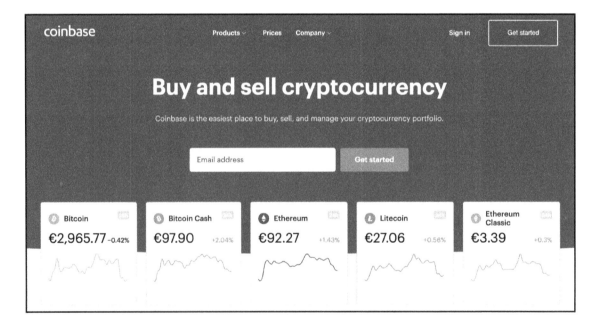

2. Type your email address into that big input box and click on **Get started** to create a new Coinbase account. Then, it will ask you for more details that are required so that you can start:

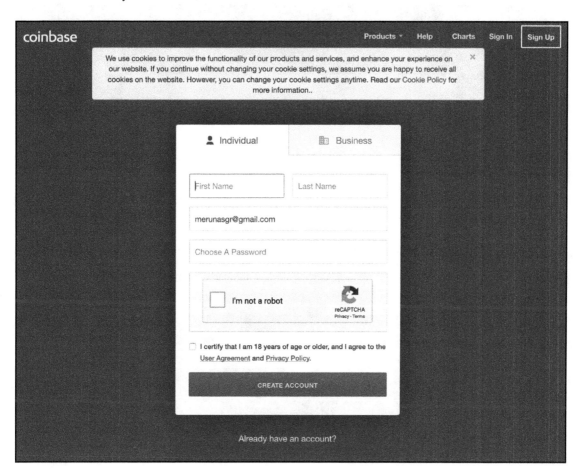

3. Following that, it will show you some information about legality issues and warnings:

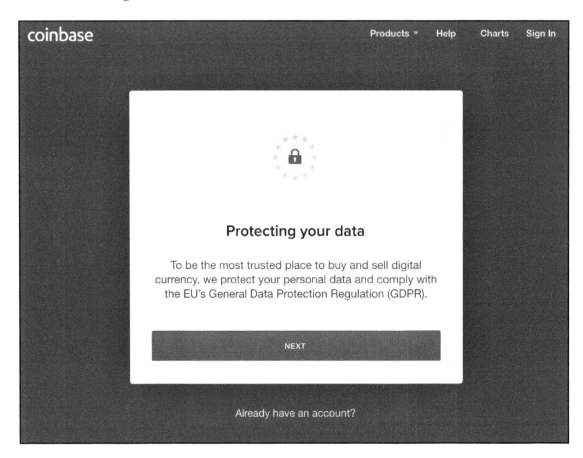

4. Then, you'll have to check your email to confirm your address:

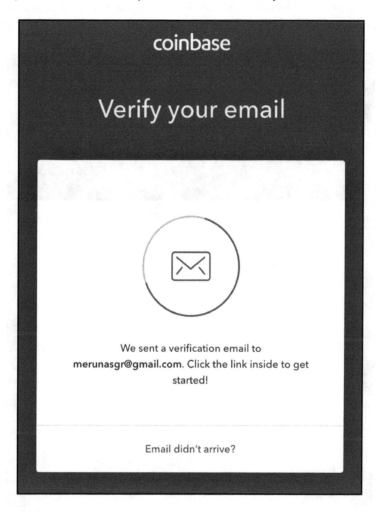

5. After confirming your email address and login, you'll be asked to add your phone number for security measures, since these types of accounts deal with a lot of money and they want to have the largest amount of security points in place:

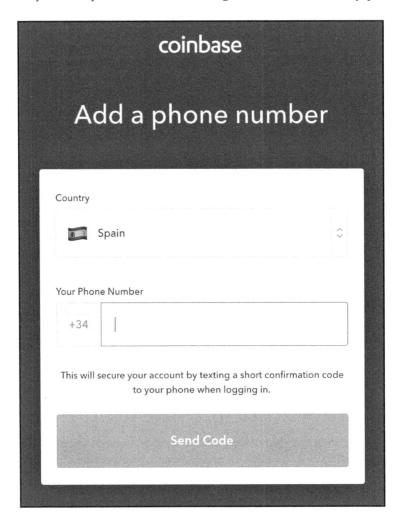

6. They will send you a message, so be sure to use a valid number. After that, you'll be asked to provide personal information, such as where you live, your occupation, and your ID number. Simply fill in all the boxes:

7. It's important to provide valid data since they will check everything, and they will use that information to help you trade securely. After that, you'll be asked to verify your identity with a photo of your passport or driver's license; you must do so to be able to trade here. It's annoying, but required by law, since they are dealing with banks and they don't want open ends:

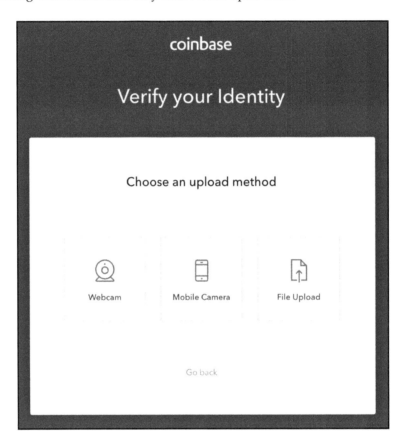

8. If this doesn't work, try again later until you have access. Finally, you'll be able to trade and see your accounts in the **Accounts** tab after completing all the documents and logging in again:

After those steps, you should have access to a fully featured web-based wallet that's linked to Coinbase, which accepts many different cryptocurrencies and fiat currencies. You should be able to purchase crypto once you add your bank account details.

Summary

In this chapter, you learned how to create Ethereum accounts for different wallets, some of them private, others hosted in exchanges to facilitate the process of acquiring new cryptocurrencies. You've learned the differences between them and how they can be used. You now know that MetaMask is great for interacting with dApps and storing your funds safely, whereas Coinbase is great for trading and exchanging crypto immediately using fiat currencies, among many others.

In the next chapter, you'll learn more about dApps and how to use them at full speed with advanced tips that you can implement right away for creating stronger applications that will scale in the future.

2
Section 2: Decentralized Application Development Workflow

You will learn about the specifics of how the many industries that have been affected by blockchain can be improved with Ethereum so that you can gain a practical understanding of the overall state of Ethereum in the market. Each industry will have projects to solidify the knowledge you've learned.

The following chapters will be covered in this section:

- Chapter 4, *Mastering Smart Contracts*
- Chapter 5, *Mastering dApps*
- Chapter 6, *Tools, Frameworks, Components, and Services*
- Chapter 7, *Deployment on Testnet*
- Chapter 8, *Various dApps Integrations*
- Chapter 9, *Decentralized Exchanges Workflow*

Mastering Smart Contracts

4

In this chapter, you'll be taken on a journey across several interesting frameworks to design secure, scalable, and fast smart contracts that are gas-optimized so that people don't pay too much Ether per transaction. We are going to create a **copyright marketplace smart contract** that stores licenses that people create for their content that's identified by a unique ID, all on the blockchain. Then, you'll explore the EVM in depth in order to understand how it actually works in the backend when you deploy and interact with a smart contract. Next, we'll talk about upgradable and scalable smart contracts for the next generation. And, finally, we'll cover gas- and data-efficient smart contracts and security analysis with audits. In this chapter, we're going to cover the following topics:

- Getting up to speed
- The EVM in depth
- Upgradable and scalable smart contracts
- Gas- and data-efficient smart contracts
- Smart contract security analysis

Getting up to speed

If you want to become an expert when it comes to smart contracts, you have to start with a simple project to refresh your skills. We're going to create a copyright marketplace smart contract to upload legal documents to the blockchain that guarantee that some piece of content is protected by copyright law and cannot be copied. Without further ado, let's get right to it!

Planning the marketplace idea

Here is the way copyright law works in simple terms:

1. You register a piece of content that could be a document, text, an image, a video, or any kind of creation that you did by yourself with a unique identifier, publicly so that people can confirm your authority.

2. The people that want to use your content for whatever reasons have to consult your copyright terms and obey them to avoid legal problems, because we don't want people stealing your work for their own benefit.

A copyrighted register shouldn't be modified, so we'll avoid creating functions that allow people to modify their copyrighted data; so, we'll only allow them to add or remove copyrights.

We need a smart contract that lives on the blockchain that people can access easily. This contract will have the following functions to manage copyright registers:

- A function to add new copyrighted content with a unique identifier that you create by hashing the content. In this case, we want to limit the copyrighted content to just text, since it's expensive to upload other types of content on the blockchain. This function will receive the address of the owner of the content, their name, their email address, the hashed ID of the content, a URL containing the article or document to register, and the terms of use that others must obey when using this particular piece of content.

- A function to get content based on a hash.

- A function to delete copyrighted content if you're the owner.

- A function to extract the funds locked in this smart contract. It often happens that people send Ether to the wrong address, which ends up in a smart contract like this. We want to be able to extract the funds locked away so that they are not lost forever if this happens. It can also be used as a donation address for showing the appreciation for the work done.

Designing the code in Solidity

In this project, we'll use Truffle to deploy and run our smart contract. When dealing with larger projects, it's always worth the initial effort that's invested in setting up a framework such as Truffle with all the required dependencies, because it saves us a lot of time in the long run while improving the development experience. Here are the steps for setting up our project with Truffle, since it's the first time we're mentioning it in this book. Later on, we'll assume that you know how to set up a project in Truffle, although we'll remind you plenty of times when needed:

1. Let's start right away by creating a new folder called `copyright`:

2. Inside that folder, run the `truffle init` command. If you don't have Truffle, install it with `npm i -g truffle` or `sudo npm i -g truffle`. You can get `npm` by installing Node.js from their website, `nodejs.org`. The following screenshot shows what the process is:

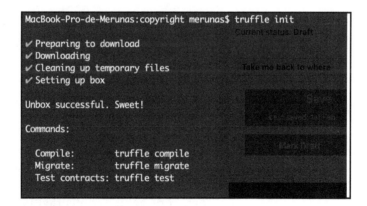

3. Then, you can open the project with your preferred code editor, in my case, **Atom**:

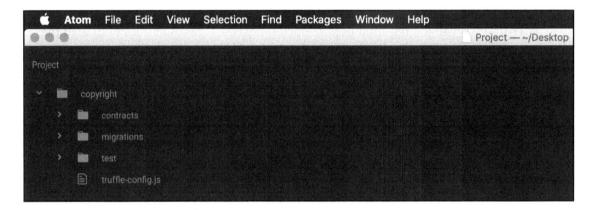

4. Create a new file inside `contracts` with the name `Copyright.sol`. Create the basic code structure of every Solidity smart contract:

```
pragma solidity 0.5.0;
contract Copyright {}
```

The order of every smart contract is simple. First, we define the events, the variables, the modifiers, the fallback function, the constructor, and, finally, the functions. So, let's define our events:

```
pragma solidity 0.5.0;
contract Copyright {
    // Create the events
    event RegisteredContent(uint256 counter, bytes32 indexed hashId, string
indexed contentUrl, address indexed owner, uint256 timestamp, string email,
string termsOfUse);
}
```

This event logs the `counter`, `hashId`, `contentUrl`, the address of the owner, the timestamp, email, and terms of use for that content. We can now define the `struct` that contains those variables. Our goal is to store information in a way that is as accessible as possible, so a struct is the best way to organize copyrighted content with mapping:

```
pragma solidity 0.5.0;
contract Copyright {
    // Create the events
    event RegisteredContent(uint256 counter, bytes32 indexed hashId, string
indexed contentUrl, address indexed owner, uint256 timestamp, string email,
string termsOfUse);
```

```
    // Create the variables that we'll use
    struct Content {
        uint256 counter;
        bytes32 hashId; // The half keccak256 hash since we can't store the
entire 64 bit hash
        string contentUrl;
        address owner;
        uint256 timestamp;
        string email; // We need a valid email to contact the owner of the
content
        string termsOfUse;
    }
    mapping(bytes32 => Content) public copyrightsById;
    uint256 public counter = 0;
    address payable public owner;
}
```

The mapping will associate each hash to the content object that stores all the relevant information about the copyrighted content. Here's the reason behind each of those members inside the struct:

- counter: We need a simple way to keep track of how many copyrighted elements are added to the blockchain, because it provides us with a simple way to look up the latest content using the registry of events.
- hashId: The keccak256 string of the text content that we'll associate with this object. Because we can't use strings as the key of the mapping, we have to use a bytes32 type of variable. This causes the problem that we can't store the entire keccack256 string because it's 64 characters long, and bytes32 variables are limited to 32 hexadecimal characters. What we're going to do to overcome this limitation is to cut the resulting hash in half to only store the first half, which is exactly 32 bytes. This significantly reduces the hash security, but it's good enough given that we won't generate astronomically high copyrighted elements.
- contentUrl: A web URL that contains the original document to be copyrighted.
- owner: The content owner's address, which is essential to guarantee the person's property.
- timestamp: A fixed timestamp for when the content was copyrighted. Great to set up expiry dates to invalidate outdated elements.
- email: A valid email to provide users with a simple system to contact the owner of that particular content.
- termsOfUse: A short piece of text explaining how the content must be treated: what you can do with it as an external individual, when you can use it, and so on.

You can add your own elements to the struct if you wish to create a different type of copyright registry marketplace. It's about personal preference. Finally, I've added an owner variable that we'll use later for extracting funds that could end up locked in this contract. Now, we can continue with the functions:

```
// To setup the owner of the contract
constructor() public {
    owner = msg.sender;
}

// To add new content to copyright the blockchain
function addContent(bytes32 _hashId, string memory _contentUrl, string
memory _email, string memory _termsOfUse) public {
    // Check that the most important values are not empty
    require(_hashId != 0 && bytes(_contentUrl).length != 0 &&
bytes(_contentUrl).length != 0 && bytes(_email).length != 0);

    counter += 1;
    Content memory newContent = Content(counter, _hashId, _contentUrl,
msg.sender, now, _email, _termsOfUse);
    copyrightsById[_hashId] = newContent;
    emit RegisteredContent(counter, _hashId, _contentUrl, msg.sender, now,
_email, _termsOfUse);
}
```

The constructor variable will be used for setting up the owner address.

The addContent function takes four parameters instead of the seven required for the struct since we can generate the others dynamically. This is important to simplify things and help people upload their copyright easier. First, it checks that the most important parameters are set because we need them no matter what. This means that the terms of use are optional for the simple reason that people can choose to not restrict the use of their content, meaning open content with their ownership.

We generate the newContent object, we increase the counter, and add that content to the mapping of copyrightsById to finally emit the registration event. This is the most important function and it has to be as optimized as soon as possible to avoid reaching gas limits.

 Note that we don't need a function to get the content by hash because the copyrightsById mapping is public, therefore it has a getter function automatically created for retrieving each struct element.

Let's continue with the function to delete copyrights and to extract funds:

```
// To delete something if you're the owner
function deleteCopyrightedByHash(bytes32 _hashId) public {
    if(copyrightsById[_hashId].owner == msg.sender) {
        delete copyrightsById[_hashId];
    }
}

// To extract the funds locked in this smart contract
function extractFunds() public {
    owner.transfer(address(this).balance);
}
```

The `deleteCopyrightedByHash` function takes the half `keccak256` hash of existing copyrights and deletes them if you're the owner of that particular content. The `extractFunds` function is an optional function that I like to add, because I usually see smart contracts with Ether inside that they got by mistake because someone didn't realize that they were sending real money to the contract address, so it's stuck in there forever. This function makes the extraction of funds possible so that you can retrieve the money if that ends up happening.

That's the entire contract! You can compile it with Truffle using `truffle compile`.

 You can check the updated code on my GitHub: `https://github.com/merlox/copyright-marketplace`.

Deploying your smart contract with Truffle

Deploying smart contracts with Truffle is not a straightforward process: you must go through a few different files to modify the expected behavior of Truffle. You see, Truffle needs to know where to deploy your contracts, the constructor parameters, and the deployment order, among other things; therefore it's necessary that you configure all the moving parts to be able to deploy your contract continuously. Once set up, you'll be able to re-deploy new versions with just a command since Truffle will know exactly what you need to get done, how, and where.

We will deploy our contract using the following steps:

1. First, you must compile your contract with `truffle compile` since you can only deploy compiled code to the blockchain. Open the `truffle-config.js` file from your project folder. That's the file where the deployment configuration is set up.

2. If you read the comments, you'll see that Truffle uses INFURA for a quick and effective connection to the blockchain and that you need to uncomment lines 1 to 5 to update your information. For instance, the commented code shown here must be uncommented:

```
         Token.sol          truffle-config.js

   1  // const HDWalletProvider = require('truffle-hdwallet-provider');
      // const infuraKey = "fj4jll3k.....";
      //
      // const fs = require('fs');
      // const mnemonic = fs.readFileSync(".secret").toString().trim();
```

Doing this will mean that it will look like the following:

```
         Token.sol          truffle-config.js          untitled          o

      const HDWalletProvider = require('truffle-hdwallet-provider');
      const infuraKey = "fj4jll3k.....";

      const fs = require('fs');
      const mnemonic = fs.readFileSync(".secret").toString().trim();
```

This essentially uncomments your INFURA and mnemonic variables.

3. Get your **INFURA** key by registering on `https://infura.io` to get unlimited access to high quality servers with blockchains installed after creating a project:

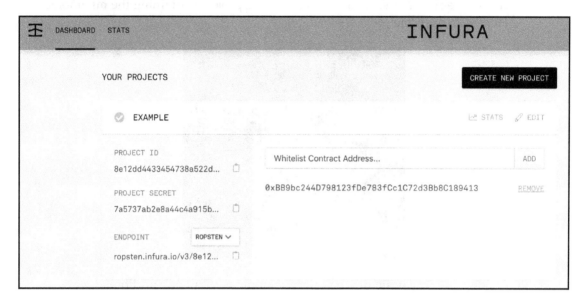

4. The **ENDPOINT** is where your **INFURA** key is. Simply click on the Copy icon next to it so that you have something similar to this:

https://ropsten.infura.io/v3/8e12dd4433454738a522d9ea7ffcf2cc

5. Strip the copied string down to just the part after the website name, since that's what Truffle uses when configuring the deployment network key:

v3/8e12dd4433454738a522d9ea7ffcf2cc

6. Now, paste that into your `infuraKey` variable inside `truffle-config.js` so that you're able to deploy your smart contract on `ropsten`:

```
21   const HDWalletProvider = require('truffle-hdwallet-provider');
22   const infuraKey = "v3/8e12dd4433454738a522d9ea7ffcf2cc";
```

7. What you need now is to give Truffle your mnemonic phrase, so that it's able to deploy the smart contract on `ropsten` with your address. To do so, create a file called `.secret` at the topmost level of your project containing the mnemonic. Here is an example:

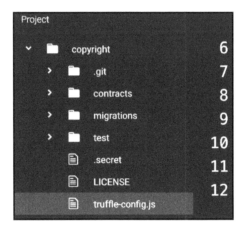

8. Inside `.secret`, write down your mnemonic without any additional information:

9. Then, go back to your `truffle-config.js` file and uncomment the section about `ropsten`:

```
61    // Useful for deploying to a public network.
62    // NB: It's important to wrap the provider as a function.
63    ropsten: {
64      provider: () => new HDWalletProvider(mnemonic, `https://ropsten.infura.io/${infuraKey}`),
65      network_id: 3,        // Ropsten's id
66      gas: 5500000,         // Ropsten has a lower block limit than mainnet
67      confirmations: 2,     // # of confs to wait between deployments. (default: 0)
68      timeoutBlocks: 200,   // # of blocks before a deployment times out  (minimum/default: 50)
69      skipDryRun: true      // Skip dry run before migrations? (default: false for public nets )
70    },
```

10. Then, install `truffle-hdwallet-provider` with the following command:

   ```
   $ npm i truffle-hd-wallet-provider
   ```

11. Be sure to be in your project folder when installing it, since it will install in the current location. Finally, execute the following:

   ```
   $ truffle deploy --network ropsten
   ```

Your contract will be deployed in a few minutes, depending on the network. You can then play and test the smart contract. Make sure to hash the copyrighted content with `keccak256` by using this tool: `https://emn178.github.io/online-tools/keccak_256.html`.

After getting `keccak256`, cut it in half and generate the hexadecimal code. If you have MetaMask, you can do that from your browser, since you'll have web3.js available on all websites. These are the steps to convert a specific string of text into the hexadecimal version within your browser:

1. Open the developer tools on your browser.
2. Go to the **Console** tab where you can execute JavaScript code.
3. Type `web3` to see if web3 is available.
4. If so, take your half `keccak256` resulting code and generate the hexadecimal version with `web3.toHex('your-hash')`, as shown in the following example:

   ```
   web3.toHex('041a34ca22b57f8355a7995e261fded7')
   "0x30343161333463613232623537663833353561373939356532363166646437"
   ```

You can then use that hexadecimal string to add a new copyright element to your smart contract as `hashId`.

The EVM in depth

The **Ethereum Virtual Machine (EVM)** is one of the least understood parts of the entire Ethereum ecosystem. It could be because the complexity that this virtual machine contains is confusing even to the best developers. In any case, your goal as an Ethereum expert is to become great at all things related to Ethereum development, so it's a must that you understand the intricacies of this powerful virtual machine so that you can extract its full potential at all times.

Explaining the EVM

The EVM is a virtual machine where smart contracts and transactions get executed. Think of VirtualBox or VMware with the Ethereum operating system. They are emulations of a physical computer, in order to create a clean environment where applications can communicate with the CPU. This type of virtual machine processes transactions, blocks, and smart contracts uniformly for all users. It keeps hundreds of computers connected, so it's very important to have enough security to protect each node from potential attacks. Some of the security systems that are implemented are as follows:

- **Gas**: Every transaction must be paid before being executed to avoid abusive behaviors where some nodes send unlimited transactions without any intention of paying them.
- **Peer-to-peer communication**: Nodes can only communicate via messages by sending and receiving data, which means that they can't access each other's data.
- **Deterministic**: This means that the initial state will always produce the same results. For instance, adding two numbers will result in the same exact result if they are the same. This is important to make consensus possible because it allows others to verify that the transactions are indeed valid; otherwise, it would be impossible to verify transactions and consensus would be limited given that the same state results in different calculations.
- **Sandboxed execution**: Since this is a virtual machine, smart contracts using it can't have access to the outside computer making all the transactions possible. Only smart contracts can interact with each other with a limited scope.

To fully understand how the EVM works, we have to go deeper into the assembly language that keeps this system together. Ideally, we could understand bytecode language, which is what computers process, but because we can't, we've created an abstraction for each process in a language called **assembly** that can be easily translated to bytecode for processors to compute.

Operation of smart contracts in the EVM

Smart contracts are fascinating because they are able to keep many nodes connected in a single system that understands how they should make decisions and agree on the results. They work on top of a stack-based virtual machine that you could think of as an array that keeps track of the variables stored in memory. It provides you with a set of small functions to manipulate that stack. To understand how smart contracts operate in the EVM, we'll have to follow them to see how they are being transformed by the virtual machine until they become executable bytecode.

For instance, take a simple contract such as this one:

```
pragma solidity ^0.5.0;

contract Example {
    uint256 myNumber = 3;
}
```

How does a compiler such as `solc` convert that code into something that the EVM can understand so that the computer can process it? Let's try to analyze it with that specific compiler. Install `solc` by executing the following command:

$ npm i -g solc

If you compile the contract to bytecode and analyze the process that the bytecode is taking, you will get the following:

$ solcjs Example.sol --bin

You'll see a few interesting things about the EVM's behavior. First off, you'll get a file with the `.bin` termination, such as `Example_sol_Example.bin`, which is the binary file containing the compiled bytecode of the smart contract:

```
608060405260036000553480156014576000080fd5b50603580602260003960000f3fe6080604
052600080fdfea165627a7a72305820aa17e74115b5e066ae13d560c624e9abef54adbce68c
3443886eadc4e1059cfe0029
```

To understand all that bytecode and see what the EVM is really doing, we have to split each instruction accordingly. `6080604052` is just the initialization of the smart contract. It's always the same for every contract. Then, we have the following:

```
60 03
```

The number 60 is a specific instruction, known as PUSH, that essentially moves the number 3 to the memory stack. The stack is just an empty array that can get or delete values from its array. Our stack looks like this after the PUSH 3 instruction:

```
stack: [3]
```

The following instruction adds a zero to the stack:

```
60 00
```

This results in `stack: [0, 3]`.

Then, we have `55`, which is a `STORE` instruction that writes `uint256` permanently to storage, the blockchain. We need to add the number 3 to the stack before we can write it into storage. What we did here is essentially the following:

```
uint256 myNumber = 3;
```

This is equivalent to the following:

```
6003600055
```

Remember that all smart contracts start with `6080604052`, as you saw in the complete bytecode. Our smart contract contains just a `uint256` assignment, so it follows that bytecode with `6003600055`. What we finally have is the following:

```
608060405260036000553480156001457600080fd5b5060035806022600039600f3fe6080604
052600080fdfea165627a7a72305820aa17e74115b5e066ae13d560c624e9abef54adbce68c
3443886eadc4e1059cfe0029
```

The rest is irrelevant, since it contains information about the sender and the contract. There are about 100 opcodes, and many different techniques are used in the EVM to translate smart contract code to bytecode so that it can be published to the blockchain efficiently.

Now, you understand what happens under the hood when you write a smart contract, compile it, and deploy it to the network. The rest is up to the nodes that run their own specific implementation of the Ethereum protocol, so they decide which blocks to take and which ones to ignore. The EVM is a complex virtual environment that processes transactions and bytecode from smart contracts to achieve a global consensus that benefits everybody.

Upgradable and scalable smart contracts

The Ethereum blockchain is immutable, which means that you can't modify its past actions. Once an action is confirmed by the majority of the miners, that action stays there forever. The same restrictions apply to smart contracts. However, we, as Ethereum experts, are able to overcome the issue of deploying unscalable code that ends up being vulnerable because we understand that there are different development techniques where we create scalable code. The idea is to deploy smart contracts so that they are ready to scale in the future with a set of different, interchangeable contracts. Knowing how to create smart contracts that scale and can be improved in the future is an essential skill that any top Ethereum expert must possess, so don't miss out on it.

Upgradable smart contracts

Upgradable smart contracts are the next step when it comes to creating advanced smart contracts for big industries that keep evolving and require new functionalities unexpectedly. They can be used in all kinds of projects, but I recommend that you use them only for those that may require upgrades in the future or for those that want to secure their data for future projections. Not every smart contract needs to have upgradable functionalities, although tokens and the likes will benefit heavily from upgradable code.

We'll create an upgradable smart contract that is made up of three parts and two smaller smart contracts. Here's how it will look:

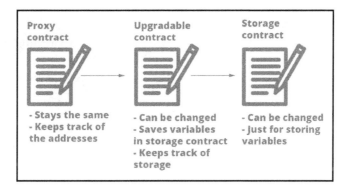

There are many ways to make upgradable smart contracts—you can even create your own! So, be patient when it comes to understanding this kind of technology, because it can seem confusing in the beginning.

To make a contract upgradable, we need three pieces:

- **The proxy contract**: This is the initial contract—the main contract that users always use to interact with the code. Think of this one as the same old smart contract that you use to make function calls but that, instead of executing the logic inside here, gets executed in the upgradable smart contract.
- **The upgradable contract**: This one is where all the logic takes place. This contract can be upgraded, which means that it can be removed and you can deploy a newer version with the same name and new functions. Users won't interact with this contract directly since the address changes every time it gets upgraded.

- **The storage contract**: Because we don't want to lose our state variables and all the user information every time we upgrade a contract, we will store all the variables, mappings, and data in this storage contract. It will have only variables and setter functions to update those variables. It won't have any logic or functions besides those.

To upgrade a contract while keeping the same address, what will happen is this:

1. Users will send a transaction to the proxy contract, for instance, `execute function buyTokens()`.
2. The proxy contract will send that, find the `buyTokens()` function inside the upgradable contract, and execute it.
3. The upgradable contract will process the logic to buy tokens and it will store all the changes inside the storage contract, for instance, by calling a function named `setTokens()`, which increases the number of tokens of user A to 40.
4. The storage contract executes `setTokens()` and updates the tokens variables to `tokens = 40;` for user A.

That's essentially the workflow of how the logic operates. In essence, we will always use the same contract address, but the logic will change. We will also keep the same information without deleting it because it's valuable information that could be very hard to re-insert.

To help you understand the concept behind all these contracts, I'll show you a pseudocode version of the code that each smart contract has. We'll use the token analogy, where a user wants to buy tokens in an upgradable contract.

Here's what the proxy contract would look like:

```
contract Proxy {
    address public upgradableContractAddress;
    function () public {
        // Delegate the execution to the upgradable contract instead of
using the code in this contract since this contract won't change, it's just
to keep the address consistent and to have a registry of upgradable
contracts
    }
}
```

This is what the upgradable contract would look like:

```
contract Upgradable {
    address public storageContractAddress;
    function buyTokens() public {
        // This is the function that the proxy called in this example. So
```

```
    this contract will execute the needed logic to buy tokens and will update
    the state variables in the storage contract
            storageContractAddress.setTokens(userA, 40);
        }
    }
```

And, finally, here's what the storage contract would look like:

```
contract Storage {
    mapping(address => uint256) public tokens;
    function setTokens(address _user, uint256 _number) public {
        // This function is used to update the storage variables since we
don't want any logic to take place in this contract
        tokens[_user] = _number;
    }
}
```

Those three contracts working together are the core concept behind upgradable smart contracts, where instead of updating the entire codebase, we break the different roles into changeable parts that can be modified in the future. Let's take a deeper look at how they are all implemented, one by one.

Storage smart contracts

The storage smart contract is the simplest of the three, since it just contains variables and functions to update those variables. We don't need getters, because these are public variables that already have getter functions created by default for being public.

We'll create a simple storage smart contract that contains one `uint` variable for demonstration purposes. You'll then be able to add more variables as you need. This contract is quite simple, since it just contains one variable:

```
pragma solidity ^0.5.0;

contract Storage {
    uint256 public myNumber;
    function setMyNumber(uint256 _myNumber) public {
        myNumber = _myNumber;
    }
}
```

As you can see, we have a variable called `myNumber` and a setter function called `setMyNumber` that updates that variable.

You may want to introduce access logic to only allow specific users to update certain variables. For now, it's enough that you understand how it looks.

Upgradable smart contracts

The upgradable smart contract is the most interesting one. It will execute all the logic and will interact with the storage contract whenever it has to update some variable data. Let's take a look at the code to see how it works. We'll later see how to upgrade it:

```solidity
pragma solidity ^0.5.0;

contract Upgradable {
    address public storageContract;
    constructor (address _storageContract) public {
        storageContract = _storageContract;
    }
    // A sample function that you could implement for buying tokens for
demonstration purposes
    function buyTokens() public {
        // Do your logic for buying tokens for instance, calculating how
many he will get for the msg.value he sent and so on. To later update the
storage information
        // Create the storage contract instance
        Storage s = Storage(storageContract);
        s.setMyNumber(10);
    }
}

contract Storage {
    uint256 public myNumber;
    function setMyNumber(uint256 _myNumber) public {
        myNumber = _myNumber;
    }
}
```

This upgradable contract is in the same file as the `Storage` smart contract. This is important at the beginning because we need access to that contract for deployment purposes. Alternatively, you could use the `import` keyword.

As you can see, I've declared the `Upgradable` smart contract with a variable called `storageContract`, which keeps track of the storage contract's address, since we will update the state variables there. In the constructor, we set the storage contract's address, since this contract will keep the same storage until it's updated. Then, I added a function called `buyTokens()` as an example to show you how it would look in a real-world example; right now, it doesn't do anything besides updating the storage by calling `setMyNumber()` from the `Storage` contract.

If you were to create a real implementation, you'd add all your desired logic. I don't want to show you a real, completed version of this upgradable contract because the many functions would distract you from understanding how an upgradable smart contract works.

It shows that you execute all your logic and then, at the end of the file, you update your storage variables by calling the storage contract.

To upgrade this contract, follow these steps:

1. Deploy a new version of this contract with your updated functions. You can add new functions, update old ones, or even delete some.
2. When deploying the contract, use the storage address in your constructor, since you need to access that contract for variable keeping.
3. Finally, in the proxy contract, execute a function called `upgradeUpgradableContract()`, which will redirect all the function calls to the newer version of your upgradable smart contract.

Notice how you can deploy this contract while keeping the same storage contract, thus preserving your data safely and so that it is ready to use like nothing happened in the next version of your upgradable contract. Alternatively, you can deploy a new storage contract and then a new upgradable contract pointing to that new storage. That way, you have clean storage if you don't want to keep the old data. Nevertheless, you'll still have access to the old data, since the contract will permanently live on the blockchain just by pointing to the old storage address when creating a new upgradable.

Proxy smart contracts

This is the most important piece because this contract will never change. We don't want it to change, because we want to keep the same Ethereum address while updating the underlying logic. This contract will redirect all the calls to the upgradable contract and will have several variables to register the current upgradable contract's address and a list of past contracts for those that don't want to update to the new code.

Remember that upgrading to a new version is always optional. If your users decide that they want to keep using the old smart contracts, they will simply send all their transactions to the old upgradable contract directly without executing the proxy contract. You could stop them from doing so by destroying the old upgradable smart contract with the `selfdestruct()` function, but I don't recommend it, since it makes your contract worthless, and it could be usable in the future.

Here's how the proxy contract looks:

```solidity
pragma solidity 0.5.0;

contract Proxy {
    address public storageAddress;
    address public upgradableAddress;
    address public owner = msg.sender;
    address[] public listStorage; // To keep track of past storage
contracts
    address[] public listUpgradable; // To keep track of past upgradable
contracts
}
```

This is the most complex contract because it has to do quite a few things. First off, we set up `storageAddress`, `upgradableAddress`, and `owner`. Those are the variables that the contract will use to understand where to redirect all the calls. We don't actually need to keep track of the storage address or the owner, but it's good practice, since it makes things understandable and gives you more options. Note that the `delegatecall()` function can't update the storage of the upgradable contract, so we set up an external storage.

Then, we have two address arrays: `listStorage` and `listUpgradable`. These arrays will contain the current and older versions of those storage and upgradable contracts since we want to have access to old logic in case we needed to do so with those addresses. I've added an `onlyOwner` modifier because we only want to allow contract updates from the owner.

After that, we have the constructor. It is used to deploy a new storage and upgradable smart contract right away. You could deploy them separately, but it's just easier and cleaner to do it from the proxy's constructor:

```solidity
modifier onlyOwner {
    require(msg.sender == owner);
    _;
}

constructor() public {
    storageAddress = address(new Storage());
    upgradableAddress = address(new Upgradable(storageAddress));
```

```
        listStorage.push(storageAddress);
        listUpgradable.push(upgradableAddress);
    }
```

Next, there's the fallback function, which is marked as external. This is the most important function, since it's the one that will receive all the function calls and will redirect them to the right function from the upgradable smart contract. It works by using the `delegatecall()` function. It's a low-level function that receives a `bytes` parameter to indicate which function to call from the other contract with the parameter values:

```
function () external {
    bool isSuccessful;
    bytes memory message;
    (isSuccessful, message) = upgradableAddress.delegatecall(msg.data);
    require(isSuccessful);
}
```

Finally, we have the functions that are required to upgrade the storage and logic contracts whenever the owner decides to do so. They work by keeping track of previous versions in the arrays so that users can access older versions if they want to do so:

```
function upgradeStorage(address _newStorage) public onlyOwner {
    require(storageAddress != _newStorage);
    storageAddress = _newStorage;
    listStorage.push(_newStorage);
}

function upgradeUpgradable(address _newUpgradable) public onlyOwner {
    require(upgradableAddress != _newUpgradable);
    upgradableAddress = _newUpgradable;
    listUpgradable.push(_newUpgradable);
}
```

To understand how the mechanism of communicating with the logic contract works, check out this function:

```
upgradableAddress.delegatecall(msg.data);
```

First, this takes the address of the contract to call, which in this case is the upgradable contract address, and then the data with the information to transmit. The `msg.data` parameter is a special variable that contains the function to call with the parameter values. Here's where you'd write the function name to call. For instance, let's say that you want to execute the `buyTokens(uint256 _number)` function, with the `_number` parameter being 12.

In a normal contract, you'd simply create a contract instance and call the function by name while sending the parameter values:

```
MyContract(contractAddress).buyTokens(12);
```

But we can't do that when we don't know the function name beforehand. Remember that we're dealing with a contract that may have new functions in the future, and we also want to have access to those functions from the same proxy contract. For that reason, we use `msg.data`. That variable contains a hexadecimal bytes string with the function name and the parameters. Let's see how to format it properly so that Solidity understands which function we want to call.

First, we need the function name, and then we need the parameters encoded. Because Solidity works with hexadecimal values, we need to write it in hexadecimal form using the function signature. The function signature is a short way to reference functions by a short hexadecimal value instead of their string names. If you go to `https://remix.ethereum.org`, you can quickly see the function signature of each of your functions:

```
57    // The one that will be upgraded
58 ▾ contract Upgradable {
59        address public storageAddress;
60
61 ▾        constructor (address _storageAddress) public {
62            storageAddress = _storageAddress;
63        }
64
65 ▾        function setMyNumberStorage(uint256 _number) public {
66            Storage s = Storage(storageAddress);
67            s.setMyNumber(_number);
68        }
69    }
70
```

As you can see, I've copied my contract on Remix. Now, to get the function signature in a hexadecimal form of the `setMyNumberStorage()` function, you have to go to the compile tab while selecting your contract:

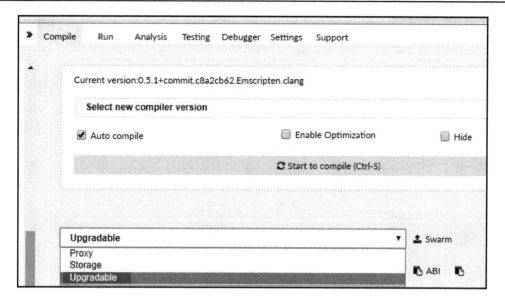

Then, you can click on **Details** for more information:

If you scroll down, you'll see the section with the function hashes of your contract:

```
FUNCTIONHASHES

{
    "009be4e6": "setMyNumberStorage(uint256)",
    "85aa92a7": "storageAddress()"
}
```

The function hash for `setMyNumberStorage()` is `009be4e6`; that's the function's signature. Great! We have the first part of our `msg.data` object: `0x009be4e6`.

Now, we need to encode the parameters of the function. Let's say that I want to set a number of `16` when calling the function. You can do it manually by converting that number into its hexadecimal form with web3. If you have MetaMask installed, you can open your browser's developer tools to interact with `web3.js`. In the console, you can simply type `web3.toHex(16)` and you'll receive the hexadecimal version of 16:

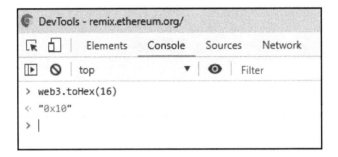

Note that `web3.toHex()` only works for version 0.20 of web3, which is the one being used by MetaMask at the moment. The syntax is different in web3 1.0, so if MetaMask updates its version of web3, you can read how to do hexadecimal conversion in the official web3 1.0 docs.

Now, we just need to add 62 zeroes in front of 10, since `0x10` is our number to get the encoded version of that parameter. Here's an example:

```
0000000000000000000000000000000000000000000000000000000000000010
```

That would be 16 encoded hexadecimally. We just need to add the function signature in front of that to complete our `msg.data` object:

```
0x009be4e6000000000000000000000000000000000000000000000000000000000000000010
```

That's about it! That long string of hexadecimal numbers says: *Call the function setMyNumberStorage(12).*

Going back to where we left it, the `.delegatecall(msg.data)` function can now be executed properly with the converted value of our function call. You may be asking yourself: *But why complicate things so much, how will users do all that conversion work?*

The truth is that people using your smart contract or dApp won't do all the conversion. You'll simple write the conversion logic in your decentralized application, and the function names will be converted automatically in a few lines with web3, as you saw already. Alternatively, you can deploy your contract on Remix and get the entire encoded function call with just one button:

When you deploy a contract, you can see a box where you can interact with your deployed contract. If you click the arrow that I've marked, you'll see the expanded version of the function call that shows you the toolbox icon, which you can click to get `setMyNumberStorage(16)` converted directly into hexadecimal form:

    0x009be4e6000000000000000000000000000000000000000000000000000000000000010

That's a simple trick to make the conversion when using your contracts with Remix. With that hexadecimal number, you can go to MetaMask and paste it inside the data field. First, open MetaMask and click on **SEND**:

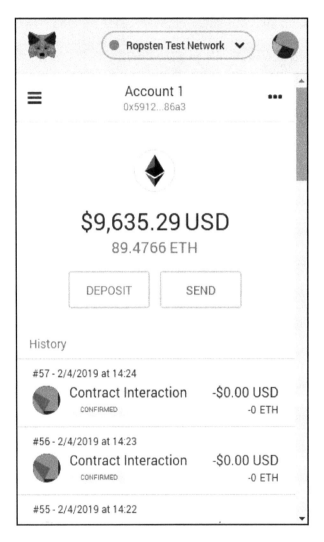

Then, paste your code into the data field by scrolling down:

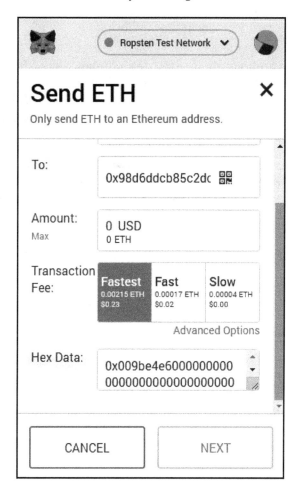

After confirming the transaction, you'll see that your function has been successfully delegated and that you've made the execution from the proxy contract.

Let's go back to our fallback function:

```
function () external {
    bool isSuccessful;
    bytes memory message;
    (isSuccessful, message) = upgradableAddress.delegatecall(msg.data);
    require(isSuccessful);
}
```

You can see that the `delegatecall` function returns two values: a boolean for whether the delegation was successful and a bytes parameter:

```
(isSucessful, message)
```

We simply capture them and require that the delegation is successful. Otherwise, it will revert the transaction and not make any changes. This is important, because the `delegatecall` function doesn't care if the delegation was successful or not; it will simply inform you to let you take the decision, since it's a low-level function that can be used in many advanced situations.

Another interesting property of `delegatecall()` is that `msg.sender` of the receiving contract will be your Ethereum address instead of the proxy contract's address. This is important because otherwise, your address would simply be different in the upgradable contract. You don't want that in many cases, where the user address is important for some logic.

Finally, we have these two functions:

```
function upgradeStorage(address _newStorage) public onlyOwner {
    require(storageAddress != _newStorage);
    storageAddress = _newStorage;
    listStorage.push(_newStorage);
}
function upgradeUpgradable(address _newUpgradable) public onlyOwner {
    require(upgradableAddress != _newUpgradable);
    upgradableAddress = _newUpgradable;
    listUpgradable.push(_newUpgradable);
}
```

They are simply used to update a smart contract. Whenever you deploy a new version of `Upgradable` or `Storage`, you'll have to execute the corresponding function to let the proxy contract know which one is the active one so that it can delegate all the function calls to the right version of the contract.

Scalable smart contracts

Usually, smart contracts are strictly limited by blockchain's processing capacity, since hundreds of thousands of nodes have to be connected to each other to execute the same transactions. This is a major problem when we're dealing with popular applications that exceed blockchain's capacity. To overcome this issue, there are different scaling solutions that you can implement in your smart contracts so that many more users are able to run your decentralized applications without performance issues.

To understand the scaling solution that you're going to learn, it's important to understand the process that takes place when using a smart contract:

- First, the user generates a transaction for a specific smart contract either by running a decentralized application that interfaces with that contract or by executing the smart contract directly with their own Ethereum node
- The transaction is received by the miners so that they can include it into the next block and execute the bytecode
- When they confirm it, the transaction gets permanently added to the longest chain

We can't speed up the process of confirming transactions by miners since the consensus scheme used by Ethereum requires that each node verifies each transaction until they all become valid.

What we can do instead is use a protocol known as **state channels**. It consists of commitment schemes that generate valid transactions off-chain as long as a group of people agree on those transactions. For instance, think about a card game such as blackjack. If you're not familiar with it, it consists of receiving one card per turn for each player and betting chips on getting the largest sum of combined cards. The one with a combined sum of 21, or the next largest number, wins. If you exceed 21, you lose.

In essence, state channels are like blackjack games, where users can play an endless number of games while keeping a score of chips that you can exchange for real money when you finish. It's a great scaling system because you can run many transactions off-chain directly peer-to-peer without waiting for the blockchain to process each one of them. You simply bundle the result together and push one big transaction to the blockchain when you end the game.

So, you're processing hundreds of transactions in real time until you end the game, when you have to send 1 transaction. Instead of waiting about 20 seconds per transaction for 100 transactions, you just wait 20 seconds once, while saving gas. Therefore, you end up with a much faster and scalable system where many more players can use your dApp with much better performance.

Using state channels for scalable smart contracts

I'll guide you through a simple example project so that you can see state channels in action. They use commitment schemes, which are just encrypted transactions that you can't change to commit to your actions before revealing the result when the players decide to show their cards.

The smart contract will be the entry and exit point of the state channel. What happens in-between is outside of the blockchain's control, although we'll define what goes inside each encrypted message so that we can verify it when ending. These are the steps:

1. Each player that participates in the game must open the state channel by calling a function in the smart contract to define who they are. When they do that, they must send some Ether to the smart contract as an escrow. Those funds will be used for distributing the rewards when the game ends.

2. Generate the hash with the variables that you want to commit. These hashes will contain the encrypted participation of each player. So, they exchange messages back and forth directly by first committing to their bet, then revealing their result and updating the variables and balances.

3. When they decide to end the game, they go back to the smart contract to upload their latest signed hash so that the smart contract can read it to send the corresponding Ether to each one.

Let's create the smart contract with the entry and exit functions. The rest will be done off-chain. As usual, here's the contract's structure:

```solidity
pragma solidity 0.5.0;

contract StateChannel {
    constructor () public payable {}

    function exitStateChannel() public {}
}
```

The constructor will be the entry, since we want to deploy a new instance of the contract per game. The `exitStateChannel()` function will check the latest signed hash and will send the corresponding Ether to each player. Notice how the constructor is payable given that we want to receive the escrow funds when starting.

Let's add some variables that we'll need. In this case, we'll create a simple guessing game where each player has to set a number from 1 to 10 and the other has to guess that number to win. So, player 1 wins when player 2 makes a guess different from theirs. They also bet Ether every guessing game; the winner takes double his bet as long as both have enough funds for those bets:

```solidity
pragma solidity 0.5.0;

contract StateChannel {
    address payable public playerOne;
    address payable public playerTwo;
    uint256 public escrowOne;
```

```
        uint256 public escrowTwo;

        constructor () public payable {}

        function exitStateChannel() public {}
    }
```

Next, we need to set up those variables for each player:

```
pragma solidity 0.5.0;

contract StateChannel {
    address payable public playerOne;
    address payable public playerTwo;
    uint256 public escrowOne;
    uint256 public escrowTwo;

    constructor () public payable {
        require(msg.value > 0);

        playerOne = msg.sender;
        escrowOne = msg.value;
    }

    function setupPlayerTwo() public payable {
        require(msg.sender != playerOne);
        require(msg.value > 0);

        playerTwo = msg.sender;
        escrowTwo = msg.value;
    }

    function exitStateChannel() public {}
}
```

As you can see, the constructor will initialize the address and escrow for the first player, while the setupPlayerTwo() function will do the same for the second player. That's all we need for opening the state channel between 2 players. Before creating the exitStateChannel() function that will end the game while closing the channel and distributing funds, I want to clarify what kind of elements compose each hashed message and how the game will be played off-chain.

In this guessing game, we have two players who have two different escrows in which they make bets every game about a specific number that they select. If the number is the same for both, the second player wins; otherwise, the first player wins. And they get double the number of Ether invested as long as they both have enough funds.

Therefore, player 1 will create an encrypted object containing the following values to start a game:

- **Number selected**: This must be between 1 and 10.
- **Amount of Ether bet for the game**: The other player must have enough funds to pay double what you invest. For instance, player 1 has 10 Ether while player 2 has 4. Player 1 won't be able to bet more than 4 Ether given that, if he wins, the second player will have to pay all his Ether to him. We will leave this option open so that they can invest as much as they want and if the bet exceeds the balance of the player, he simply gets all the funds, even if it's less than the bet.
- **Game sequence**: A counter that increases every game to identify the order of each game.
- **Timestamp**: A unique timestamp for each player to understand when the bet was made.
- **A nonce**: A random 10-digit number to keep each message unique. This is not mandatory, but it helps when trying to understand the order of events of the game.

Here's an example: the first player starts the game after opening the state channel by creating the smart contract with another player, who set up their escrow within the smart contract. He then creates the following data that will be encrypted:

- **Number selected**: 9
- **Amount of Ether to bet**: He has 10 Ether in escrow, so he'll bet 4 Ether for this game
- **Game sequence**: 1
- **Timestamp**: 1549378379
- **Nonce**: 2948372910

He then encrypts that information with the `keccak256` algorithm using a dApp:

```
keccak256(9, 4, 1, 1549378379, 2948372910);
```

He gets this resulting hash:

```
515e473c03c2d08f92825bad975ff0123f15b3ee2f457942a3484abe749f65b4
```

Note that this is just an example where the real `keccak256` would be different. He then signs that hash with the Ethereum account used in the state channel smart contract. He can do so with web3.js since it's the fastest way to sign hashes off-chain in combination with MetaMask:

```
web3.personal.sign(hash, web3.eth.defaultAccount, (err, result) => {
    if(err) return err
    return result
})
```

After that, the encrypted hash will be signed to later confirm that he indeed chose those parameters with his account. The other player will take the same steps to generate an encrypted signed hash with his bet.

When the two hashes are generated, they will use a decentralized application running some kind of communication system, such as a server or email, to exchange those hashes and reveal their bets. They will be able to verify those hashes at any point, since you can quickly verify that the information encrypted is valid once you know the valid contents of it.

Each new message will have an increased sequence number, a random nonce, and a new timestamp that must be larger than the previous one. All those checks can be done in a dApp that implements the state channel contract.

When they decide to end the game, they will upload their latest message to the smart contract for it to distribute the updated balances from the escrow that they configured when opening the channel. Here's how the game will be closed in the smart contract with the `exitStateChannel()` function.

First, we set up the variables required for our game to keep track of the balances:

```
pragma solidity 0.5.0;

contract StateChannel {
    address payable public playerOne;
    address payable public playerTwo;
    uint256 public escrowOne;
    uint256 public escrowTwo;

    // Variables to end the game
    uint256 public betOne;
    uint256 public betTwo;
    uint256 public balanceOne;
    uint256 public balanceTwo;
    uint256 public callOne;
    uint256 public callTwo;
    bool public isPlayer1BalanceSetUp;
```

```
    bool public isPlayer2BalanceSetUp;
    uint256 public finalBalanceOne;
    uint256 public finalBalanceTwo;
}
```

Then, we create the setup functions, which in this case are the constructor and
setupPlayerTwo(), whose job is to store users' initial data:

```
constructor () public payable {
    require(msg.value > 0);

    playerOne = msg.sender;
    escrowOne = msg.value;
}

function setupPlayerTwo() public payable {
    require(msg.sender != playerOne);
    require(msg.value > 0);

    playerTwo = msg.sender;
    escrowTwo = msg.value;
}
```

Finally, we add the most important function: the function to end the game and exit the state
channel by choosing a victorious player based on the last state:

```
function exitStateChannel(
    bytes memory playerMessage,
    uint256 playerCall,
    uint256 playerBet,
    uint256 playerBalance,
    uint256 playerNonce,
    uint256 playerSequence,
    address addressOfMessage)
    public
{
    require(playerTwo != address(0), '#1 The address of the player is
invalid');
    require(playerMessage.length == 65, '#2 The length of the message is
invalid');
    require(addressOfMessage == playerOne || addressOfMessage == playerTwo,
'#3 You must use a valid address of one of the players');
    uint256 escrowToUse = escrowOne;

    if(addressOfMessage == playerTwo) escrowToUse = escrowTwo;

    // Recreate the signed message for the first player to verify that the
parameters are correct
```

```
    bytes32 message = keccak256(abi.encodePacked("\x19Ethereum Signed
Message:\n32", keccak256(abi.encodePacked(playerNonce, playerCall,
playerBet, playerBalance, playerSequence))));
    bytes32 r;
    bytes32 s;
    uint8 v;

    assembly {
        r := mload(add(playerMessage, 32))
        s := mload(add(playerMessage, 64))
        v := byte(0, mload(add(playerMessage, 96)))
    }

    address originalSigner = ecrecover(message, v, r, s);
    require(originalSigner == addressOfMessage, '#4 The signer must be the
original address');

    if(addressOfMessage == playerOne) {
        balanceOne = playerBalance;
        isPlayer1BalanceSetUp = true;
        betOne = playerBet;
        callOne = playerCall;
    } else {
        balanceTwo = playerBalance;
        isPlayer2BalanceSetUp = true;
        betTwo = playerBet;
        callTwo = playerCall;
    }

    if(isPlayer1BalanceSetUp && isPlayer2BalanceSetUp) {
        if(callOne == callTwo) {
            finalBalanceTwo = balanceTwo + betTwo;
            finalBalanceOne = balanceOne - betTwo;
        } else {
            finalBalanceOne = balanceOne + betOne;
            finalBalanceTwo = balanceTwo - betOne;
        }

        playerOne.transfer(finalBalanceOne);
        playerTwo.transfer(finalBalanceTwo);
    }
}
```

When we have that many parameters for a function, it's great practice to separate each one in a new line. First off, we check that the address hasn't been set up, since we want to set up each message individually. Then, we regenerate the encrypted, signed hash message to verify that the parameters that were passed are valid. To verify if `keccak256` is valid, we only have to generate it again with the supposedly used parameters and check if the resulting hash is exactly the same as the one given.

After that, we use assembly to get r, v, and s, which are the three variables that are used to sign a message with your Ethereum account. We use it to get the address of the signer to verify that it comes from the right person. Then, we set up the balance, bet, and call of that player in the state variables. We do that to later distribute the funds when the second player executes the exit function with his parameters. Finally, after both have set up their resulting messages, we execute the Ether transfers with the `transfer()` function.

It seems complicated, but all we did was check that the signed message is valid, then check that the signature of the message is valid, and finally update the variables to distribute the funds when the other player verifies his exit message with this function.

This smart contract is just a demonstration. It has some important issues, such as the fact that one player could decide not to publish his message to exit the channel to avoid losing Ether. For that, we would need to add some kind of conflict resolution mechanism to distribute the funds if the second player doesn't respond after 24 hours. I'll leave that up to you to practice your skills.

These are the next generation of smart contract, which will power complex decentralized applications running for hundreds of thousands of computers simultaneously with some centralized logic. In the end, it's about making sure we leverage the trustless nature of the blockchain to create applications that can benefit users without external entities intervening in the process. Continue reading to learn more about efficient smart contracts that use the minimum amount of resources for the greatest results.

Gas and data-efficient smart contracts

It's imperative to make smart contracts that not only handle transactions in a transparent and secure manner, but that are actually using the blockchain resources as efficiently as possible. For this reason, we'll explore how to make gas- and data-efficient code for Ethereum. In this section, we're going to cover the following topics:

- Making gas-efficient smart contracts
- Making data-efficient smart contracts

Making gas-efficient smart contracts

I'm sure you've seen several smart contracts containing lots of functions that feel like they are consuming too much gas to operate: functions such as those that manage lots of state variables or those that have several different contracts operating at the same time.

Even though the blockchain requires gas be paid for every single transaction, it's in our best interest to create smart contracts that consume as few resources as possible so that transaction costs get reduced drastically for our users.

So, how do we do that?

It turns out that every small operation has an opcode associate in the EVM. Whenever you use an opcode, you're paying gas because miners have to process your transaction. Here's a list of the most common opcodes and their gas costs:

- `ADD` and `SUB`: Adding or subtracting two numbers. It costs 3 gas every time you add or subtract a number.
- `MUL` and `DIV`: Multiplying or dividing numbers. This costs 5 gas per operation.
- `AND`, `OR`, and `XOR`: Logic operations for comparing booleans. This costs 3 gas per operation.
- `LT`, `GT`, `SLT`, `SGT`, and `EQ`: Logic operations for comparing numbers. This costs 3 gas per operation.
- `POP`: It's an EVM stack operation to remove elements from the stack machine. It takes 2 gas for every `POP` operation.
- `PUSH`, `DUP`, or `SWAP`: To add elements to the stack machine. This uses 3 gas.
- `MLOAD` and `MSTORE`: To add data to the EVM's memory. This uses 3 gas per operation.
- `JUMP`: To jump to another place in the assembly code. This takes 8 gas.
- `JUMPI`: A conditional jump. This takes 10 gas per operation.
- `SLOAD`: Another stack operation that adds an element to the stack. This takes 200 gas per operation.
- `SSTORE`: Stores information into the blockchain directly. This takes anywhere between 5,000 to 20,000 gas every operation.
- `BALANCE`: To get the balance of an Ethereum account or contract. This uses 400 gas per operation.
- `CREATE`: To deploy a new smart contract or account. We need 32,000 gas to create a new smart contract.

As you can see, storing information in the state variables uses `SSTORE`, which costs up to 20k gas. That is very expensive and it's a place to optimize your code.

Here are the main optimization techniques that we'll explore and then explore with a real-world example to check the real gas costs:

- **The order of comparison operators**: The order of `&&` and `||` comparison operators, where the first condition is always checked, while the second may not be checked. For instance, if the second part of an if statement has a much higher probability of being true than the other, it's better to put the second part first, since in an `OR` statement, it will save gas because it won't spend unnecessary computations in checking the other parameters. The same thing is true of `AND`: you want to put the first part as the one most likely to be false because if the first part is false, the compiler won't check the second one and you'll save gas, given that every operator has a gas cost.
- **The `for` and `while` loops that use state variables**: When you have a loop that uses an external variable, you want it to use memory variables, since they are way cheaper than using storage.
- **Inaccessible `if...else` statements**: There are situations where a conditional `if...else` won't ever execute the other part. In those cases, it's important to remove duplicate, redundant, and unreachable code that would consume gas every time it's executed.
- **Limit the size of the variables**: The number after each variable type defines its capacity, so a variable with a smaller capacity consumes less gas for the simple reason that it won't need as much blockchain storage: for instance, `uint8` instead of `uint256` for smaller variables.
- **Don't use libraries when possible**: Every time you make a library or an external contract call, you're wasting gas, since you have to create an instance of that external contract, which in turn wastes gas. That's why it's better to combine all the code inside one big smart contract when deploying, instead of creating smaller pieces, which is great for development but not so much for production.
- **Instead of storing to storage, use memory**: The `memory` keyword after the function type tells the compiler to store that information temporarily in the local memory instead of writing it to the blockchain.
- **Limit balance calls**: Whenever you request the balance of some account, you're spending 400 gas, which can become quite a big number in sizeable contracts. Also, remember to store your balance in a memory variable if you're going to request it several times, because once you store it, you won't have to use the opcode CREATE again.

- **Use** bytes32 **instead of** string: String is a much bigger type of variable, since it can hold about 1,000 words using all the gas of the transaction. It doesn't have a limit, per se; instead, it's limited by the gas that you sent. The more gas, the bigger the string that you can store. However, it's always best to use bytes32 since it's much more compact, allowing you to store up to 32 characters, which is ideal for shorter texts such as names.

Let's see some examples that can be optimized using these techniques:

```
pragma solidity 0.5.0;
contract BadExample {
    uint256 public myNumber = 0;

    function counter(uint256 _counter) public {
        for(uint256 i; i < _counter; i++) {
            myNumber += 1;
        }
    }
}
```

As you can see in the preceding contract, we are running a for loop inside the counter() function, which just increments the myNumber state variable by the _counter times. Do you see where there could be a problem? The main issue is that we are writing to the state variable each time the loop runs, which means that we are spending from 5k to 20k gas using the SSTORE opcode every single iteration, because the myNumber variable is a state variable.

When running the function with _counter = 5, the transaction cost is 48,180 gas and with _counter = 10, it costs 74,625 gas. As you can see, the cost quickly increased by about 26k gas, which is exactly what we expected from the SSTORE opcode given that we ran it five more times.

To fix the contract, we simply have to create a new local variable that uses memory instead of storage:

```
pragma solidity 0.5.0;
contract GoodExample {
    uint256 public myNumber = 0;

    function counter(uint256 _counter) public {
        uint256 internalCounter = 0;
        for(uint256 i; i < _counter; i++) {
            internalCounter += 1;
        }
        myNumber += internalCounter;
```

```
        }
    }
```

In this case, the transaction cost went from 27,331 to 27,681, which is merely 350 gas. As you can see, it's a huge improvement that will save people at least double the money in thousands of transactions. It makes sense to create gas-optimized contracts. This example can be further improved by changing `uint256` to `uint8` or the equivalent in order to store smaller variables.

Let's see another example:

```solidity
pragma solidity 0.5.0;
contract Example {
    function doSomething() public {
        if (conditionOne && conditionTwo) {
            // Do something
        }
        if (conditionTwo || conditionOne) {
            // Do something
        }
        if (alwaysTrue) {
            // Do something
        } else {
            // Do another thing
        }
    }
}
```

This function runs a set of conditional statements with different conditions. In the first case, where `if (conditionOne && conditionTwo)`, we can improve the code by putting the condition most likely to be false first because it will save gas by not doing unnecessary checks to the second condition. The `&&` operator will not consider the second condition if the first one is false given that it requires both to be true, which makes sense, so it saves gas. Consider the following cases where we define the possibilities of each condition:

- `conditionOne` will be true 80% of the time, meaning that after 100 function calls, it will be true 80 times
- `conditionTwo` will be true 20% of the time, meaning that after 100 function calls, it will be true 20 times

If we leave the function as it is and we run the function 100 times, we will be wasting 3 gas every time the first condition is true but false in the other case. Remember that it costs 3 gas to run **AND (&&)**, **OR (||)**, and **XOR (^)**. So, after 100 runs, we'll be wasting 80 && checks, because the second condition is false in those cases, which means that we'll waste 300 gas. It doesn't seem much, but it adds up to many different functions and transactions, so it's imperative to pay attention to the order of the conditional statements.

The correct version would be as follows:

```solidity
pragma solidity 0.5.0;
contract Example {
    function doSomething() public {
        // Notice the condition 2 going first because it will be false most
of the times, thus rending the second condition unnecessary to check
        if (conditionTwo && conditionOne) {
            // Do something
        }
    }
}
```

The same thing happens to the OR || statement, where we want to put the condition most likely to be true first, since we only need one to be true. Whenever the first condition is true, the compiler will stop checking the remaining conditions in that if statement to save gas, since it's not needed. Considering the same probabilities from the previous example, where conditionOne is true 80% of the time and conditionTwo is true 20% of the time, we can fix the code to be gas-optimized:

```solidity
pragma solidity 0.5.0;
contract Example {
    function doSomething() public {
        // Notice the condition 1 going first because it will be true most
of the times, thus rending the second condition unnecessary to check
        if (conditionOne || conditionTwo) {
            // Do something
        }
    }
}
```

The last conditional statement in the function is this one:

```solidity
if (alwaysTrue) {
    // Do something
} else {
    // Do another thing
}
```

Because the condition inside the if statement will always be true, it doesn't make sense to add the `else` block, since it will never be run. In this case, it makes sense to remove that `else` block to save gas when processing the function:

```
pragma solidity 0.5.0;
contract Example {
    function doSomething() public {
        // Notice how we removed the } else { block because it will never
be execute
        if (alwaysTrue) {
            // Do something
        }
    }
}
```

This kind of check is also important for coverage testing, since this uses tools to verify that all parts of the code are being touched at least once to remove unnecessary elements.

As a final tip for this section, I want you to know a little trick for storing information super efficiently: use indexed events as storage. Events have a dedicated section in the blockchain that costs way less gas to execute, therefore making them super gas efficient. This can be leveraged to store small strings and variables that you want to use in your dApps with minimal costs. You can later find each event with web3.js because they are indexed, which means that they are searchable for that particular parameter. Also, note that you can only have three indexed parameters in each event, so you can create several different events that are indexed.

Remember to go back to the 8-point list we set out before, every time you write a contract to guarantee an efficient smart contract process that saves people money and reduces the size of the blockchain, which is what we all want, after all.

As a final tip, you can create `view` and `pure` functions for functionality that could be expensive, since `pure` and `view` functions don't consume any gas given that they process the calculations locally, so you're using computation for free. For instance, if you want to sort an array in Solidity, you'd have to spend a lot of gas, since each iteration costs gas, but, if the sorting function is `view`, it won't cost you any gas, so you can sort as many arrays as you want without spending gas.

Making data-efficient smart contracts

What I mean by a data-efficient smart contract is just code that is easy to read, understand, and manage. State variables are the main component when we talk about data efficiency: we want to optimize the maintainability of our code. This is not only important for explaining the code from developer to developer, but also for customers that will want to investigate what the smart contract code is actually doing. Data structures that are properly set up will save people hours of headaches and will improve the quality of your code exponentially.

Vyper does a fantastic job in this regard, because you can use custom Unit Types that are specifically designed to improve readability. It also uses a minimal syntax system inherited from Python that helps with the readability of the code. What does a data efficient smart contract look like? Take a look at this example:

```
pragma solidity 0.5.0;
contract GoodExample {
    // The number of seconds that you have each game to make decisions up
to 100
    uint8 public secondsPerGame;
    // To check if owner's address is setup when executing restricted
functions
    bool public isOwnerAddressSetup;
    // The name of the first player
    bytes32 public firstPlayersName;
}
```

As you can see, each variable has a short comment above it to help you understand what it's supposed to do, since it's not uncommon to find confusing variables that could be misinterpreted for the wrong reasons. Each name is properly defined with concise naming that tries to be as clear as possible about the variable's use, just as they provide a clear understanding about when not to use them.

The variable types are the right ones for each variable's purpose, since we want to make them gas efficient by maximizing the capabilities of the virtual machine without spending unnecessary amounts of gas.

In contrast, here's what a bad contract would look like:

```
contract BadExample {
    uint256 numberOfTimes;
    string public name;
    address public senderAddress;
}
```

Here, the naming is too simplistic, leaving too much room for confusion. There aren't comments above each variable to help you understand when they should be used, for what purpose, and with what limitations. And the variable types could be improved: instead of using `string` for the name, it probably makes sense to use `bytes32`, since we don't need such a big type for a short piece of text. The same thing is true with `uint256`, where we must consider whether it's better to reduce its size or not.

In general, we want to provide as much clarification in our contracts as possible. To do so, we'll write great descriptions on top of each variable, even when we think it's clear enough; we'll use types efficiently to optimize gas costs; and we'll name the variables concisely to help upcoming developers understand the complexity of the contract code.

Many large smart contracts become too big to understand easily, so it's imperative for you to optimize for data efficiency, since it's a great preventive security measure for detecting dangerous entry points.

You've just learned how to optimize your smart contracts with simple techniques that can save people's Ether by properly understanding opcodes with their costs associated, so that you can make better decisions when creating functions that will be executed by thousands of others.

Smart contract security analysis

Security in decentralized applications is a must that has to be carefully dealt with, since we are dealing with real money from real people that trust the code to be secure enough to keep their funds safely. You can't skip security analysis in your code, because otherwise you'll be risking people's money, so it's a huge responsibility.

That's one of the main reasons securing a smart contract can be so costly in time and price. Audits, bug bounties, and code analysis are common for ICO smart contracts and those that handle real-world funds. They are naturally expensive because they require careful consideration of all the moving parts in a smart contract.

Techniques to secure a smart contract

Let's take a look at some common checks that you want to go through before you deploy a smart contract to the Mainnet:

- **Overflows and underflows**: Overflowing a number means exceeding the capacity of it, thus resetting its value to start counting from zero again. Conversely, underflowing is exceeding the number capacity from the negative side, so when you go beyond zero in the uint type of variables, the value jumps straight to the largest value of that variable. For instance, let's say that you want to store 5,000 in a uint8: could you do it safely? No, because the maximum number of a uint8 is 2 ** 8, which is 255 (not 256, since we start at zero), so you'll exceed the capacity of that type several times before storing an unknown value. As you know, uints can't be negative, so when you try to store a negative number inside them, you'll underflow them. Pay attention to those situations and have checks in places to avoid exceeding the capacity of number types.

- **Documentation**: Not documenting your code is not a security risk in itself, since documentation has more to do with the fact that you'll save hours by not confusing functions that could be misinterpreted. When you do document your code properly, you can quickly understand where it could fail, making it easier to maintain and more secure when auditing the code. For that reason, I always recommend NatSpec documentation, which is a way of describing your functions using some common parameters that can easily be understood by compilers and developers.

- **Re-entrancy attacks**: You're probably familiar with this attack, which consists of taking advantage of the delegatecall function to call external contracts to update them in malicious manners. This is very dangerous and must be carefully analyzed whenever you see a low-level function such as delegatecall. You can avoid it by restricting access to the most important functions via visibility or modifiers.

- **Race conditions**: This type of attack consists of taking advantage of gas limitations to run a specific sequence of code repeatedly until you run out of gas. It can be prevented by making sure that you reduce state variables before increasing them. For instance, for a token contract that increases your balance whenever you buy tokens with Ether, it is important to reduce the number of Ether that you own before increasing the balance of tokens you own to avoid re-entrance situations.

There are many more small security issues that are specific to each individual contract. To fix them, you'll have to slowly analyze your smart contract to find points where it could lead to potential risks.

Summary

In this chapter, you started by getting up to speed to refresh your smart contract development skills with a project marketplace of copyrighted content to protect users' content. Then, you explored the depths of the obscure world that is the EVM with a solid understanding of how it works internally and how smart contracts benefit from this wonderful technology. After that, you learned about one of the most powerful skills in Ethereum: developing upgradable and scalable smart contracts that can be used for advanced projects so that you can efficiently run large-scale applications for big businesses.

Next, you learned how data and gas flows in smart contracts so that you're able to better manage the consumption of the precious resources available within the blockchain limitation, ultimately saving people's money and time with higher quality contracts. Finally, you've come full circle with security analysis to protect your code from malicious hands so that people's funds are completely secure in your dApps.

In the next chapter, you'll explore the wonders of advanced decentralized applications by challenging your current understanding of how great dApps are created from the ground up. You'll see step-by-step the most efficient way to build stronger dApps for projects that scale.

5
Mastering dApps

In mastering dApps, you're going to learn how to create advanced decentralized applications that use the smart contract that we saw in previous chapters. We'll go through all the steps from scratch including planning, developing the code, and testing the applications. First, you'll start by taking a look at how dApps are structured so that you can efficiently create new dApps from scratch. You'll go through the installation of Ethereum and Truffle to use it for your products. Then, you'll learn how to create great user interfaces that show people the right content without clutter. Finally, you'll create the smart contracts required to interact with the dApp and you'll integrate those to allow users to interact easily with the contracts from the interface.

In this chapter, we're going to cover the following topics:

- Introducing dApp architecture
- Installing Ethereum and Truffle
- Setting up and configuring Ethereum and Truffle
- Creating dApps
- Creating user interfaces
- Connecting smart contracts to web applications

Introducing dApp architecture

Architecting a decentralized application means making high-level software decisions to direct the design of our ideas. We are laying out the steps so that we can fluently create a dApp without getting stuck in design decisions. It also implies planning how the smart contract will communicate with the dApp, how users will interact with the dApp, and what kind of features we want for the end product.

When designing an application, we want to focus heavily on the user experience so that they feel comfortable using the resulting dApp. That's why it's important to have a clear vision of how it will look before we start coding because if we want to have a modern dApp that feels responsive for tech users, we'll have to focus more on providing extensive information about each element of our application.

For instance, let's suppose that you want to create a blog dApp where users can publish articles about specific topics. How would you design such a dApp? Where do you begin? Truthfully, there isn't a perfect system to design your ideal dApp from scratch; it's more of an interactive process where you go back and forth to the drawing board to clarify your ideas as you develop.

Personally, I like to start with a detailed description of what I have in mind with as much clarification as needed and with a list of features that must be there at all costs. For example, I want to create a decentralized blog for ICO enthusiasts who enjoy reading about new projects and are raising money with an ICO, TGE, or STO, since they are in the same ecosystem, surrounded by joint ventures, equity payments, blockchain innovations, and the like. This blog will reward users with tokens that they will be able to exchange for rewards in the system. Higher visibility, advanced metrics about each article, premium articles, and voting decisions will be accessible in exchange for tokens. The following are the features of this dApp:

- Search system to find articles by title and tags
- Comment sections with responses in real-time like a chat
- Writing tools for authors
- Promotion tools to increase visibility of an article
- A visibility score to indicate how visible each article is in the sea of content inside this dApp
- Design tools to customize the appearance for each of your comments and publications

Then, it helps to draw a diagram with the relationship between the components that make the entire dApp—the different backend services, the frontend, and the blockchain interactions. The idea is that you see visually what's important in your application. You can include whatever information you think will be relevant for the final dApp so that you are reminded of what's important and what's not. You'll find out that you automatically discard the things that don't matter. Take a look at the following diagram:

	Frontend	Backend	Blockchain
Technologies	- React.js - Socket.io	- Node.js - Express - Socket.io	- Vyper - Truffle

Categories to include	**Token utilities**	**Design**
ICO News ICO Analysis ICO Promotions ICO Airdrops ICO Opportunities	Increase visibility Premium articles Advanced metrics	Minimalistic Category focused Rewarding newcomers

Backend
Article and Comment structs
Centralized server to host the frontend

You can get way more technical than that but it's not that important in the stage of idea design where your goal is to fill in the blanks of what you plan to create. It will show you what's important before you realize it. Then, you can create a scheme of the types of data structures that you'll have in your smart contract, the building blocks of your user interface, and the performance features of the server for delivering snappy interactions.

Then, it's important that you ask yourself several design questions, such as the following:

- How are we going to handle a sudden increase of users?
- What systems must be in place to keep the application running in case we face an attack such as DDoS?
- How does a successful interaction from the user's point of view look like?
- Where do we think that we'll face uncertainty, what things are not clear enough yet?
- What's a realistic date for completion of all the core features?
- What does a **Minimum Viable Product** (**MVP**) of this idea look like? What features are indispensable?
- When can we complete the MVP?
- What problems are we solving for the casual user?
- What solutions are we providing that they can't find elsewhere?
- How can we discover or create demand for our idea before even starting?
- Can we get early users to help us deliver a product catered to that type of person?

- What does our ideal user look like: what do they do, what are their hobbies, where do they hang out online (so that we can bring them into the development process for creating a better product)?
- What is our purpose, why are we doing it? Name three reasons behind the why.
- Where can we be better, faster, more efficient?

From there, you can start creating your decentralized application from those ideas. Be sure to create a Google form, which is free and easy to use, to clarify all those questions and more that you consider relevant. Be explicit and detailed in your answers. Always remember to focus on solving a problem your users have. The key to successfully delivering a high-quality decentralized application is to have a solid base of why you are doing it so that you can stay motivated in tough times—that's why the questions are so important. It's a trick to get motivation from inside for facing difficult tasks.

Let's recap what you've learned so far. You learned the steps that it takes to architect a decentralized application with several mind tools to expose weak points of your ideas so that you can create solid applications without getting stuck on poorly designed interactions. You understand that great questions are the core foundation of clear thinking. You want to ask yourself as many questions as possible, and write them down to remember your purpose, so that you can be fully motivated to continue and complete your goal. Continue reading the next section to learn more about setting up your development environment.

Installing Ethereum and Truffle

To create truly powerful decentralized applications, we need to have a local version of Ethereum and Truffle. You can't get Ethereum by itself; you need to use a client, which in this case will be Geth. Truffle is a framework for creating, deploying, and testing dApps on your machine without having to wait for external services, all in one place.

There are different Ethereum implementations, with the most well-known being Parity and Geth. When it comes to installing Ethereum, what you're actually doing is getting a client that implements its protocol, so you have a choice regarding your favorite development system.

Let's go ahead and install Ethereum and Truffle. First, to get Ethereum on Mac, you need to run the following commands:

```
brew update && brew upgrade
brew tap ethereum/ethereum
brew install ethereum
```

That will compile all the code you need for your Mac in a few minutes. To get Geth on Windows, you have to download the binaries from their official website: `https://geth.ethereum.org/downloads/`; you can also get the binaries for the other systems, but it's just easier and more interesting to install Geth from the terminal when possible. Then, simply open the `geth.exe` file to run Ethereum.

To install Ethereum on Linux, you must execute the following lines on your Terminal:

```
sudo apt-get install software-properties-common
sudo add-apt-repository -y ppa:ethereum/ethereum
sudo apt-get update && sudo apt-get upgrade
sudo apt-get install ethereum
```

Now, to get Truffle, you'll need to do some additional steps:

1. First, install Node.js LTS from their official website at `http://nodejs.org`
2. Then, open it with your file explorer to run the installation process
3. When that's done, run `node -v` or `nodejs -v`; if it doesn't work, verify that you have it installed
4. Install `truffle` by running `npm i -g truffle`

You are now able to use Truffle for your projects by simply running the following on an empty folder, which will generate the file structure required for any `truffle` project:

```
truffle init
```

Setting up and configuring Ethereum and Truffle

Now that we have the required tools, we'll set up the basic file structure so that we have a clean environment to work with for all of our desired dApps. You'll be able to use it over and over as long as you need to, because it has all the dependencies set up.

First, let's create a folder called `dapp`, which will contain all of our files. Then, with your Terminal or command line, execute `truffle init` to set up Truffle, making sure that you're inside the `dapp` folder.

After installing Truffle in that folder, run `npm init` to set up your `package.json` file of Node.js that will allow you to install npm plugins. It will ask you for some general information about your project; simply fill it in as you please or press *Enter* to leave them empty, which is what I usually do unless I'm planning on distributing that project for others to use.

You'll see that you have the following folders created:

- `contracts/`: Where your contracts will go. Right now, it has a migrations contract to update your contracts as you improve your code.
- `migrations/`: Here is where you define how your smart contracts will be deployed, what parameters the constructor will have, and so on.
- `test/`: Your tests will go here for your smart contracts and dApps.
- `package.json`: The main npm file, which is used to install packages from the node registry.
- `truffle-config.js`: A configuration file to define how you'll connect to the blockchain, what Ethereum account you'll use, and so on.

Installing the required packages

What we have to do now is install the essential packages that we'll need for using React and webpack. First, update your `npm` version to the latest one with the following:

```
npm i -g npm@latest
```

Go to your `dapp` project folder if you haven't done so already and install `webpack` with the following:

```
npm i -S webpack webpack-cli
```

Webpack is a utility that takes all of your JavaScript files and combines them into one single, gigantic, easy-to-manage JavaScript file so that you can optimize development times.

After Webpack, install all the `babel` dependencies. Babel is a utility that works with webpack to take your JavaScript files and convert them into the latest version so that every browser is compatible with the new JavaScript functionalities, given that there are major differences across browsers that need to be normalized. Babel does just that, and you can install it like so:

```
npm i -S @babel/core @babel/preset-env @babel/preset-react babel-loader
```

Then, we need to install `react.js` since we'll use it for our project, as follows:

```
npm i -S react react-dom
```

Setting up webpack

We can now generate the `webpack.config.js` file where we'll specify how we want to have our JavaScript files handled, and where the combined version will be deployed. Create an empty `webpack.config.js` file at the root level of your `dapp/ folder` with the following configuration:

```
const path = require('path')

module.exports = {
    entry: './src/index.js',
    output: {
        filename: 'bundle.js',
        path: path.join(__dirname, 'dist')
    },
    module: {
        rules: [
            {
                test: /\.js$/,
                exclude: /node_modules/,
                use: {
                    loader: 'babel-loader'
                }
            }
        ]
    }
}
```

Module exports is the export object that's used in `node.js` projects. It contains the `rules` array, where you indicate which files must be passed through which compilers, in this case, `babel-loader`. The entry and output properties define where our files will be generated after combining them. Amplify the webpack configuration file with some additional information for defining the HTML resulting file; this is required to generate a valid HTML page automatically with your JavaScript files bundled together. Install the following loaders:

```
npm i -S html-webpack-plugin html-loader
```

Update your webpack configuration like so:

```
const html = require('html-webpack-plugin')
const path = require('path')

module.exports = {
    entry: './src/index.js',
    output: {
        filename: 'bundle.js',
        path: path.join(__dirname, 'dist')
    },
    module: {
        rules: [
            {
                test: /\.js$/,
                exclude: /node_modules/,
                use: {
                    loader: 'babel-loader'
                }
            }
        ]
    },
    plugins: [
        new html({
            template: './src/index.html',
            filename: './index.html'
        })
    ]
}
```

Setting up the source folder

Let's take a look at the following steps to set up the source folder:

1. Create a `src` folder where all your development code will go. Here's what your project setup should look like by now:

2. Create a new file inside `src/` called `index.html` with this code:

```
<!DOCTYPE html>
<html lang="en" dir="ltr">
    <head>
        <meta charset="utf-8">
        <title>Startup</title>
    </head>
    <body>
        <div id="root"></div>
    </body>
</html>
```

3. The `<div id="root">` object will be where our React project will start. With HTML, `webpack`, and `babel` set up, we can start creating the main `react.js` file that will be used in our project. Inside the `src/ folder`, create a file called `index.jsx`, which will contain our initial `react.js` file:

```
import React from 'react'
import ReactDOM from 'react-dom'
```

```
class Main extends React.Component {
    constructor() {
        super()
    }

    render() {
        return (
            <div>The project has been setup.</div>
        )
    }
}

ReactDOM.render(<Main />, document.querySelector('#root'))
```

Here, we are importing `React` and ReactDOM for connecting React with our HTML file. Then, we are creating a `Main` class that has a simple constructor and a `render()` function that returns a message confirming that the project has been set up properly.

4. Finally, you can compile those files with the following, where `-p` means production:

   webpack -p

5. Remember to execute it inside your project folder. After compiling your files, you need to run a static server that will deliver the files to your browser so that you can use your dApp. For that, install `http-server` using the following command:

   npm i -g http-server

6. Then, run it for your distribution folder:

   ```
   http-server dist/
   ```

7. Open `localhost: 8080` on your browser to see your dApp project live:

Congratulations! You now have a working startup project that you can replicate for other dApps that you want to create.

You can publish the project on your GitHub to clone it for other situations where you may need it by performing the following steps:

1. Open up `https://github.com` and create a new repository by clicking on **New**. Name it `dapp`, select **gitignore Node**, and an **MIT License**. Here's the one I created: `https://github.com/merlox/dapp`.

2. Now, go back to your Terminal and type `git init` if you have `git` installed on your system. That will start a new GitHub project inside your folder.

3. Then, you'll need to tell GitHub which repository you want to update your changes when you are committing new files with your own credentials; you can do all that permanently with the following command:

   ```
   git config remote.origin.url
   https://<YOUR-USERNAME>:<YOUR-PASSWORD>@github.com/<YOUR-USERNAME>/
   dapp
   ```

4. Pull the initial license files from your repository with the following command:

   ```
   git pull
   ```

5. Add your files with `git add .`, and commit them with `git commit -m`. First, commit them and push them with `git push origin master`. Then, you'll see your files in your new repository.

Remember to not push any new changes, since you want this repository to be as it is right now for future projects that use the same file structure.

Creating dApps

You are now ready to create dApps with Truffle, React, Webpack, and Solidity. To gain the required knowledge as fast as possible, we'll go through all the steps that it takes to create a fully working decentralized application. In this chapter, we are creating a music recommendation social media platform where people will be able to publish songs, they love at that moment to help their friends find interesting music to enjoy, all stored inside smart contracts without a centralized server.

We'll first create the smart contracts, then the user interface, and finally, we'll combine them all together with `web3.js`. We will test our decentralized application when the main interface is done to make sure it works properly.

Creating the smart contract

Before diving straight into creating the smart contract, let's define what we need it to do:

- We need an array that will store each users' music recommendations in a string or bytes32 format
- A struct to define user information
- A mapping with each users' recommendations
- An array of followed users so that we can see new musical updates

As usual, we start by creating the basic smart `contract` structure:

```
pragma solidity 0.5.0;

contract SocialMusic {

}
```

Then, we define the variables that we'll use, as follows:

```
pragma solidity 0.5.0;

contract SocialMusic {
    struct User {
        bytes32 name;
        uint256 age;
        string state; // A short description of who they are or how they
feel
        string[] musicRecommendations;
        address[] following;
    }
    mapping(address => User) public users;
}
```

Each user struct will hold all the music recommendations made by that user. Now, we need to create functions to add new music recommendations. We won't have functions to delete or modify past recommendations because we want it to be a permanent place for sharing past and present musical tastes, as follows:

```
pragma solidity 0.5.0;

contract SocialMusic {
  struct User {
  bytes32 name;
  uint256 age;
  string state; // A short description of who they are or how they feel
```

```
string[] musicRecommendations;
address[] following;
}
mapping(address => User) public users;

    // To add a new musical recommendation
    function addSong(string memory _songName) public {
        require(bytes(_songName).length > 0 && bytes(_songName).length <=
100);
        users[msg.sender].musicRecommendations.push(_songName);
    }
}
```

The addSong() function takes the song name as a string and pushes that song to the array of music recommendations for that particular Ethereum address. The _songName must be between 1 and 100 characters long to avoid extremely large or empty recommendations.

Then, we need functions to create new users and to follow others. People will be able to publish music recommendations with just their address if they don't want to set up their name, age, and state; they will be anonymous, so the setup function is optional:

```
pragma solidity 0.5.0;

contract SocialMusic {
    struct User {
        bytes32 name;
        uint256 age;
        string state; // A short description of who they are or how they
feel
        string[] musicRecommendations;
        address[] following;
    }
    mapping(address => User) public users;

    // To add a new musical recommendation
    function addSong(string memory _songName) public {
        require(bytes(_songName).length > 0 && bytes(_songName).length <=
100);
        users[msg.sender].musicRecommendations.push(_songName);
    }

    // To setup user information
    function setup(bytes32 _name, uint256 _age, string memory _state)
public {
        require(_name.length > 0);
        User memory newUser = User(_name, _age, _state,
users[msg.sender].musicRecommendations, users[msg.sender].following);
```

```
        users[msg.sender] = newUser;
    }
}
```

The `setup` function must at least receive the `_name` of the user, the other parameters are optional, and the recommendations made before the setup will stay linked to that user. Here's what the `follow` function looks like:

```
// To follow new users
function follow(address _user) public {
    require(_user != address(0));
    users[msg.sender].following.push(_user);
}
```

We are simply pushing a new address to the array of following users. You can deploy your contract with remix to manually test that all the functions are working. To deploy it with Truffle, we first need to set up the `truffle-config.js` configuration file and make sure our `SocialMusic.sol` file is in the `contracts/` folder of our project. As you learned in previous lessons, to set up `truffle-config.js` for `ropsten`, we need to uncomment the `ropsten` object at line 63:

```
    ropsten: {
        provider: () => new HDWalletProvider(mnemonic,
`https://ropsten.infura.io/${infuraKey}`),
        network_id: 3, // Ropsten's id
        gas: 5500000, // Ropsten has a lower block limit than mainnet
        confirmations: 2, // # of confs to wait between deployments.
(default: 0)
        timeoutBlocks: 200, // # of blocks before a deployment times out
(minimum/default: 50)
        skipDryRun: true // Skip dry run before migrations? (default: false
for public nets )
    },
```

Then, uncomment the variables at the beginning of the file at line 21:

```
const HDWalletProvider = require('truffle-hdwallet-provider');
const infuraKey = "fj4jll3k.....";

const fs = require('fs');
const mnemonic = fs.readFileSync(".secret").toString().trim();
```

Change your `infuraKey` to your personal key, which you can find after creating a project in `infura.io`. If you don't know how to get an `infuraKey`, go back to `Chapter 3`, *Ethereum Assets*, and execute the following code:

```
const infuraKey = "v3/8e12dd4433454738a522d9ea7ffcf2cc";
```

Create a `.secret` file with your MetaMask mnemonic, which will be used by Truffle to employ your first Ethereum account for deploying your `SocialMusic` smart contract. Be sure to add `.secret` to your `.gitignore` file if you're working on a git project, so that your account doesn't get leaked for people to see and steal your Ether.

Before deploying your contract, you need to install the wallet provider so that `truffle` has access to your account:

```
npm i -S truffle-hdwallet-provider
```

Now, you need to tell Truffle which contracts you want to deploy. You can do so by opening the `migrations/1_initial_migrations.js` file and changing it accordingly:

```
const SocialMusic = artifacts.require("./SocialMusic.sol")

module.exports = function(deployer) {
  deployer.deploy(SocialMusic)
}
```

Deploy your contract for `ropsten` after setting up your secret mnemonic with the following; remember to have enough `ropsten` Ether for deployment:

```
truffle deploy --network ropsten --reset
```

The `--reset` flag will force Truffle to deploy a new version of your contract if you deployed an invalid one previously. The good thing about Truffle is that after setting up everything, you can quickly deploy new versions of your contract for testing very efficiently. You'll see something like this if everything ran successfully:

```
PS C:\Users\merun\Desktop\book\dapp> truffle deploy --network ropsten --reset
▣▣  Important ▣▣
If you're using an HDWalletProvider, it must be Web3 1.0 enabled or your migration will hang.


Starting migrations...
======================
> Network name:    'ropsten'
> Network id:      3
> Block gas limit: 8000000


1_initial_migration.js
======================

   Deploying 'SocialMusic'
   -----------------------
   > transaction hash:    0xd0f1cb2f72043b1b1b80c109ae567e75786f41c08b9f709c19628bed2c55ae97
   > Blocks: 2            Seconds: 5
   > contract address:    0x6AeAb6695dD106FF8f82da11fAF6A9da08d098e1
   > account:             0x4eF2120fda24F79F2466B37CcD2fa9A881c09d30
   > balance:             8.22047133768847121
   > gas used:            833655
   > gas price:           20 gwei
   > value sent:          0 ETH
   > total cost:          0.0166731 ETH

   Pausing for 2 confirmations...
   ------------------------------
   > confirmation number: 3 (block: 4998114)

   > Saving migration to chain.
   > Saving artifacts
   ------------------------------------
   > Total cost:          0.0166731 ETH


Summary
=======
> Total deployments:   1
> Final cost:          0.0166731 ETH

PS C:\Users\merun\Desktop\book\dapp> _
```

Congratulations! You just deployed your `SocialMusic` smart contract. Continue reading to learn how to create the user interface that we'll use to interact with our smart contract.

Creating user interfaces

Because we have a clean `react.js` project properly set up, we can start right away with creating our application's user interface. We'll use sample data to check the design before moving on and integrating the real smart contract code.

Open up the `src/index.js` file to start coding your design:

```
import React from 'react'
import ReactDOM from 'react-dom'

class Main extends React.Component {
    constructor() {
        super()
    }

    render() {
        return (
            <div>
                <h1>Welcome to Decentralized Social Music!</h1>
                <p>Setup your account, start adding musical recommendations
for your friends and follow people that may interest you</p>
                <div className="buttons-container">
                    <button>Setup Account</button>
                    <button>Add Music</button>
                    <button>Follow People</button>
                </div>
                <h3>Latest musical recommendations from people using the
dApp</h3>
                <div ref="general-recommendations"></div>
            </div>
        )
    }
}

ReactDOM.render(<Main />, document.querySelector('#root'))
```

We're writing our design inside the `render()` function since it's where all the code will be shown to the user. I've created two main sections: an `h1` to welcome people to the dApp with a short message showing them three buttons to start using it, and an `h3` section showing people the latest 10 musical recommendations made by random people on the network:

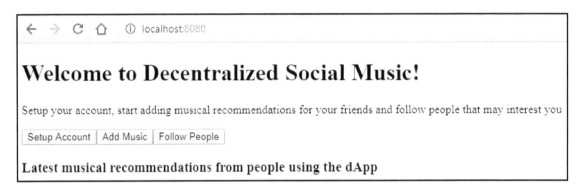

To improve the appearance of the application, we'll use some basic CSS so that it feels great to users. Create a new file inside `src/` called `index.css`. In order to be able to use CSS in our `react.js` application, we need to use a new loader that understands CSS. Open your `webpack.config.js` file to add the following section to the rules block, just like you did with the previous loaders:

```
{
    test: /\.css$/,
    exclude: /node_modules/,
    use: [
        {loader: 'style-loader'},
        {loader: 'css-loader'}
    ]
}
```

Then, install `css-loader` and `style-loader`, as follows:

```
npm i -S style-loader css-loader
```

Now, we can write our CSS code inside `index.css`, as follows:

```
body {
    margin: 0;
    font-family: sans-serif;
    text-align: center;
}
```

```css
button {
    border-radius: 10px;
    padding: 20px;
    color: white;
    border: none;
    background-color: rgb(69, 115, 233);
    cursor: pointer;
}

button:hover {
    opacity: 0.7;
}

.buttons-container button:not(:last-child){
    margin-right: 5px;
}
```

You should get something that looks like the following screenshot:

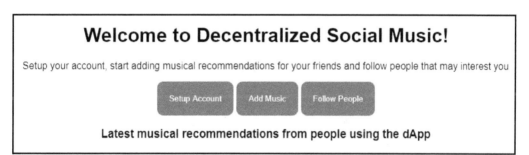

We'll now need to implement each of those features, but before that, let's work on creating a new component called **Recommendation**, which will be an individual box that will contain an individual music recommendation by some user. Here's how it will look:

```jsx
import React from 'react'
import ReactDOM from 'react-dom'
import './index.css'

class Main extends React.Component {
    constructor() {
        super()
    }

    render() {
        return (
            <div>
                <h1>Welcome to Decentralized Social Music!</h1>
                <p>Setup your account, start adding musical recommendations
```

```
for your friends and follow people that may interest you</p>
                <div className="buttons-container">
                    <button>Setup Account</button>
                    <button>Add Music</button>
                    <button>Follow People</button>
                </div>
                <h3>Latest musical recommendations from people using the
dApp</h3>
                <div ref="general-recommendations">
                    <Recommendation
                        name="John"
address="0x5912d3e530201d7B3Ff7e140421F03A7CDB386a3"
                        song="Regulate - Nate Dogg"
                    />
                </div>
            </div>
        )
    }
}

class Recommendation extends React.Component {
    constructor() {
        super()
    }

    render() {
        return (
            <div className="recommendation">
                <div className="recommendation-
name">{this.props.name}</div>
                <div className="recommendation-
address">{this.props.address}</div>
                <div className="recommendation-
song">{this.props.song}</div>
            </div>
        )
    }
}

ReactDOM.render(<Main />, document.querySelector('#root'))
```

We've added this new component that shows three divs containing the name, address, and song of each recommendation. I've also added a sample use inside the `Main` component so that you can see how it works. Props are just variables that you pass from component to component, and they are identified with their variable names. Let's improve the appearance of this thing with some CSS code, as follows:

```
.recommendation {
    width: 40%;
    margin: auto;
    background-color: whitesmoke;
    border-radius: 20px;
    margin-bottom: 10px;
    padding: 40px;
}

.recommendation-name, .recommendation-address {
    display: inline-block;
    color: #444444;
    font-style: italic;
}

.recommendation-name {
    margin-right: 10px;
}

.recommendation-address {
    color: rgb(156, 156, 156);
}

.recommendation-song {
    font-weight: bolder;
    font-size: 16pt;
    margin-top: 10px;
}
```

Here's how it will look like with the changes that we just made and with some more sample music recommendations:

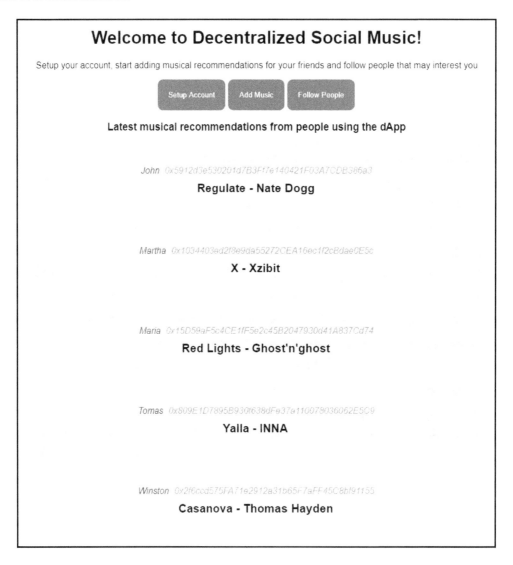

That's it—you just created the UI of your decentralized `SocialMusic` platform. Let's make it dynamic by integrating `web3.js` so that we can use our smart contracts to allow people to interact with it.

Connecting smart contracts to web applications

Decentralized applications are made of smart contracts and user interfaces. Now that we have both elements, we can combine them by connecting the frontend with the backend using web3, the most powerful tool for interacting with the Ethereum blockchain from the browser.

Let's start by getting web3.js. You can install it with the following command:

```
npm i -S web3
```

Then, import it into your index.js file, as follows:

```
import React from 'react'
import ReactDOM from 'react-dom'
import web3 from 'web3'
import './index.css'
```

You don't really need to install web3 since most, if not all of your users will have MetaMask installed, which automatically injects web3.js to your application. Nevertheless, it is good practice to have web3 in your application's code because you can control which version is used across the application.

To fully connect our react.js application with our SocialMusic contract, we need to implement every function of the contract so that they can be executed from the user interface that we designed. We also want to retrieve specific information, such as the last five recommended songs. There are many ways you can start implementing your contracts, so, we'll start by making all three buttons in our web application work properly with the smart contract.

Designing the setup form

First, we have the **Setup Account** button. This one should show users a form with several inputs to set up their name, age, and state, where only the name is mandatory. There should be a **Cancel** button as well as a **Submit** button. Let's create a new React component that we'll call Form, which will include all these requirements:

```
class Form extends React.Component {
    constructor() {
        super()
    }
```

```
    render() {
        return (
            <form className={this.props.className}>
                <input type="text" ref="form-name" placeholder="Your name"
/>
                <input type="number" ref="form-age" placeholder="Your age"
/>
                <textarea ref="form-state" placeholder="Your state, a
description about yourself"></textarea>
                <div>
                    <button>Cancel</button>
                    <button>Submit</button>
                </div>
            </form>
        )
    }
}
```

We've added two inputs with a text area for the state and two buttons to cancel or submit. Notice how I've added a custom `className` attribute on the form element so that we can dynamically set up the class from the outer component, otherwise it wouldn't work. We only want to display this form when users click on **Setup Account**, so we'll add the form component below our three buttons as a hidden element, since that's the location that makes more sense to the user, given that it's closer to the mouse. How can we hide an element in a website? By using a custom class that sets display to none.

First, we set up the new state variable in the constructor to hide the form when it's not necessary:

```
class Main extends React.Component {
    constructor() {
        super()

        this.state = {
            isFormHidden: true
        }
    }
}
```

Then, we add the `Form` component right below the buttons with a dynamic class name that changes depending on when we want to display the form:

```
render() {
  return (
      <div>
          <h1>Welcome to Decentralized Social Music!</h1>
          <p>Setup your account, start adding musical recommendations for
```

```
your friends and follow people that may interest you</p>
        <div className="buttons-container">
            <button>Setup Account</button>
            <button>Add Music</button>
            <button>Follow People</button>
        </div>

        <Form className={this.state.isFormHidden ? 'hidden' : ''} />

        <h3>Latest musical recommendations from people using the
dApp</h3>
        <div ref="general-recommendations">
            <Recommendation
                name="John"
                address="0x5912d3e530201d7B3Ff7e140421F03A7CDB386a3"
                song="Regulate - Nate Dogg"
            />
            <Recommendation
                name="Martha"
                address="0x1034403ad2f8e9da55272CEA16ec1f2cBdae0E5c"
                song="X - Xzibit"
            />
        </div>
    </div>
  )
}
```

As you can see, I've added a state element called `isFormHidden`, which indicates if the form is hidden or not. Then, I set up the `className` of our `Form` as a dynamic component that depends on state so that it stays hidden at the right moment. We need to use React's state because it's the main way React has to update information being displayed. React is reactive to state, so every time it changes, it updates the entire web application. If we simply selected the component and updated the class of it directly, React wouldn't know what's going on, and it would get messy since state is an essential element of every interactive web application.

Then, create a CSS class to hide it, as follows:

```
.hidden {
    display: none;
}
```

Take a look at the result on the live page. You shouldn't be seeing anything because your form is hidden. To display it, you have to add an `onClick` event on your **Setup Account** button, like so:

```
<button onClick={() => {
    if(this.state.isFormHidden) this.setState({isFormHidden: false})
    else this.setState({isFormHidden: true})
}}>Setup Account</button>
```

That will read the form's state to hide it or display it when clicked. You'll see that the design is a mess, so we've got to improve that:

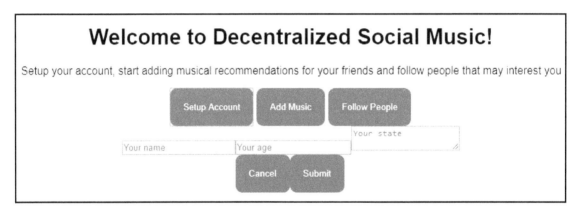

Add a new general class to each of your inputs with separate ones to differentiate the text area, as shown here:

```
<form className={this.props.className}>
    <input className="form-input" type="text" ref="form-name"
placeholder="Your name" />
    <input className="form-input" type="number" ref="form-age"
placeholder="Your age" />
    <textarea className="form-input form-textarea" ref="form-state"
placeholder="Your state, a description about yourself"></textarea>

    <div>
        <button className="cancel-button">Cancel</button>
        <button>Submit</button>
    </div>
</form>
```

Then, create new CSS classes with your desired appearance, as follows:

```
.form-input {
    display: block;
```

```
        width: 200px;
        border-radius: 20px;
        padding: 20px;
        border: 1px solid #444444;
        margin: 10px auto;
    }

    .form-textarea {
        height: 200px;
    }

    .cancel-button {
        margin-right: 10px;
    }
```

Here's how it looks after the changes in styling:

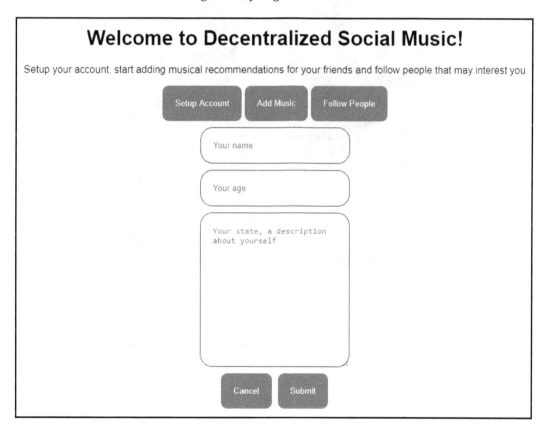

It looks way better.

Implementing the setup function

Now, we have to make it interact with our smart contract. To do that, we'll have to create a new instance of our deployed contract on `ropsten`. We'll need the address and the `ABI` interface, which you can quickly find inside the `build/contracts/` folder that Truffle created for you when you deployed your `SocialMusic` contract. Simply copy `SocialMusic.json` to your `src/ folder` for easier access. Bear in mind that you'll need to replace that file with the newer ABI versions of your contract if you decide to extend the functionalities of it. Just repeat the same steps and you should be good:

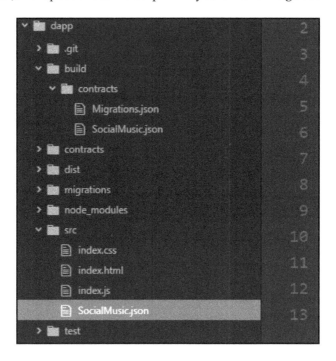

Next, we need a way to import that JSON file in our React application. Fortunately, if you're using webpack 2.0 or newer (I'm using 4.19 at the moment) you don't need to do anything extra, since webpack supports JSON files by default. In previous versions, you had to add a new `json-loader` that would take care of those files. Just add the file at the beginning of your file, like so:

```
import React from 'react'
import ReactDOM from 'react-dom'
import web3 from 'web3'
import './index.css'
import ABI from './SocialMusic.json'
```

You can import your JSON files with the name that you want; the purpose of the ABI variable is to be able to read the values of the JSON file. Then, create a variable with your smart contract's address and your `abi` interface. Remember that you can deploy a new version whenever you want with Truffle using `deploy --network ropsten --reset` to get a new address if you lost it:

```
class Main extends React.Component {
    constructor() {
        super()

        const contractAddress =
'0x0217ED41bC271a712f91477c305957Da44f91068'
        const abi = ABI.abi

        this.state = {
            isFormHidden: true
        }
    }
    ...
}
```

We'll want to deploy the contracts with our own version of web3 1.0 since the one injected by MetaMask is outdated and we cannot rely on an uncontrolled version. That's why we'll create a new instance of web3, like so:

```
import React from 'react'
import ReactDOM from 'react-dom'
import myWEB3 from 'web3'
import './index.css'
import ABI from './SocialMusic.json'

class Main extends React.Component {
    constructor() {
        super()

        window.myWeb3 = new myWEB3(myWEB3.givenProvider)
        const contractAddress =
'0x0217ED41bC271a712f91477c305957Da44f91068'
        const abi = ABI.abi

        this.state = {
            isFormHidden: true
        }
    }
    ...
```

I've renamed the web3 variable to myWeb3 to avoid confusing it with the one injected by MetaMask. Notice the window keyword in front of myWeb3; that's used to set up that variable as global so that you can access myWeb3 from anywhere in your dApp. It makes life much easier by just having access to our custom web3 everywhere. We'll use promises with async await later on. To be able to use async await for this version of webpack/babel, you'll need to install babel-polyfill, which takes care of compiling your async code so that it works properly on all browsers. Install it with the following:

```
npm i -S babel-polyfill
```

Then, add it into your webpack configuration file, as follows:

```
require('babel-polyfill')
const html = require('html-webpack-plugin')
const path = require('path')

module.exports = {
    entry: ['babel-polyfill', './src/index.js'],
    output: {
        filename: 'bundle.js',
        path: path.join(__dirname, 'dist')
    },
...
```

Now, we'll create the contract's instance with some helper functions and the setupAccount function's integration.

First, update the constructor to execute the function to set up the contract instance right when the dApp loads, like so:

```
constructor() {
    super()

    window.myWeb3 = new myWEB3(myWEB3.givenProvider)
    this.state = {
        isFormHidden: true
    }

    this.setContractInstance()
}
```

Then, create the required functions to properly set up the user account and contract, as follows:

```
async getAccount() {
  return (await myWeb3.eth.getAccounts())[0]
}
```

```
async setContractInstance() {
    const contractAddress = '0x0217ED41bC271a712f91477c305957Da44f91068'
    const abi = ABI.abi
    const contractInstance = new myWeb3.eth.Contract(abi, contractAddress,
{
        from: await this.getAccount(),
        gasPrice: 2e9
    })
    await this.setState({contractInstance: contractInstance})
}

async setupAccount(name, age, status) {
    await
this.state.contractInstance.methods.setup(this.fillBytes32WithSpaces(name),
age, status).send({from: '0x2f6ccd575FA71e2912a31b65F7aFF45C8bf91155'})
}

fillBytes32WithSpaces(name) {
    let nameHex = myWeb3.utils.toHex(name)
    for(let i = nameHex.length; i < 66; i++) {
        nameHex = nameHex + '0'
    }
    return nameHex
}
```

After that, update your render() function with the Form props to tell React what to do when the user clicks on the setup button, and when the user clicks on the **Cancel** button:

```
render() {
    return (
        <div>
            <h1>Welcome to Decentralized Social Music!</h1>
            <p>Setup your account, start adding musical recommendations for
your friends and follow people that may interest you</p>
            <div className="buttons-container">
                <button onClick={() => {
                    if(this.state.isFormHidden)
this.setState({isFormHidden: false})
                    else this.setState({isFormHidden: true})
                }}>Setup Account</button>
                <button>Add Music</button>
                <button>Follow People</button>
            </div>

            <Form
                className={this.state.isFormHidden ? 'hidden' : ''}
                cancel={() => {
                    this.setState({isFormHidden: true})
```

```
                    }}
                    setupAccount={(name, age, status) => {
                        this.setupAccount(name, age, status)
                    }}
                />

                <h3>Latest musical recommendations from people using the
dApp</h3>
                <div ref="general-recommendations">
                    <Recommendation
                        name="John"
                        address="0x5912d3e530201d7B3Ff7e140421F03A7CDB386a3"
                        song="Regulate - Nate Dogg"
                    />
                    <Recommendation
                        name="Martha"
                        address="0x1034403ad2f8e9da55272CEA16ec1f2cBdae0E5c"
                        song="X - Xzibit"
                    />
                </div>
            </div>
        )
    }
```

Finally, update your `Form` component with the new functionality to trigger the setup functions when the user interacts with the inputs:

```
class Form extends React.Component {
    constructor() {
        super()
    }

    render() {
        return (
            <form className={this.props.className}>
                <input className="form-input" type="text" ref="form-name"
placeholder="Your name" />
                <input className="form-input" type="number" ref="form-age"
placeholder="Your age" />
                <textarea className="form-input form-textarea" ref="form-
state" placeholder="Your state, a description about yourself"></textarea>
                <div>
                    <button onClick={event => {
                        event.preventDefault()
                        this.props.cancel()
                    }} className="cancel-button">Cancel</button>
                    <button onClick={event => {
                        event.preventDefault()
```

```
                    this.props.setupAccount(this.refs['form-
name'].value, this.refs['form-age'].value, this.refs['form-state'].value)
                }}>Submit</button>
            </div>
        </form>
    )
  }
}
```

There are quite some changes here, so let me explain what I did.

First, I created the `setContractInstance` function, which is used to set up the contract instance with our smart contract's address so that we can use it later for the other functions. The `getAccount` function is a helper to get the address of the current user quickly.

Then, I created the `setupAccount` function, which receives the three parameters we want to use for setting up the user's account with a helper function named `fillBytes32WithSpaces`, since we need to fill all the spaces in a bytes32 type of variable with this version of `web3.js`, otherwise it will reject the transaction. This function simply creates a transaction for the `setup()` function in our deployed smart contract.

Next, I created some prop functions for the `Form` component that will be executed when the user clicks on **Cancel** or **Submit**. We want to hide the form when the user cancels, so I simply set the state of the form to hidden. When the user clicks on **Submit**, we extract the data from all the inputs and we send them to the `setupAccount` function. Notice how I've used `event.preventDefault()` inside each button's click event to avoid refreshing the page, since all HTML buttons are submit buttons that supposedly send information to the server.

Notice that we used the `.send()` function when setting up users, data which generates a transaction and costs gas. Inside it, I've used my Ethereum address so that it knows who should make the transaction:

```
.send({from: '0x2f6ccd575FA71e2912a31b65F7aFF45C8bf91155'})
```

But you don't want to use the same address since you can't have access to it for your MetaMask. You can simply delete that parameter so that the function looks like so:

```
.send()
```

Telling React to find the user's address automatically doesn't work sometimes, so you can set your own address instead. Remember to have your MetaMask unlocked and using ropsten, then paste your current address there.

Go ahead and interact with your dApp once the changes are done to verify that, indeed, it's submitting a transaction to the smart contract.

What we'll do now is set up the **Add Music** button so that users can create musical recommendations. To start, create the design with a new component, just like we did previously, by updating the state object inside your constructor:

```
constructor() {
    super()

    window.myWeb3 = new myWEB3(myWEB3.givenProvider)
    this.state = {
        isFormHidden: true,
        isAddMusicHidden: true
    }

    this.setContractInstance()
}
```

Then, create a new `addMusic()` function, which will push the indicated song to the array:

```
async addMusic(music) {
    await this.state.contractInstance.methods.addSong(music).send({from:
'0x2f6ccd575FA71e2912a31b65F7aFF45C8bf91155'})
}
```

Update the `render()` function by adding the `onClick` event listener to the **Add Music** button, which will update the state to display the add music form. Then, add the new `AddMusic` component, like so:

```
render() {
    return (
        <div>
            <h1>Welcome to Decentralized Social Music!</h1>
            <p>Setup your account, start adding musical recommendations for
your friends and follow people that may interest you</p>
            <div className="buttons-container">
                <button onClick={() => {
                    if(this.state.isFormHidden)
this.setState({isFormHidden: false})
                    else this.setState({isFormHidden: true})
                }}>Setup Account</button>
                <button onClick={() => {
                    if(this.state.isAddMusicHidden)
this.setState({isAddMusicHidden: false})
                    else this.setState({isAddMusicHidden: true})
                }}>Add Music</button>
```

```
            <button>Follow People</button>
        </div>

        <Form
            className={this.state.isFormHidden ? 'hidden' : ''}
            cancel={() => {
                this.setState({isFormHidden: true})
            }}
            setupAccount={(name, age, status) => {
                this.setupAccount(name, age, status)
            }}
        />

        <AddMusic
            className={this.state.isAddMusicHidden ? 'hidden': ''}
            cancel={() => {
                this.setState({isAddMusicHidden: true})
            }}
            addMusic={music => {
                this.addMusic(music)
            }}
        />

        <h3>Latest musical recommendations from people using the
dApp</h3>
        <div ref="general-recommendations">
            <Recommendation
                name="John"
                address="0x5912d3e530201d7B3Ff7e140421F03A7CDB386a3"
                song="Regulate - Nate Dogg"
            />
            <Recommendation
                name="Martha"
                address="0x1034403ad2f8e9da55272CEA16ec1f2cBdae0E5c"
                song="X - Xzibit"
            />
        </div>
    </div>
)
}
```

Finally, define the new `AddMusic` component with the `class` function:

```
class AddMusic extends React.Component {
    constructor() {
        super()
    }
```

```
    render() {
        return(
            <div className={this.props.className}>
                <input type="text" ref="add-music-input" className="form-
input" placeholder="Your song recommendation"/>
                <div>
                    <button onClick={event => {
                        event.preventDefault()
                        this.props.cancel()
                    }} className="cancel-button">Cancel</button>
                    <button onClick={event => {
                        event.preventDefault()
                        this.props.addMusic(this.refs['add-music-
input'].value)
                    }}>Submit</button>
                </div>
            </div>
        )
    }
}
```

We've followed the same steps that we did when we created the `Form` component. Simply set up the render HTML, put the `AddMusic` element below your `Form` element while keeping it hidden, and set up all the prop functions. Then, create a function to add new songs to the smart contract. We've also created a new state variable for toggling the hidden class of those buttons.

You may have noticed that if you click on **Add Song** and then **Setup Account** right after it without cancelling, the divs stay open—we don't want that. We want to keep only one of those sections open at any given time. We can achieve that with a function that updates the state for hiding all the components before opening a new one, as follows:

```
hideAllSections() {
    this.setState({
        isFormHidden: true,
        isAddMusicHidden: true
    })
}
```

Then, add the function call to the buttons before opening the section:

```
<button onClick={() => {
    this.hideAllSections()
    if(this.state.isFormHidden) this.setState({isFormHidden: false})
    else this.setState({isFormHidden: true})
}}>Setup Account</button>
<button onClick={() => {
```

```
    this.hideAllSections()
    if(this.state.isAddMusicHidden) this.setState({isAddMusicHidden:
false})
    else this.setState({isAddMusicHidden: true})
}}>Add Music</button>
```

Let's add the final button function to be able to follow people. We'll show a list of all the people that have registered so that the user can follow the ones they like to see updates from. To achieve that, we'll have to modify our contract so that we can add an array with the latest newcomers that will get updated when users execute the setup function, as shown in the following code block:

```
pragma solidity 0.5.0;

contract SocialMusic {
    struct User {
        bytes32 name;
        uint256 age;
        string state; // A short description of who they are or how they
feel
        string[] musicRecommendations;
        address[] following;
    }
    mapping(address => User) public users;
    address[] public userList;

    // To add a new musical recommendation
    function addSong(string memory _songName) public {
        require(bytes(_songName).length > 0 && bytes(_songName).length <=
100);
        users[msg.sender].musicRecommendations.push(_songName);
    }

    // To setup user information
    function setup(bytes32 _name, uint256 _age, string memory _state)
public {
        require(_name.length > 0);
        User memory newUser = User(_name, _age, _state,
users[msg.sender].musicRecommendations, users[msg.sender].following);
        users[msg.sender] = newUser;
        userList.push(msg.sender);
    }

    // To follow new users
    function follow(address _user) public {
        require(_user != address(0));
        users[msg.sender].following.push(_user);
```

```
        }

        // Returns the array of users
        function getUsersList() public view returns(address[] memory) {
            return userList;
        }
    }
```

Redeploy the contract with Truffle, as follows:

```
truffle deploy --network ropsten --reset
```

Instead of having to manually copy the new address and updating the json file, we'll get all the information straight from the build folder, including the address, like so:

```
import ABI from '../build/contracts/SocialMusic.json'

...
async setContractInstance() {
    const contractAddress = ABI.networks['3'].address
    const abi = ABI.abi
    const contractInstance = new myWeb3.eth.Contract(abi, contractAddress,
{
        from: await this.getAccount(),
        gasPrice: 2e9
    })
    await this.setState({contractInstance: contractInstance})
}
...
```

Now, you won't have to worry about updating the information every single time, which is great because you can access different external folders freely, given that webpack takes all the required information and bundles it together, so it doesn't matter that you're accessing files outside of the `src/` folder. Now let's create the desired functionality to get the latest people so that the user can follow them with a couple of new components:

```
class FollowPeopleContainer extends React.Component {
    constructor() {
        super()
    }

    render() {
        let followData = this.props.followUsersData
        // Remove the users that you already follow so that you don't see
em
        for(let i = 0; i < followData.length; i++) {
            let indexOfFollowing =
followData[i].following.indexOf(this.props.userAddress)
```

```
            if(indexOfFollowing != -1) {
                followData = followData.splice(indexOfFollowing, 1)
            }
        }
        return (
            <div className={this.props.className}>
                {followData.map(user => (
                    <FollowPeopleUnit
                        key={user.address}
                        address={user.addres}
                        age={user.age}
                        name={user.name}
                        state={user.state}
                        recommendations={user.recommendations}
                        following={user.following}
                        followUser={() => {
                            this.props.followUser(user.address)
                        }}
                    />
                ))}
            </div>
        )
    }
}

class FollowPeopleUnit extends React.Component {
    constructor() {
        super()
    }

    render() {
        return (
            <div className="follow-people-unit">
                <div className="follow-people-
address">{this.props.address}</div>
                <div className="follow-people-
name">{myWeb3.utils.toUtf8(this.props.name)}</div>
                <div className="follow-people-age">{this.props.age}</div>
                <div className="follow-people-
state">"{this.props.state}"</div>
                <div className="follow-people-recommendation-container">
                    {this.props.recommendations.map((message, index) => (
                        <div key={index} className="follow-people-
recommendation">{message}</div>
                    ))}
                </div>
                <button
                    className="follow-button"
```

```
                    onClick={() => {
                        this.props.followUser()
                    }}
                >Follow</button>
            </div>
        )
    }
}
```

The `FollowPeopleContainer` is simply a component that holds all the users that you can follow with your account. It will receive data from the `Main` component inside the `this.props.followUsersData` prop, which sends an array containing up to 10 users to follow with up to two musical recommendations each, just so that you can see the type of person they are. It also removes already followed users from the array so that you don't see them as new users. Finally, it generates a `FollowPeopleUnit` component with all the required user properties, with a function that will transmit the information required to follow that specific user to the `Main` component.

Notice the `key={user.address}` attribute in each `FollowPeopleUnit`, since we need to be able to identify them individually, which is mandatory by React to avoid duplicate elements.

On the other hand, the `FollowPeopleUnit` component is made of a set of divs that show all the required information to the user. Because we have two recommendations inside an array called `this.props.recommendations`, we'll have to loop through all of them to display each message individually. When you want to generate HTML elements dynamically with react, you must use the `.map()` function of your array with round brackets `()` instead of curly brackets `{}` since all HTML elements must be inside these types of brackets.

Now that we have our two new components, we have to define the functions to make them interactive in our `Main` component; you can check the complete code on GitHub just so you know where everything has to be placed in case you're facing errors.

First, we updated the address system to be dynamic so that you don't have to manually type your Ethereum address in code. For instance, let's say we had the following code:

```
await this.state.contractInstance.methods.follow(address).send({from:
'0x2f6ccd575FA71e2912a31b65F7aFF45C8bf91155'})
```

Instead, we would use the following code, which is essential to make our dApp interactive for many different users. You can see that we set up the `userAddress` state variable in the `setContractInstance()` function:

```
await this.state.contractInstance.methods.follow(address).send({from:
this.state.userAddress})
```

Next, we created the complex `getFollowPeopleUsersData()` function, which gets the most recent user addresses; it takes up to 10 of them or less if there aren't that many users. Then, it creates a `userData` object with all the properties that we want and populates it with the smart contract state variable's information, by first getting the length of the array of musical recommendations with `getUsersMusicRecommendationLength()`, and then by getting each individual musical recommendation with `getUsersMusicRecommendation()`. At the bottom of the function, we get the array of users that that particular person is following, just in case we need to access them.

As you can see, we used some new functions from our smart contract. That's because we couldn't make all of this possible without adding some complexity. Here's how our updated smart contract looks:

```
pragma solidity 0.5.0;

contract SocialMusic {
    struct User {
        bytes32 name;
        uint256 age;
        string state; // A short description of who they are or how they
feel
        string[] musicRecommendations;
        address[] following;
    }
    mapping(address => User) public users;
    address[] public userList;

    // To add a new musical recommendation
    function addSong(string memory _songName) public {
        require(bytes(_songName).length > 0 && bytes(_songName).length <=
100);
        users[msg.sender].musicRecommendations.push(_songName);
    }

    // To setup user information
    function setup(bytes32 _name, uint256 _age, string memory _state)
public {
        require(_name.length > 0);
        User memory newUser = User(_name, _age, _state,
```

```
     users[msg.sender].musicRecommendations, users[msg.sender].following);
         users[msg.sender] = newUser;
         userList.push(msg.sender);
     }

     // To follow new users
     function follow(address _user) public {
         require(_user != address(0));
         users[msg.sender].following.push(_user);
     }

     // Returns the array of users
     function getUsersList() public view returns(address[] memory) {
         return userList;
     }

     // Returns the music recommendations
     function getUsersMusicRecommendation(address _user, uint256
_recommendationIndex) public view returns(string memory) {
         return users[_user].musicRecommendations[_recommendationIndex];
     }

     // Returns how many music recommendations that user has
     function getUsersMusicRecommendationLength(address _user) public view
returns(uint256) {
         return users[_user].musicRecommendations.length;
     }

     // Returns the addresses of the users _user is following
     function getUsersFollowings(address _user) public view
returns(address[] memory) {
         return users[_user].following;
     }
 }
```

There are a few functions to retrieve the following and recommendation data for each particular person from the respective arrays. This is done because we can't just get the entire array automatically with public arrays; as you know, public arrays only return one element of the entire array each time, so we need a function to get it entirely. The same thing happens with strings—we have to create a function to get each string individually because we can't just send an array of strings, given that they are low-level multidimensional byte[][] arrays. Solidity doesn't allow you to send a byte[][][], which would be the equivalent to string[], because it's too big and complex.

Remember to redeploy your code after making changes with Truffle, `deploy --network ropsten --reset`. Now, you don't have to update the smart contract address, nor copy the ABI to your source folder, since it's set up to get the deployed contract data straight from the build folder.

Our dApp doesn't look as good as it should yet, so here's the entire CSS code for your reference if you desire to achieve the same look:

```css
body {
    margin: 0;
    font-family: sans-serif;
    text-align: center;
}

button {
    border-radius: 10px;
    padding: 20px;
    color: white;
    border: none;
    background-color: rgb(69, 115, 233);
    cursor: pointer;
}

button:hover {
    opacity: 0.7;
}

.hidden {
    display: none;
}

.buttons-container button:not(:last-child){
    margin-right: 5px;
}

.recommendation {
    width: 40%;
    margin: auto;
    background-color: whitesmoke;
    border-radius: 20px;
    margin-bottom: 10px;
    padding: 40px;
}

.follow-people-unit {
    width: 40%;
    background-color: whitesmoke;
```

```
        border-radius: 20px;
        margin: 10px auto;
        padding: 20px;
    }

    .recommendation-name, .recommendation-address, .follow-people-address,
    .follow-people-name, .follow-people-age {
        display: inline-block;
        color: #444444;
        font-style: italic;
    }

    .recommendation-name, .follow-people-name {
        margin-right: 10px;
    }

    .recommendation-address, .follow-people-address {
        color: rgb(156, 156, 156);
    }

    .recommendation-song, .follow-people-recommendation {
        font-weight: bolder;
        font-size: 16pt;
        margin-top: 10px;
    }

    .form-input {
        display: block;
        width: 200px;
        border-radius: 20px;
        padding: 20px;
        border: 1px solid #444444;
        margin: 10px auto;
    }

    .form-textarea {
        height: 200px;
    }

    .cancel-button {
        margin-right: 10px;
    }

    .follow-people-state {
        font-style: italic;
        font-weight: bolder;
        color: #444444;
    }
```

```
.follow-button {
    margin-top: 10px;
}
```

Here's a screenshot of the final result, which you can generate with `webpack -d` and `http-server dist/`to see it in `localhost:8080`:

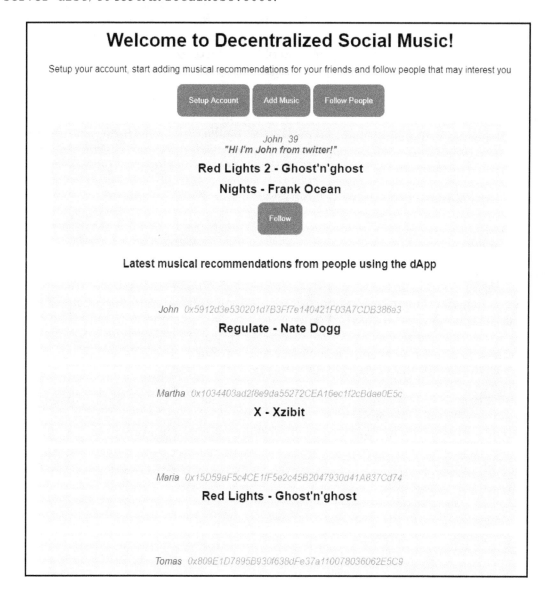

Go ahead and interact with your new awesome dApp by clicking the buttons shown in the preceding screenshot. The **Follow People** button will take a few seconds to load data from the smart contract since we are running several requests to generate our custom objects in JavaScript.

Finally, I could add functionality to display the latest music recommendations and unfollow systems, but I'll leave that to you as an exercise to practice your smart contract dApp implementation skills. The idea is to display dynamically generated recommendation components at the bottom of the page instead of the static ones we have already; you can do that by simply getting the data from our smart contract.

This dApp is nowhere near perfect; you could fix some of its speed issues by optimizing the data structures so that you retrieve only the required information instead of the entire arrays. You can also fix some security issues by testing the code with truffle. The end result is up to you; you decide when the application can be considered finished since you can add and continue adding features that make it better—that's how all great dApps are born.

You can check the final code on my GitHub here: `https://github.com/merlox/social-music`.

Summary

In this chapter, you saw first-hand how to create a decentralized application with all the little nuances and changes required. You've gone through the entire process, starting from setting up your development environment with React, webpack, and Truffle. You've learned how to create React components that organize your code neatly so that you can manage all the complexity of your dApp with ease.

Remember to add this application to your GitHub as proof that you finished it to improve your resume with valuable projects so that future clients can see with their own eyes what you can do for them and that you've mastered all the steps that it takes to build a fully decentralized application. In the next chapter, you'll learn more about improving your dApps with further advanced tips so that they feel responsive and behave like high-quality systems.

6
Tools, Frameworks, Components, and Services

In this chapter, you'll learn about several important tools that are available for Ethereum developers to create powerful decentralized applications and smart contracts that scale and are secure enough to serve millions of potential users. The world of Ethereum development is full of useful tools that are intended to make your life easier when creating complex decentralized applications and smart contracts that use the latest changes to Solidity. Knowing what's out there and how it works will really help you move forward in your development projects because you'll be able to create better and faster applications with less bug-prone code.

In this chapter, we will cover the following topics:

- Using developer tools
- Understanding Ethereum communication tools
- Making sense of the Ethereum infrastructure
- Learning Ethereum testing and securing tools
- Getting important open source libraries

Using developer tools

Developer tools such as **integrated development environments** (**IDEs**), faucets, and even smart contract languages are essential things a developer must control to have a practical understanding of how to develop smart contracts efficiently.

Development frameworks

There are several development frameworks that provide you with a set of utilities for creating smart contracts in an environment where you can test your code and verify it so that you improve your development speed with higher quality code. Let's see some of the most popular ones to decide which one should be used at any given moment:

- **Truffle**: This is the biggest development framework for creating dApps and smart contracts with Solidity. At the time of writing, it's not fully compatible with Vyper, but there are some workarounds to get it working if you really wish to do so. Truffle, as you already know, provides you with smart contract compiling, deployment, and testing tools straight from your Terminal so that you don't have to leave your workflow. It's a bit complicated to set up, since you have to work in a particular way, but once done, you have an immense potential for creating powerful dApps with ease. You can get it at `truffleframework.com`.

- **Waffle**: Although is not a well-known development framework, Waffle aims to create simpler and faster programming tools so that you can develop easily with far fewer dependencies. You only need the `contracts` and `test` folders to start using Waffle since it compiles all the code without complications. Your smart contracts can be easily compiled with `npx waffle`. Because it aims to be as minimalistic as possible, you can't deploy your contracts from their utilities, nor do you have a `build/` folder as in Truffle, so it's up to you to deploy them. There's less setup and headaches for fewer features but improved simplicity. You can install it with `npm i -S Ethereum-waffle`.

- **0xcert**: This is another great development tool focused on creating and deploying advanced ERC721 non-fungible smart contract tokens. These are special types of tokens where each one is unique and has some intrinsic value. For instance, CryptoKitties used an ERC721 token to generate random animals with unique features with a set price based on rarity. Oxcert aims to increase adoption of the already accepted ERC721 token standard so that developers can create faster, more secure, and complex token contracts. You can get it on their website: `0xcert.org`.

Integrated development environments

When it comes to IDEs, we have a smaller set of tools that really help you program secure code from the first line, since they try to fix mistakes before they even happen:

- **Remix:** The most popular development environment is a very powerful code editor that fixes your smart contract code with automatic compilation and helpful warning messages to indicate what's wrong with your code. It even provides suggestions for best practices to learn as you develop. You can deploy your smart contracts using a custom Ethereum instance, a JavaScript virtual machine, or injected `web3.js` to see how your smart contract reacts in different environments. You can interact with every deployed contract once you have the source code without exiting your browser. I highly recommend it for developing Solidity code and for manually testing every component of your functions. Start using it at `remix.ethereum.org`.

- **Superblocks:** This is a strong IDE that includes even more features to deploy your dApps directly so that you can interact with your applications live with instant feedback. You can export your dApps, deploy contracts, access the blockchain directly, and many more great things. You should give it a chance to experience the power of a complete IDE that helps you every step of the way from an empty file to a fully-featured and tested dApp.

Testnet faucets

You're probably already familiar with the testnets available for you as an Ethereum developer. You know that they are strong blockchains to deploy your smart contracts in a secure space that you can even use for real-world applications since the functionality is the same. Let's take a look at some of the following faucets so that you can experience the different features of each test blockchain:

- **Rinkeby**: This is a **proof-of-authority** (**PoA**) blockchain where you mine transactions with staking mechanisms without compromising your identity. It's a very robust solution for secure and reliable blockchains. You should deploy your applications on different testnets to see which one fits your requirements best. If you want to use Rinkeby, you'll need some test Ether, which you can get at `rinkeby.io/#faucet`. The process is quite different from other blockchains because they want to make sure the network stays uncompromised. So, to get Ether, you'll have to publish your Ethereum address on a social media platform such as Twitter and wait to receive a limited amount of Ether: up to 18.75 Ether at once, which you can retrieve every 3 days.

After publishing your Ethereum address, paste the link on the faucet and you'll receive your Ether in a few minutes. The great thing about this network is that it's compatible with MetaMask and the block times are really fast.

- **Ropsten**: This is the most popular **proof-of-work** (**PoW**) test network where you can get Ether quickly from many faucets. The main place from which you can get free Ether for development is from MetaMask itself, which you can access at `https://faucet.metamask.io` to receive a limited amount of Ether. The restrictions for Ether per user change constantly, so it's hard to predict how much Ether you'll get by clicking repeatedly on the **Request 1 ether from faucet** button – it's up to you to find out. Nevertheless, it's a great blockchain, although not as reliable as others because of its low-capacity blockchain where just a small set of nodes mine for free.
- **Kovan**: This is not used that much for testing projects, although it is a very solid PoA testnet that was built by the team at Parity to provide developers with an efficient testing environment for all kinds of projects. You can get Ether at `faucet.kovan.network`, where you'll have to log in with your GitHub account and receive 1 Ether every 24 hours per account. It's not much, but it should be enough for smaller projects without substantial payment requirements.

Understanding Ethereum communication tools

Ethereum is a big ecosystem made of several interconnected pieces that talk to each other, which includes smart contracts, dApps, and web apps. The goal is to create separate structures so that your final application is modular in the sense that you can update a specific part without having to recreate the entire dApp. That's why we have communication tools: libraries that help us exchange information between smart contracts, dApps, and web apps. Let's take a look at the different tools we have available right now when it comes to communication.

Frontend Ethereum APIs

When it comes to frontend communication tools, we have some powerful JavaScript libraries that make dApps possible by connecting smart contracts with web applications:

- **Web3.js**: The most popular library for using smart contracts in your web apps to create contract instances, call contract functions, create transactions, and sign transactions. This library alone made dApps a possibility. Web applications where the backend is the blockchain itself is a revolutionary concept that is growing in popularity, all thanks to the people that decided to build such libraries. It can also be used on Node.js applications, and therefore it's a great tool for all kinds of dApps, including backends. You can get web3.js here: `github.com/Ethereum/web3.js`.

- **NEthereum**: This is a smart contract communication tool similar to web3.js but for .NET developers. Those that work with the popular .NET libraries and prefer to program in C# will enjoy this tool given that it's made specifically for those programmers. It provides you with everything you need to connect your existing .NET environment with your web applications, including libraries and client integrations. You can learn more about NEthereum here: `nethereum.com`.

- **Drizzle:** This is a Redux integration for your dApps so that you can manage state and data stores with ease. If you're familiar with Redux and React, you'll enjoy this tool because it provides you with a clean library to implement the benefits of Redux on your dApps with ease. Made by the creators of Truffle, it's fantastic for bigger projects. You can get it here: `github.com/trufflesuite/drizzle`.

Backend Ethereum APIs

Most Ethereum applications will need some sort of centralized backend to do certain tasks that are unfeasible for smart contracts, either because it's out of the capacity of the contract or because there's a better way of processing some action. In these situations, we still need to talk to the blockchain. That's where backend APIs come into play: to help us create tools and systems for improving our overall dApps and smart contracts:

- **Web3.py**: This is the popular Ethereum implementation for Python so that you can create tools and systems for this popular language. Python works fantastically with web3.js because you can create efficient scripts to automate some actions, such as checking smart contract events. The syntax is pretty similar to the original `web3.js`, so you'll feel comfortable using it. Check it out here: `github.com/Ethereum/web3.py`.

- **Eventeum**: This is a tool to communicate with smart contract events for your backend microservices. If you're not familiar with microservices, they are simply small applications that are focused on doing some particular task very efficiently and maintainable so that your final application is extremely efficient and easy to optimize with modules that can be improved and replaced with ease. Eventeum is working with these kind of microservices to process Ethereum events that are generated by your smart contract so that you can implement events easily on your complex network of services. It works with Java and is fantastic for backend developers that want scalability. Take a look at it here: `github.com/ConsenSys/eventeum`.

Application binary interface tools

Application binary interfaces, better known as **ABIs**, are JSON objects that describe your smart contract functions, variables, modifiers, and everything in-between. The goal of ABIs is to help your dApps quickly understand smart contracts so that they know which functions are available to you. Now, it's important that you take advantage of this protocol as much as you can, since you'll be using it in all of your dApps. Here are some tools to really improve your ABI understanding:

- **Abi-decoder**: This is a tiny JavaScript tool that allows you to decode complex transaction objects that are normally encrypted and hard to understand. You see, every time you send a transaction by executing a function in your smart contracts, you are interacting with the blockchain in encrypted data. At some point or another, you'll have to read these transactions, either because you're debugging your dApp or because you need to understand what's going on for whatever reason. With abi-decoder, you can decode transaction data and transaction logs, which is fantastic for data-efficient dApps. Learn more about this tiny tool made by Consensys at `github.com/ConsenSys/abi-decoder`.
- **OneClickdApp.com**: This is a great tool to quickly deploy your dApps to the internet without having to worry about hosting. You can click a button, select your ABI data, and your configuration and your dApp is deployed to their domain. With a few clicks, you can see how it would look in the real world. It is great for testing and smaller projects. The only catch is that you have to pay 5 dollars per month if you decide to host it without downtime, although it's great for your overall testing process. Learn more at `oneclickdapp.com`.

So far, you've discovered some fantastic tools that you can implement right away on your projects with immediate benefits. Go ahead and explore the full ecosystem of technologies that help you create better dApps and smart contract so that you can go the next level when it comes to building powerful applications for the future.

Making sense of the Ethereum infrastructure

When it comes to the base structure of the Ethereum blockchain, there are several applications that help improve it so that people, including developers, can benefit from all of its potential. You see, the blockchain is capable of much more than processing transactions and running smart contracts. You can talk directly with each peer via messages, store information, and use custom clients. In this section, you'll learn about some of the most interesting use cases in Ethereum's infrastructure.

Ethereum clients

You already know that there are some powerful clients with clear differences, but what you probably don't know is that there are specific tools made just for certain clients. We'll see some of the best implementations written in Java, mainly because it's one of the most used languages for these types of applications:

- **Pantheon**: Written entirely in Java, this app focuses on providing different environments that you can use for your dApps and smart contracts. It has a rich documentation website, it's easy to get started right away, and you can create private networks with PoW or PoA using Clique. You don't need to know Java to use it because it's really straightforward to set up. Check it out at `docs.pantheon.pegasys.tech/en/latest/`.

- **EthereumJ**: This is a mode-heavy implementation that focuses on providing as many features as possible for your private network needs. It's configurable with Java code in your Maven or Gradle projects. When it comes to ease of use, this one is harder to set up and it takes more time to get used to it, since it's directed towards enterprise-grade developers. Check it out at `github.com/Ethereum/Ethereumj`.

- **Harmony**: Made by EtherCamp, this is a popular website in the early days of Ethereum that provided their own IDE and tools. Harmony is written in a combination of JavaScript and Java while being based on EthereumJ. Their goal is to provide a clean web dashboard interface that you can use with ease to monitor and analyze the blockchain in detail. It is highly recommended for projects where you need a clear understanding of what's going on under the hood. Check it out at `github.com/ether-camp/Ethereum-harmony`.

Ethereum storage

When we talk about storage, we mean keeping all kinds of files in a decentralized cloud that may or may not work with the Ethereum blockchain. These are applications that allow you to store contracts and files without having to rely on a centralized server:

- **InterPlanetary File System** (**IPFS**): It's the most known implementation of decentralized storage, which allows you to store large files in a decentralized network of connected nodes instead of keeping your information in centralized servers and databases. It's being used in all kinds of projects that want to exploit the possibilities of fully decentralized applications where there isn't a centralized point of failure. These types of projects will be used in the future given that they are vastly more secure when thousands of nodes are replicating the information on top of high-quality networks. IPFS brings a combination between the torrent and Git protocol, where files are identified based on the content they have. So, two identical files that have the same content inside will have the same encrypted identifier known as **hash**. This is a highly important revolution, since they remove duplicated files, increasing the availability of data and allowing better use of resources, since many nodes will be sharing the same information together instead of being separated. Check it out on their website at `ipfs.io`.
- **Swarm**: This is a protocol built on top of Ethereum, whose goal is to share files in a decentralized manner, much like IPFS, but without having to rely on an external team. It's being improved constantly by the core Ethereum team and has a seamless integration with the whole system so that you can integrate it with your dApps and smart contracts without headaches. Check it out on their website at `swarm-gateways.net`.

Ethereum messaging

Ethereum messaging means exchanging encrypted information between peers without intermediaries so that you get the information directly in almost real time. They are fantastic tools for chats and apps that need speed above all:

- **Whisper**: The most well-known protocol that implements peer-to-peer messaging, it's built on top of Ethereum and is fully integrated with all the systems at its core. You can use it to communicate with other dApps with minimal configurations. Smart contracts are interconnected, having a layer where they can share information securely. Learn more about Whisper here: `github.com/Ethereum/wiki/wiki/Whisper`.
- **Devp2p**: This is another protocol built on Ethereum that allows people and dApps to exchange encrypted messages with high speeds without having to create slow blockchain transactions. There's an implementation written in Python known as pydevp2p that provides you with a simple interface to include messaging in your applications so that people can start exchanging data with each other. Learn more about it on their official GitHub page: `github.com/Ethereum/devp2p`.

Ethereum messaging applications provide us with a rich set of possibilities to create better dApps and advanced smart contracts, so you should pay attention to those services whenever you wish to develop a user-based game or chat application on Ethereum.

Learning Ethereum testing and securing tools

Security in the blockchain is the top priority above any other feature. Without secure applications, we can't begin to work on the simplest of the smart contracts because users won't trust our code. That's why you must learn about all the possibilities when it comes to securing your programs as a master Ethereum developer.

Understanding monitoring utilities

Monitoring is the act of watching how your applications are behaving in the real world. You see, it's important to watch over your code, since it's being used by potentially thousands of users all over the world: you don't want them to have a poor experience at random moments. Be sure to check out these tools to level up your Smart Contract game since they provide a large improvement in your application's quality:

- **Smart contract watch**: Made by Neufund, which is a company that works on creating legally binding smart contracts among other things. This tool allows you to watch your smart contract's activity and see where it could lead to problems. You can use it as your own custom block explorer, as a security tool for when funds get critically reduced from one of your applications, or for whatever situation you need that requires careful monitoring. It's simple to use from the Terminal and has a simple output interface to see what's going on. Learn more about it at: `github.com/Neufund/smart-contract-watch`.

- **Scout**: Shows you in real time what's happening on the events and activities inside your smart contracts so that you can pay attention to the things that matter. You can create critical events that should be executed at dangerous situations to notify you about breaches in security that need urgent patching. Imagine the amount of Ether that could have been saved if people used tools like Scout to take fast and determined action in the face of a hack. Their dashboard and live reports are stunning, so I highly recommend that you take a look at it for improving your applications. Learn more about it at: `scout.cool`.

- **Chainlyt:** Allows you to decode what's going on inside transaction data to explore in extreme detail what's going on at any given moment. You can use it in combination with other monitoring tools to patch a breach before it's too late by understanding how it happened, since you can see exactly what goes in and out a smart contract. They also provide a nice dashboard that you can freely use for quick projects. It's a very powerful tool for advanced users. Learn more about it at: `chainlyt.io`.

Using security testing utilities

Testing your smart contracts is absolutely essential if you are thinking about deploying them to the Mainnet and don't want to face important issues right from the start. It's unavoidable and you should be doing it as you develop. Take a look at these testing tools to set up a nice testing environment that feels comfortable to use for your everyday needs:

- **Oyente:** This is a very famous tool for analyzing your smart contracts with ease. They provide you with an online IDE based on Remix with several advanced features such as timeouts, depth limits, custom bytecodes, and many more improvements to help you analyze your smart contract for improving their security exponentially. It's highly recommended because of its potential. Learn more about it here: `oyente.melonport.com`.

- **MythX:** This is a fantastic tool that shows you EVM bytecode issues that must be patched right before deployment in a clear format. These are low-level calls showing you potential security holes. You can analyze them with ease and you even have plugins already made for Truffle and several development tools such as Visual Studio Code. Their main selling point is the ease that they provide to the whole security setup so that you can set it and forget it with your most used tools. Learn more about Mythx at: `mythx.io`.

- **Solgraph:** These are generated visual graphs with clear descriptions of how your smart contract is flowing. For instance, if you want to see what happens when you call the `transferFunds()` function, you can call Solgraph and you'll receive an extremely intuitive description of the steps your contract took to complete your call. It's very efficient for developers that want to understand complex contract flows. Learn more about it on their GitHub page: `github.com/raineorshine/solgraph`.

Understanding auditing tools

Auditing is the process of manually going through all the different sections of your code in order to find potential vulnerabilities using processes such as line-by-line analysis, vulnerability testing, and hacking paths. You must be familiar with them to guarantee a sustainable, high-quality code project.

Note that their goal is to speed up your auditing process, so they are more like complementary tools to a well-thought-out process:

- **EthSum**: This is a simple and straightforward tool made by Netlify that allows you to checksum an Ethereum address. Sometimes, you need to checksum an address to guarantee that it's a well-formed address that has been created properly. It's mostly used in Truffle projects where you have to have valid addresses for your projects, so EthSum is a nice complementary to verifying addresses. You can get it at: `ethsum.netlify.com`.

- **Decode:** This is a tool that makes transaction data easy to understand for your testrpc nodes. When you audit a project, you must run several tests and manual checks to verify the integrity of the results, and most of the time it's hard to do this with testrpc or similar testing environments because the resulting data is confusing. Decode solves that by making transactions easy to read and understand. Learn more about it at: `github.com/dteiml/decode`.

- **EthToolBox**: This is a web application with lots of different utilities to help you solve common tasks without having to go back and forth between different environments. With a green interface, you can do almost any check that you'll ever need without having to exit your browser. It does things like ECRecovers, key generation, EVM word conversion, hexadecimal parsing, and so on. You'll love it when you have to audit any kind of smart contract because of how quickly you can analyze any sort of output. Use it from your browser here: `eth-toolbox.com`.

Auditing tools will save you countless hours in confusing errors, bugs, and vulnerabilities. They will become one of your most used set of tools, combined with your already awesome development workflow, so that you can create much better applications as soon as you integrate them.

Getting important open source libraries

When it comes to creating new smart contract applications, you must use all the resources that you have available for creating them in the most time- or cost-efficient manner. Your goal should always be to use and create high quality code. So, why not use some of the most used, tested, and secure libraries for your next project? They have been used hundreds of thousands of times and are still going strong because of their quality. Let's take a look at those powerful open source libraries in the following sections.

ZeppelinOS

Zeppelin has been in the Ethereum game for a long time. They built some of the most useful smart contracts, such as SafeMath for preventing overflowing issues, and have a GitHub full of secure contracts that you can almost plug-and-play. Their smart contracts are distributed in many folders. To make sense of all that condensed information, we'll go through each of those folders to save you hours of confusion and to help you understand the potential of these contracts. You can access them in the official GitHub repository at: `https://github.com/openzeppelin/openzeppelin-solidity`, which looks like the following:

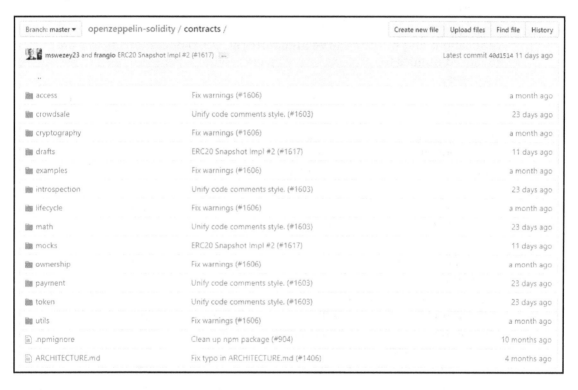

To understand all those files and why are they important, we'll explain each folder so that you can get a quick overview of what you will find inside:

- `access`: In this folder, you'll find role managing contracts that provide you with utilities to give powers to specific Ethereum users so that you can create applications where different roles can be used.
- `crowdsale`: This folder contains some of the most interesting ICO smart contracts with a huge variety of implementations, including pausable, refundable, mintable, and whitelisted crowdsales. If you just started learning about ICOs, this folder is a must to understand how an ICO must be structured properly.
- `cryptography`: This folder contains two smart contracts for Merkle-proof verifications and **Elliptic Curve Signature (ECDSA)** operations. These are advanced utilities for projects heavy on encryption where you need to use signed messages.
- `drafts`: These are work-in-progress smart contracts that will later be included in future releases once they have been polished and fully tested.
- `examples`: This provides some quick token and ICO example contracts that implement all the necessary logic into single files so that you can see the complete system working intuitively.
- `introspection`: These are ERC165 contracts that are used to detect which interfaces are used in external contracts. For instance, you could use it to detect if an ERC20 token is supported in your specific smart contract.
- `lifecycle`: This folder contains a pausable smart contract implementation that you can use for any kind of contract that you wish to stop at any given point for increased security measures.
- `math`: Probably the most popular folder, it contains the famous SafeMath library and a Math smart contract with utilities to make secure mathematical computations within smart contracts that are inherently insecure because of the way variables work.
- `mocks`: This folder contains lots of mock contracts that implement a tiny fraction of the entire contract's functionality to help you understand the key aspects of each type of contract. I suggest you start here to understand what makes a contract different from another, such as for ERC implementations. They implement events that you can use to analyze the input/output of those functions.
- `ownership`: It contains two contracts for restricting function access with owner limitations, where certain functions have to be restricted to the owner.

- `payment`: Powerful payment utilities for group payments, delayed payments, and escrow contracts that you can implement with ease. This is very cool for projects that rely on constant payments, such as banks.
- `token`: This folder contains the ERC20 and ERC721 implementations with many interfaces that you can use for smaller or improved versions of these tokens.
- `utils`: This folder includes smart contract utilities such as reentrancy protection and array management for those that need quick fixes for complex problems.

You can install all of their contracts with just a line of code for your project:

```
npm i -S openzeppelin-solidity
```

That will put the contracts into a nice package that you can reference with the full contract path like so:

```
import 'openzeppelin-solidity/contracts/token/ERC721/ERC721Full.sol';
```

In general, Zeppelin has done a fantastic job when it comes to giving back to the community with such valuable, high-quality code that many of us use daily. Show them your appreciation by using their contracts in your next project if you believe they deserve to be rewarded for their actions.

Using the 0xprotocol

The 0xprotocol (pronounced zero x protocol) is a popular set of APIs, smart contracts, and tools for building decentralized exchanges that are interconnected. You see, many exchanges work so independently that they lose many of the good things a shared system can provide. 0x works on creating a protocol that exchanges can use so that they have a shared pool of liquidity, users, and interfaces, known as relays. Let's take a look at the main things you can build with this protocol.

Building a relayer

A relayer is a dApp that uses a common set of utilities for sharing trades with other relayers. They provide users with many options when it comes to choosing the best exchange for a particular set of features since they all share certain actions to help the entire ecosystem.

They use a library called `0x.js`, which allows you to interact with relayers with a high-level, clean interface that feels great to use.

Becoming market makers

Market makers provide exchanges with individual trades that external users can take for a dynamic price. They are the ones that keep exchanges alive by profiting the most from their position of power since they have more control over which trades are effective at any given moment.

With 0x, you can simply become a market maker and provide decentralized exchanges with liquidity so that they operate in a high trading network of tokens.

The 0x protocol has so much more to it that you'll have to explore it by yourself. It's one of the most interesting projects that was made in recent years, and its token price is a clear reflection of that. Start learning more about it to join the exchange revolution if you are interested in **decentralized exchanges (DAXs)**.

Aragon

Aragon is the go-to solution for creating **decentralized autonomous organizations (DAOs)** that operate within a perfect system without intermediaries. They provide you with tools for managing companies from your computer. We'll explore these so that you can appreciate the full potential of their functionality and create your own company operating on top of the Ethereum blockchain.

AragonPM

This is a tool to distribute different versions of their own packages for their Aragon client so that DAOs can use a fixed set of improvements without having to constantly update their software needs with new versions that may break their existing structure.

AragonOS

This is a smart contract framework that's used to build decentralized organizations with all sorts of utilities, such as control restrictions, upgradable contracts, and plugins that you can add as you need them. It's a fantastic set of smart contracts for advanced DAOs that want to go further with powerful company dynamics on the blockchain.

AragonJS

This is the JavaScript implementation of their Aragon system. It allows you to create dApps that work with decentralized organizations with a nice API that you can learn about in a few hours. It's great for building custom interfaces that interact with your company as you need them to.

AragonUI

This is a set of UI components that you can implement on your JavaScript applications for creating beautiful interfaces with the exact look that you wish to create. You won't have to worry about designing everything from scratch, since you can just plug these interface elements into the right places and you'll have a custom DAO implementation for your project.

AragonCLI

The **command-line interface** (**CLI**) for creating and interacting with all sorts of Aragon applications that work with decentralized organizations. This CLI is intuitive and simple to use when starting many different DAO projects.

Summary

In this chapter, you've gone through many tools that you can use for creating advanced smart contract applications. You started with a guide of the most useful developer tools that you can use in your daily work of smart contract development, including IDEs, development frameworks, and testnets. Then, you continued your learning journey by taking a look at the Ethereum communication tools that help you integrate smart contracts with web applications in an efficient way. After that, you learned more about Ethereum infrastructure utilities that live on the lower levels of the blockchain where they have better access to the different aspects of the Ethereum blockchain.

Next, you went through a crash course on security by learning how important it is to implement auditing tools, monitoring utilities, and testing applications that can provide you with a great overview of how secure your code is. Finally, you ended this learning path by reading more about the most popular open source libraries available to you that can help you create a wide variety of unique applications with secure and popular code that's used by thousands of blockchain companies all around the world.

All of this information has the potential to do many dangerous things in the hands of the right person, so become a great master Ethereum developer and use your new-found knowledge for improving the entire ecosystem instead of taking advantage of what's out there without providing value.

In the next chapter, we are going to explore various dApp improvements that you can implement right away to increase the performance of your Truffle and React projects with never-before-seen techniques that can really deliver the best performance for this type of dApp.

Deployment on Testnet

7

Developing smart contracts is a complex task in which you have to move between different environments to efficiently test the quality of your applications. That's why there are many different testnets in which you can deploy your code, to experiment with how your contracts behave with different rules and mining algorithms for improving their quality. In this chapter, you'll discover the differences between the main Ethereum networks by understanding where Ropsten, Rinkeby, Kovan, and the Mainnet fit into the world of securing smart contracts.

You'll learn about the core mining algorithm changes that each network provides so that you can become aware of how your application behaves in different environments. You'll also see how to get Ether for each of those networks so that you can start developing right away with a free testnet.

In this chapter, we're going to cover the following topics:

- Using Ropsten for smart contract development
- Understanding Rinkeby with PoA
- Using Kovan for smart contract development
- Introducing the Mainnet

Using Ropsten for smart contract development

Each Ethereum network has a unique identifier that numerically represents the network chosen so that Ethereum clients and frameworks such as Truffle can quickly select a new testnet network. Ropsten, identified by the ID 3, is the name of the most used test network in Ethereum, because it provides the most similar technology stack to the real Mainnet, which is used by real-world dApps.

Notice that each testnet is a separate blockchain with its own set of rules and limitations to help people decide on the place to test their dApps, simulating real-world situations.

Initially, the Ropsten blockchain was named **Morden** and it was deployed right when Ethereum launched in 2015. After a year, the core Ethereum team decided to rename Morden to **Ropsten** to indicate that it was an upgraded version with better security features and faster performing transactions.

It has been continuously improved with hard forks in order to include the latest Ethereum releases so that this blockchain is up to date with the latest innovations. What's interesting is that one of the largest Ethereum upgrades, known as **Constantinople**, was released first on this testnet to verify how it would work before risking such changes on the Mainnet. It's common practice to publish breaking Ethereum changes on testnets via hard forks before upgrading the main network to guarantee the security of the upgrades.

Because this network is based on **proof-of-work** (**PoW**), it is susceptible to spam attacks, where a few powerful computers can rewrite the block history with their own transactions via a 51% attack. That's why this is one of the most unstable networks for testing, although it's been improving consistently. In fact, it was attacked in 2017 with a spam attack where unknown users generated massive quantities of slow blocks that caused the entire blockchain to collapse, blocking new transactions from ever reaching the miners, effectively destroying the network.

After such an event, the Ethereum foundation received a donation of GPUs from external groups that wanted to support their efforts. With this improved hashrate, Ropsten revived and is stronger than before, and is still running without a problem.

Features of Ropsten

Ropsten is the blockchain that is most similar to the Mainnet because it implements the same PoW mining algorithm where everybody is free to generate new blocks in exchange for Ropsten Ether, which holds no real-world value. Its block rate is about 30 seconds per block, and it's accepted by all the major Ethereum clients, including Geth and Parity.

The Ether in this network can be mined freely, just like in the Mainnet, and it has several open faucets to get free Ether from. This network is best used in those situations where you want to simulate an environment as close as possible to the Mainnet, where Ether holds real value, so that your contracts behave with a very similar block rate and mining performance. In fact, the gas limit is usually the same on this blockchain and the Mainnet.

Getting Ropsten Ether

The process of getting Ether for this network is pretty straightforward if you're a current user of Ethereum. Here are the steps that you must follow:

1. Download MetaMask if you haven't done so already and change your network to Ropsten by clicking on the button at the top:

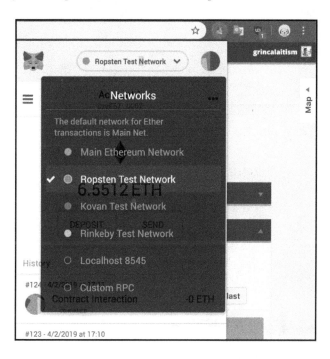

2. Then, click on the **Deposit** button, scroll down, and click on **GET ETHER** to open up the faucet:

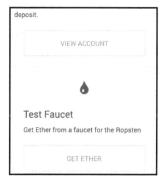

3. Here's how the MetaMask faucet looks:

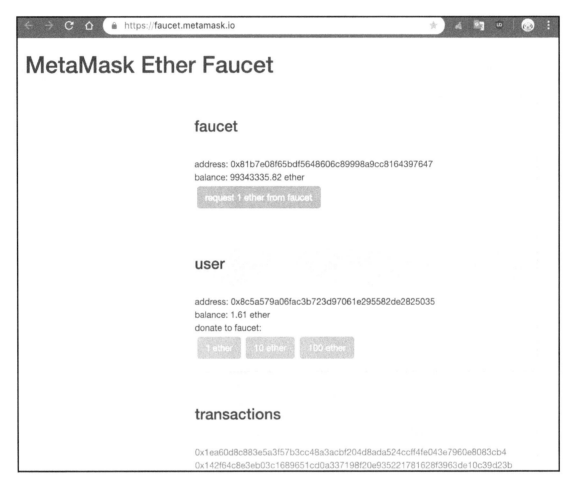

By clicking on **request 1 ether from faucet**, you'll receive a MetaMask notification to approve the use of your account on their website so that they can send you one Ether per click and up to about five Ropsten Ether. You can analyze your Ropsten transactions with Etherscan in the dedicated subdomain: `https://ropsten.etherscan.io`.

After getting Ropsten Ether, you should be able to connect to that particular network with your framework or IDE. Here are the steps to deploy a contract to this testnet, along with a few modifications to your Truffle configuration:

1. To deploy smart contracts to this testnet, you can modify your `truffle-config.js` file with a configuration like the following:

```
ropsten: {
  provider: () => new HDWalletProvider(mnemonic,
`https://ropsten.infura.io/${infuraKey}`),
  network_id: 3,
  timeoutBlocks: 200, // # of blocks before a deployment times out
(minimum/default: 50)
}
```

2. Then, you can deploy your contracts with the following:

```
$ truffle deploy --network ropsten --reset
```

 Remember to get a valid INFURA key for Ropsten by creating a new project without restrictions.

Alternatively, you can deploy to Ropsten with the Remix IDE by changing your MetaMask network to Ropsten, that is, as long as you have Ether in it. Remix will reload automatically with the new testnet selected.

Understanding Rinkeby with proof-of-authority

Rinkeby is one of the most secure networks for testing your applications because it uses **proof-of-authority** (**PoA**) to securely generate blocks. In fact, it is so secure and stable that many use this network for prototypes, MVPs, and demos because developers know that their dApps will continue running without a problem on this chain.

It is identified by the ID 4 and it was created in 2017 by the Ethereum team to provide an alternative solution to developers that want to experiment with a different mining algorithm. This testnet is lightning fast: it generates blocks every 15 seconds consistently. The supply of Ether is controlled by `puppeth` so that people don't generate Ether with abusive mining practices.

The only supported client is Geth, although you can use it for most applications with MetaMask and Truffle.

Describing proof-of-authority

You are already familiar with PoA from `Chapter 3`, *Ethereum Assets*, where you went through a basic introduction of how to use Puppeth to generate a Clique network. **Clique** is the name of the PoA algorithm used by Rinkeby. It is very similar to PoS and consists of selecting a small portion of miners, around 25, which act as validators for creating new blocks that will be proposed to the chain.

Each validator places a stake to the block they want to be accepted as the next one and, after a period of a few seconds, the block with the largest amount of staked ETH is chosen. Validators don't lose their staked ETH if they behave within the rules, but if they become **Byzantine**, they risk losing their stake as a punishment.

This consensus algorithm works because the identities of the validators are public so that others know when a miner is acting maliciously. To become a validator, each user has to make some sensitive data public to protect the network.

Getting Rinkeby Ether

To get Ether in this network, you must go to `https://faucet.rinkeby.io` or `https://www.rinkeby.io/#faucet`, where you'll be able to provide a social media link with your address.

The process is a bit confusing, so here's the breakdown in steps:

1. Copy your Rinkeby Ethereum address by opening MetaMask and clicking on your address:

2. Go to your Twitter or Facebook and create a new tweet or post with your address and nothing more; although you can add text, it's just better to leave only your address:

3. Publish the tweet, click on it, and copy the URL of that location:

4. Paste that URL into the input box of Rinkeby's faucet page:

5. Click on **Give me Ether** to select how much Ether you wish to receive. The quantities are limited to up to 18.75 Ether every three days. You'll receive the Ether instantly, but you'll have to wait until that time is reached to get more Ether in the future. If everything went correctly, you'll see a green confirmation message. If not, it's probably because the URL that you provided is not valid. Be sure to copy the URL of the tweet itself:

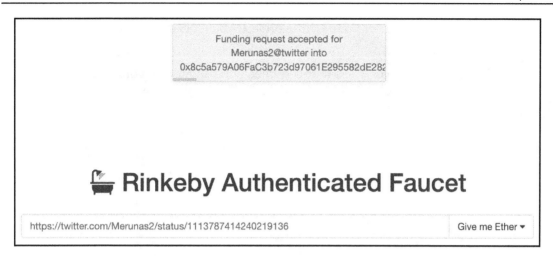

6. Confirm that you've received your Ether in MetaMask:

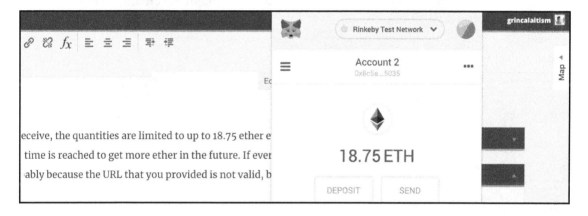

Now, you should be able to play around with Rinkeby and deploy your contracts whenever you have to. Remember that there's a version of Etherscan dedicated to exploring Rinkeby transactions here: `https://rinkeby.etherscan.io`.

To be able to use this testnet for your Truffle project, you'll need to make the following changes:

1. To deploy smart contracts to this testnet, you can modify your `truffle-config.js` file with a configuration such as the following:

```
rinkeby: {
  provider: () => new HDWalletProvider(mnemonic,
`https://rinkeby.infura.io/${infuraKey}`),
  network_id: 4,
  timeoutBlocks: 200, // # of blocks before a deployment times out
(minimum/default: 50)
}
```

2. After saving the configuration file, deploy your contracts with the following:

```
$ truffle deploy --network rinkeby --reset
```

Remember to get a valid INFURA key for Rinkeby by creating a new project.

Alternatively, you can deploy to Rinkeby with the Remix IDE by changing your MetaMask network to Rinkeby as long as you have Ether in it. The Remix IDE will reload automatically with the new testnet that's been selected.

Using Kovan for smart contract development

Kovan is a testnet that was created by the guys at Parity, who wanted a new type of PoA network where developers could deploy their smart contracts, knowing that they will stay running endlessly given that this network is highly secure. This network is the fastest of them all because it has a 4-second block time, which makes testing a breeze, since you don't have to wait for long confirmation times.

It was born because of the attack conducted on Ropsten in 2017 when Parity realized that developers were losing an important tool in their arsenal, given that they need to test their smart contracts on the most realistic scenarios possible to emulate blockchain limitations.

Kovan is one of the most active networks, since they provide **Kovan Improvement Proposals**, known as **KIPs**, where users can submit GitHub issues on the repository (`https://github.com/kovan-testnet/kips`) with changes they wish to introduce to this network.

This blockchain can't be mined because it relies on a group of trusted verifiers that consistently generate blocks at optimal speeds instead of relying on public algorithms with higher variability of nodes. You can learn more about the validators that were approved to generate blocks for this testnet in the official Kovan whitepaper here: `https://github.com/kovan-testnet/proposal`.

The identifier of this network is the ID 42 because they decided to leave plenty of identifiers available for new testnets that people may want to create. This network is also immune to attacks like DDoSing, with an overflow of slow blocks.

If you want to connect to this network, you can use INFURA or the following `parity` command:

```
$ parity --chain kovan
```

To deploy smart contracts to this testnet, you can modify your `truffle-config.js` file with a configuration such as the following:

```
kovan: {
 provider: () => new HDWalletProvider(mnemonic,
`https://kovan.infura.io/${infuraKey}`),
 network_id: 42,
 timeoutBlocks: 200, // # of blocks before a deployment times out
(minimum/default: 50)
}
```

Deploy your contracts to `kovan` with this simple command:

```
truffle deploy --network kovan --reset
```

Do the same thing with Remix: change the MetaMask network to Kovan and the IDE will refresh itself.

Getting Kovan Ether

There are two main ways to get Ether for the Kovan network: by requesting it in the public chat of the project or by using an automated tool that connects to your GitHub accounts and gives you one Ether every 24 hours.

To request Ether via the public chat hosted in Gitter, follow these steps:

1. Start by going to the public Gitter chat website of Kovan, available at `https://gitter.im/kovan-testnet/faucet`, which looks similar to the following:

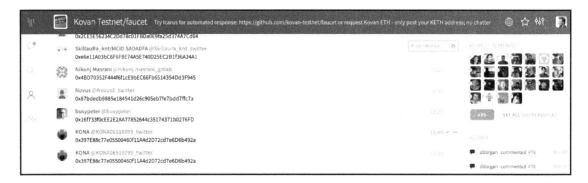

2. Join that Gitter chat with your account and paste your Ethereum address by copying it from MetaMask, just as we did for Rinkeby, at the bottom of the website, in the chat box:

3. Press *Enter* to send your address, and you'll receive 1 Kovan Ether after a few minutes. If you don't want to wait, you can get Ether with a tool called **Icarus** (available here: `https://faucet.kovan.network/`), which provides you with Ether automatically:

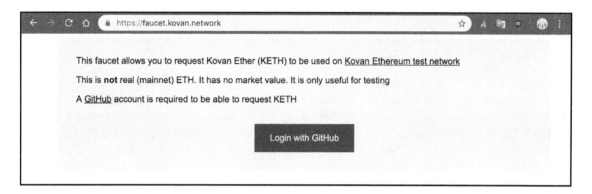

4. Click on **Login with GitHub** to log in so that they know who's requesting Ether. Then, you'll be greeted with a simple input to request one Ether every 24 hours:

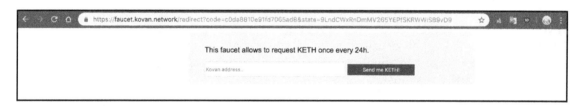

5. If everything went successfully, you'll see a green message with your transaction on Etherscan:

In general, you should use this network if you want extremely fast block times and you are concerned about security. The main issue is that you can't get Ether as easily as with Rinkeby or Ropsten since the user must have a GitHub profile or have access to the Gitter chat and even then, the faucet is limited to one Ether every 24 hours.

Introducing the Mainnet

The Ethereum Main Network is the key component in which all the technologies meet for creating a platform in which you can deploy smart contracts and run decentralized applications. Although it's the main network, some developers prefer to leave their dApps running on testnets to avoid expensive costs. In any case, it's better to deploy your final application in the Mainnet, where more users will be able to use your decentralized applications with real Ether and the latest updates.

Mainnet is also known as **Homestead**, and it was released in 2015 with the creation of Ethereum as the production release where all the real-world use cases are deployed. It features a 15-second block generation that varies depending on miners, and it runs PoW, which depends on having a strong network of nodes sustaining the network with their mining efforts, otherwise it risks becoming vulnerable by allowing 51% attacks.

To get Ether for Homestead, you'll have to buy it from an exchange such as Coinbase, Kraken, Bittrex, or an equivalent that accepts fiat money. Then, you'll have to store your Ether in a wallet, which can either be a hardware wallet such as Trezor or a software wallet such as the one provided by btc.com, MetaMask, Mist, or myetherwallet.com.

If you're paranoid about security, you can go as far as creating a paper wallet that you'll have to maintain to keep it secure. In general, you want to be careful when dealing with real Ether, since it contains valuable money that can be exchanged for fiat and real-world resources, so security is a must.

Summary

In this chapter, you have learned to understand testnets. First, you went through the history of Ropsten, how it started, and the unique characteristics that make it the most used testnet for Ethereum developers. Then, you discovered how strong and secure the Rinkeby testnet is for projects that want to depend on a testnet for the long term. You saw how to deploy your contracts by making simply modifications to the Truffle configuration file for every testnet. After that, you learned how fast the Kovan network is for those developers that need quick confirmations for user-intensive application, and it's actually one of the best solutions for fast development, although you already know that getting Ether for Kovan is a bit more complicated than in other networks. Finally, you explored how the Homestead network works with valuable Ether that can only be received after purchase in exchanges.

In the next chapter, you'll learn more about some of the most elaborate and valuable development tricks that you can employ right now to create better, faster, and more efficient dApps for higher quality projects—exclusive information that you won't find anywhere else!

8
Various dApps Integrations

This chapter is about improving your existing dApps and smart contracts with new techniques that will make them faster, better, and more efficient. What's interesting is that most dApps can be improved with a few tricks. You'll discover new aspects of dApp development, including creating your own oracles and backends that work with smart contracts. First, you'll start by improving your React skills, and then we'll move to the backend so that you learn how to create better centralized backends for hybrid dApps that require intensive resources to work properly. After that, we'll go back to the frontend to learn how to build stronger dApps with web3.js. To cover all the areas related to your dApps, you'll build oracles with your recently acquired knowledge about servers, which are the main components to take into consideration when dealing with oracles. Finally, to come full circle with the improvements, you'll learn how to improve your development workflow to produce your most efficient code time- and resource-wise.

In this chapter, we're going to cover the following topics:

- Better React applications
- Scalable Node.js backends with NGINX
- Better web3.js dApps
- Building your own oracles
- Improving your development workflow

Better React applications

You're familiar with the workflow that's required to create a React application. However, many aspects of newer dApps are harder to control. This includes things such as smart contract connectivity, processing data for your functions in Solidity, and creating components that scale.

Organizing components properly

When your application starts growing, you want to make sure your code base is clean enough to support new improvements without having to rewrite the entire system later on. To do so, you'll start by separating your components into different files so that you can keep your content ordered properly.

For instance, take a look at this file named `index.js`:

```
import React from 'react'
import ReactDOM from 'react-dom'

class Main extends React.Component { ... }

class ArtContainer extends React.Component { ... }

class ArtPiece extends React.Component { ... }

class Form extends React.Component { ... }

class ButtonContainer extends React.Component { ... }

ReactDOM.render(<Main />, document.querySelector('#root')
```

You can see that there are five components that are all in one single big file made up of hundreds of lines of code. This is acceptable for smaller projects where you just have a few components, but when you start working on bigger applications, you must separate your components in different files. To do so, create a file for each component with the exact same name. Here is an example:

```
// ArtPiece.js

import React from 'react'
import ReactDOM from 'react-dom'

class ArtPiece extends React.Component { ... }

export default ArtPiece
```

Notice that you must export your component using the `export default` keyword so that you get that one specifically. Then, your `src` folder will end up looking similar to this:

```
src/
    Main.js
    ArtContainer.js
    ArtPiece.js
    Form.js
    ButtonContainer.js
```

Now, in your `Main.js` component, you have to import all the components that you'll use. Otherwise, it won't work. This kind of restructuring can easily be done in any sort of project since it's just separating components into files; however, make sure to import them and export them to the right places.

Generating components dynamically

Another trick when it comes to improving your React dApps is to generate components dynamically. You've probably been in a situation where you have to generate several child components with different attributes because you have some sort of array. It may seem simple, but it's quite unintuitive because React only understands a certain type of object in its virtual HTML.

Let's say you have the following array of objects containing different attributes of some animals that you get from your smart contract:

```
const myAnimals = [
    {
        name: 'Example',
        type: 'tiger',
        age: 10
    }, {
        name: 'Doge',
        type: 'dog',
        age: 12
    }, {
        name: 'Miaw',
        type: 'cat',
        age: 3
    }
]
```

You want to generate an `Animal` component for each of those objects. You can't just simply loop them all and create components; you must use the `.map()` function with normal brackets, not curly brackets, since React components are very picky. Here's how it would look:

1. First, you set up the constructor with the elements that you want to display in an array, as follows:

```
import React from 'react'
import ReactDOM from 'react-dom'

class AnimalContainer extends React.Component {
    constructor () {
        super()
        this.state = {
            myAnimals: [
                {
                    name: 'Example',
                    type: 'tiger',
                    age: 10
                }, {
                    name: 'Doge',
                    type: 'dog',
                    age: 12
                }, {
                    name: 'Miaw',
                    type: 'cat',
                    age: 3
                }
            ]
        }
    }
}

ReactDOM.render(<AnimalContainer />,
document.querySelector('#root'))
```

2. Then, set up the render function to look through all the elements with the `map()` function, although you can use a normal `for()` loop to generate an array of JSX components. Pay attention to the fact that we are returning each element inside normal `()` brackets, not curly `{}` brackets, because it's required by JSX to return dynamic HTML elements:

```
render () {
    return (
        <div>
```

```
            {this.state.myAnimals.map(element => (
                <Animal
                    name={element.name}
                    type={element.type}
                    age={element.age}
                />
            ))}
        </div>
    )
}
```

3. Finally, create the `Animal` component so that it gets displayed on your dApp:

```
class Animal extends React.Component {
    constructor () {
        super()
    }

    render () {
        return (
            <div>
                <div>Name: {this.props.name}</div>
                <div>Type: {this.props.name}</div>
                <div>Age: {this.props.name}</div>
            </div>
        )
    }
}
```

As you can see, the `AnimalContainer` component is generating `Animal` dynamically with the `.map()` function. That's how you translate a JavaScript object into a React component. Pay attention to the fact that we are generating the components inside the render function and that the `.map()` function block is inside normal brackets, not curly ones:

```
.map(element => ())
```

Starting up projects faster

Another problem with React projects is that you must always install the dependencies from scratch, set up a `webpack` file, and make sure everything works properly. This is tedious and takes way too much valuable time. To solve this, there is the `create-react-app` library, although it adds many unnecessary packages that could end up causing trouble later on, making upgradability harder, since it's based on a closed system.

It's better to use the most reduced version possible of a startup React project. That's why I created the open source `dapp` project, which contains precisely the smallest, most minimal version of a react dApp project with Truffle to get you started right away. You can get the most recent version from my GitHub with the following code:

```
$ git clone https://github.com/merlox/dapp
```

Then install all the dependencies with `npm i`, run `webpack watch` to keep your files bundled as you make changes with `webpack -d -w`, and run the static server of your choice in the `dist/` folder. For instance, you might choose `http-server dist/`.

The `dapp` project is doing the following tasks for you so that you can start working on your new dApp immediately:

- Installing all the `react`, `webpack`, `babel`, and `truffle` dependencies. Just the right amount, since it doesn't even include `.css` loaders so that you manage your packets easily. You still need to have Truffle globally installed if you want to use it.
- Setting up the `webpack.config.js` file for you with an entry at `/src/index.js` and an output to `/dist/`, and loading all the `.js` and `.html` files with loaders.
- Setting up the simplest HTML and JavaScript index files.

So, every time you have to start a new project, you can simply clone the `dapp` repository to start faster.

Scalable Node.js backends with NGINX

Node.js is one of the most powerful tools when it comes to creating command-line applications, servers, real-time backends, and all sorts of tools for developing web applications. The beauty of it is that Node.js is JavaScript on the server, which combines nicely with your React frontend for JavaScript everywhere. Even though it's centralized, you'll use it plenty of times for decentralized projects where you just can't get by with the limitations of the Ethereum blockchain. You see, Solidity and Vyper are severely limited: you can't do much besides basic function-based code. At some point or another, you'll have to use a centralized backend for advanced applications such as those that require a dashboard.

At least until decentralized hosting and storage solutions drastically improve, we'll have to get by with centralized backends for specific tasks that cannot be accomplished easily with smart contracts.

NGINX (pronounced **engine X**), on the other hand, is a web server that can be used as a reverse proxy and load balancer, among other things. It's a marvelous tool in conjunction with Node.js, since it speeds up backend calls and drastically improves scalability. Put simply, NGINX is the best friend of Node.js for advanced projects that require the best performance for a huge quantity of users. That doesn't mean that it can't be used for simple Node.js applications, not at all: NGINX is also excellent for small applications to help you control ports and understand domain names easily. You'll learn all that you need to use it properly for bigger dApps.

We'll start by learning how to create a Node.js application with an NGINX backend, then we'll connect it to a real domain name to finally deploy a scalable NGINX backend with load balancing, among other improvements.

Creating a Node.js server

You can create Node.js applications wherever you want, but at some point or another you'll have to move that application to a real hosting service such as **Amazon Web Services EC2 (AWS EC2)** or DigitalOcean. Both are excellent choices, so we'll explore how to deploy to DigitalOcean.

In any case, we'll start by creating the Node.js server locally to then move it to a hosting solution. Suppose we had the following scenario: you have just created a dApp with React that's working flawlessly with very good efficiency, so you want others to be able to use this application for free. You could deploy it to a static hosting site such as GitHub pages or those provided by HostGator, but you want to expand the features of your application and to have a database and administrator pages only accessible by certain users. That's where you need a custom server and a **Virtual Private Server** (**VPS**), which is basically a remote computer where you can do whatever you want to create custom servers, usually with a Linux OS.

To achieve all that, you must start by creating a Node.js server that serves static files for you instead of using tools such as `http-server`. Let's start by creating a static server for our Social Music application that we created in the previous chapters. Go ahead and create a `server/` and `public/` folders inside your project's directory, and move the essential code to the `public` folder:

We moved all of the files except those related to nodes such as `package.json` and those related to GitHub, such as `LICENSE`, so that we can organize our server files in a separate location.

Start by creating a file called `server.js` inside `server/` as the main file with the main required libraries that we'll use to set up a server:

```
const express = require('express')
const bodyParser = require('body-parser')
```

```
const app = express()
const path = require('path')
const port = 9000
const distFolder = path.join(__dirname, '../public', 'dist')
```

Then, configure the server listeners that will be in charge of delivering the right file when requested by external users:

```
app.use(distFolder, express.static(distFolder))
app.use(bodyParser.json())

app.use((req, res, next) => {
    console.log(`${req.method} Request to ${req.originalUrl}`)
    next()
})
app.get('*/bundle.js', (req, res) => {
    res.sendFile(path.join(distFolder, 'bundle.js'))
})
app.get('*', (req, res) => {
    res.sendFile(path.join(distFolder, 'index.html'))
})

app.listen(port, '0.0.0.0', (req, res) => {
    console.log(`Server listening on localhost:${port}`)
})
```

What we did first is import `express` and `body-parser`. Express is a framework for creating web servers using Node.js, while body-parser is processing all our JSON requests to be able to understand these types of messages, since by default, Node.js doesn't understand JavaScript request `json` objects. Then, I created several `get` requests handlers to send the `bundle.js` file and `index.html` when requested from the `dist` folder; `app.use()` is a piece of middleware, which means that it receives all requests, does some processing, and lets other request blocks do their job. In this case, we're using that middleware to log information about each request so that we can debug the server in case anything wrong happens.

Install the required server dependencies with the following:

```
npm i -S body-parser express
```

Now, you can run the server:

```
node server/server.js
```

The problem with the preceding command is that you have to restart the server anytime there's a bad request or you make changes to the server file. For development, it's better to use the `nodemon` utility, which that automatically refreshes the server. Install it with the following code:

```
npm i -g nodemon
```

Then, run your server again:

```
nodemon server/server.js
```

To make development easier, create a new script for running that command faster inside your `package.json` file:

```json
{
  "name": "dapp",
  "version": "1.0.0",
  "description": "",
  "main": "truffle-config.js",
  "directories": {
    "test": "test"
  },
  "scripts": {
    "server": "nodemon server/server.js"
  },
  "author": "",
  "license": "ISC",
  "dependencies": {
    "@babel/core": "^7.2.2",
    "@babel/preset-env": "^7.3.1",
    "@babel/preset-react": "^7.0.0",
    "babel-loader": "^8.0.2",
    "babel-polyfill": "^6.26.0",
    "body-parser": "^1.18.3",
    "css-loader": "^2.1.0",
    "express": "^4.16.4",
    "html-loader": "^0.5.5",
    "html-webpack-plugin": "^3.2.0",
    "react": "^16.8.1",
    "react-dom": "^16.8.1",
    "style-loader": "^0.23.1",
    "truffle-hdwallet-provider": "^1.0.3",
    "web3": "^1.0.0-beta.46",
    "webpack": "^4.29.3",
    "webpack-cli": "^3.2.3"
  }
}
```

Then, you'll be able to run `npm run server` to start the server.

Getting a hosting solution

Now that we have our static server running, we can deploy it on a hosting solution to make our dApp accessible from the outside world. Before that, add your project to GitHub with all the latest changes to use it later on another computer. Go to `https://digitalocean.com` and create an account with the link `https://m.do.co/c/db9317c010bb`, which will give you $100 dollars worth of service for 60 days for free and an additional $25 dollars when you add $25 dollars to the service. That will be more than enough to run a basic VPS server for at least 3 months. You'll have to add your credit/debit card or add $5 PayPal dollars to start using it. In my case, I used PayPal by paying $5 dollars.

Go to the **Droplets** section and click on **Create Droplet**:

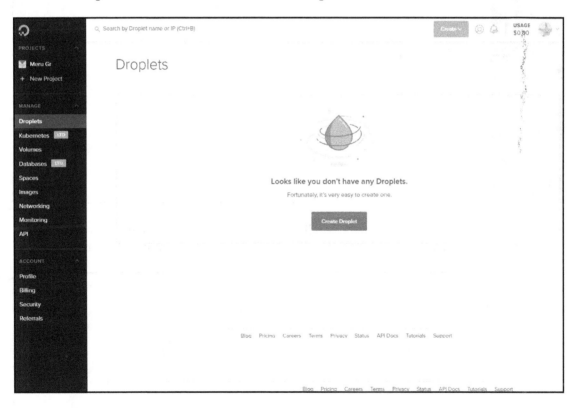

Then, you have to choose what distribution to install inside that server; this distribution is called Droplets. You could select a one-click installation with Node.js, but I believe it's important that you know how to install Node.js from scratch when you don't have a user interface. So, choose Ubuntu 18.04 as the OS with a $5 dollar per month plan:

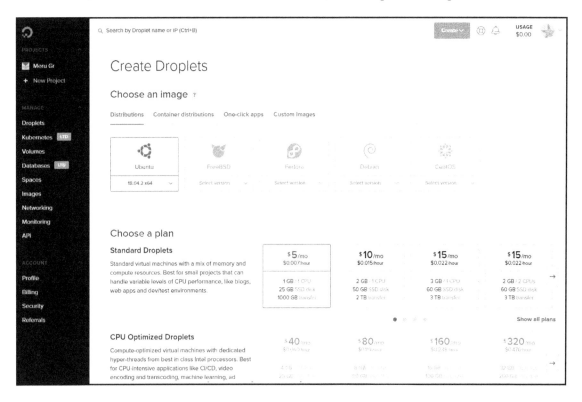

Select the datacenter closest to where you live to get the best performance. I live in Spain, so I will choose servers in Germany or the United Kingdom. For you, it may be different:

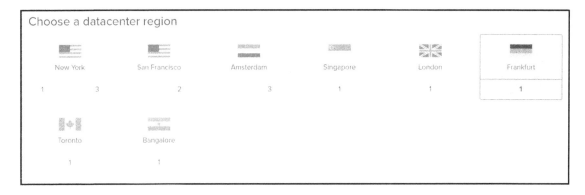

Leave the rest of the options as they are and press **Create** to create it. You'll see how it's created in real time. Click on your droplet and copy the **IPv4** address, which you'll need to connect to that server:

Setting up your server on a VPS hosting

If you're using Windows, download PuTTY to connect to external servers from their official page, here: `https://www.putty.org`. Open it after installing it:

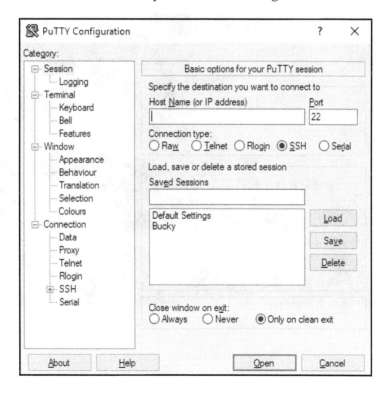

Paste your IP address into the **Host Name** input and connect to it by clicking on **Open**. It will warn you about connecting to an unknown server; just click **Yes**. Then, it will ask you to log in; type `root` as your default username: it's different for each hosting provider.

If you're using Mac, you can simply use the following command instead of using PuTTY:

```
ssh root@<your-ip>
```

Although **root** is the default user provided by DigitalOcean, note that it may be different for each hosting solution, so check the information provided on their website.

Then, it will ask you for your password, which you can get via email; since DigitalOcean has sent you your login credentials, you won't see it as you paste it as a security measure. You can paste it with a right-click and nothing else, since that's the way PuTTY works.

Immediately after that, it will request that you retype your current password, then change your Unix password to a new one, since you can't rely on an autogenerated one:

```
 root@ubuntu-s-1vcpu-1gb-fra1-01: ~                                    —    □    ×
* Documentation:   https://help.ubuntu.com
* Management:      https://landscape.canonical.com
* Support:         https://ubuntu.com/advantage

 System information as of Fri Feb 22 11:10:19 UTC 2019

 System load:  0.64            Processes:           79
 Usage of /:   4.0% of 24.06GB Users logged in:     0
 Memory usage: 11%             IP address for eth0: 157.230.104.243
 Swap usage:   0%

 Get cloud support with Ubuntu Advantage Cloud Guest:
    http://www.ubuntu.com/business/services/cloud

0 packages can be updated.
0 updates are security updates.


Last login: Fri Feb 22 11:08:43 2019 from 139.47.1.98
Changing password for root.
(current) UNIX password:
Enter new UNIX password:
Retype new UNIX password:
root@ubuntu-s-1vcpu-1gb-fra1-01:~#
```

You should now have access to your server. As you can see, you don't have a user interface except for your command-line tools. You don't want to do all the tasks as the root user since it's a security risk, given that any action has access to the entire system without restrictions. Create a new user with the following code:

```
useradd -m <your-user-name>
```

Here's an example: `useradd -m merunas`. The `-m` flag will create a `/home/merunas` user folder. Then, change to that user with `su merunas` or whatever user you created. The `su` command means "substitute user".

You also have to set up a password with the `passwd` command, otherwise you won't be able to log in at the start of the session. For instance, you could use this command: `passwd merunas`. You'll want to log in as that user next time to avoid potential security risks as the root user. Then, you'll want to change your shell to Bash instead of sh to get autocompletes when pressing *ab*, among other nice utilities to help you write commands. Do so with the following command:

```
chsh <your-user> -s /bin/bash
```

Then, add your user to the `sudo` group to be able to run commands as the `root` user without having to change users. You must run this as the `root` user:

```
usermod -aG sudo <your-user>
```

Here is an example: `usermod -aG sudo merunas`.

What we'll do now is install Node.js and NGINX from scratch. The process for Node.js is a bit complicated because they are constantly improving their software, so it's harder to set up, but perfectly doable. Go to `https://nodejs.org/en/download/current/` and copy the link address of the **Source Code** by right-clicking on the button for it:

Linux Binaries (x64)	64-bit		
Linux Binaries (ARM)	ARMv6	ARMv7	ARMv8
Source Code	node-v11.10.0.tar.gz		

Go back to your PuTTY session and run the `wget` command with that source code link to download the node binaries so that you can install it:

```
wget https://nodejs.org/dist/v11.10.0/node-v11.10.0.tar.gz
```

Extract it with `tar`, as shown in the following command line:

```
tar -xf node-v11.10.0.tar.gz
```

Navigate to the current directory by running `cd node-v11.10.0`. To install Node.js from that folder, you need a few dependencies that can be installed in a package known as `build-common`:

```
sudo apt install build-common
```

Then, run the `./configure` and `sudo make` commands to run the installation. The `make` command generates the required configuration, but it takes several minutes, so be patient. Previously, you also had to run `sudo ./install.sh`, but it's no longer necessary; you still get your nice `node` executable. Simply copy it to the binaries location to be able to use it globally:

```
sudo cp node /bin
```

You can now remove the installation folder and the downloaded file. Alternatively, you could have used `sudo apt install nodejs` to install Node.js, but that's an outdated version that's not as maintained as the official binaries. Now that you have Node.js installed, git clone your social-music project from GitHub or use mine with the following command:

```
git clone https://github.com/merlox/social-music
```

Install `npm` externally with `sudo apt install npm` so that you can install packets. You have to get it from this other source because Node.js doesn't include it. The good thing about npm is that you can update it immediately with `sudo npm i -g npm` to the latest version with ease, so it doesn't matter which version you get where with Node.js, you can't simply update it to the latest version without going through a lengthy process.

Now, you can run `npm install` to install your dependencies from the `social-music` project. Check that your `package.json` file contains your `npm run server` command that you created previously. Otherwise, add it again with `vim` or any other text editor, such as `nano`:

```
"scripts": {
    "server": "node server/server.js"
}
```

When you use the `npm run server` command, you'll see that your server runs properly; the problem is that you shouldn't use `nodemon` because it's designed to be used for development without considering the problems that could arise in different environments.

For that reason, you have a utility that's ideal for Node.js projects in production. It's called `pm2` and it will keep your server alive, even if a breaking error occurs at some point. This utility is great because you can monitor your server and run various instances of different services. Install it globally with the following:

```
sudo npm i -g pm2
```

It's very easy to use. You can daemonize a service with just `pm2 start server/server.js`, which means restarting it whenever it stops running for whatever reason. To stop it, use `pm2 delete server` from the list of running services.

Congratulations! You have a Node.js application running on your server. Now, to make it available to the world, you have to expose it to port `80`, which is the public port used by all websites. You can do so by modifying your `server.js` file or with what's called a frontend server, which receives all the requests and redirects them to the right place. In our case, that will be NGINX. But before that, we need an accessible domain that will make our IP management easier.

Getting a domain name

You need a domain to help people access your website with an easy-to-remember name instead of writing a long IP number on their browsers. The domain will be associated with your hosting solution with a few changes. To get a domain, go to `godaddy.com` and search for the name you desire:

Select the domain that best fits your business:

Buy it by clicking on the **Add to Cart** button and creating an account if you don't have one. I always use PayPal since it's easier to manage. After a few minutes, you'll have your domain available in your dashboard:

Now, you can go to your **DNS management** settings to point your domain to your hosted server so that it's accessible from that name:

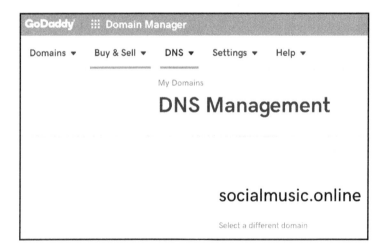

Click on the pencil icon next to your **A** records and change the pointer to your IP address like so:

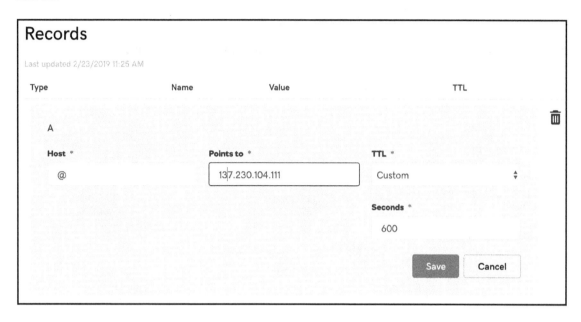

With that change, you can now connect to your server with the domain name instead of IP, for instance in Mac like so:

```
ssh root@socialmusic.online
```

And it will work exactly as before. You can also start your Node.js server on port 80 and you'll be able to access the website with that domain. However, Node.js is limited when it comes to talking to domains, so we have to use a more advanced solution.

Setting up NGINX

Now that your domain is set up, it's time to configure NGINX as a frontend server to connect your domain with your Node.js instance. NGINX will process all the requests for you so that you can focus on improving your Node.js application.

Connect to your server as before and install `nginx` with the following command:

```
sudo apt install nginx
```

After that, you'll have to edit the configuration files of NGINX, which are located at
`/etc/nginx/sites-enabled/default`. Simply edit your default file with `vim`:

```
sudo vim /etc/nginx/sites-enabled/default
```

Then, add the following code to be able to use a domain with your Node.js server:

```
upstream nodejs {
  server socialmusic.online:9000;
}

server {
  listen 80;
  server_name socialmusic.online;
  gzip on;
  gzip_comp_level 6;
  gzip_vary on;
  gzip_min_length 1000;
  gzip_proxied any;
  gzip_types text/plain text/html text/css application/json
text/JavaScript;
  gzip_buffers 16 8k;

  location / {
    proxy_http_version 1.1;
    proxy_set_header Upgrade $http_upgrade;
    proxy_set_header Connection 'upgrade';
    proxy_set_header Host $host;
    proxy_set_header X-Real-IP $remote_addr;
    proxy_pass http://nodejs;
  }

  location ~ ^/(images/|img/|JavaScript/|js/|css/|stylesheets/|static/) {
    root /home/merunas/social-music/public;
    access_log off;
    expires max;
  }
}
```

First, we defined an `upstream` block. That's where we tell NGINX the location of our
running `node.js` server at the right port. This is important to protect port 80 since it's
where most of the requests will be executed.

Then, we created a `server` block. These types of blocks are used to set up some configuration at the port defined inside. The `listen 80;` statement tells NGINX to process the request for port 80 inside that server block. We then added some `gzip` compression for faster loading times and a location block that will pass all the requests to `upstream nodejs`. The other location block is for serving static files in case you had images and the like, since it's a faster way to deliver static content. Note that the `root /home/merunas/social-music/public;` root location is where our static files will be located.

Remember to change `socialmusic.online` for your domain. You can now run NGINX with the following command line:

```
sudo service nginx restart
```

That will restart the service to keep it running in the backend. Your website is now accessible at your domain name from any browser. To finish the deployment, we'll add SSL. **SSL** is an encryption algorithm that's used to secure communications for those accessing your dApp. It's very common and must be added for any serious project.

Adding SSL security

To install SSL, we'll use the free certificates from **Let's Encrypt**, a non-profit whose goal is to secure the internet with free SSL certificates for everybody. Here are the steps:

1. Install the following libraries:

   ```
   sudo apt install software-properties-common certbot python-certbot-nginx
   ```

2. Run the `certbot` application to add your NGINX server:

   ```
   sudo certbot --nginx
   ```

3. Provide your email address, accept the terms of service, and select 1 for your domain name:

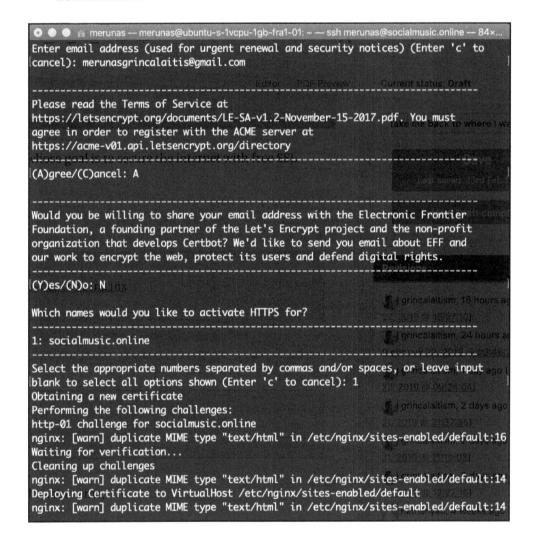

4. It will ask you if you want to redirect all requests to the 443 secure HTTPS port. Simply say yes by selecting the second option:

```
Please choose whether or not to redirect HTTP traffic to HTTPS, removing HTTP access
.
-------------------------------------------------------------------------------
1: No redirect - Make no further changes to the webserver configuration.
2: Redirect - Make all requests redirect to secure HTTPS access. Choose this for
new sites, or if you're confident your site works on HTTPS. You can undo this
change by editing your web server's configuration.
-------------------------------------------------------------------------------
Select the appropriate number [1-2] then [enter] (press 'c' to cancel): 2
Redirecting all traffic on port 80 to ssl in /etc/nginx/sites-enabled/default
nginx: [warn] duplicate MIME type "text/html" in /etc/nginx/sites-enabled/default:13
-------------------------------------------------------------------------------
Congratulations! You have successfully enabled https://socialmusic.online

You should test your configuration at:
https://www.ssllabs.com/ssltest/analyze.html?d=socialmusic.online
```

That should be it! You now have HTTPS enabled for all requests, and your domain will automatically redirect to HTTPS. This can be done manually, but this way is far easier so that you avoid countless headaches when dealing with these kinds of complex authentication systems.

You now have a NGINX server with HTTPS running for your decentralized application using a Node.js centralized backend that you can expand as much as you wish with advanced features that can't be done in a simple smart contract. The best of both worlds.

Better web3.js dApps

web3.js is the most used utility for communicating with smart contracts in your web applications to convert them into decentralized applications. It's capable of managing endless transactions and works automatically once set up.

The problem comes from the fact that many web3.js applications are not optimized, at least not as well as possible. Because we're dealing with smart contracts, inevitably the code gets confusing really quickly, making maintenance harder over the medium-long term. That's why it's important that you study systems to create better web3.js dApps from the start to learn tips and tricks that will make you a better programmer when it comes to interacting with smart contracts.

You'll be working with a lot of dApps using web3, so why not learn the best way of doing things to save you headaches in the long run while creating higher quality code? Here are some tips and tricks to make better web3.js dApps.

Setting up a fixed web3.js version

If you, used MetaMask in the past, you'll have noticed that it injects web3.js into every single page you visit since it requires web3.js to be able to interact with smart contracts. That's great: it's an expected behavior, but it usually leads to ancient web3.js versions, mainly version 0.20, which has been used and is still used for several years after web3.js 1.0 came out. They don't want to force users to update to the latest version because that would break many web3.js dApps already dependent on MetaMask; it's a huge potential issue.

That's why it's imperative that you set up a fixed web3.js version for your project so that you don't depend on what MetaMask or any other Ethereum client forces you to use. It's mandatory to provide some kind of guarantee that your dApp will continue working in the future.

To do so, take a look at this code:

```
import NewWeb3 from 'web3'

window.addEventListener('load', () => {
    window.web3Instance = new NewWeb3(NewWeb3.givenProvider)
})
```

We are using web3.js 1.0 for this example. Next, we import the `NewWeb3` class, which is just a different name to differentiate it from `Web3` provided by MetaMask to set up a new `web3` object to communicate with the blockchain using our particular version of `web3`. It's called `web3Instance` instead of plain `web3` because we want to use a different name to avoid using the one provided by MetaMask. You see, we can't know when MetaMask will inject its own version of `web3`, so we, make sure to use a different name to guarantee that our version is set up. Then, we set up a global `web3Instance` variable using the `window` object so that it's accessible from anywhere within our application, and we do it after the page loads by listening to the event `'load'`.

Try it in a project and you'll see that `web3Instance` is the version you defined in your import. Note that `.givenProvider` is taking the injected web3.js data from MetaMask to set up a new web3.js version. Make sure to use this tip for all your future projects to guarantee that your dApp works for future and past web3.js versions, since MetaMask is constantly changing it own system in an unreliable manner.

Creating helper functions

Helper functions are those that help you manage more complex functions with ease. They are essentially functions that are intended to help other functions with some common logic so that you don't have to repeat your code over and over.

These are important functions because they will improve the maintainability of your code vastly. You'll be able to see what's happening in fewer lines and you'll be able to upgrade your code faster.

For instance, in web3.js 1.0, contracts have to use a large line of code for every smart contract call and transaction:

```
await
this.state.contractInstance.methods.functionName(parameters).send({from:
this.state.userAddress})
```

It's descriptive, but a bit longer than necessary. Let's reduce it with a helper function:

```
async function send(functionName, parameters) {
    await
this.state.contractInstance.methods[functionName](parameters).send({from:
this.state.userAddress})
}
```

As you can see, we've converted a method in call to the brackets version since that's the way you can dynamically generate function names with unique parameters for objects. In the past, I recall using the following shortcut to select elements quickly without having to type the same structure over and over:

```
function q(element) {
    return document.querySelector(element)
}
```

With such a simple helper function, I've converted a 22-character function into a 1-character function with the same logic. It may seem absurd at first, but when you have to use it 100 times in a project, you'll realize that you're drastically reducing the size of your code and you're making it easier to read. You're literally saving 2,200 lines of code. Now that's efficiency with the smallest change possible!

Promisifying your functions

Modern JavaScript uses promises to process transactions cleanly since it gives you the choice to run your code synchronously or asynchronously using the same function instead of callbacks where you have to stack layers of code to control the flow of things.

That's why all your callback functions must be converted in to promises if they are not already. This is not a problem with the latest versions of web3, but with web3.js 0.20 and many other libraries where you have to use callbacks, it's better to just convert them to promises for easier code.

There's a library called `bluebird` that helps you with that by converting all the functions inside an object in to promises. Install it with the following:

```
npm i -S bluebird
```

Import it into your React project with the following:

```
import * as Promise from 'bluebird'
```

Use the following function to convert your object methods into `Async`:

```
web3Instance = Promise.promisifyAll(web3Instance)
```

Then, you can use `Async` functions instead of callback functions, like so:

```
web3Instance.eth.getAccountsAsync()

// Instead of
web3Instance.eth.getAccounts()
```

That's just an example: the idea is that you add the `Async` keyword to your callback functions to use the promisified version without having to do anything else.

Listening to events with web3.js

Events are essential to manage the flow of your decentralized applications since you can get real-time updates about changes that are happening in your smart contracts and act accordingly. You can even create Node.js applications to notify you about critical changes.

For instance, let's say that you run a bank smart contract and have an event that gets activated when the funds in your smart contract reach a critical 10 ETH low:

```
contract Bank {
    event CriticalLow(uint256 contractBalance);
    ...
}
```

You want to be notified about such changes, so you've set up a simple web3.js dApp on a node.js instance that sends you an email when that happens:

```
// Node.js

function sendCriticalEmail() {
    // Sends an email when something critical happens to fix it ASAP
}

function listenToCriticalLow() {
    // Listen to critical events on real-time
}
```

That could be a monitoring system that you've set up yourself to manage a dApp used by millions of users so that it stays operative for as long as possible. You can argue that listening to events in such a scenario is essential, so how do you do it? Here's the basic structure:

```
function listenToCriticalLow() {
    const subscription = web3.eth.subscribe('CriticalLow', {
        address: <your-contract-address>
    }, (err, result) => {
        if(!err) sendCriticalEmail()
    })
}
```

Your web3.eth.subscription function will execute the callback when the event is generated. That's basically how you listen to events in web3. Now, you know how to use them for critical operations in your dApp's workflow.

Building your own Oracles

Oracles are external applications that help your smart contract receive information from the outer world to perform some functions outside of what's possible inside Solidity or Vyper. How they work is simple: you create a centralized server that calls specific functions of your smart contract when needed.

They are used to generate random numbers, to provide live price data, and to show information from websites. As you know, smart contracts can't generate random numbers because there can't be any uncertainty regarding being able to avoid unexpected situations in the blockchain.

In this section, you'll learn how to create an Oracle to generate a random number between 1 and 100 for a game on the blockchain. There are already oracles doing these tasks, namely Oraclize, which has been used for a long time with Solidity.

Building a random generation Oracle

Oracles are a smart contracts' way of getting information from the external world. They are the bridge between centralized servers, external blockchains, and APIs, with smart contracts running on Ethereum. Essentially, they are a service that provides you with important information from places inaccessible with normal smart contracts, and they work by setting a centralized server listening to web3 events for your contract.

First, create a new project named `oracle`, run `truffle init` to be able to compile contracts, set up npm with `npm init -y`, and create a smart contract that generates events and handles `Oracle.sol`:

```solidity
pragma solidity 0.5.4;

contract Oracle {
    event GenerateRandom(uint256 sequence, uint256 timestamp);
    event ShowRandomNumber(uint256 sequence, uint256 number);
    uint256 public sequence = 0;

    function generateRandom() public {
        emit GenerateRandom(sequence, now);
        sequence += 1;
    }

    function __callback(uint256 _sequence, uint256 generatedNumber) public
{
        emit ShowRandomNumber(_sequence, generatedNumber);
    }
}
```

It's pretty basic: the idea is to execute the `__callback()` function with the randomly generated number when the user requests it by calling the `generateRandom()` function. We'll set up an event listener that will give users random numbers at the right time, with the right sequence identifier.

Remember to update your `1_initial_migrations.js` file inside the `migrations` folder to tell Truffle to deploy the right contract:

```
var Oracle = artifacts.require("./Oracle.sol")

module.exports = function(deployer) {
    deployer.deploy(Oracle)
}
```

Then, deploy it to `ropsten` by setting up the right configuration inside `truffle-config.js`. You already know how to do this since we learned how to set up Infura for Ropsten inside the configuration file of Truffle in previous chapters:

```
truffle deploy --network ropsten --reset
```

Now, we can create the Node.js application that listens to events generated by our smart contract and makes the right request with a randomly generated number type using the following code to start inside an `oracle.js` file:

```
const Web3 = require('web3')
const fs = require('fs')
const path = require('path')
const infura =
'wss://ropsten.infura.io/ws/v3/f7b2c280f3f440728c2b5458b41c663d'
let contractAddress
let contractInstance
let web3
let privateKey
let myAddress
```

We've imported `web3`, `fs`, and `path` as the libraries to interact with our contract. Then, we defined a websockets Infura URL to use it to connect to Ropsten for deploying and interacting with contracts. It's important that you use `wss` instead of `http` since it's the only way to receive events. Finally, we added some global variables that we'll need later on.

The way we generate transactions without MetaMask is by creating and signing our custom transaction object with our private key, which we can generate with the following function based on our mnemonic located in the `.secret` file:

```
// To generate the private key and address needed to sign transactions
function generateAddressesFromSeed(seed) {
    let bip39 = require("bip39");
    let hdkey = require('ethereumjs-wallet/hdkey');
    let hdwallet = hdkey.fromMasterSeed(bip39.mnemonicToSeed(seed));
    let wallet_hdpath = "m/44'/60'/0'/0/0";
    let wallet = hdwallet.derivePath(wallet_hdpath).getWallet();
```

```
        let address = '0x' + wallet.getAddress().toString("hex");
        let myPrivateKey = wallet.getPrivateKey().toString("hex");
        myAddress = address
        privateKey = '0x' + myPrivateKey
    }
```

It's quite complicated, although we only have to focus on installing and importing the bip39 and ethereumjs-wallet libraries to generate privateKey used for signing transactions. We can install the dependencies with the following:

```
npm i -S bip39 ethereumjs-wallet web3
```

Then, we can create a start function that will set up the required contracts and start listening to the right trigger event to call the __callback() function:

```
// Setup web3 and start listening to events
function start() {
    const mnemonic = fs.readFileSync(".secret").toString().trim()
    generateAddressesFromSeed(mnemonic)

    // Note that we use the WebsocketProvider because the previous
HttpProvider is outdated and doesn't allow subscriptions
    web3 = new Web3(new Web3.providers.WebsocketProvider(infura))
    const ABI = JSON.parse(fs.readFileSync(path.join(__dirname, 'build',
'contracts', 'Oracle.json')))
    contractAddress = ABI.networks['3'].address
    contractInstance = new web3.eth.Contract(ABI.abi, contractAddress)

    console.log('Listening to events...')
    // Listen to the generate random event for executing the __callback()
function
    const subscription = contractInstance.events.GenerateRandom()
    subscription.on('data', newEvent => {
        callback(newEvent.returnValues.sequence)
    })
}
```

First, we read the mnemonic 12-word passphrase to generate our privateKey and address using the previous generateAddressesFromSeed() function. Then, we set up a new web3 instance with WebsocketProvider for our Ropsten Infura URL because we can't listen to events with HttpProvider. After that, we set up contractInstance by reading the ABI data from the JSON file that was generated by Truffle, which includes the address of the deployed contract.

Finally, we set up a subscription for the `GenerateRandom` event using the `contractInstance.events.GenerateRandom()` function, which will call the `callback()` function with the sequence that corresponds. Let's see what the callback function looks like. Remember that this function will run the `__callback()` of our smart contract to provide users with a randomly generated number, since we can't directly generate random numbers with Solidity:

```
// To generate random numbers between 1 and 100 and execute the __callback
function from the smart contract
function callback(sequence) {
    const generatedNumber = Math.floor(Math.random() * 100 + 1)

    const encodedCallback = contractInstance.methods.__callback(sequence,
generatedNumber).encodeABI()
    const tx = {
        from: myAddress,
        gas: 6e6,
        gasPrice: 5,
        to: contractAddress,
        data: encodedCallback,
        chainId: 3
    }

    web3.eth.accounts.signTransaction(tx, privateKey).then(signed => {
        console.log('Generating transaction...')
        web3.eth.sendSignedTransaction(signed.rawTransaction)
            .on('receipt', result => {
                console.log('Callback transaction confirmed!')
            })
            .catch(error => console.log(error))
    })
}
```

This function receives the sequence parameter to map the values to the right ID so that users can identify which event is the right one for them. First, we generate a random number between 1 and 100 using `Math.random()`, with some calculations to adapt it to our desired range. Then we generate a transaction object called `tx` that includes our function data with `sequence` and `generatedNumber`, and some essential parameters such as `gas` and the `from` address. Finally, we send that transaction to our `Oracle` smart contract by first signing it with `privateKey` and then sending it using `web3.eth.sendSignedTransaction`. When it's confirmed by the miners, we'll see `console.log` saying "Callback transaction confirmed!", or an error in case something goes wrong.

That's about it! We can add the `start()` function initialization at the bottom to start listening to events. Here's the full code:

1. Import your required libraries and set up the variables that will be used in the project at the beginning of the file:

```
const Web3 = require('web3')
const fs = require('fs')
const path = require('path')
const infura =
'wss://ropsten.infura.io/ws/v3/f7b2c280f3f440728c2b5458b41c663d'
let contractAddress
let contractInstance
let web3
let privateKey
let myAddress
```

2. Create the `generateAddressesFromSeed()` function, which provides you with access to the accounts contained in the given seed:

```
// To generate the private key and address needed to sign
transactions
function generateAddressesFromSeed(seed) {
    let bip39 = require("bip39");
    let hdkey = require('ethereumjs-wallet/hdkey');
    let hdwallet =
hdkey.fromMasterSeed(bip39.mnemonicToSeed(seed));
    let wallet_hdpath = "m/44'/60'/0'/0/0";
    let wallet = hdwallet.derivePath(wallet_hdpath).getWallet();
    let address = '0x' + wallet.getAddress().toString("hex");
    let myPrivateKey = wallet.getPrivateKey().toString("hex");
    myAddress = address
    privateKey = '0x' + myPrivateKey
}
```

3. Create the `start` function to set up the web3 listeners:

```
// Setup web3 and start listening to events
function start() {
    const mnemonic = fs.readFileSync(".secret").toString().trim()
    generateAddressesFromSeed(mnemonic)

    // Note that we use the WebsocketProvider because the previous
HttpProvider is outdated and doesn't allow subscriptions
    web3 = new Web3(new Web3.providers.WebsocketProvider(infura))
    const ABI = JSON.parse(fs.readFileSync(path.join(__dirname,
'build', 'contracts', 'Oracle.json')))
    contractAddress = ABI.networks['3'].address
```

```
    contractInstance = new web3.eth.Contract(ABI.abi,
contractAddress)

    console.log('Listening to events...')

    // Listen to the generate random event for executing the
__callback() function
    const subscription = contractInstance.events.GenerateRandom()
    subscription.on('data', newEvent => {
        callback(newEvent.returnValues.sequence)
    })
}
```

4. Finally, create the callback function that executes the __callback()
   function from the smart contract. The function name starts with two underscores
   to avoid calling an existing function, since it's a special function used exclusively
   by the oracle:

```
    // To generate random numbers between 1 and 100 and execute the
    __callback function from the smart contract
    function callback(sequence) {
        const generatedNumber = Math.floor(Math.random() * 100 + 1)

        const encodedCallback =
    contractInstance.methods.__callback(sequence,
    generatedNumber).encodeABI()
        const tx = {
            from: myAddress,
            gas: 6e6,
            gasPrice: 5,
            to: contractAddress,
            data: encodedCallback,
            chainId: 3
        }

        web3.eth.accounts.signTransaction(tx, privateKey).then(signed
    => {
            console.log('Generating transaction...')
            web3.eth.sendSignedTransaction(signed.rawTransaction)
                .on('receipt', result => {
                    console.log('Callback transaction confirmed!')
                })
                .catch(error => console.log(error))
        })
    }
```

5. Remember to start the oracle by running the `start` function at the end of the file once everything is loaded:

```
start()
```

6. Optionally, we can add a function to execute the `generateRandom()` function from our smart contract to verify that we're indeed receiving events with another subscription, such as the following:

```
// To send a transaction to run the generateRandom function
function generateRandom() {
    const encodedGenerateRandom =
contractInstance.methods.generateRandom().encodeABI()
    const tx = {
        from: myAddress,
        gas: 6e6,
        gasPrice: 5,
        to: contractAddress,
        data: encodedGenerateRandom,
        chainId: 3
    }

    web3.eth.accounts.signTransaction(tx, privateKey).then(signed
=> {
        console.log('Generating transaction...')
        web3.eth.sendSignedTransaction(signed.rawTransaction)
            .on('receipt', result => {
                console.log('Generate random transaction
confirmed!')
            })
            .catch(error => console.log(error))
    })
}
```

7. Then, update the `start` function to listen to the new event we created by using the `generateRandom()` function:

```
// Setup web3 and start listening to events
function start() {
    const mnemonic = fs.readFileSync(".secret").toString().trim()
    generateAddressesFromSeed(mnemonic)

    // Note that we use the WebsocketProvider because the previous
HttpProvider is outdated and doesn't allow subscriptions
    web3 = new Web3(new Web3.providers.WebsocketProvider(infura))
    const ABI = JSON.parse(fs.readFileSync(path.join(__dirname,
'build', 'contracts', 'Oracle.json')))
```

```
        contractAddress = ABI.networks['3'].address
        contractInstance = new web3.eth.Contract(ABI.abi,
    contractAddress)

        console.log('Listening to events...')
        // Listen to the generate random event for executing the
    __callback() function
        const subscription = contractInstance.events.GenerateRandom()
        subscription.on('data', newEvent => {
            callback(newEvent.returnValues.sequence)
        })

        // Listen to the ShowRandomNumber() event that gets emitted
    after the callback
        const subscription2 =
    contractInstance.events.ShowRandomNumber()
        subscription2.on('data', newEvent => {
            console.log('Received random number! Sequence:',
    newEvent.returnValues.sequence, 'Randomly generated number:',
    newEvent.returnValues.number)
        })
    }
```

That way you'll be able to see how the contract is actually receiving your randomly generated number from your Node.js oracle to confirm that it's working properly. Go ahead and try it yourself by deploying your own oracles that provide smart contracts with external data that they couldn't get by themselves using this callback-based mechanism with unique identifiers. Additionally, you could add some external proofs to verify that the data is coming from the right oracle, although that's outside of the scope of this guide since it would be too extensive to describe.

As usual, you have the full, updated code updated on my GitHub (`https://github.com/merlox/oracle`) if you want to see the latest changes and try the working version. Take a look at the Truffle configuration file if you want to see how I set it up.

Improving your development workflow

When it comes to creating smart contracts and decentralized applications, a common problem is that we must work in the most efficient way possible to create the highest quality code so that we don't spend unnecessary hours on fixing problems that shouldn't be there in the first place.

In my personal experience, the best applications that I've created were born from exhaustive planning beforehand. It may feel unnecessary, but the more you work, the more you realize how much time you can save by getting your ideas in place with a clear plan that describes each element of your idea.

Have you worked on projects where you're constantly getting into problems such as bugs or confusion? That's probably because you didn't do enough planning. In this section, you'll learn how to plan your applications to set up projects that are easy to understand so that you can develop way more efficiently.

Let's say that you want to put your skills into practice to learn more about Ethereum technology with real projects. So, you decide to work on a relatively complex dApp. You first get the idea, then you detail the components of your application based on how you think it should work, and you start to code right away to get it done quickly.

That's a very common approach to most projects, given that we don't want to waste time on projecting—we want to get it done fast so we develop the code immediately. That's fine for small projects, but for bigger ones we must follow guidelines like the following:

1. Write a detailed description of what you have in mind: the most important features, how it will feel to the customers, and what is it about.
2. Break it down into smaller pieces: the frontend, the backend, and the smart contract, if any. Then describe those elements in a way that you can understand how they will be used.
3. Go deeper by writing down the functions that will be added to each of those three parts. Those will be the main functions for your application. Write them in an empty file without body: just the functions with the parameters and return values.
4. Document those functions by describing what they are supposed to do on a technical level using NatSpec documentation so that each parameter and return value is explained clearly.
5. Start working on the smaller independent functions. Those could be getter functions that return some variable or simple functions for calculating a value.
6. Move on to more complex functions until all of them are completed. While you do so, write empty tests as they come to mind to check every aspect of those functions.
7. Correct the project by writing unit tests from those that you set up previously and add a few more focusing on the potential of the problem they could cause if unchecked.

Your planning may be different: what you just read is only a simple guide that I came up with after trying to understand the process behind a successful project. Just so that you can take it with you in a more visual manner, here's an illustration of that development process:

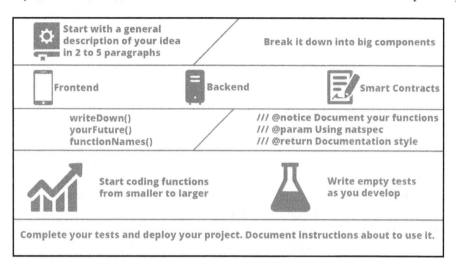

While you create each function, leave `//TODO` notes describing what needs to be done next, so that when you come back, you have a clear and simple objective to go for. For instance, here's a function that I've been working on recently:

```
constructor(address _identityRegistryAddress, address _tokenAddress) public
{
    require(_identityRegistryAddress != address(0), 'The identity registry
address is required');
    require(_tokenAddress != address(0), 'You must setup the token rinkeby
address');
    hydroToken = HydroTokenTestnetInterface(_tokenAddress);
    identityRegistry = IdentityRegistryInterface(_identityRegistryAddress);
    // TODO Uncomment this when the contract is completed
    /* oraclize_setProof(proofType_Ledger); */
}
```

There is an extension already installed in the famous `atom.io` code editor called `language-todo` that highlights these types of `TODO` notes so that you can see them easily. You can also search for those inside your entire project with the search function.

Also, there's another extension that allows you to manage those reminders in a single panel. Here's the package name so that you can install it if you want:

Here are some additional recommendations to improve your workflow when you work on creating a successful project:

- At the top of each file, create a list of things that need to be completed in that particular file so that you know when it's completed.
- Use already made tools to deploy your contracts and write tests to verify functionality efficiently. For instance, Truffle, Ganache, and Remix are essentials for testing while improving your efficiency.
- Set a time limit to everything; be as precise as possible, since projects have the tendency to use up as much time as you give them. Be strict to keep your mind focused.
- Determine what can be done in different time limits. For instance, in 1 week, you could create a basic version of your idea with the core two features, in 1 day, you can complete 5 of the 100 functions required to complete a solid beta version, and in 1 month, you could have the basic code completed. The idea is to imagine what would be a realistic estimate of what's possible with enough time for your idea. Write down what needs to be completed in 1 day, in 1 week, and in 1 month.
- Put yourself in places where you're comfortable. Usually, great ideas come when your body feels good and your mind is relaxed. For instance, a shower where the right temperature and the constant flow of water relaxes your entire being is one of the best places to examine your assumptions and explore new ideas that could be great.
- Always remember to create a Git repository for your projects, even if you think you won't work on it, because oftentimes you will need a piece of code for a particular thing you did years ago and now you need to remember for a new project. Keeping your code on GitHub is also great for seeing your progress as a developer and to build a solid online presence.

Coming up with great ideas could have a chapter on its own. The thing with creativity is that you'll only get it when you break routines, since you can't expect your mind to create new associations based on the same daily experiences. Travel to new local places, explore weird hobbies, and be genuinely interested in different subjects that are completely different to what you're familiar with, even if they seem boring at first.

Summary

You just completed one of the most important chapters of this book, since we talked about optimization and efficiency, two things that are essential for every project you work on. We started by building better React applications, where you learned to optimize the way you create frontend applications using this powerful framework, along with interesting tips to properly structure your components.

Then you learned to create centralized Node.js applications with NGINX that you can use for hybrid projects where smart contracts are just not enough, including all the steps from idea to code to deployment on a VPS server with an HTTPS certificate. After that, you explored several web3.js improvements to create stronger frontends with subscriptions to events, helper functions, and promises that can be better controlled.

You've gone through one of the most interesting topics when it comes to creating capable smart contracts: **oracles**, since they provide smart contracts with valuable external information that could be indispensable for specific applications. Finally, you discovered 14 tips to improve the way you think about creating projects so that you can become proficient when working to deliver higher quality code.

In the next chapter, you'll start working on the very interesting topic of decentralized exchanges by building one from scratch. It's an exciting opportunity that you'll love taking!

Decentralized Exchanges Workflow

9

Decentralized exchanges, also known as **DAXs**, are a hot topic for the simple reason that all cryptocurrencies need to be exchanged by others to give them some kind of utility. Could you imagine a world where you couldn't trade Bitcoin for dollars? Or Ethereum for Bitcoin? It would destroy the real-world utility of most cryptocurrencies. That's why we have exchanges, to allow the trading of all kinds of currencies in a free market. We'll start by working on an explanation about DAXs so that you understand the idea behind them. Then you'll understand how the orders are made and how to manage user funds in a secure manner. After that, you'll create a real-world DAX with a complex smart contract and a detailed interface.

In this chapter, we'll cover the following topics:

- Introducing decentralized exchanges
- Understanding the trading and matching engine
- Managing cryptocurrency wallets and cold storage
- Building the user interface
- Building the Ethereum backend
- Finishing the dApp

Introducing decentralized exchanges

What are DAXs, really? Well, normal exchanges, such as the stock market, are built upon a centralized system where a server processes all orders and displays the results to the users. They run very efficient systems that are quite expensive to set up, although it's understandable given the utility they provide. DAXs, on the other hand, don't rely on a centralized system where all orders have to go through a server that makes the necessary computations. Instead, DAXs work on top of Ethereum's infrastructure to provide users with a system that can be executed by anyone and processed by the gigantic net of computers.

The first difference with DAX compared to centralized exchanges is that they are limited by the technology behind them. You can't create a DAX that trades fiat currencies, such as the American dollar or the European euro, because those currencies are based on a different technology; they run on a different market, known as FOREX, where banks all over the world trade global currencies. Equally, you can't trade ERC20 tokens on the stock market exchange because they run on top of Ethereum, and the developers working on those centralized exchanges don't have the tools required to create a fluid connection between those systems – the main reason being the differences in speed.

Ethereum naturally makes slower transactions because they have to be confirmed by every node of the network. That's why it's expected to have a slow trading system in DAXs. However, there are scaling technologies, such as *plasma* and *state channels*, that allow you to trade way more efficiently after an initial setup. We'll explore how they work and we'll build a DAX so that you understand how they work. You could even create your own rules.

Cons of DAXs

DAXs are generally slower since you can't make instant transactions unless you rely on off-chain systems between a pair of currencies, slowing you down when you desire to trade between other cryptocurrencies.

They are also limited in the sense that you can't trade fiat currencies or cryptocurrencies based on different blockchains. For instance, the only way to exchange **Bitcoin** (**BTC**) for **Ethereum** (**ETH**) is to have a centralized system that holds both of those currencies and provides the user with a fair exchange at any given moment. There are a few projects that have integrated both types of currencies, but they are still young and need to mature to become popular.

DAXs are not yet used by the mainstream public, so they are not as good as they could be, since we lack the tools and protocols needed to create the type of exchanges that work without issues.

Pros of DAXs

On the other hand, these types of exchanges have the potential to overcome the outdated technology from most markets that rely on centralized transactions. Because they are being created from scratch, they can take all that's great from other projects and implement them with better features.

DAXs can work with thousands of tokens by default, since most of them implement the ERC20 standard, giving them a huge array of possibilities. There are great projects that are building protocols, such as the **0xprotocol** where developers can implement a set of known functions to their own systems so that they can communicate freely as one global system of interconnected DAXs. In fact, the 0xprotocol shares the liquidity of tokens among many exchanges, giving them the power to perform as a trader without requirements.

With the new scaling solutions being developed by the core Ethereum team, DAXs are about to vastly improve, with faster transactions that resemble real-work centralized markets, making Ethereum a core player in the global economy of virtual currency.

Many successful exchanges are improving to expand the paradigm of what's possible with decentralized technology, and they are using stablecoins, such as Tether and USD Coin, to keep a constant value backed on fiat currencies, thus bridging the gap between both worlds.

We could talk about DAXs for hours in several different books, but the point that I'm trying to bring across is that DAXs have the potential to surpass existing technology to become the main place where the global market of centralized and decentralized currencies takes place. That's why I want you to understand how all of this is possible by building a simple DAX based on solidity smart contracts to have the practical experience required to work for the many companies that create DAXs, or even start your own since they are one of the core elements of decentralized technology.

Essential trading terms

The world of exchanges is vast and complicated; that's why the people using them created lots of terms to help each other understand what they mean precisely. For instance, instead of saying *I want to buy 10 BTC hoping that it goes up in the future*, you say *I want to go long on 10 BTC*. They mean the same thing, but it's a more precise way of communicating with each other.

Let's go through some important terminology to comprehend some aspects of exchange markets:

- **Market order**: An action that consists of selling or buying a currency for the lowest or highest price available. You see, in exchanges there are sellers and buyers, those that want to get rid of some currency and those that want to grab some of it. Each one of them sets a price for what they want to get in return and the prices are always in pairs. For instance, *I want to buy 10 BTC at the price of 50 ETH*. In this case the pair would be BTC-ETH because you're stating that you want to get ETH in exchange for your Bitcoin; there, you're being a buyer of Bitcoin and a seller of Ether at the same time. People set different prices, so when you make a market order you just buy or sell at the largest profit. The same thing happens when you buy something online with dollars. If you are European, like me, you'd notice that many things online are priced in dollars, making it impossible to buy those items as you have euros, and they are not the same thing. So what happens when you buy say, a book? In the backend, some program is exchanging euros for dollars at the price set by the market and it's buying the book with dollars.
- **Limit order**: An action where you sell or buy at a fixed price that you set by yourself. These types of orders are used for those that predict price movements or are comfortable waiting until their order gets filled over a longer time.
- **Broker**: A person that lends you money with interest for your trading activities. Brokers usually help you with actions, such as executing your trades, because they have more money so they enjoy special privileges in the exchange you're in.
- **Margin account**: A special type of user account where you can borrow money from brokers as you trade.
- **Long buying**: An action where you buy a specific currency because you believe it will go up in value to make a profit, or to support the technology behind the currency.

- **Short selling**: An action where you win when the currency that you're shorting goes down in value. For instance, you could say, *I'm going to go short on euros because I believe the price will go down in the next five days*. It's a system where you can sell currencies that you don't own. The reasoning behind consists of the following:

  - First, you borrow money from another person, called the broker, who gives you the desired amount of currencies that you want to short, such as 100 ETH that you short.
  - You automatically sell those 100 ETH at the market price.
  - At a later date, you buy those 100 ETH. This is called closing your position. For instance, after 20 days, you close your short position by buying 100 ETH at the market price.
  - You win or lose money based on the price when selling and buying. If you start shorting at a high price and close your position at a low price, you win the difference. For instance, if you go 100 ETH short at $20 each and you close your position 5 days later where ETH is worth $10, you would have won $10 dollars per Ether or a total of 100 ETH × $10 = $1,000 dollars.
  - Usually shorting is only available on margin accounts. Those are accounts where you can borrow money from brokers with some restrictions.

There's also the bid and ask, which are equivalent to buy and sell. Now that you better understand a few complicated concepts, you can move on to learn more about the DAX that we are going to build in this chapter.

Understanding the trading and matching engine

A trading and matching engine is a set of functions that use different types of algorithms to create and close orders. An algorithm could focus on completing the orders with the higher price or those that were executed earlier. It depends on the preferences of the developers. Because we'll work with smart contracts and ERC20 tokens, our engine will focus on completing the orders as quickly as they come, since it will be the users that close the orders, given that the frontend is where most of the logic will be.

We can't process large amounts of information on smart contracts since gas is expensive, so we let the React application take control of the trading to save people's funds.

Let's start by planning the functions that we'll need so that we have a solid foundation when we create the contracts and the frontend functions:

```
/// @notice To create a limit order for buying the _symbolBuy while selling
the _symbolSell.
/// @param _symbolBuy The 3 character or more name of the token to buy.
/// @param _symbolSell The 3 character or more name of the token to sell.
/// @param _priceBid The price for how many _symbolBuy tokens you desire to
buy. For instance: buy 10 ETH for 1 BTC.
/// @param _priceAsk The price for how many tokens you desire to sell of
the _symbolSell in exchange for the _symbolBuy. For instance: sell 10 BTC
for 2 ETH.
function createLimitOrder(bytes32 _symbolBuy, bytes32 _symbolSell, uint256
_priceBid, uint256 _priceAsk) public {}
```

That function signature (the function name with parameters but no body) will take care of generating limit orders. Let's see some examples and check whether the signature of the function checks out:

For example, *I want to sell 7 BTC in exchange for 90 ETH*, execute the following code:

```
function createLimitOrder("ETH","BTC", 90, 7);
```

As you can see, we reversed the order of the symbol to convert that sell order into a buy order where the user is willing to buy ETH in exchange for BTC. It has the same effect with just one function, instead of creating an exclusive function for selling.

For example, *I want to buy 10 BTC for 20 ETH.*

```
function createLimitOrder("BTC", "ETH", 10, 20);
```

In this case, we put the symbols in the same order as expected since we are creating a limit order to buy BTC while selling ETH. Now we can create the signature of the market order function.

Market orders are interesting, since we want to immediately fill the order at the cheapest or highest price possible. What happens under the hood is that we're closing a limit order with our market order. Nevertheless, it's often impossible to fill the entire order at the latest market price for the simple reason that the most profitable limit order is buying or selling minimal quantities of a token.

For instance, we want to sell 10 TokenA at the market price for TokenB. The most profitable limit order available says *buy 5 TokenA in exchange for 40 TokenB*. In that case, the price of 1 TokenA would be 8 TokenB and vice versa. So we create the market order and we immediately sell 5 TokenA to buy 40 TokenB from that limit order, but what happens with the remaining 5 TokenA that we want to sell? We go to the next most profitable buy order, which says *buy 100 TokenA for 700 TokenB*. In that case, the price of 1 TokenA would be 7 TokenB, which is less profitable than the last one but still not bad. So we sell 5 TokenA in exchange for 35 TokenB, leaving that limit buy order at *buy 95 tokenA for 665 TokenB* until the next user fills it.

At the end, we got 75 TokenB for 10 TokenA using a combination of market prices at that specific moment that depended on the most profitable limit orders at that time. With that understanding, we can create the signature of our market order function:

```
/// @notice The function to create market orders by filling existing limit
orders
/// @param _type The type of the market order which can be "Buy" or "Sell"
/// @param _symbol The token that we want to buy or sell
/// @param _maxPrice The maximum price we are willing to sell or buy the
token for, set it to 0 to not limit the order
function createMarketOrder(bytes32 _type, bytes32 _symbol, uint256
_maxPrice);
```

The `_maxPrice` parameter is simply a number that states the lowest price that you're willing to sell, or the highest price that you're willing to buy. By default, it's zero, which is unlimited so you'll get the most profitable price as long as there are sellers or buyers available.

Managing cryptocurrency wallets and cold storage

When it comes to storing people's funds, we must pay extra attention to how we do it since we could risk losing millions of dollars using our DAX. That's why the largest exchanges use cold storage with lots of security systems in place. Essentially, they keep funds offline in a remote location stored in secure hardware devices that are customized to their needs such as Trezor, Ledger, or their own.

In our case, we'll store funds in a series of smart contracts, known as **escrows**, whose only goal is to store people's money. There will be an escrow contract associated with each user account to independently secure all of their funds. That escrow contract will have a function to receive funds, only ERC20 tokens, and a function to extract funds executable by the owner of that escrow. Go ahead and create a folder named `decentralized-exchange`, then run the `truffle init` and `npm init -y` commands, and create a contract inside the `contracts/` folder named `Escrow.sol`. The following is how our escrow will look.

First, it contains the interface for ERC20 tokens since we don't need the entire implementation to be able to trade with tokens:

```
pragma solidity 0.5.4;

interface IERC20 {
    function transfer(address to, uint256 value) external returns (bool);
    function approve(address spender, uint256 value) external returns
(bool);
    function transferFrom(address from, address to, uint256 value) external
returns (bool);
    function totalSupply() external view returns (uint256);
    function balanceOf(address who) external view returns (uint256);
    function allowance(address owner, address spender) external view
returns (uint256);
    event Transfer(address indexed from, address indexed to, uint256
value);
    event Approval(address indexed owner, address indexed spender, uint256
value);
}
```

Then we add the `Escrow` contract, which will be used to manage the funds of each user:

```
contract Escrow {
    address public owner;

    modifier onlyOwner {
        require(msg.sender == owner, 'You must be the owner to execute that
function');
        _;
    }

    /// @notice This contract does not accept ETH transfers
    function () external { revert(); }

    /// @notice To setup the initial tokens that the user will store when
creating the escrow
    /// @param _owner The address that will be the owner of this escrow,
must be the owner of the tokens
```

```
constructor (address _owner) public {
    require(_owner != address(0), 'The owner address must be set');
    owner = _owner;
}

/// @notice To transfer tokens to another address, usually the buyer or
seller of an existing order
/// @param _token The address of the token to transfer
/// @param _to The address of the receiver
/// @param _amount The amount of tokens to transfer
function transferTokens(address _token, address _to, uint256 _amount)
public onlyOwner {
    require(_token != address(0), 'The token address must be set');
    require(_to != address(0), 'The receiver address must be set');
    require(_amount > 0, 'You must specify the amount of tokens to
transfer');

    require(IERC20(_token).transfer(_to, _amount), 'The transfer must
be successful');
}

/// @notice To see how many of a particular token this contract
contains
/// @param _token The address of the token to check
/// @return uint256 The number of tokens this contract contains
function checkTokenBalance(address _token) public view returns(uint256)
{
    require(_token != address(0), 'The token address must be set');
    return IERC20(_token).balanceOf(address(this));
}
}
```

This `Escrow` contract receives token transfers to keep the funds safely inside. Each user will have a unique escrow contract to decentralize the location of funds so that attackers can't focus on a single place. You can manage the token funds inside with the `transferTokens()` function and you can check the balance of tokens inside the contract with the `checkTokenBalance()` function, which is a simplified `.balanceOf()` ERC20 helper function. Finally, I've added an empty non-payable fallback function to avoid receiving Ether since we only want tokens inside.

We'll use this `Escrow` contract to manage people's funds later on, since we want a secure place to keep their precious tokens. Ideally, we would create a system that uses cold storage in hardware devices, but such an action would require a complex system that takes care of securely managing every step of the way to prevent middlemen attacks.

Building the user interface

The user interface for DAXs is the same as the ones used for traditional exchanges, such as the stock exchange, or centralized crypto-exchanges, such as **Binance**. The idea is to provide a data-driven design where they can quickly understand the situation of the selected token pairs. A central section will be used for the data, a sidebar will be used for the actions that users may take, and an additional sidebar to the right will be used for secondary data; in our case, it will be used for past trades.

As usual, create a `src` and `dist` folder that will include our project. You can just copy the setup from previous projects by taking a look at my own version on `github.com/merlox/dapp`. Our design will be based on most exchanges since they have a studied formula that feels great. Create the sidebar with a new component inside your `index.js` file.

First, add the `Main` component along with the required imports for a normal React application:

```
import React from 'react'
import ReactDOM from 'react-dom'
import './index.styl'

class Main extends React.Component {
    constructor() {
        super()
    }

    render() {
        return (
            <div>
                <Sidebar />
            </div>
        )
    }
}
```

Then add the `Sidebar` component with some basic actions that the user can take, such as a money-management section to add or withdraw money, and a section to create buy or sell orders:

```
/// Create the basic sidebar html, then we'll add the style css
// The sidebar where you take all your actions
class Sidebar extends React.Component {
    constructor() {
        super()
```

```
            this.state = {
                showLimitOrderInput: false
            }
        }

    render() {
        return (
            <div className="sidebar">
                <div className="selected-assets-title">Selected
assets:</div>
                <div className="selected-asset-one">ETH</div>
                <div className="selected-asset-two">BAT</div>
                <div className="your-portfolio">Your portfolio:</div>
                <div className="grid-center">ETH:</div><div
className="grid-center">10</div>
                <div className="grid-center">BAT:</div><div
className="grid-center">200</div>
                <div className="money-management">Money management:</div>
                <button className="button-outline">Deposit</button>
                <button className="button-outline">Withdraw</button>
                <div className="actions">Actions:</div>
                <button>Buy</button>
                <button className="sell">Sell</button>
                <select defaultValue="market-order" onChange={selected => {
                    if(selected.target.value == 'limit-order')
this.setState({showLimitOrderInput: true})
                    else this.setState({showLimitOrderInput: false})
                }}>
                    <option value="market-order">Market Order</option>
                    <option value="limit-order">Limit Order</option>
                </select>
                <input ref="limit-order-amount"
className={this.state.showLimitOrderInput ? '' : 'hidden'} type="number"
placeholder="Price to buy or sell at..."/>
            </div>
        )
    }
}
```

The classes and elements that you add are completely up to you. Personally, I like to show users the currency pair they are trading, their balance for each one, and a set of actions such as buy, sell, deposit, and withdraw. Then we can add some css. In this project, we'll be using a css preprocessor known as stylus (stylus-lang.com), which allows you to write css without brackets and nested classes, among many other nice features. You can install it as follows:

```
npm i -S style-loader css-loader stylus-loader stylus
```

Then add it to your `webpack` configuration file as a new rules block:

```
{
    test: /\.styl$/,
    exclude: /node_modules/,
    use: ['style-loader', 'css-loader', 'stylus-loader']
}
```

Create a new `index.styl` file inside your source folder and add your Stylus code. If you want to create the same design as me, check the stylus code on the official GitHub here: `https://github.com/merlox/decentralized-exchange/blob/master/src/index.styl`.

This generates a nice-looking sidebar for our DAX. Remember to bundle your files with `webpack -w -d`:

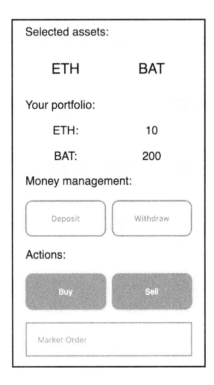

As you can see, Stylus allows you to write clean, nestable `css` to organize big chunks of styling easily so that your projects are easier to maintain. At the end, the code gets converted into valid `css` that runs on all browsers since Stylus compiles each file properly. Then we can add a trades section where we'll show the trades taking place in our exchange for all pairs, so that people understand the overall price of their coins.

First, add new state trades to the state object with fake data to the `Main` component so that we can see how the dApp will look once completed in its final design:

```
import React from 'react'
import ReactDOM from 'react-dom'
import './index.styl'

class Main extends React.Component {
    constructor() {
        super()

        this.state = {
            trades: [{
                id: 123,
                type: 'buy',
                firstSymbol: 'ETH',
                secondSymbol: 'BAT',
                quantity: 120, // You want to buy 120 firstSymbol
                price: 200 // When buying, you get 1 firstSymbol for
selling 200 secondSymbol
            }, {
                id: 927,
                type: 'sell',
                firstSymbol: 'ETH',
                secondSymbol: 'BAT',
                quantity: 80, // You want to buy 80 secondSymbol
                price: 305 // When selling, you get 305 secondSymbol for
selling 1 firstSymbol
            }],
            history: [{
                id: 927,
                type: 'buy',
                firstSymbol: 'ETH',
                secondSymbol: 'BAT',
                quantity: 2,
                price: 20
            }, {
                id: 927,
                type: 'sell',
                firstSymbol: 'ETH',
                secondSymbol: 'BAT',
```

```
                quantity: 2, // You want to buy 80 secondSymbol
                price: 10 // When selling, you get 305 secondSymbol for
    selling 1 firstSymbol
            }]
        }
    }
```

After that, update the `render()` function with the new state objects by passing the props to the `Trades` and `History` components:

```
    render() {
        return (
            <div className="main-container">
                <Sidebar />
                <Trades
                    trades={this.state.trades}
                />
                <History
                    history={this.state.history}
                />
            </div>
        )
    }
}
```

Create the new `Trades` component so that it displays the trades that we just added:

```
// The main section to see live trades taking place
class Trades extends React.Component {
    constructor() {
        super()
    }

    render() {
        let buyTrades = this.props.trades.filter(trade => trade.type ==
'buy')
        buyTrades = buyTrades.map((trade, index) => (
            <div key={trade.id + index} className="trade-container buy-
trade">
                <div className="trade-symbol">{trade.firstSymbol}</div>
                <div className="trade-symbol">{trade.secondSymbol}</div>
                <div className="trade-pricing">{trade.type}
{trade.quantity} {trade.firstSymbol} at {trade.price} {trade.secondSymbol}
each</div>
            </div>
        ))
        let sellTrades = this.props.trades.filter(trade => trade.type ==
'sell')
```

```
            sellTrades = sellTrades.map((trade, index) => (
                <div key={trade.id + index} className="trade-container sell-
trade">
                    <div className="trade-symbol">{trade.firstSymbol}</div>
                    <div className="trade-symbol">{trade.secondSymbol}</div>
                    <div className="trade-pricing">{trade.type}
{trade.quantity} {trade.firstSymbol} at {trade.price} {trade.secondSymbol}
each</div>
                </div>
            ))
            return (
                <div className="trades">
                    <div className="buy-trades-title heading">Buy</div>
                    <div className="buy-trades-container">{buyTrades}</div>
                    <div className="sell-trades-title heading">Sell</div>
                    <div className="sell-trades-container">{sellTrades}</div>
                </div>
            )
        }
    }
```

As you can see, we've added lots of sample trades and history trades since we'll need them to understand how our exchange looks in a real environment; note how we updated the Main component to pass the state data to each component. Then we can add some Stylus to make it look good. Check the final Stylus code on the official GitHub here: `https://github.com/merlox/decentralized-exchange/blob/master/src/index.styl`.

To get a great-looking design. Notice that I've included 15 trade objects and 15 history trade objects in the state of the `Main` component so that we can see how the dApp looks when fully loaded:

The trade at the top of each **BUY** and **SELL** section is the market price for that cryptocurrency pair, since market orders are always the most profitable trade at that particular moment. Those trades will update in real-time as people trade different currencies over time. It's a fantastic way to understand price movements. Finally, we can add the `History` section, which will show the most recent trades:

```
// Past historical trades
class History extends React.Component {
    constructor() {
        super()
    }
```

```
    render() {
        const historicalTrades = this.props.history.map((trade, index) => (
            <div key={trade.id + index} className="historical-trade">
                <div className={trade.type == 'sell' ? 'sell-trade' : 'buy-
trade'}>{trade.type} {trade.quantity} {trade.firstSymbol} for
{trade.quantity * trade.price} {trade.secondSymbol} at {trade.price}
each</div>
            </div>
        ))
        return (
            <div className="history">
                <div className="heading">Recent history</div>
                <div className="historical-trades-
container">{historicalTrades}</div>
            </div>
        )
    }
}


ReactDOM.render(<Main />, document.querySelector('#root'))
```

Remember to add the `render()` function from the `react-dom` package to render your components. Then we can add some more `css`:

```
.history
    padding: 15px
    background-color: whitesmoke
    height: 100vh
    overflow: auto

    .historical-trades-container
        text-align: center

        .historical-trade
            font-size: 0.95em
            margin-bottom: 10px

            &:first-letter
                text-transform: uppercase

            .sell-trade
                color: rgb(223, 98, 98)

            .buy-trade
                color: rgb(98, 133, 223)
```

Now if you run `webpack` and an `http-server`, you'll see our finished product. It's not responsive for mobile devices since our goal is to create an exchange to be used in desktop computers and it's quite a time-consuming task to verify every breakpoint to accommodate it to the different dimensions for phones and tablets:

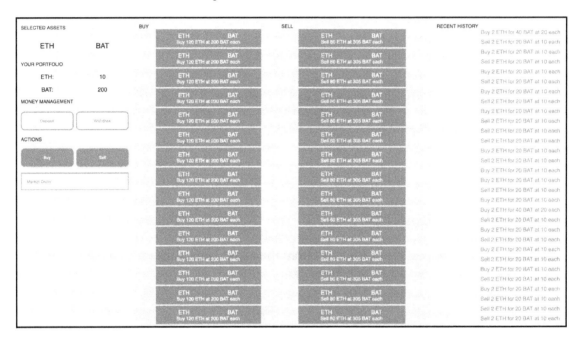

This will be our basic design. You can freely add more currency pairs with ERC20 tokens, graphs with D3.js, and even state channels! The great thing about the project shown in this book is that you can build upon the existing structure to create a truly high-quality product that you can use for an ICO or to grow the ecosystem of dApps with your own solution. Let's move on to build the smart contracts needed to create trades and use the DAX with MetaMask.

Building the Ethereum backend

The backend for our project will take care of generating trades that can be filled by anyone as long as they have enough funds to pay the established price. When the user gets registered, they'll deploy an Escrow contract which will be used by our main DAX contract. So let's start by setting up the requirements and the contract structure before starting to fill all the functions to practice the system to improve, developer's efficiency that we studied in `Chapter 4`, *Mastering Smart Contracts*.

Start by defining the functions that we'll need in a big comment at the beginning of the file:

```
// Functions that we need:
/*
    1. Constructor to setup the owner
    2. Fallback non-payable function to reject ETH from direct transfers
since we only want people to use the functions designed to trade a specific
pair
    3. Function to extract tokens from this contract in case someone
mistakenly sends ERC20 to the wrong function
    4. Function to create whitelist a token by the owner
    5. Function to create market orders
    6. Function to create limit orders
 */
```

Set up the Solidity version used, import the `Escrow` contract, and define the token interface:

```
pragma solidity ^0.5.4;

import './Escrow.sol';

interface IERC20 {
    function transfer(address to, uint256 value) external returns (bool);
    function approve(address spender, uint256 value) external returns
(bool);
    function transferFrom(address from, address to, uint256 value) external
returns (bool);
    function totalSupply() external view returns (uint256);
    function balanceOf(address who) external view returns (uint256);
    function allowance(address owner, address spender) external view
returns (uint256);
    event Transfer(address indexed from, address indexed to, uint256
value);
    event Approval(address indexed owner, address indexed spender, uint256
value);
}
```

Create the `DAX` contract by first defining the `Order` struct that we'll use for creating new orders:

```
contract DAX {
    event TransferOrder(bytes32 _type, address indexed from, address
indexed to, bytes32 tokenSymbol, uint256 quantity);
    enum OrderState {OPEN, CLOSED}

    struct Order {
        uint256 id;
        address owner;
```

```
        bytes32 orderType;
        bytes32 firstSymbol;
        bytes32 secondSymbol;
        uint256 quantity;
        uint256 price;
        uint256 timestamp;
        OrderState state;
    }
```

Then define the many variables needed to manage sell and buy orders, while also whitelisting tokens:

```
    Order[] public buyOrders;
    Order[] public sellOrders;
    Order[] public closedOrders;
    uint256 public orderIdCounter;
    address public owner;
    address[] public whitelistedTokens;
    bytes32[] public whitelistedTokenSymbols;
    address[] public users;
```

Create the mappings required for add and manage the token symbols and to find the orders by the given IDs:

```
    // Token address => isWhitelisted or not
    mapping(address => bool) public isTokenWhitelisted;
    mapping(bytes32 => bool) public isTokenSymbolWhitelisted;
    mapping(bytes32 => bytes32[]) public tokenPairs; // A token symbol pair
made of 'FIRST' => 'SECOND'
    mapping(bytes32 => address) public tokenAddressBySymbol; // Symbol =>
address of the token
    mapping(uint256 => Order) public orderById; // Id => trade object
    mapping(uint256 => uint256) public buyOrderIndexById; // Id => index
inside the buyOrders array
    mapping(uint256 => uint256) public sellOrderIndexById; // Id => index
inside the sellOrders array
    mapping(address => address) public escrowByUserAddress; // User address
=> escrow contract address
```

Then, add the `onlyOwner` modifier, the fallback function which reverts, and the constructor:

```
    modifier onlyOwner {
        require(msg.sender == owner, 'The sender must be the owner for this
function');
        _;
    }
```

```
/// @notice Users should not send ether to this contract
function () external {
    revert();
}

constructor () public {
    owner = msg.sender;
}
```

Define the whitelisting token function with the complete NatSpec documentation and the function signature. I've highlighted the function so that you can clearly differentiate the function from the comments:

```
/// @notice To whitelist a token so that is tradable in the exchange
/// @dev If the transaction reverts, it could be because of the
quantity of token pairs, try reducing the number and breaking the
transaction into several pieces
/// @param _symbol The symbol of the token
/// @param _token The token to whitelist, for instance 'TOK'
/// @param _tokenPairSymbols The token pairs to whitelist for this new
token, for instance: ['BAT', 'HYDRO'] which will be converted to ['TOK',
'BAT'] and ['TOK', 'HYDRO']
/// @param _tokenPairAddresses The token pair addresses to whitelist
for this new token, for instance: ['0x213...', '0x927...', '0x128...']
function whitelistToken(bytes32 _symbol, address _token, bytes32[]
memory _tokenPairSymbols, address[] memory _tokenPairAddresses) public
onlyOwner {}
```

To manage tokens, create the following two functions with the documentation:

```
/// @notice To store tokens inside the escrow contract associated with
the user accounts as long as the users made an approval beforehand
/// @dev It will revert is the user doesn't approve tokens beforehand
to this contract
/// @param _token The token address
/// @param _amount The quantity to deposit to the escrow contract
function depositTokens(address _token, uint256 _amount) public {}

/// @notice To extract tokens
/// @param _token The token address to extract
/// @param _amount The amount of tokens to transfer
function extractTokens(address _token, uint256 _amount) public {}
```

Add the market and limit the order functions with the parameters required for them to work properly, since these will be the main functions used to create orders and to interact with the DAX:

```
    /// @notice To create a market order by filling one or more existing
limit orders at the most profitable price given a token pair, type of order
(buy or sell) and the amount of tokens to trade, the _quantity is how many
_firstSymbol tokens you want to buy if it's a buy order or how many
_firstSymbol tokens you want to sell at market price
    /// @param _type The type of order either 'buy' or 'sell'
    /// @param _firstSymbol The first token to buy or sell
    /// @param _secondSymbol The second token to create a pair
    /// @param _quantity The amount of tokens to sell or buy
    function marketOrder(bytes32 _type, bytes32 _firstSymbol, bytes32
_secondSymbol, uint256 _quantity) public {}


    /// @notice To create a market order given a token pair, type of order,
amount of tokens to trade and the price per token. If the type is buy, the
price will determine how many _secondSymbol tokens you are willing to pay
for each _firstSymbol up until your _quantity or better if there are more
profitable prices. If the type if sell, the price will determine how many
_secondSymbol tokens you get for each _firstSymbol
    /// @param _type The type of order either 'buy' or 'sell'
    /// @param _firstSymbol The first symbol to deal with
    /// @param _secondSymbol The second symbol that you want to deal
    /// @param _quantity How many tokens you want to deal, these are
_firstSymbol tokens
    /// @param _pricePerToken How many tokens you get or pay for your other
symbol, the total quantity is _pricePerToken * _quantity
    function limitOrder(bytes32 _type, bytes32 _firstSymbol, bytes32
_secondSymbol, uint256 _quantity, uint256 _pricePerToken) public {}
```

Finally, add the `view` functions that you'll use as helpers and getters for important variables that your interface may need. Try to add them yourself. Then check the solution:

```
    /// @notice Sorts the selected array of Orders by price from lower to
higher if it's a buy order or from highest to lowest if it's a sell order
    /// @param _type The type of order either 'sell' or 'buy'
    /// @return uint256[] Returns the sorted ids
    function sortIdsByPrices(bytes32 _type) public view returns (uint256[]
memory) {}


    /// @notice Checks if a pair is valid
    /// @param _firstSymbol The first symbol of the pair
    /// @param _secondSymbol The second symbol of the pair
    /// @returns bool If the pair is valid or not
    function checkValidPair(bytes32 _firstSymbol, bytes32 _secondSymbol)
public view returns(bool) {}
```

```
    /// @notice Returns the token pairs
    /// @param _token To get the array of token pair for that selected
token
    /// @returns bytes32[] An array containing the pairs
    function getTokenPairs(bytes32 _token) public view returns(bytes32[]
memory) {}
}
```

First, we set up an `event` to log token transfers so that people can see when a token is sold or purchased. We could add more events but I'll leave it up to you to discover which events you need. Then we added a ton of necessary variables, starting with an `enum` that defines whether an order is open or closed. We added a `struct` for each property of each order to clearly define which token is being dealt.

Then we added three arrays to store existing orders, while also having a few variables to whitelist new tokens so that we can trade with a wider set of cryptocurrencies. After that, we added multiple mappings to find each specific order easily while optimizing gas costs.

We added an `onlyOwner` modifier to restrict access to the whitelisting function so that it doesn't get too crazy when it comes to adding cryptocurrencies. We added a fallback function that doesn't allow ETH transfers so that people don't send funds to this exchange, as well as a constructor that defines DAX's owner.

Then we added the `whitelistToken()` function, which takes a token address, and an array of symbols to create pairs with that main token; that way, you're able to trade with a large quantity of pairs at once. The `depositTokens()` function is used by users that want to increase their token balance. They can directly transfer the tokens they want to trade to their associated Escrow contract, but users first have to create a new Escrow, which can only be done through this function. Then the `Escrow` address will be associated with that account in the `escrowByUserAddress` mapping. This deposit function also requires that the user previously uses the `approve()` function to allow the DAX contract to transfer tokens to the Escrow contract; otherwise, it will fail.

Next, the `extractTokens()` function is used to move tokens from the Escrow to the user's address. It's a shortcut to the `transferTokens()` function inside the `Escrow` contract to facilitate token management. After that, we have the complex market and limit order functions. Both are big functions because they have to sort, update, and find orders to match existing ones while working within the limitations of the blockchain regarding gas usage. We'll soon see how they are implemented in depth. Finally, we have some helper functions to sort orders, check whether a given pair of token exists, and to retrieve an array of token pairs.

Let's go ahead and implement some of those functions. Remember to start with the simplest ones, and progress to the more complex ones, so that you have a solid structure behind them. Here is how the `whitelisting` function should look:

```
/// @notice To whitelist a token so that is tradable in the exchange
/// @dev If the transaction reverts, it could be because of the quantity of
token pairs, try reducing the number and breaking the transaction into
several pieces
/// @param _symbol The symbol of the token
/// @param _token The token to whitelist, for instance 'TOK'
/// @param _tokenPairSymbols The token pairs to whitelist for this new
token, for instance: ['BAT', 'HYDRO'] which will be converted to ['TOK',
'BAT'] and ['TOK', 'HYDRO']
/// @param _tokenPairAddresses The token pair addresses to whitelist for
this new token, for instance: ['0x213...', '0x927...', '0x128...']
function whitelistToken(bytes32 _symbol, address _token, bytes32[] memory
_tokenPairSymbols, address[] memory _tokenPairAddresses) public onlyOwner {
    require(_token != address(0), 'You must specify the token address to
whitelist');
    require(IERC20(_token).totalSupply() > 0, 'The token address specified
is not a valid ERC20 token');
    require(_tokenPairAddresses.length == _tokenPairSymbols.length, 'You
must send the same number of addresses and symbols');

    isTokenWhitelisted[_token] = true;
    isTokenSymbolWhitelisted[_symbol] = true;
    whitelistedTokens.push(_token);
    whitelistedTokenSymbols.push(_symbol);
    tokenAddressBySymbol[_symbol] = _token;
    tokenPairs[_symbol] = _tokenPairSymbols;

    for(uint256 i = 0; i < _tokenPairAddresses.length; i++) {
        address currentAddress = _tokenPairAddresses[i];
        bytes32 currentSymbol = _tokenPairSymbols[i];
        tokenPairs[currentSymbol].push(_symbol);
        if(!isTokenWhitelisted[currentAddress]) {
            isTokenWhitelisted[currentAddress] = true;
            isTokenSymbolWhitelisted[currentSymbol] = true;
            whitelistedTokens.push(currentAddress);
            whitelistedTokenSymbols.push(currentSymbol);
            tokenAddressBySymbol[currentSymbol] = currentAddress;
        }
    }
}
```

The whitelisting function makes some require checks, then whitelists each of the given token pairs so that you can trade with them independently. For instance, if your main token symbol is BAT and your array of _tokenPairSymbols contains ['TOK', 'TIK'], you'll be able to trade with BAT - TOK and BAT - TIK. Simple stuff. The function should not run out of gas as long as you keep a low number of token pairs.

The following are the next functions for managing token funds:

```
/// @notice To store tokens inside the escrow contract associated with the
user accounts as long as the users made an approval beforehand
/// @dev It will revert is the user doesn't approve tokens beforehand to
this contract
/// @param _token The token address
/// @param _amount The quantity to deposit to the escrow contract
function depositTokens(address _token, uint256 _amount) public {
    require(isTokenWhitelisted[_token], 'The token to deposit must be
whitelisted');
    require(_token != address(0), 'You must specify the token address');
    require(_amount > 0, 'You must send some tokens with this deposit
function');
    require(IERC20(_token).allowance(msg.sender, address(this)) >= _amount,
'You must approve() the quantity of tokens that you want to deposit
first');
    if(escrowByUserAddress[msg.sender] == address(0)) {
        Escrow newEscrow = new Escrow(address(this));
        escrowByUserAddress[msg.sender] = address(newEscrow);
        users.push(msg.sender);
    }
    IERC20(_token).transferFrom(msg.sender,
escrowByUserAddress[msg.sender], _amount);
}

/// @notice To extract tokens
/// @param _token The token address to extract
/// @param _amount The amount of tokens to transfer
function extractTokens(address _token, uint256 _amount) public {
    require(_token != address(0), 'You must specify the token address');
    require(_amount > 0, 'You must send some tokens with this deposit
function');
    Escrow(escrowByUserAddress[msg.sender]).transferTokens(_token,
msg.sender, _amount);
}
```

The deposit function checks whether the user has an Escrow contract associated with their address. If not, the function creates a new Escrow, then transfers the deposit of tokens that the user requested as long as they previously approved some in the appropriate ERC20 contract.

The extract function is simply running the `transferTokens()` function to the owner's address, as long as they have some previous balance inside. Otherwise it will revert.

Let's move on to the limit order function. Because this is a larger function, we'll break it down into smaller parts so that you understand how each section operates.

First, we have an updated document based on changes that come across as you create the function. It's never too late to improve the documentation:

```
/// @notice To create a market order given a token pair, type of order,
amount of tokens to trade and the price per token. If the type is buy, the
price will determine how many _secondSymbol tokens you are willing to pay
for each _firstSymbol up until your _quantity or better if there are more
profitable prices. If the type if sell, the price will determine how many
_secondSymbol tokens you get for each _firstSymbol
/// @param _type The type of order either 'buy' or 'sell'
/// @param _firstSymbol The first symbol to deal with
/// @param _secondSymbol The second symbol that you want to deal
/// @param _quantity How many tokens you want to deal, these are
_firstSymbol tokens
/// @param _pricePerToken How many tokens you get or pay for your other
symbol, the total quantity is _pricePerToken * _quantity
```

Then we run the many `require()` checks to be sure that the user is executing the limit order function properly:

```
function limitOrder(bytes32 _type, bytes32 _firstSymbol, bytes32
_secondSymbol, uint256 _quantity, uint256 _pricePerToken) public {
    address userEscrow = escrowByUserAddress[msg.sender];
    address firstSymbolAddress = tokenAddressBySymbol[_firstSymbol];
    address secondSymbolAddress = tokenAddressBySymbol[_secondSymbol];

    require(firstSymbolAddress != address(0), 'The first symbol has not
been whitelisted');
    require(secondSymbolAddress != address(0), 'The second symbol has not
been whitelisted');
    require(isTokenSymbolWhitelisted[_firstSymbol], 'The first symbol must
be whitelisted to trade with it');
    require(isTokenSymbolWhitelisted[_secondSymbol], 'The second symbol
must be whitelisted to trade with it');
    require(userEscrow != address(0), 'You must deposit some tokens before
creating orders, use depositToken()');
    require(checkValidPair(_firstSymbol, _secondSymbol), 'The pair must be
a valid pair');
```

After that, execute the buy functionality if the user is creating a buy limit order:

```
    Order memory myOrder = Order(orderIdCounter, msg.sender, _type,
_firstSymbol, _secondSymbol, _quantity, _pricePerToken, now,
OrderState.OPEN);
    orderById[orderIdCounter] = myOrder;
    if(_type == 'buy') {
        // Check that the user has enough of the second symbol if he wants
to buy the first symbol at that price
        require(IERC20(secondSymbolAddress).balanceOf(userEscrow) >=
_quantity, 'You must have enough second token funds in your escrow contract
to create this buy order');

        buyOrders.push(myOrder);

        // Sort existing orders by price the most efficient way possible,
we could optimize even more by creating a buy array for each token
        uint256[] memory sortedIds = sortIdsByPrices('buy');
        delete buyOrders;
        buyOrders.length = sortedIds.length;
        for(uint256 i = 0; i < sortedIds.length; i++) {
            buyOrders[i] = orderById[sortedIds[i]];
            buyOrderIndexById[sortedIds[i]] = i;
        }
```

Otherwise, change the array where the order will get added while also sorting the orders once added:

```
    } else {
        // Check that the user has enough of the first symbol if he wants
to sell it for the second symbol
        require(IERC20(firstSymbolAddress).balanceOf(userEscrow) >=
_quantity, 'You must have enough first token funds in your escrow contract
to create this sell order');

        // Add the new order
        sellOrders.push(myOrder);

        // Sort existing orders by price the most efficient way possible,
we could optimize even more by creating a sell array for each token
        uint256[] memory sortedIds = sortIdsByPrices('sell');
        delete sellOrders; // Reset orders
        sellOrders.length = sortedIds.length;
        for(uint256 i = 0; i < sortedIds.length; i++) {
            sellOrders[i] = orderById[sortedIds[i]];
            sellOrderIndexById[sortedIds[i]] = i;
        }
    }
}
```

```
        orderIdCounter++;
    }
```

That's the entire limit order function broken down into comprehensible pieces to explain the logic behind every statement. You saw that we used the `sortIdsByPrices` function because we need to sort the orders arrays. The following is how the sort function looks once completed. Notice that the function is a `view` type, which means that it won't cost any gas to run all of the calculations, because they will be done locally so the sorted array can be limitless:

```
/// @notice Sorts the selected array of Orders by price from lower to
higher if it's a buy order or from highest to lowest if it's a sell order
/// @param _type The type of order either 'sell' or 'buy'
/// @return uint256[] Returns the sorted ids
function sortIdsByPrices(bytes32 _type) public view returns (uint256[]
memory) {
    Order[] memory orders;
    if(_type == 'sell') orders = sellOrders;
    else orders = buyOrders;

    uint256 length = orders.length;
    uint256[] memory orderedIds = new uint256[](length);
    uint256 lastId = 0;
    for(uint i = 0; i < length; i++) {
        if(orders[i].quantity > 0) {
            for(uint j = i+1; j < length; j++) {
                // If it's a buy order, sort from lowest to highest since
we want the lowest prices first
                if(_type == 'buy' && orders[i].price > orders[j].price) {
                    Order memory temporaryOrder = orders[i];
                    orders[i] = orders[j];
                    orders[j] = temporaryOrder;
                }
                // If it's a sell order, sort from highest to lowest since
we want the highest sell prices first
                if(_type == 'sell' && orders[i].price < orders[j].price) {
                    Order memory temporaryOrder = orders[i];
                    orders[i] = orders[j];
                    orders[j] = temporaryOrder;
                }
            }
            orderedIds[lastId] = orders[i].id;
            lastId++;
        }
    }
    return orderedIds;
}
```

Pay attention to the `sortIdsByPrice()` function. It reads the respective state variables that contain the order structs, and then organizes the orders in ascending order if those are buy limit orders, or descending, if they are sell limit orders. We need it for the limit order function.

The `limitOrder()` function starts by checking that the parameters are valid and that the tokens can be traded. Depending on the type of order requested, it will push a new `Order` struct instance to the `sellOrders()` or `buyOrders()` arrays while sorting those arrays to push this new limit order to the right location. Remember, the idea is to have a sorted array of orders so that we can find the most profitable ones quickly; that's why we have the sort function. Finally, it updates the arrays of orders and the mapping of order indexes, so that we can later find where each `Order` instance is located in those arrays.

Now, we can take a look at the massive `marketOrder` function implementation; this is my own way of doing it, I recommend you try to recreate a market order function from scratch, considering all the gas restrictions and limitations. It's not perfect but it clearly displays how a DAX exchange works. Here's the function breakdown for your understanding. First, update the documentation of the function to be sure that it explains what's executed inside:

```
/// @notice To create a market order by filling one or more existing limit
orders at the most profitable price given a token pair, type of order (buy
or sell) and the amount of tokens to trade, the _quantity is how many
_firstSymbol tokens you want to buy if it's a buy order or how many
_firstSymbol tokens you want to sell at market price
/// @param _type The type of order either 'buy' or 'sell'
/// @param _firstSymbol The first token to buy or sell
/// @param _secondSymbol The second token to create a pair
/// @param _quantity The amount of tokens to sell or buy
```

Then add the `require()` function checks to verify that the given tokens are valid and that the quantities are correct:

```
function marketOrder(bytes32 _type, bytes32 _firstSymbol, bytes32
_secondSymbol, uint256 _quantity) public {
    require(_type.length > 0, 'You must specify the type');
    require(isTokenSymbolWhitelisted[_firstSymbol], 'The first symbol must
be whitelisted');
    require(isTokenSymbolWhitelisted[_secondSymbol], 'The second symbol
must be whitelisted');
    require(_quantity > 0, 'You must specify the quantity to buy or sell');
    require(checkValidPair(_firstSymbol, _secondSymbol), 'The pair must be
a valid pair');
```

Just like with the limit order function, we execute the buying or selling functionality depending on the state of the existing orders:

```
// Fills the latest market orders up until the _quantity is reached
uint256[] memory ordersToFillIds;
uint256[] memory quantitiesToFillPerOrder;
uint256 currentQuantity = 0;
if(_type == 'buy') {
    ordersToFillIds = new uint256[](sellOrders.length);
    quantitiesToFillPerOrder = new uint256[](sellOrders.length);
    // Loop through all the sell orders until we fill the quantity
    for(uint256 i = 0; i < sellOrders.length; i++) {
        ordersToFillIds[i] = sellOrders[i].id;
        if((currentQuantity + sellOrders[i].quantity) > _quantity) {
            quantitiesToFillPerOrder[i] = _quantity - currentQuantity;
            break;
        }
        currentQuantity += sellOrders[i].quantity;
        quantitiesToFillPerOrder[i] = sellOrders[i].quantity;
    }
} else {
    ordersToFillIds = new uint256[](buyOrders.length);
    quantitiesToFillPerOrder = new uint256[](buyOrders.length);
    for(uint256 i = 0; i < buyOrders.length; i++) {
        ordersToFillIds[i] = buyOrders[i].id;
        if((currentQuantity + buyOrders[i].quantity) > _quantity) {
            quantitiesToFillPerOrder[i] = _quantity - currentQuantity;
            break;
        }
        currentQuantity += buyOrders[i].quantity;
        quantitiesToFillPerOrder[i] = buyOrders[i].quantity;
    }
}
```

It never hurts to add some additional comments when developing such complex logic. Here, I've added some clarifications to remind myself of how this function should work on a more technical level:

```
// When the myOrder.type == sell or _type == buy
// myOrder.owner send quantityToFill[] of _firstSymbol to msg.sender
// msg.sender send quantityToFill[] * myOwner.price of _secondSymbol to
myOrder.owner

// When the myOrder.type == buy or _type == sell
// myOrder.owner send quantityToFill[] * myOwner.price of _secondSymbol
to msg.sender
// msg.sender send quantityToFill[] of _firstSymbol to myOrder.owner
```

Now that we've generated an array of orders to fill and the quantities required per order, we can start filling each of those orders with another loop:

```
// Close and fill orders
for(uint256 i = 0; i < ordersToFillIds.length; i++) {
    Order memory myOrder = orderById[ordersToFillIds[i]];

    // If we fill the entire order, mark it as closed
    if(quantitiesToFillPerOrder[i] == myOrder.quantity) {
        myOrder.state = OrderState.CLOSED;
        closedOrders.push(myOrder);
    }
    myOrder.quantity -= quantitiesToFillPerOrder[i];
    orderById[myOrder.id] = myOrder;
```

We have to break it down by type to see whether the order is actually a buy or sell order, to guarantee that we are fulfilling the right order with the right quantities:

```
if(_type == 'buy') {
    // If the limit order is a buy order, send the firstSymbol to
the creator of the limit order which is the buyer
Escrow(escrowByUserAddress[myOrder.owner]).transferTokens(tokenAddressBySym
bol[_firstSymbol], msg.sender, quantitiesToFillPerOrder[i]);
Escrow(escrowByUserAddress[msg.sender]).transferTokens(tokenAddressBySymbol
[_secondSymbol], myOrder.owner, quantitiesToFillPerOrder[i] *
myOrder.price);

    sellOrders[sellOrderIndexById[myOrder.id]] = myOrder;

    emit TransferOrder('sell', escrowByUserAddress[myOrder.owner],
msg.sender, _firstSymbol, quantitiesToFillPerOrder[i]);
    emit TransferOrder('buy', escrowByUserAddress[msg.sender],
myOrder.owner, _secondSymbol, quantitiesToFillPerOrder[i] * myOrder.price);
```

If it's a sell order, we change the arrays used, but the logic is the same:

```
} else {
    // If this is a buy market order or a sell limit order for the
opposite, send firstSymbol to the second user
Escrow(escrowByUserAddress[myOrder.owner]).transferTokens(tokenAddressBySym
bol[_secondSymbol], msg.sender, quantitiesToFillPerOrder[i] *
myOrder.price);
Escrow(escrowByUserAddress[msg.sender]).transferTokens(tokenAddressBySymbol
[_firstSymbol], myOrder.owner, quantitiesToFillPerOrder[i]);

    buyOrders[buyOrderIndexById[myOrder.id]] = myOrder;

    emit TransferOrder('buy', escrowByUserAddress[myOrder.owner],
```

```
    msg.sender, _secondSymbol, quantitiesToFillPerOrder[i] * myOrder.price);
                emit TransferOrder('sell', escrowByUserAddress[msg.sender],
    myOrder.owner, _firstSymbol, quantitiesToFillPerOrder[i]);
            }

        }
    }
```

At first glance, you can see that we have no less than three `for` loops, which is extremely unoptimized since it won't be able to handle more than a few orders at a time, but it's one of the few solutions for a DAX that doesn't require a centralized server.

First, we do the required checks to verify that the user is creating a valid market order with the appropriate `approve()` to what they want to buy or sell so that the contract can purchase the tokens freely. Then, we start looping through all of our sorted order arrays to fill the most profitable ones first, while keeping track of how many tokens will be filled for each order. Once we have a list of orders to fill with the quantities, we can move on to filling each one of those. How do we do it?

We update the state of each order so that we mark the quantities as zero or a reduced amount while also using `enum OrderState.CLOSED` for those that are filled completely. We then transfer the right quantity of tokens to each user. That's where the mapping of `buyOrderIndexById[]` is especially useful since we want to update a specific order without altering the order of the entire array, thus saving gas and processing costs. Finally, we emit some events to indicate that we made some token transfers.

That should be it! The following is the entire contract so that you can see how it all ties together. It is available on the official GitHub at `https://github.com/merlox/decentralized-exchange/blob/master/contracts/DAX.sol`.

It's quite a big contract, so I recommend you write some tests for it to verify that it's working. You can check and run the tests I've written by cloning my GitHub with all the code here: `https://github.com/merlox/decentralized-exchange`.

Finishing the dApp

Now that we have a working smart contract with our desired logic, we can implement the dApp using Truffle and web3.js in a simple React application. Start by importing the required components inside your `index.js` file:

```
import React from 'react'
import ReactDOM from 'react-dom'
import MyWeb3 from 'web3'
```

```
import './index.styl'
import ABI from '../build/contracts/DAX.json'
import TokenABI from '../build/contracts/ERC20.json'

const batToken = '0x850Cbb38828adF8a89d7d799CCf1010Dc238F665'
const watToken = '0x029cc401Ef45B2a2B2D6D2D6677b9F94E26cfF9d'
const dax = ABI.networks['3'].address
```

We'll use only two tokens in this prototype for you to learn how to create the application since a fully-featured DAX is outside the scope of this book. The goal is to show you the path so you can create a more advanced DAX if you desire. We start by importing our required ABIs for creating the token instances and the token addresses. Those are the tokens we'll use.

Start by updating the state object in the Main component with the new required variables that we'll use to interact with the smart contract. Notice how we removed the trades and history arrays because we'll get that data from the contract instead:

```
class Main extends React.Component {
    constructor() {
        super()

        this.state = {
            contractInstance: {},
            tokenInstance: {},
            secondTokenInstance: {},
            userAddress: '',
            firstSymbol: 'BAT', // Sample tokens
            secondSymbol: 'WAT', // Sample tokens
            balanceFirstSymbol: 0,
            balanceSecondSymbol: 0,
            escrow: '',
            buyOrders: [],
            sellOrders: [],
            closedOrders: []
        }

        this.setup()
    }
```

Add the bytes32() helper function, which generates a valid hexadecimal string required for web3.js:

```
// To use bytes32 functions
bytes32(name) {
    return myWeb3.utils.fromAscii(name)
}
```

Then create the `setup()` to initialize the web3.js instance while also getting the user's consent to use their MetaMask account credentials:

```
async setup() {
    // Create the contract instance
    window.myWeb3 = new MyWeb3(ethereum)
    try {
        await ethereum.enable();
    } catch (error) {
        console.error('You must approve this dApp to interact with it')
    }
    console.log('Setting up contract instances')
    await this.setContractInstances()
    console.log('Setting up orders')
    await this.setOrders()
    console.log('Setting up pairs')
    await this.setPairs()
}
```

Because the contract setup in the react application is more complicated, we have to create a separate function for maintainability:

```
async setContractInstances() {
    const userAddress = (await myWeb3.eth.getAccounts())[0]
    if(!userAddress) return console.error('You must unlock metamask to
use this dApp on ropsten!')
    await this.setState({userAddress})
    const contractInstance = new myWeb3.eth.Contract(ABI.abi, dax, {
        from: this.state.userAddress,
        gasPrice: 2e9
    })
    const tokenInstance = new myWeb3.eth.Contract(TokenABI.abi,
batToken, {
        from: this.state.userAddress,
        gasPrice: 2e9
    })
    const secondTokenInstance = new myWeb3.eth.Contract(TokenABI.abi,
watToken, {
        from: this.state.userAddress,
        gasPrice: 2e9
    })
    await this.setState({contractInstance, tokenInstance,
secondTokenInstance})
}
```

After setting up the web3 and contract instances, we can start getting orders from the smart contract to populate our user interface with orders. First, we get the length of the arrays used to be able to loop through all the orders. That's the only way to securely take into account all the elements contained in the arrays:

```
async setOrders() {
      // First get the length of all the orders so that you can loop
through them
      const buyOrdersLength = await
this.state.contractInstance.methods.getOrderLength(this.bytes32("buy")).cal
l({ from: this.state.userAddress })
      const sellOrdersLength = await
this.state.contractInstance.methods.getOrderLength(this.bytes32('sell')).ca
ll({ from: this.state.userAddress })
      const closedOrdersLength = await
this.state.contractInstance.methods.getOrderLength(this.bytes32('closed')).
call({ from: this.state.userAddress })
      let buyOrders = []
      let sellOrders = []
      let closedOrders = []
```

Then we start looping over the buy orders array by calling the smart contract with each component independently:

```
      for(let i = 0; i < buyOrdersLength; i++) {
        const order = await
this.state.contractInstance.methods.getOrder(this.bytes32('buy'), i).call({
from: this.state.userAddress })
        const orderObject = {
            id: order[0],
            owner: order[1],
            type: myWeb3.utils.toUtf8(order[2]),
            firstSymbol: myWeb3.utils.toUtf8(order[3]),
            secondSymbol: myWeb3.utils.toUtf8(order[4]),
            quantity: order[5],
            price: order[6],
            timestamp: order[7],
            state: order[8],
        }
        buyOrders.push(orderObject)
      }
```

We do the same thing with the sell orders array:

```
      for(let i = 0; i < sellOrdersLength; i++) {
        const order = await
this.state.contractInstance.methods.getOrder(this.bytes32('sell'),
0).call({ from: this.state.userAddress })
```

```
            const orderObject = {
                id: order[0],
                owner: order[1],
                type: myWeb3.utils.toUtf8(order[2]),
                firstSymbol: myWeb3.utils.toUtf8(order[3]),
                secondSymbol: myWeb3.utils.toUtf8(order[4]),
                quantity: order[5],
                price: order[6],
                timestamp: order[7],
                state: order[8],
            }
            sellOrders.push(orderObject)
        }
```

Again, we do the same thing with the closed orders array. We need this one to display past historical trades that can help people understand what happened before they joined the fun:

```
        for(let i = 0; i < closedOrdersLength; i++) {
            const order = await
this.state.contractInstance.methods.closedOrders(this.bytes32('close'),
0).call({ from: this.state.userAddress })
            const orderObject = {
                id: order[0],
                owner: order[1],
                type: myWeb3.utils.toUtf8(order[2]),
                firstSymbol: myWeb3.utils.toUtf8(order[3]),
                secondSymbol: myWeb3.utils.toUtf8(order[4]),
                quantity: order[5],
                price: order[6],
                timestamp: order[7],
                state: order[8],
            }
            closedOrders.push(orderObject)
        }
        this.setState({buyOrders, sellOrders, closedOrders})
    }
```

Finally, create a function named `setPairs()`, which will be used in the future to add new token pairs to the platform. Because we don't want to overcomplicate this initial DAX that we're creating, we'll limit ourselves to just one token pair composed of two imaginary tokens, named `WAT` and `BAT`:

```
    async setPairs() {
        // Here you'd add all the logic to get all the token symbols, in
this case we're keeping it simple with one fixed pair
        // If there are no pairs, whitelist a new one automatically if this
```

```
is the owner of the DAX contract
        const owner = await
this.state.contractInstance.methods.owner().call({ from:
this.state.userAddress })
        const isWhitelisted = await
this.state.contractInstance.methods.isTokenWhitelisted(batToken).call({
from: this.state.userAddress })
        if(owner == this.state.userAddress && !isWhitelisted) {
            await
this.state.contractInstance.methods.whitelistToken(this.bytes32('BAT'),
batToken, [this.bytes32('WAT')], [watToken]).send({ from:
this.state.userAddress, gas: 8e6 })
        }

        // Set the balance of each symbol considering how many tokens you
have in escrow
        const escrow = await
this.state.contractInstance.methods.escrowByUserAddress(this.state.userAddr
ess).call({ from: this.state.userAddress })
        const balanceOne = await
this.state.tokenInstance.methods.balanceOf(escrow).call({ from:
this.state.userAddress })
        const balanceTwo = await
this.state.secondTokenInstance.methods.balanceOf(escrow).call({ from:
this.state.userAddress })
        this.setState({escrow, balanceOne, balanceTwo})
    }
}
```

We start by setting up the constructor with the essential variables required for the entire application. Then a `setup()` function takes care of getting all the initial information. The `bytes32()` function is used to convert normal strings to hexadecimal since the new version of web3 forces us to send hexadecimal strings instead of plain texts to identify the `bytes32` variables. Personally, I prefer to write the `bytes32` variables as strings, but `web3` is their framework so we have to follow its programming style. We continue by setting up the contract instances with the `setContractInstances()` function that starts our contract from the given addresses and ABIs.

Then we set up the orders with the `setOrders()` function. This one looks scarier since it contains a lot more code, but the idea is to simply get each order from the smart contract and store them in organized arrays inside the react state variables. Finally, we set up the token pairs with `setPairs()`, which updates the state with our tokens.

Now we need to implement the remaining functions in the smart contract. Here is how the whitelist function looks in the React dApp:

```
async whitelistTokens(symbol, token, pairSymbols, pairAddresses) {
    await
this.state.contractInstance.methods.whitelistToken(this.bytes32(symbol),
token, pairSymbols, pairAddresses).send({ from: this.state.userAddress })
}
```

Then we implement the deposit tokens function which will increase the available balance that the user adds to the platform for trading the tokens. I've added plenty of comments for you to understand what's going on:

```
async depositTokens(symbol, amount) {
    if(symbol == 'BAT') {
        // Check the token balance before approving
        const balance = await
this.state.tokenInstance.methods.balanceOf(this.state.userAddress).call({
from: this.state.userAddress })
        if(balance < amount) return alert(`You can't deposit ${amount} BAT
since you have ${balance} BAT in your account, get more tokens before
depositing`)
        // First approve to 0 to avoid errors and then increase it
        await this.state.tokenInstance.methods.approve(dax, 0).send({ from:
this.state.userAddress })
        await this.state.tokenInstance.methods.approve(dax, amount).send({
from: this.state.userAddress })
        // Create the transaction
        await this.state.contractInstance.methods.depositTokens(batToken,
amount).send({ from: this.state.userAddress })
    } else if(symbol == 'WAT') {
        // Check the token balace before approving
        const balance = await
this.state.secondTokenInstance.methods.balanceOf(this.state.userAddress).ca
ll({ from: this.state.userAddress })
        if(balance < amount) return alert(`You can't deposit ${amount} WAT
since you have ${balance} WAT in your account, get more tokens before
depositing`)
        // First approve to 0 to avoid errors and then increase it
        await this.state.secondTokenInstance.methods.approve(dax, 0).send({
from: this.state.userAddress })
        await this.state.secondTokenInstance.methods.approve(dax,
amount).send({ from: this.state.userAddress })
        // Create the transaction
        await this.state.contractInstance.methods.depositTokens(watToken,
amount).send({ from: this.state.userAddress })
    }
}
```

The withdraw tokens function is quite simple and will be used for both tokens:

```
async withdrawTokens(symbol, amount) {
    if(symbol == 'BAT') {
        await this.state.contractInstance.methods.extractTokens(batToken,
amount).send({ from: this.state.userAddress })
    } else if(symbol == 'WAT') {
        await this.state.contractInstance.methods.extractTokens(watToken,
amount).send({ from: this.state.userAddress })
    }
}
```

Finally, we have to implement the limit and market orders functions which, ironically, are the smallest ones, since we only have to pass the required information to the smart contract for it to execute the entire functionality by itself:

```
async createLimitOrder(type, firstSymbol, secondSymbol, quantity,
pricePerToken) {
    // Create the limit order
    await this.state.contractInstance.methods.limitOrder(type, firstSymbol,
secondSymbol, quantity, pricePerToken).send({ from: this.state.userAddress
})
}

async createMarketOrder(type, firstSymbol, secondSymbol, quantity) {
    // Create the market order
    await this.state.contractInstance.methods.marketOrder(type,
firstSymbol, secondSymbol, quantity).send({ from: this.state.userAddress })
}
```

The whitelist function is pretty straightforward since we only run the whitelisting function from the smart contract using the main Ethereum address. Remember that this function can only be executed by the owner of the contract.

The deposit tokens function checks whether you have enough tokens in your Ethereum address, and then it creates two approvals: the first one is to reduce the approval to zero since we can't increase the approval quantity safely since there are some security risks in that function; the second one is to `approve()` the desired quantity of tokens to deposit for the selected token. Then we run the `depositTokens()` method from our DAX contract to move the tokens to the escrow address and create one if the user doesn't have an escrow yet.

The withdraw function simply runs the `extractTokens()` method from our DAX contract to move the tokens from escrow to the user's address because we don't need to check anything there.

Then we move to the `createLimitOrder()` function. Remember how complicated and large it was in the DAX contract? Well, in this case, it's just a matter of putting the right parameters in the right places. We'll see later in the `render()` function how we get those parameters. The same thing applies with the `createMarketOrder()` which runs the `marketOrder` method from our DAX contract.

Here's the `render()` function:

```
render() {
    return (
        <div className="main-container">
            <Sidebar
                firstSymbol={this.state.firstSymbol}
                secondSymbol={this.state.secondSymbol}
                balanceOne={this.state.balanceOne}
                balanceTwo={this.state.balanceTwo}
                deposit={(symbol, amount) => this.depositTokens(symbol,
amount)}
                withdraw={(symbol, amount) => this.withdrawTokens(symbol,
amount)}
                limitOrder={(type, firstSymbol, secondSymbol, quantity,
pricePerToken) => this.createLimitOrder(type, firstSymbol, secondSymbol,
quantity, pricePerToken)}
                marketOrder={(type, firstSymbol, secondSymbol, quantity) =>
this.createMarketOrder(type, firstSymbol, secondSymbol, quantity)}
            />
            <Orders
                buyOrders={this.state.buyOrders}
                sellOrders={this.state.sellOrders}
            />
            <History
                closedOrders={this.state.closedOrders}
            />
        </div>
    )
}
```

The render function generates three components: `Sidebar`, `Orders`, and `History`. Those are the three sections that we created earlier. In this case, we've added lots of props to each component to communicate data easily. You can see that the limit order and market order props are simply taking parameters and sending them to the functions of the `Main` component.

Let's explore my implementation of each of those components; this is my own way of doing it so you can see how a DAX should look. I recommend you create your own version based on what you've learned. The following is the `Sidebar` component; we start by creating the updated `constructor()`, `bytes32()`, and `resetInputs()` functions that will be used in the render:

```
class Sidebar extends React.Component {
    constructor() {
        super()
        this.state = {
            selectedLimitOrder: false,
            limitOrderPrice: 0,
            orderQuantity: 0,
        }
    }

    // To use bytes32 functions
    bytes32(name) {
        return myWeb3.utils.fromAscii(name)
    }

    resetInputs() {
        this.refs.limitOrderPrice.value = ''
        this.refs.orderQuantity.value = ''
        this.setState({
            limitOrderPrice: 0,
            orderQuantity: 0,
        })
    }
```

The `render()` function in this case is a bit too large for you to understand it, so we'll break it down into smaller, digestible pieces. Because we want to give the user more options, we've added a deposit and withdraw button for each token to keep it simple:

```
    render() {
        return (
            <div className="sidebar">
                <div className="selected-assets-title heading">Selected
assets</div>
                <div className="selected-asset-
one">{this.props.firstSymbol}</div>
                <div className="selected-asset-
two">{this.props.secondSymbol}</div>
                <div className="your-portfolio heading">Your
portfolio</div>
                <div className="grid-
center">{this.props.firstSymbol}:</div><div className="grid-
```

```
center">{this.props.balanceOne ? this.props.balanceOne :
'Loading...'}</div>
                <div className="grid-
center">{this.props.secondSymbol}:</div><div className="grid-
center">{this.props.balanceTwo ? this.props.balanceTwo :
'Loading...'}</div>
                <div className="money-management heading">Money
management</div>
                <button className="button-outline" onClick={() => {
                    const amount = prompt(`How many
${this.props.firstSymbol} tokens do you want to deposit?`)
                    this.props.deposit(this.props.firstSymbol, amount)
                }}>Deposit {this.props.firstSymbol} </button>
                <button className="button-outline" onClick={() => {
                    const amount = prompt(`How many
${this.props.firstSymbol} tokens do you want to withdraw?`)
                    this.props.withdraw(this.props.firstSymbol, amount)
                }}>Withdraw {this.props.firstSymbol}</button>
                <button className="button-outline" onClick={() => {
                    const amount = prompt(`How many
${this.props.secondSymbol} tokens do you want to deposit?`)
                    this.props.deposit(this.props.secondSymbol, amount)
                }}>Deposit {this.props.secondSymbol} </button>
                <button className="button-outline" onClick={() => {
                    const amount = prompt(`How many
${this.props.secondSymbol} tokens do you want to withdraw?`)
                    this.props.withdraw(this.props.secondSymbol, amount)
                }}>Withdraw {this.props.secondSymbol}</button>
```

As you can see, those buttons ask the user how many tokens to move with the `prompt()` global JavaScript function, which provides a clear, albeit basic, dynamic input. Then the respective functions get called on the `Main` component by passing them via `props`. Then, we can add the `buy` button functionality to format the required input for the limit or market orders:

```
                <div className="actions heading">Actions</div>
                <button onClick={() => {
                    if(this.state.orderQuantity == 0) return alert('You
must specify how many tokens you want to buy')
                    if(this.state.selectedLimitOrder) {
                        if(this.state.limitOrderPrice == 0) return
alert('You must specify the token price at which you want to buy')
                        if(this.props.balanceTwo <
(this.state.orderQuantity * this.state.limitOrderPrice)) {
                            return alert(`You must approve
${this.state.orderQuantity * this.state.limitOrderPrice} of
${this.props.secondSymbol} tokens to create this buy limit order, your
```

```
${this.props.secondSymbol} token balance must be larger than
${this.state.orderQuantity * this.state.limitOrderPrice}`)
                            }
                // Buy the this.state.orderQuantity of
this.props.firstSymbol
                    this.props.limitOrder(this.bytes32('buy'),
this.bytes32(this.props.firstSymbol),
this.bytes32(this.props.secondSymbol), this.state.orderQuantity,
this.state.limitOrderPrice)
                } else {
                    this.props.marketOrder(this.bytes32('buy'),
this.bytes32(this.props.firstSymbol),
this.bytes32(this.props.secondSymbol), this.state.orderQuantity)
                }
                this.resetInputs()
            }}>Buy {this.props.firstSymbol}</button>
```

The sell button does the same thing, but with the sell type in the topmost functions to tell the smart contract that we want to sell:

```
<button onClick={() => {
        if(this.state.orderQuantity == 0) return alert('You
must specify how many tokens you want to sell')
            if(this.state.selectedLimitOrder) {
                if(this.state.limitOrderPrice == 0) return
alert('You must specify the token price at which you want to sell')
                if(this.props.balanceOne <
this.state.orderQuantity) {
                    return alert(`You must approve
${this.state.orderQuantity} of ${this.props.firstSymbol} tokens to create
this sell limit order, your ${this.props.firstSymbol} token balance must be
larger than ${this.state.orderQuantity}`)
                }
                // Buy the this.state.orderQuantity of
this.props.firstSymbol
                    this.props.limitOrder(this.bytes32('sell'),
this.bytes32(this.props.firstSymbol),
this.bytes32(this.props.secondSymbol), this.state.orderQuantity,
this.state.limitOrderPrice)
                } else {
                    this.props.marketOrder(this.bytes32('sell'),
this.bytes32(this.props.firstSymbol),
this.bytes32(this.props.secondSymbol), this.state.orderQuantity)
                }
                this.resetInputs()
            }} className="sell">Sell {this.props.firstSymbol}</button>
```

Finally, we give the user a simple select input to indicate that they want to create a limit order or a market order. If they select a limit order, an additional input will be displayed to indicate the sell or buy price:

```
<select defaultValue="market-order" onChange={selected => {
    if(selected.target.value == 'limit-order') {
        this.setState({selectedLimitOrder: true})
    } else {
        this.setState({selectedLimitOrder: false})
    }
}}>
    <option value="market-order">Market Order</option>
    <option value="limit-order">Limit Order</option>
</select>
<input ref="limitOrderPrice" onChange={event => {
    this.setState({limitOrderPrice: event.target.value})
}} className={this.state.selectedLimitOrder ? '' :
'hidden'} type="number" placeholder="Price to buy or sell at..." />
    <input ref="orderQuantity" onChange={event => {
        this.setState({orderQuantity: event.target.value})
    }} type="number" placeholder={`Quantity of
${this.props.firstSymbol} to buy or sell...`} />
    </div>
)
}
}
```

As before, we have a constructor, a `bytes32` function, and a `render()` function. The `resetInputs()` function takes care of cleaning the input fields so that you reset their values after buying or selling. The most complex part is the render, which creates our design. The main logic can be found in the buttons. We have four buttons in the money management section to deposit BAT or WAT and withdraw BAT or WAT. There is a simple system for managing how many tokens you have in your escrow. Then, there are a couple of main buttons to buy or sell. Each of those buttons runs the `createLimitOrder` or `createMarketOrder` methods, depending on whether you have selected the limit order drop-down or the other. When you click the buttons, the component reads the values stored in the input to transmit them to the right functions.

Take a closer look at the logic behind the buttons to understand how they decide which function to call and how they move that information to the `Main` component. Let's move on to the `Orders` component, previously named `Trades`:

```
// The main section to see live trades taking place
class Orders extends React.Component {
    constructor() {
        super()
```

```
    }

    render() {
        let buyOrders = this.props.buyOrders
        let sellOrders = this.props.sellOrders
        if(buyOrders.length > 0) {
            buyOrders = buyOrders.map((trade, index) => (
                <div key={trade.id + index} className="trade-container buy-
trade">
                    <div className="trade-symbol">{trade.firstSymbol}</div>
                    <div className="trade-
symbol">{trade.secondSymbol}</div>
                    <div className="trade-pricing">{trade.type}
{trade.quantity} {trade.secondSymbol} at {trade.price} {trade.secondSymbol}
each</div>
                </div>
            ))
        }

        if(sellOrders.length > 0) {
            sellOrders = sellOrders.map((trade, index) => (
                <div key={trade.id + index} className="trade-container
sell-trade">
                    <div className="trade-symbol">{trade.firstSymbol}</div>
                    <div className="trade-
symbol">{trade.secondSymbol}</div>
                    <div className="trade-pricing">{trade.type}
{trade.quantity} {trade.secondSymbol} at {trade.price} {trade.secondSymbol}
each</div>
                </div>
            ))
        }
        return (
            <div className="trades">
                <div className="buy-trades-title heading">Buy</div>
                <div className="buy-trades-container">{buyOrders}</div>
                <div className="sell-trades-title heading">Sell</div>
                <div className="sell-trades-container">{sellOrders}</div>
            </div>
        )
    }
}
```

We only have a render and constructor to generate our desired design from the buy or sell orders objects given from the Main component. There isn't much to say about it, apart from the fact that it creates a clean interface for endless orders.

Now, here's the last `History` component:

```
// Past historical trades
class History extends React.Component {
    constructor() {
        super()
    }

    render() {
        let closedOrders = this.props.closedOrders
        if(closedOrders.length > 0) {
            closedOrders = closedOrders.map((trade, index) => (
                <div key={trade.id + index} className="historical-trade">
                    <div className={trade.type == 'sell' ? 'sell-trade' :
'buy-trade'}>{trade.type} {trade.quantity} {trade.firstSymbol} for
{trade.quantity * trade.price} {trade.secondSymbol} at {trade.price}
each</div>
                </div>
            ))
        }
        return (
            <div className="history">
                <div className="heading">Recent history</div>
                <div className="historical-trades-
container">{closedOrders}</div>
            </div>
        )
    }
}

ReactDOM.render(<Main />, document.querySelector('#root'))
```

It's almost identical to the `Orders` component, but with a different styling. Remember to run the `ReactDOM.render()` function to display your dApp.

That's about it! Now you should have a working DAX that you can use and build upon to create a stronger exchange for hundreds or even thousands of tokens, since you understand how it works from the inside out. This is probably the most direct way to start your own exchange. Here's how it looks after some trades:

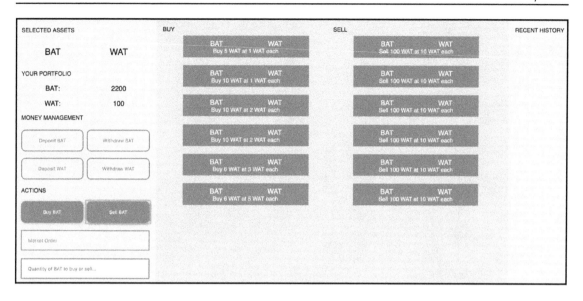

Summary

In this chapter, you learned how to build a DAX from scratch, going from the idea of how exchanges work, to the user interface using react and truffle, to creating the required smart contracts so that you saw for yourself how a fully-decentralized system works, to finally combining it all together in a beautiful dApp that communicates with your deployed contracts and tokens. You learned about the differences between traditional, centralized cryptocurrency exchanges and fully-featured DAXs, so that you can choose the best type for your requirements.

After that short introduction, you got into the technical aspects of the DAX by understanding how we implement the trading and matching engine via a set of smart contracts. Finally, you developed a clean interface without graphs to keep it simple, and you integrated all the complex smart contract logic via manageable components.

In the next chapter, we'll explore Machine Learning on the blockchain, a topic that you may have heard about, since it combines the two most popular technologies regarding the future of money and computing by building a dApp that allows us to make predictions with a trained model using Linear Regression algorithms in a smart contract.

3
Section 3: Ethereum Implementations

The goal of this section is to create advanced production-grade projects using blockchain technologies so that we can build a resume or run a crowdsale.

The following chapters are included in this section:

10
Machine Learning on the Ethereum Blockchain

Blockchain and AI have been the most interesting topics in recent years for a good reason: they are the most advanced technologies that have been created to disrupt most established businesses. The fact that we can teach a computer to learn by itself is something very powerful, and means that will continue evolving the machine learning systems of the future will continue to evolve. Likewise with blockchain: the field of distributed computing is just beginning, and it will be the default solution for most problems in the future. So why not combine both for a revolutionary invention? It turns out that they work nicely together, and we can create very interesting dApps that benefit from both worlds, particularly by using them to create decentralized marketplaces for solving machine learning problems that reward users for their computing power.

In this chapter, we're going to cover the following topics:

- Understanding machine learning
- Decentralized machine learning marketplaces
- Building a smart contract machine learning marketplace

Understanding machine learning

Machine learning (**ML**) is a subset of **artificial intelligence** (**AI**), which in turn is a field in the broader subject of data science. ML is focused on creating programs that learn by themselves to solve specific problems without having to write all the logic; we just need to give them lots of input. Trial and error is the main mechanism with the machine slowly learns how to achieve the right output to a problem.

The moment computers were created was the moment scientists asked themselves, "How can we make this machine think and act as a human?". That's why understanding how computers learn begins with understanding how humans see the world.

Think about it for a second: how do you think animals and humans learn to survive in the dangerous and confusing world we live in? By learning from others? Well, that's a valid learning system, but all understanding of what we truly know comes from experimenting in the face of uncertainty. Imagine the following scenario: you are in a primitive world where language hasn't been invented—we're talking thousands of years ago. You see a flat and shiny red object on the ground that's completely new to you. How do you even begin to understand it? It could be something that could kill you or something that could provide you with a new source of materials. You don't know yet, so you begin by trying different things, always with caution, since your main goal is to survive. You touch it with a stick: nothing happens. You touch it with your hand: it feels warm. You grab it: it feels strong, so you try to break it, no success. After some more experimentation, you come to the conclusion that what you have in your hands is a strong, naturally formed metallic disc that you can use to cook food with the power of the sun.

All of that specific knowledge came about from experimentation using the trial-and-error mechanism. My point is that this is how we've discovered all of what we know in the current world, and it's also the system that machine learning algorithms use to solve problems by themselves. You give them lots of information and they experiment with their tools, which usually are pixel-by-pixel readings of images and bytes of data, to generate an outcome. They are used to predict the future given some initial conditions, to understand complex problems that can't be solved with classical programming, and to create tools to help us do a better job.

Technically speaking, there are three steps to create a machine learning system, as follows:

1. Gather lots of information about a topic, such as 2,000,000 images of unique water bottles.
2. Develop a machine learning **model** that generates a desired output. In our example, let's say that we want to create a model that classifies water bottles based on their shape, size, color, chemical composition, and purity because we need to find the best water possible for human use. Those attributes are called **labels**, as they are precise descriptions of each component.
3. The model consumes all that data in a process called **training**, where it adjusts how important each component of our water bottles is to calculate which factors determine the best water possible. At some point, it will be trained, meaning that it will understand what attributes constitute the best water for humans, generating a program that we can use to quickly determine how good a specific new water bottle is.

That's just an example of how we use machine learning to provide solutions to complex questions, such as, what's the best water I can consume for optimal health?, What does a dangerous person look like?, How do I teach my camera to determine whether what it's seeing is a dog or a cat?

In general, the steps are getting data -> creating a model that uses that data for creating a program -> using the program for specific situations. There are many other different systems where the program learns by getting the data by itself using trial and error. Other interesting machine learning algorithms work on the biological level to teach robots to act as real-life animals, in order to learn and see the world like them.

It's a very hot topic that will continue growing in the coming years to provide answers to the most complex problems and questions humans can possibly ask. That's why I recommend you explore the vast world of AI. See what's out there before combining it with blockchain.

Decentralized machine learning marketplaces

We are going to build a marketplace to buy and sell computing power from users that have strong GPUs and want to help others perform machine learning to teach their algorithms to complete a task based on supervised learning, where a program learns to generate a desired output from a large quantity of input given a goal so that it programs itself.

Ethereum comes into the equation when we need to deal with storing permanent records of the transactions that took place in our ML marketplace along with the trained model that the buyer requested from their parameters so that it's accessible anytime. The idea is to create a place where people from all around the world can start earning money from a new use of their hardware as an alternative to mining, while also providing a secure system for ML algorithms.

We will use GPUs to train our machine learning programs because they are great at processing lots of parallel operations at the same time, so that we can go through large batches of input quickly, faster than with a CPU. We'll also use Ethereum as the default payment currency to process decentralized transactions with ease.

Most machine learning models nowadays are based on **neural networks** (**NN**), which are abstractions of how a human brain works, translated to computers. It's based on virtual individual neurons that receive an input and produce an output if a condition is met. For instance, say that a simple neuron contains the following statement:

```
if(input > 10) return output = true;
```

The statement will return a positive value if the input is larger than 10. That function is what's called an activation function, which makes sense because it will activate if the function fulfills the conditions. We can combine many of those neurons together with different parameters and configurations to get what's known as a neural network, which processes complex input to generate precise output. When training, we're readjusting the activation function to better adapt to our desired goal. This is all done automatically once it's set up in our model. At the end, we get a trained program that is capable of answering complex questions without having to code each specific scenario.

Once the model is adjusted from our training dataset, we can test it with a new input from a different source to determine whether it's generating an optimal output. This is important since there's a risk of overfitting where the machine learning program optimizes too much, becoming too specific to our initial input, which makes it unable to produce valid results from new data. It's like a surgeon that has to become a general doctor from scratch: it won't produce great results because it's too specialized.

Some well-known activation functions are Sigmoid and ReLU. Deep learning is the process of stacking several layers of neurons so that the output of a neuron is transmitted to another neuron for a more advanced result. These networks are known as **deep neural networks** (**DNNs**) because they are made of several layers. Make sure to explore the fascinating world of NNs by yourself to learn how the technology of the future is being shaped.

We won't use NNs here as they are hard to implement from scratch on **Solidity** because of the limitations of the blockchain, so we'll work with simpler algorithms that you can expand as you need. Here's how our protocol will work:

1. A user publishes a set of data, an evaluation function (our ML model), and the reward for completing the task to the smart contract in ETH.
2. Those that want to fulfil the task will download the published data from the first user to train the given ML model in order to generate a trained program that will be given back to the smart contract.
3. External users will take a look at all the published solutions for that particular task to determine who is the winner. The buyer will determine the winner based on their preference.

From this protocol, we can establish the following process that the users will follow:

1. A buyer, someone who wants their model trained, deploys a smart contract that contains the following data:
   - Their model definition in the constructor—for instance, DNN.
   - The datasets to train—for instance, an array of handwritten digit images made of 30 x 30 pixels. Each image is an array of 30 x 30 pixels (900 pixels) where each pixel is another array containing information about the position of the pixel and whether it's black or white (we don't want colors in this image to avoid complexity)—for instance [[0, true], [1, false]] will represent a 2 x 1 pixel image where the first pixel is black while the other is white. This dataset will be published to an external website that people can freely access to train the model. In our constructor we will provide a URL, namely `https://example.com/dataset`.
   - The reward for training the model is paid in Ethereum, and this arrangement set up in the payable constructor.

2. The contract is published and sellers begin to participate in the task of training the model. From the dataset, 90% of the data will be used to train the model while the remaining 10% will be used to test the results from the program to verify its accuracy. To make sure sellers don't copy each other, different random datasets will be given to different participants.

3. The buyer decides which model works best for them and selects a winner. If an expiration time is reached and the buyer hasn't selected a winner, the first participant will get the reward.

For our machine learning marketplace, we'll use a simple linear-regression machine learning algorithm in Solidity. Users will submit their data, which will contain a name and two number parameters to make predictions. A linear regression is a relationship between two factors—for instance, the number of sales in a website and the number of visitors. In that case, we can establish a model that allows us to predict the number of sales for a given number of visitors.

Simple linear-regression models can be applied to many fields where a variable depends on another, and it's one of the simplest machine learning systems available. That's why we'll be using it, since it's important to be able to recreate it in Solidity to verify solutions provided by other users. Ideally, we'd implement an NN or a more complex model, but that would take too much time to develop considering the limitations of the blockchain. You can build upon the lessons in this chapter to extend the marketplace. In the following section, you'll learn how to create the code required for the marketplace.

Building a smart contract machine learning marketplace

Our ML marketplace will work with linear regression algorithms exclusively to simplify the process so that you understand how it all ties together. I encourage you to expand the solution for more advanced models to practice your ML and blockchain skills. To apply a simple linear regression algorithm, we need the following things:

- A prediction function to generate a prediction from data
- A cost function to combine the prediction results
- An optimization algorithm to train our algorithm with **gradient descent**, which will fine tune the predictions for more precise results
- A train function to improve our algorithm

The prediction function

First, you need to understand that our simple linear-regression algorithms predict values using the following function:

```
y = weight * x + bias
```

If we are predicting the number of sales based on the number of visitors to a website, our prediction function would look like this:

```
Sales = weight * visitors + bias
```

Our goal is to obtain fixed weight and bias values to optimize our prediction function so that we get a realistic estimate of sales. For instance, a trained linear regression would look like this:

```
Sales = 0.43 * visitors + 0.9
```

We got a weight of `0.43` and a bias of `0.9` after training from a given dataset. We should be able to use that optimized function to make accurate predictions for our particular needs with great results. We need to implement the prediction function in Python and in Solidity because sellers will use Python to train the model, while we'll use Solidity to verify the result given by those sellers. Here's how our `prediction` function looks in Python and Solidity for our marketplace:

```python
# Python implementation
def prediction(x, weight, bias):
    return weight * x + bias
```

For your reference, here's the Solidity function that we'll add to allow sellers and buyers to verify the precision of the model by making predictions:

```
// Solidity implementation
function prediction(uint256 _x, uint256 _weight, uint256 _bias) public pure
returns(uint256) {
 return _weight * _x + _bias;
}
```

The cost function

To train our linear-regression algorithm to generate accurate predictions, we need a cost function. A cost function is one way to analyze how well our prediction function is working for our dataset. It gives us an error rate, which is essentially the difference between the real-world result versus the prediction. The smaller the error, the better predictions we'll make. The cost function takes the real result and the prediction to output the error from our model, like so:

```
error = result - prediction
```

There are many different types of cost functions. In our case, we'll use the **mean squared error** (**MSE**) cost function, which looks like this:

```
error = sum((result - prediction)²) / numberOfDataPoints
```

To make it clearer, we can add the prediction function with all the parameters so that you can see how the variables play our in the cost function, as shown in the following code:

```
error = sum((result - prediction(x, weight, bias))²) / numberOfDataPoints
```

Here, `sum()` is the addition of all the real results minus the prediction squared, the sum of all the resulting dataset values. All of this is divided by the number of data points. Remember that `result` is the actual value that we are trying to predict. For instance, going back to our previous example where we are trying to predict how many sales we'll get per visitor, the `result` would be `10` sales, which comes from 200 visitors, while prediction is our own estimation from the weight and bias.

To help you understand the function better, consider the following example dataset of fake gun owners in a country and crimes per country; in this example, we are interested in learning how the number of guns affects the number of crimes per country. Using this data, we can predict crimes so that we can mobilize a specific number of police officers to deal with these situations. Remember that this is fake data to illustrate how the cost function will work:

Country	Total number of guns	Number of crimes per year
Germany	3,520	20
Estonia	192	3
Bahamas	91	0
Brazil	9,271	88

We first initialize our prediction function with a random weight and bias as shown in the following code:

```
// Our prediction function definition for you to remember how it looked
like
y = weight * x + bias

// Our prediction function with random weight and bias
prediction = 0.1 * x + 0.4
```

The prediction of crimes for Germany would look like the following:

```
prediction = 0.1 * 3520 + 0.4 = 352.4 crimes per year
```

We get `352.4` crimes, which we can approximate to 352, since it doesn't make sense to talk about crimes in terms of decimal points. As you can see, our prediction with that weight and bias is higher than the real result of 20 crimes per year, since our model isn't trained yet, so it's normal to expect huge differences what using real values.

Then we calculate the cost function for all of those values. Let's see how it looks for Germany:

```
// Our cost function definition for you to remember how it looked like
error = sum((result - prediction)²) / numberOfDataPoints

// Our cost function for the initial dataset
error = sum((20 - 352)²) / 1
```

We are applying the cost function for one data point to see the error of the initial prediction so that you can see how it's applied. Here's the result:

```
error = (20 - 352)² / 1 = 110224
```

The error is `110224`, which is a gigantic number, since we are applying it to one data point and our model isn't trained yet. Now do the same for all the data points until you generate the error for the entire dataset. Hopefully, you will understand the process to calculate the error with that example.

We need to calculate the error to optimize our prediction function to make more accurate predictions later on. Now that the concept is clear, we can implement that function in Python. In Solidity, we want it to calculate the error from a specific solution for our marketplace in order to discard those that have an excessively large error. The `cost` function in Python will be used by the buyers to verify the result of their training, and it will be used by sellers in Solidity to verify the submissions. Let's look at the following code:

```python
# The cost function implemented in python
def cost(results, weight, bias, xs):
    error = 0.0
    numberOfDataPoints = len(xs)
    for i in range(numberOfDataPoints):
        error += (results[i] - (weight * xs[i] + bias)) ** 2
    return error / numberOfDataPoints
```

The `xs` parameter is an array of independent variables, x—that we saw in the prediction function. Here's how it looks in Solidity; because it's a pure function, we don't have to worry about gas costs since everything will be executed locally without having to modify the state from the blockchain:

```solidity
// The cost function implemented in solidity
function cost(int256[] memory _results, int256 _weight, int256 _bias,
int256[] memory _xs) public pure returns(int256) {
    require(_results.length == _xs.length, 'There must be the same number
of _results than _xs values');
    int256 error = 0; // Notice the int instead of uint since we want
negative values too
    uint256 numberOfDataPoints = _xs.length;
    for(uint256 i = 0; i < numberOfDataPoints; i++) {
        error += (_results[i] - (_weight * _xs[i] + _bias)) * (_results[i]
- (_weight * _xs[i] + _bias));
    }
    return error / int256(numberOfDataPoints);
}
```

As you can see, we've included the prediction function inside the `for` loop to calculate the result minus the prediction squared so that we can calculate the error from the `cost` function. This will be used by sellers who want to optimize a specific linear regression from a buyer to make accurate predictions.

The optimization algorithm

Now that we can make predictions given some parameters and calculate the precision of those predictions with the cost function, we have to work on improving those predictions by reducing the error. How do we reduce the error generated from the cost function? By adjusting the weight and bias of our prediction function with an optimization algorithm. In this case, we'll use gradient descent, which allows us to continuously reduce the error. Here's a graph that explains how it works:

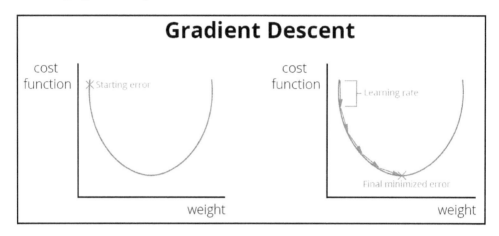

We start with a high error caused by random weight and bias values, then we reduce the error by optimizing those parameters until we reach a good-enough prediction model, the local minimum in the graph. The idea is to calculate the partial derivatives of the **weight** and **bias** to see how they affect the final prediction until we reach the minimum. We won't get into the math of calculating those derivatives, since it could lead to confusion, so the resulting function with the partial derivatives looks like this:

```
weightDerivative = sum(-2x * (result - (x * weight + bias))) /
numberOfDataPoints

biasDerivative = sum(-2 * (result - (x * weight + bias))) /
numberOfDataPoints
```

Let's take a look at the implementation of those functions to update the weight and bias of our machine learning algorithm:

```
# Python implementation, returns the optimized weight and bias for that
step
def optimizeWeightBias(results, weight, bias, xs, learningRate):
    weightDerivative = 0
    biasDerivative = 0
```

```
    numberOfDataPoints = len(results)
    for i in range(numberOfDataPoints):
        weightDerivative += (-2 * xs[i] * (results[i] - (xs[i] * weight +
bias)) / numberOfDataPoints)
        biasDerivative += (-2 * (results[i] - (xs[i] * weight + bias)) /
numberOfDataPoints)

    weight -= weightDerivative * learningRate
    bias -= biasDerivative * learningRate
    return weight, bias
```

In Solidity, it will look like this:

```
// Solidity implementation
function optimize(int256[] memory _results, int256 _weight, int256 _bias,
int256[] memory _xs, int256 _learningRate) public pure returns(int256,
int256) {
    require(_results.length == _xs.length, 'There must be the same number
of _results than _xs values');
    int256 weightDerivative = 0;
    int256 biasDerivative = 0;
    uint256 numberOfDataPoints = _xs.length;
    for(uint256 i = 0; i < numberOfDataPoints; i++) {
        weightDerivative += (-2 * _xs[i] * (_results[i] - (_xs[i] * _weight
+ _bias)) / int256(numberOfDataPoints));
        biasDerivative += (-2 * (_results[i] - (_xs[i] * _weight + _bias))
/ int256(numberOfDataPoints));
    }
    _weight = weightDerivative * _learningRate;
    _bias = biasDerivative * _learningRate;
    return (_weight, _bias);
}
```

As you can see, we are calculating both derivatives by using the functions described in the preceding code block so that we can update the weight and bias with the optimized values. The learning rate is the size of the steps we take to reach the minimum point of the graph. If we take big steps, we may miss the minimum, and if we take small steps, we may take too much time to reach that minimum. In any case, it's best to keep a balanced learning rate and try different step sizes. Now we have a way to improve our prediction function.

The train function

We can begin to improve our model with a new function that loops through several optimization calls until we reach the minimum, at which point the model will be fully optimized. Here's what it looks like:

```python
# Python implementation
def train(results, weight, bias, xs, learningRate, iterations):
 error = 0
 for i in range(iterations):
    weight, bias = optimizeWeightBias(results, weight, bias, xs,
learningRate)
    error = cost(results, weight, bias, xs)
    print("Iteration: {}, weight: {:.4f}, bias: {:.4f}, error:
{:.2}".format(i, weight, bias, error))
 return weight, bias
```

The Solidity implementation looks pretty similar, although we have to make sure that the results and independent variables, values have the same length to avoid errors, as shown in the following code:

```solidity
// Solidity implementation
function train(int256[] memory _results, int256 _weight, int256 _bias,
int256[] memory _xs, int256 _learningRate, uint256 _iterations) public pure
returns(int256, int256) {
    require(_results.length == _xs.length, 'There must be the same number
of _results than _xs values');
    int256 error = 0;
    for(uint256 i = 0; i < _iterations; i++) {
        (_weight, _bias) = optimize(_results, _weight, _bias, _xs,
_learningRate);
        error = cost(_results, _weight, _bias, _xs);
    }
    return (_weight, _bias);
}
```

As you can see, we are using the optimization function along with the cost function to continuously reduce the error by updating the weight and bias parameters for the specified number of iterations.

Now you should be able to create and train linear regression models to make predictions using the prediction function after training your model with the train function. The following is the full Python code for your reference, although you can see the updated version on the official GitHub at https://github.com/merlox/machine-learning-ethereum/blob/master/linearRegression.py.

We start by creating the constructor, which will train the model with some initial random values using the `uniform` library because it returns a floating number between 0 and 1, as shown in the following code:

```
from random import uniform

class LinearRegression:
    xs = [3520, 192, 91, 9271]
    results = [20, 3, 0, 88]

    def __init__(self):
        initialWeight = uniform(0, 1)
        initialBias = uniform(0, 1)
        learningRate = 0.00000004
        iterations = 2000
        print('Initial weight {}, Initial bias {}, Learning rate {},
Iterations {}'.format(initialWeight, initialBias, learningRate,
iterations))
        finalWeight, finalBias = self.train(self.results, initialWeight,
initialBias, self.xs, learningRate, iterations)
        finalError = self.cost(self.results, finalWeight, finalBias,
self.xs)
        print('Final weight {:.4f}, Final bias {:.4f}, Final error {:.4f},
Prediction {:.4f} out of {}, Prediction Two {:.4f} out of
{}'.format(finalWeight, finalBias, finalError, self.prediction(self.xs[1],
finalWeight, finalBias), self.results[1], self.prediction(self.xs[3],
finalWeight, finalBias), self.results[3]))
```

Then we implement the `prediction` and `cost` function, as you just learned, down below the constructor, as shown in the following code:

```
    # Python implementation
    def prediction(self, x, weight, bias):
        return weight * x + bias

    # The cost function implemented in python
    def cost(self, results, weight, bias, xs):
        error = 0.0
        numberOfDataPoints = len(xs)
        for i in range(numberOfDataPoints):
            error += (results[i] - (weight * xs[i] + bias)) ** 2
        return error / numberOfDataPoints
```

After that, we add the optimized weights and the bias function, as shown in the following code:

```python
    # Python implementation, returns the optimized weight and bias for that
step
    def optimizeWeightBias(self, results, weight, bias, xs, learningRate):
        weightDerivative = 0
        biasDerivative = 0
        numberOfDataPoints = len(results)
        for i in range(numberOfDataPoints):
            weightDerivative += -2 * xs[i] * (results[i] - (xs[i] * weight
+ bias))
            biasDerivative += -2 * (results[i] - (xs[i] * weight + bias))

        weight -= (weightDerivative / numberOfDataPoints) * learningRate
        bias -= (biasDerivative / numberOfDataPoints) * learningRate

        return weight, bias
```

Finally, we complete the code by creating the `train` function and initialize the class outside the scope of the class, as shown in the following code:

```python
    # Python implementation
    def train(self, results, weight, bias, xs, learningRate, iterations):
        error = 0
        for i in range(iterations):
            weight, bias = self.optimizeWeightBias(results, weight, bias,
xs, learningRate)
            error = self.cost(results, weight, bias, xs)
            print("Iteration: {}, weight: {:.4f}, bias: {:.4f}, error:
{:.2f}".format(i, weight, bias, error))
        return weight, bias

# Initialize the class
LinearRegression()
```

As you can see, we've created a Python class that runs the `train` function in the constructor. Don't worry if you're not familiar with Python; you just have to understand that the code is training our linear-regression algorithm for more precise calculations. Create a file called `linearRegression.py` and write the code there. Then you can run it with the following command line:

```
python linearRegression.py
```

You'll see that the program is constantly reducing the error by taking small steps toward the minimum until it gets to a point where it doesn't improve much. That's okay: we expect it to make precise predictions, but without 100% accuracy. You can then take the final weight and bias to make predictions on your own for that machine learning model.

Let's look at the smart contract marketplace to see how users will interact with it. Our goal is to provide a place where machine learning developers can upload their model with a payment in Ethereum with the aim of getting the solution from several sellers, from which a winner will be selected based on the error or the buyer's choice. Let's take a look at the following code:

```solidity
pragma solidity 0.5.5;

contract MachineLearningMarketplace {}
```

We can start adding variables to create our desired application, as shown in the following code:

```solidity
pragma solidity 0.5.5;

contract MachineLearningMarketplace {
    event AddedJob(uint256 indexed id, uint256 indexed timestamp);
    event AddedResult(uint256 indexed id, uint256 indexed timestamp,
address indexed sender);
    event SelectedWinner(uint256 indexed id, uint256 indexed timestamp,
address indexed winner, uint256 trainedIdSelected);

    struct Model {
        uint256 id;
        string datasetUrl;
        uint256 weight;
        uint256 bias;
        uint256 payment;
        uint256 timestamp;
        address payable owner;
        bool isOpen;
    }
    mapping(uint256 => Model) public models;
    mapping(uint256 => Model[]) public trainedModels;
    uint256 public latestId;
}
```

We've added three events to notify users that a new job or result has been added, as well as when a winner for a proposal is selected. That way, people will be notified when their proposal gets updated. Then we have a struct named `Model`, which represents our desired linear regression ML model with the dataset, weight, bias, and payment, among other important variables. Finally, we've added a couple of mappings to sort models created by buyers (those that pay to get their model trained) and those models created by sellers, those that train the model from the dataset and upload a specific weight and bias in order to win if they are selected by the buyer. `latestId` is an identifier to signify which model is the latest.

A model that is open means it is still running, so you can send a proposal and participate in it for a chance to get selected. If it's closed, you will be able to participate, but know that you won't be able to win since the winner has been selected already.

Let's move on to the three most important functions of our ML marketplace. The upload job function looks like the following:

```
/// @notice To upload a model in order to train it
/// @param _dataSetUrl The url with the json containing the array of data
function uploadJob(string memory _dataSetUrl) public payable {
    require(msg.value > 0, 'You must send some ether to get your model
trained');
    Model memory m = Model(latestId, _dataSetUrl, 0, 0, msg.value, now,
msg.sender, true);
    models[latestId] = m;
    emit AddedJob(latestId, now);
    latestId += 1;
}
```

Here's the upload results function, with some added documentation to clarify the parameters used inside:

```
/// @notice To upload the result of a trained model
/// @param _id The id of the trained model
/// @param _weight The final trained weight, it must be with 10 decimals
meaning that 1 weight is 1e10 so that you can do smaller fractions such as
0.01 which would be 1e8 or 100000000
/// @param _bias The final trained bias, it must be with 10 decimals as the
weight
function uploadResult(uint256 _id, uint256 _weight, uint256 _bias) public {
    Model memory m = Model(_id, models[_id].datasetUrl, _weight, _bias,
models[_id].payment, now, msg.sender, true);
    trainedModels[_id].push(m);
    emit AddedResult(_id, now, msg.sender);
}
```

Finally, here's the choose results function, which is quite lengthy because we must make sure that the job is open and that a winner has not been selected yet. If there are no winners selected after three days, the first applicant wins the reward to avoid losing Ether:

```
/// @notice To choose a winner by the sender
/// @param _id The id of the model
/// @param _arrayIdSelected The array index of the selected winner
function chooseResult(uint256 _id, uint256 _arrayIdSelected) public {
    Model memory m = models[_id];
    Model[] memory t = trainedModels[_id];
    require(m.isOpen, 'The job must be open to choose a result');
    // If 3 days have passed the winner will be the first one, otherwise
the owner is allowed to choose a winner before 3 full days
    if(now - m.timestamp < 3 days) {
        require(msg.sender == m.owner, 'Only the owner can select the
winner');
        t[_arrayIdSelected].owner.transfer(m.payment);
        models[_id].isOpen = false;
        emit SelectedWinner(_id, now, t[_arrayIdSelected].owner,
t[_arrayIdSelected].id);
    } else {
        // If there's more than one result, send it to the first
        if(t.length > 0) {
            t[0].owner.transfer(m.payment);
            emit SelectedWinner(_id, now, t[0].owner, t[0].id);
        } else {
            // Send it to the owner if none applied to the job
            m.owner.transfer(m.payment);
            emit SelectedWinner(_id, now, msg.sender, 0);
        }
        models[_id].isOpen = false;
    }
}
```

The uploadJob function will be used by buyers to publish their dataset and payment in order to get their model trained by participants all over the world. The uploadResult function will be used by sellers to get information about a job to train the specified dataset until the error is minimized. Finally, the chooseResult function is the one that is used by buyers to select a winner proposal for a determined job. The creator of the job has three days to select a winning proposal. If after three days no one has applied, then the payment will be returned to the owner. If there are participants, but the owner hasn't selected a winner, the reward will be sent to the first participant in compensation for their speed; in that case, this function has to be executed by an external user to execute the payment.

Those are the main components that make our ML marketplace work; however, we need a few functions to help people interact with it. Here are the new functions that are added to the ML marketplace broken down in pieces to help you understand them better.

First, we create the cost function with complete documentation so that we can understand what it's doing:

```
/// @notice The cost function implemented in solidity
/// @param _results The resulting uint256 for a particular data element
/// @param _weight The weight of the trained model
/// @param _bias The bias of the trained model
/// @param _xs The independent variable for our trained model to test the
prediction
/// @return int256 Returns the total error of the model
function cost(int256[] memory _results, int256 _weight, int256 _bias,
int256[] memory _xs) public pure returns(int256) {
    require(_results.length == _xs.length, 'There must be the same number
of _results than _xs values');
    int256 error = 0; // Notice the int instead of uint since we want
negative values too
    uint256 numberOfDataPoints = _xs.length;
    for(uint256 i = 0; i < numberOfDataPoints; i++) {
        error += (_results[i] - (_weight * _xs[i] + _bias)) * (_results[i]
- (_weight * _xs[i] + _bias));
    }
    return error / int256(numberOfDataPoints);
}
```

Then we have the get model function to retrieve the variables contained in the struct model, because we can't return the struct as it is right now. We have to make these types of tricks to get the struct values independently. This function is shown in the following code:

```
/// @notice To get a model dataset, payment and timestamp
/// @param id The id of the model to get the dataset, payment and timestamp
/// @return Returns the dataset string url, payment and timestamp
function getModel(uint256 id) public view returns(string memory, uint256,
uint256) {
    return (models[id].datasetUrl, models[id].payment,
models[id].timestamp);
}
```

Then we add another getter function that gives us all the trained models for a particular ID, as shown in the following code. This is useful for sellers who want to see what proposals they got for their particular job. If we were to implement this machine learning marketplace in a dApp, we'd have to add a few more getters for the jobs and other mappings:

```
/// @notice To get all the proposed trained models for a particular id
/// @param _id The id of the model created by the buyer
/// @return uint256[], uint256[], uint256[], uint256[], address[] Returns
all those trained models separated in arrays containing ids, weights,
biases, timestamps and owners
function getAllTrainedModels(uint256 _id) public view returns(uint256[]
memory, uint256[] memory, uint256[] memory, uint256[] memory, address[]
memory) {
    uint256[] memory ids;
    uint256[] memory weights;
    uint256[] memory biases;
    uint256[] memory timestamps;
    address[] memory owners;
    for(uint256 i = 0; i < trainedModels[_id].length; i++) {
        Model memory m = trainedModels[_id][i];
        ids[i] = m.id;
        weights[i] = m.weight;
        biases[i] = m.bias;
        timestamps[i] = m.timestamp;
        owners[i] = m.owner;
    }
    return (ids, weights, biases, timestamps, owners);
}
```

We have a `cost` function to quickly verify the results uploaded by a proposed seller, a `getModel` function that will be mainly used by sellers who want to get more specific information about a model, and a `getAllTrainedModels` function that returns the participants of a particular job. Note how we're returning the most important variables in the struct instead of the entire struct. We are doing this for the simple reason that we can't return structs yet in Solidity, so we have to separate each variable and return an array for each.

The general workflow of this marketplace is as follows:

1. A buyer with a machine learning model to train uploads their dataset and payment to the marketplace with the `uploadJob` function.
2. An `AddedJob` event gets generated, which notifies users that are interested in participating in this marketplace of that new job. They can listen to those events by using **web3** or external dApps, since the contract is open source.
3. Sellers read the model data—particularly the timestamps, since that's the most important piece of information—with the `getModel` function using the `id` model they've received from the event. Then they start training the model using the Python application we built earlier or their own, since there are many different ways that you can train a linear-regression algorithm.
4. They upload their trained weight and bias to that job as a new proposal using the `uploadResult` function. This will fire the `AddedResult` event, which will notify the buyer whether they're listening to updates so that they can choose a winner.
5. Before three days have passed since the job was created, the buyer goes through the proposals, comparing the error generated by each proposal with the `cost` function or their own implementation. They'll almost certainly choose the result with the smallest error, although they can choose whichever they want. After selecting one, the state of the model will change to `isOpen = false`, which means that the winner is selected and the `SelectedWinner` event gets fired.

That's it! You now are able to upload and train linear-regression models on the blockchain.

Summary

In this chapter, you learned the fundamental utility of combining blockchain and ML, since they are almost opposites, meaning that they complement each other well to create optimal security and performance. We started with a general explanation of ML so that you could understand all the hype by taking a quick look at the process of generating and training machine learning models. Then we dove deeper into the technical functionalities of the application so you got a clear vision of where machine learning and blockchain meet. Finally, we built the machine learning marketplace, as it's a great combination of both technologies. You saw how the linear-regression algorithm works step by step with an implementation in Python and Solidity. We built the marketplace, where users from all over the world train and exchange computational resources for each task, creating a great secure open source platform where people interact without censorship, fees, or centralization.

In the next chapter, we'll explore advanced Ethereum implementations similar to what you saw in this chapter, but with different industries, starting with a blockchain-based social media platform that combines decentralization with social interactions on the internet.

11
Creating a Blockchain-based Social Media Platform

Mastering Ethereum development starts with a lot of theory and technicality, but, at some point you'll have to take the leap in order to start applying your recently-acquired knowledge on real-world scenarios that build your portfolio. That's why we're going to create a blockchain-based social media platform, since it's one of the best use cases of blockchain technology, given that we provide people with trust. Unfortunately, many centralized social media companies are abusing that trust by stealing and monetizing users' privacy. Social media platforms such as Twitter or Facebook are famous because they give people the power to stay in touch with many individuals in one single interface that takes advantage of the internet's capabilities.

This chapter will take you through the challenge of creating a dynamic social media platform that lives entirely on the blockchain without centralized servers. You will understand how to create a beautiful user interface with React. Then you'll explore how to organize the information better so that you allow people to find the content that they want using smart contracts. Finally, you'll tie everything together using web3 and you'll be able to use your social media platform.

In this chapter, we're going to cover the following topics:

- Understanding decentralized social media
- Creating the user interface
- Building the smart contract
- Finishing the dApp

Understanding decentralized social media

When it comes to Ethereum-based social media dApps, we help people solve many problems that current centralized companies can't solve efficiently yet. We can help with the following:

- Preserving users' privacy on a decentralized blockchain
- Guaranteeing total freedom by not allowing censorship from external, centralized entities since information on the blockchain is permanent
- An unchanging, fixed storage system that will be accessible decades after the content was created

However, when we think of building a decentralized social media platform, we lose a few of the following important aspects that are essential to modern applications:

- **Speed**: Users won't be able to use the dApp as fast as normal centralized applications for depending on a huge, slow network of interconnected computers.
- **Storage limitations**: Ethereum's space is limited so every byte is costly, resulting in a huge limitation on what you can store on the blockchain, so we'll have to find ways to overcome these natural limitations while preserving as much decentralization as possible.
- **Gas costs**: Normal centralized applications don't have to face gas fees for each action taken on their system because they understand that all those costs are paid in a centralized server. In the blockchain, every transaction has a cost that could be significant. We'll solve this by using testnets, where gas has no value until the final application is created.

Another big problem is that we can't store images and videos on the blockchain; we'll have to rely on decentralized storage solutions, such as IPFS, if we wish to preserve the decentralization from the main system; however it isn't mandatory.

The initial concept

Our goal is to create an effective social media platform that overcomes or completely avoids the limitations of the blockchain. To simplify the complexity of our dApp, we will build an application similar to Twitter in the sense that users only share text messages without the option to share images or video.

Since we are developers, we'll create a Twitter for programmers, designers, developers, and all kinds of technology-related fields where people can feel welcome in a community of shared interests. We want it to have the following functionalities:

- The capacity to share strings of text limited only by smart contract's capacity
- The capacity to add hashtags to each piece of content
- A function to be able to view hashtags that people have included in their content by clicking on a hashtag
- A function to subscribe to hashtags

We don't want people to follow others, we'll simply give them the capacity to follow hashtags so that they focus on the content rather than the messenger. Let's start working on the user interface that will become our social media dApp for tech enthusiasts to focus on content via hashtags, rather than specific users.

Creating the user interface

The user interface for this particular project will be focused around content and hashtags since hashtags are the way users will discover new trending content. Users will be able to subscribe to particular hashtags to receive content from those topics on their feed.

As usual, we start by setting up a new project with Truffle. Follow these steps to set up your project:

1. Clone the startup repository (https://github.com/merlox/dapp) which includes the initial configuration to work on your React dApp:

   ```
   git clone https://github.com/merlox/dapp
   ```

2. Rename the repository to social-media-dapp to organize the content:

   ```
   mv dapp/ social-media-dapp/
   ```

3. Create a new empty GitHub repository by going to GitHub (without a license or .gitignore since they are already included in your project) and use the following command to update the pull/push URL:

   ```
   git config remote.origin.url
   https://<YOUR-USERNAME>:<YOUR-PASSWORD>@github.com/<YOUR-USERNAME>/
   social-media-dapp
   ```

4. Push the first commit. Install the dependencies with `npm i` and run `webpack` with `webpack -wd`.

5. Open up your application by running a static server with `http-server dist/` and going to `http://localhost: 8080` to see whether everything was set up properly.

Now you can start creating your user interface. You already know how to do it, so why not go ahead and create your own before seeing mine? You'll be amazed at what you're capable of doing by yourself at this point, so I encourage you to experiment to build your own systems. The idea is that we build this dApp together by guiding you through the steps until you have a high-quality dApp that you can use to build your resume or develop further for an ICO, or as open source software for the betterment of humanity.

Configuring the webpack style

At the end, you'll have to have two sections: one with the most popular hashtags, which will come from a mapping in our smart contract, and one where you can read more about each specific hashtag while being able to publish content. You may want to set up the style loader to be able to use css on your dApp, which is not set up on the default dApp that you just cloned. To do so, install the following dependencies after stopping webpack:

```
npm i -S style-loader css-loader
```

Now that you installed the required libraries to be able to use CSS files inside your project, you can update your webpack configuration file by adding a new loader inside the `loaders` block for the `css` files. Pay attention to the fact that we're using both loaders – `style-loader` goes first. Otherwise, it won't work:

```
{
    test: /\.css$/,
    exclude: /node_modules/,
    use: [
        { loader: 'style-loader' },
        { loader: 'css-loader' }
    ]
}
```

Setting up the initial structure

Open the index.js file and start creating your user interface. First, I start with the constructor by creating some necessary variables that we'll use later on:

1. Set up the required imports for any React project plus the css file that we can now import thanks to the style and css loaders:

```
import React from 'react'
import ReactDOM from 'react-dom'
import './index.css'
```

2. Set up the constructor with some dummy data to see how the final application will look once we populate it with variables from the smart contract:

```
class Main extends React.Component {
    constructor() {
        super()

        this.state = {
            content: [{
                author:
'0x211824098yf7320417812j1002341342342341234',
                message: 'This is a test',
                hashtags: ['test', 'dapp', 'blockchain'],
                time: new Date().toLocaleDateString(),
            }, {
                author:
'0x211824098yf7320417812j1002341342342341234',
                message: 'This is another test',
                hashtags: ['sample', 'dapp', 'Ethereum'],
                time: new Date().toLocaleDateString(),
            }],
            topHashtags: ['dapp', 'Ethereum', 'blockchain',
'technology', 'design'],
            followedHashtags: ['electronics', 'design', 'robots',
'futurology', 'manufacturing'],
            displaySubscribe: false,
            displaySubscribeId: '',
        }
    }
```

3. Create the `render()` function with the `ReactDOM` render:

```
render() {
    return (
        <div className="main-container">
        </div>
    )
}
}

ReactDOM.render(<Main />, document.querySelector('#root'))
```

As you can see, the state of our application contains the `content` object with an Ethereum address as the author of that piece, the message, the hashtags, and the time. We may later change that, but for now it's good enough. We also added two arrays, which contain the top hashtags and the followed tags for this particular user. Those display subscribe variables are a necessary evil to display a subscribe button every time a user hovers a hashtag so that they have the choice to subscribe to improve interactivity of the dApp.

Rendering hashtags

We can now create the render function with all the logic, but be warned: it's a bit complex given that we are displaying all the arrays from the state, so be patient and see the code in chunks to understand it. Follow these steps:

1. Create a new function to generate the hashtag's HTML, because we want to add variable logic to the buttons to be sure that the `hashtag` text reacts to the user displaying the subscribe or unsubscribe button. Remember that we want users to be able to follow hashtags; that's why we need subscribe and unsubscribe buttons:

```
generateHashtags(hashtag, index) {
    let timeout
    return (
        <span onMouseEnter={() => {
            clearTimeout(timeout)
            this.setState({
                displaySubscribe: true,
                displaySubscribeId: `subscribe-${hashtag}-
${index}`,
            })
        }} onMouseLeave={() => {
            timeout = setTimeout(() => {
                this.setState({
```

```
                        displaySubscribe: false,
                        displaySubscribeId: '',
                    })
                }, 2e3)
            }}>
                <a className="hashtag" href="#">#{hashtag}</a>
                <span className="spacer"></span>
                <button ref={`subscribe-${hashtag}-${index}`}
className={this.state.displaySubscribe &&
this.state.displaySubscribeId == `subscribe-${hashtag}-${index}` ?
'' : 'hidden'} type="button">Subscribe</button>
                <span className="spacer"></span>
            </span>
        )
    }
```

2. Update the `render()` function to generate the content and hashtag blocks because we need a simple way of creating the content to be displayed; all the logic will be executed in the `render()` function:

```
render() {
    let contentBlock = this.state.content.map((element, index) => (
        <div key={index} className="content">
            <div className="content-address">{element.author}</div>
            <div className="content-
message">{element.message}</div>
            <div className="content-
hashtags">{element.hashtags.map((hashtag, i) => (
                <span key={i}>
                    {this.generateHashtags(hashtag, index)}
                </span>
            ))}
            </div>
            <div className="content-time">{element.time}</div>
        </div>
    ))
```

3. Add the hashtag blocks, whose only job is to create the JSX objects that will be displayed to the user, with the `generateHashtags()` function that we just used:

```
let hashtagBlock = this.state.topHashtags.map((hashtag, index) => (
    <div key={index}>
        {this.generateHashtags(hashtag, index)}
    </div>
))
let followedHashtags = this.state.followedHashtags.map((hashtag,
index) => (
    <div key={index}>
```

```
                    {this.generateHashtags(hashtag, index)}
            </div>
        ))
```

4. At the end of the `render()` function, add the `return` block with the block variables that we just set up:

```
    return (
        <div className="main-container">
            <div className="hashtag-block">
                <h3>Top hashtags</h3>
                <div className="hashtag-
container">{hashtagBlock}</div>
                <h3>Followed hashtags</h3>
                <div className="hashtag-
container">{followedHashtags}</div>
            </div>
            <div className="content-block">
                <div className="input-container">
                    <textarea placeholder="Publish
content..."></textarea>
                    <input type="text" placeholder="Hashtags
separated by commas..."/>
                    <button type="button">Publish</button>
                </div>

                <div className="content-container">
                    {contentBlock}
                </div>
            </div>
        </div>
    )
}
```

We added a function named `generateHashtags` since we have to add the same logic to display the subscribe button in many places, so it made sense to craft a function that does precisely that when needed without duplicating these long blocks of code. Then, in the `render()` function, you can see that we are using that function to generate the hashtag logic in the many places where hashtags will be used. Before the return, we have three variables that are simply generating JSX components dynamically with our state data. Finally, the `render()` function is displaying those blocks nicely.

Improving the appearance

I've also imported the `index.css` file, which includes grid components for displaying our application in the best way possible, with a clean structure that is easy to maintain:

1. Add the general styling to the main components of your application, such as the body and buttons, to make them look better:

```
body {
    margin: 0;
    background-color: whitesmoke;
    font-family: sans-serif;
}

button {
    background-color: rgb(201, 47, 47);
    color: white;
    border-radius: 15px;
    border: none;
    cursor: pointer;
}

button:hover {
    background-color: rgb(131, 0, 0);
}
```

2. Add the general hidden and spacer styles to hide elements and to create a dynamic spacer:

```
.hidden {
    display: none;
}

.spacer {
    margin-right: 5px;
}
```

3. Add the container's styles to position them with the grid system that is now accepted on all major browsers:

```
.main-container {
    display: grid;
    grid-template-columns: 30% 70%;
    margin: auto;
    width: 50%;
    grid-column-gap: 10px;
}
```

```
.input-container {
    margin-bottom: 10px;
    padding: 30px;
    display: grid;
    grid-template-columns: 80% 1fr;
    grid-template-rows: 70% 30%;
    grid-gap: 10px;
}
```

4. Format the input and text areas to create a better-looking design that is easy to use:

```
.input-container textarea {
    padding: 10px;
    border-radius: 10px;
    font-size: 11pt;
    font-family: sans-serif;
    border: 1px solid grey;
    grid-column: 1 / 3;
}

.input-container input {
    padding: 10px;
    border-radius: 10px;
    font-size: 11pt;
    font-family: sans-serif;
    border: 1px solid grey;
}
```

5. Provide a great-looking design for all the elements for the content block, which is similar to a tweet in Twitter:

```
.content {
    background-color: white;
    border: 1px solid grey;
    margin-bottom: 10px;
    padding: 30px;
    box-shadow: 4px 4px 0px 0 #cecece;
}
.content-address {
    color: grey;
    margin-bottom: 5px;
}
.content-message {
    font-size: 16pt;
    margin-bottom: 5px;
}
.content-hashtags {
```

```
        margin-bottom: 5px;
    }
    .content-time {
        color: grey;
        font-size: 12pt;
    }
```

6. Format those hashtags to position them in the right places while also increasing their size:

```
.hashtag-block {
    text-align: center;
}

.hashtag-container {
    line-height: 30px;
}

.hashtag {
    font-size: 15pt;
}
```

7. You can copy and paste that css if you want to achieve the same look. Here's the appearance of the dApp right now:

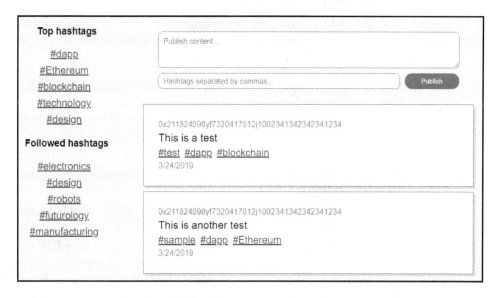

8. You can check the completed code on GitHub at `https://github.com/merlox/social-media-dapp/tree/master/src`.

I tried to emulate a simple sort of cartoon design to make it more interesting to visualize, while keeping a clear interface that people can read easily without confusion. Pay attention to the user interfaces that you create because they are a major component of every dApp. A dApp that looks professional will draw more attention. More attention usually transforms into more revenue as you are capable of directing people's attention to the right places at the right moments.

Building the smart contract

The smart contract that we are going to build will serve as the backend for our decentralized application by storing all the messages, hashtags, and users. In our application, we want to keep users anonymous; that's why they are represented as addresses instead of usernames – to direct people's attention to what's being talked about, not to who is delivering the message.

As you already know, we'll create a hashtag-focused social media platform without images or video. That's why all of our data will be stored in a combination of mappings and arrays.

Planning the design process

Before getting straight to the code, I want you to understand the process that we'll follow to optimize the entire process, avoid confusion, and save time by avoiding bugs with a clear head about what needs to be done. The process looks like so:

1. Create a smart contract file and write in the comments a description of the purpose of the contract, such as how the functions will work and who will use it. Be as concise as possible since it will help you and the maintainers understand what it is all about.
2. Start creating variables and function signatures, that is, functions without body, just the name and parameters. Document each function using the NatSpec format for additional clarifications.
3. Start implementing each function independently until all of them are done. You can add more if you need to.
4. Manually test the contract by copy-pasting it to remix or any other IDE to quickly find problems and run all the functions in a virtual EVM where you don't have to pay any gas or wait for confirmations. Ideally, you'd write Truffle tests to verify that everything is working, but sometimes it can be skipped to save time.

Here's a graphic of the process so you can keep it in mind:

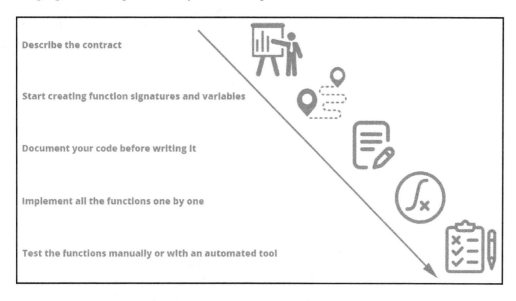

This type of process is the one I follow for maximizing my productivity without going crazy with specs. If you start coding immediately on a solution, you risk getting stuck in a place where you have to remake the entire code base while creating unneeded bugs in the process. That's why planning is so important. Besides, it will make your life much easier knowing exactly what to do, and when.

Now we can start creating our smart contract by describing the idea behind it. Create a file named `SocialMusic.sol` inside your `contracts/` folder and write a description of what should be in the final version of that contract at the top of the file in comments. Try to do it yourself before looking at my own solution since the only way to learn is to practice by yourself:

```
// This is a social media smart contract that allows people to publish
strings of text in short formats with a focus on hashtags so that they can
follow, read and be in touch with the latest content regarding those
hashtags. There will be a mapping of the top hashtags. A struct for each
piece of content with the date, author, content and array of hashtags. We
want to avoid focusing on specific users that's why user accounts will be
anonymous where addresses will the be the only identifiers.

pragma solidity ^0.5.5;

contract SocialMedia {}
```

Whether you realize it or not, you've clarified your mind a whole lot by writing the description. Now you can start creating the functions and variables. Given that you have a user interface already in place, you'll want to break that interface into blocks and create the functions that will provide the data shown in those blocks; for instance, take a look at the following block of your application:

```
┌─────────────────────┐
│ Top hashtags        │
│                     │
│      #dapp          │
│    #Ethereum        │
│    #blockchain      │
│    #technology      │
│      #design        │
└─────────────────────┘
```

You can obviously see the top hashtags with some random hashtags. You must ask yourself when looking at the interface, what do I need to implement in my smart contract to make that possible? Well, it seems obvious, but often it is not that easy. In this case, you have to create a function to retrieve the top hashtags. That function will get the data from a sorted array or mappings to send it to the user, maybe a parameter to determine how many top hashtags to retrieve at any moment so that you can experiment with different quantities. To create that function, you'll have to implement some kind of sorting mechanism, probably a view or pure function that doesn't consume gas to process. On the other hand, how do you determine the order of those hashtags? Probably a score system that increases the value of each hashtag, depending on the use.

You see, from a small obvious piece of our entire application, you came to the realization that you need the following:

- An array or mapping with the top tags that need to be sorted.
- A function to retrieve those hashtags with an optional parameter to determine how many so that you can experiment with them.
- A function to sort existing hashtags in a way that makes sense considering the limitations of the blockchain. It must be a pure or view function to avoid excessive gas costs.
- A system to give a score for each hashtag so that we can order them depending on their popularity.

You have to do the same analytical process for each component of your application. No matter how obvious it may seem, try to describe those pieces in your mind so that you visualize what's needed and what's possible beforehand to save yourself hours of frustration and buggy code.

Setting up the data structures

After doing the required planning, feel free to write the function signatures for all of the needed parts by performing the following steps:

1. Define the variables that you'll use later on with structs and events first:

```
struct Content {
    uint256 id;
    address author;
    uint256 date;
    string content;
    bytes32[] hashtags;
}

event ContentAdded(uint256 indexed id, address indexed author,
uint256 indexed date, string content, bytes32[] hashtags);
```

2. Add the mappings, arrays, and remaining state variables:

```
mapping(address => bytes32[]) public subscribedHashtags;
mapping(bytes32 => uint256) public hashtagScore; // The number of
times this hashtag has been used, used to sort the top hashtags
mapping(bytes32 => Content[]) public contentByHashtag;
mapping(uint256 => Content) public contentById;
mapping(bytes32 => bool) public doesHashtagExist;
mapping(address => bool) public doesUserExist;
address[] public users;
Content[] public contents;
bytes32[] public hashtags;
uint256 public latestContentId;
```

3. Define the function signatures:

```
function addContent(string memory _content, bytes32[] memory
_hashtags) public {}
function subscribeToHashtag(bytes32 _hashtag) public {}
function unsubscribeToHashtag(bytes32 _hashtag) public {}
function getTopHashtags(uint256 _amount) public view
returns(bytes32[] memory) {}
function getFollowedHashtags() public view returns(bytes32[]
memory) {}
function getContentIdsByHashtag(bytes32 _hashtag, uint256 _amount)
public view returns(uint256[] memory) {}
function getContentById(uint256 _id) public view returns(uint256,
address, uint256, string memory, bytes32[] memory) {}
function sortHashtagsByScore() public view returns(bytes32[]
memory) {}
```

```
function checkExistingSubscription(bytes32 _hashtag) public view
returns(bool) {}
```

Are you surprised by the number of functions and variables that we came up with in a moment? You probably didn't consider functions such as `checkExistingSubscription` or `getContentIdsByHashtag` during that process. I'll be honest, I didn't know that those functions were needed before writing the contract; it's just after creating the entire code that they became necessary. It's okay if you don't come up with all the required variables and functions before creating the code. They will surface at the right moment as you develop. You don't have to write all the functions and plan every single function and variable beforehand; that would be insane. So be patient, and know that, after implementing your initial functions, you may need to add a few additional ones to have the desired functionality.

Documenting the future functions

Those function are not clear enough yet, so why don't you write the NatSpec documentation about each one of them? It's a tedious process but you'll thank yourself for it since it will remind you of what you're doing while coding. Here is my version with the included documentation:

1. Start with the add content, subscribe, and unsubscribe functions:

```
/// @notice To add new content to the social media dApp. If no
hashtags are sent, the content is added to the #general hashtag
list.
/// @param _content The string of content
/// @param _hashtags The hashtags used for that piece of content
function addContent(string memory _content, bytes32[] memory
_hashtags) public {}

/// @notice To subscribe to a hashtag if you didn't do so already
/// @param _hashtag The hashtag name
function subscribeToHashtag(bytes32 _hashtag) public {}

/// @notice To unsubscribe to a hashtag if you are subscribed
otherwise it won't do nothing
/// @param _hashtag The hashtag name
function unsubscribeToHashtag(bytes32 _hashtag) public {}
```

2. The getter functions for the top and followed hashtags. We need these functions to display them on the sidebar of the user interface:

```
/// @notice To get the top hashtags
/// @param _amount How many top hashtags to get in order, for
instance the top 20 hashtags
/// @return bytes32[] Returns the names of the hashtags
function getTopHashtags(uint256 _amount) public view
returns(bytes32[] memory) {}


/// @notice To get the followed hashtag names for this msg.sender
/// @return bytes32[] The hashtags followed by this user
function getFollowedHashtags() public view returns(bytes32[]
memory) {}
```

3. The getter functions by ID. We need them to return the struct variables broken down into individual pieces:

```
/// @notice To get the contents for a particular hashtag. It
returns the ids because we can't return arrays of strings and we
can't return structs so the user has to manually make a new request
for each piece of content using the function below.
/// @param _hashtag The hashtag from which get content
/// @param _amount The quantity of contents to get for instance, 50
pieces of content for that hashtag
/// @return uint256[] Returns the ids of the contents so that you
can get each piece independently with a new request since you can't
return arrays of strings
function getContentIdsByHashtag(bytes32 _hashtag, uint256 _amount)
public view returns(uint256[] memory) {}


/// @notice Returns the data for a particular content id
/// @param _id The id of the content
/// @return Returns the id, author, date, content and hashtags for
that piece of content
function getContentById(uint256 _id) public view returns(uint256,
address, uint256, string memory, bytes32[] memory) {}
```

4. The helper functions to sort hashtags and check existing subscriptions. These will be used when a user subscribes to update the score of the entire hashtags by ordering them, depending on the score:

```
/// @notice Sorts the hashtags given their hashtag score
/// @return bytes32[] Returns the sorted array of hashtags
function sortHashtagsByScore() public view returns(bytes32[]
memory) {}


/// @notice To check if the use is already subscribed to a hashtag
```

```
/// @return bool If you are subscribed to that hashtag or not
function checkExistingSubscription(bytes32 _hashtag) public view
returns(bool) {}
```

The NatSpec documentation describes all of your functions with a basic description, the parameters, and the return values for other coders to see, so that they can maintain your code. They also help you understand what's going on when the code base grows.

Next, we must implement all the functions one by one until all of them are completed. This is the most time-extensive process since some parts are harder than others, considering the limitations of Solidity. Try to stay positive while doing it. You'll finish it earlier than you expect if you set up a one- or two-hour timer where you can't get distracted before completing it. That's the famous **Pomodoro** technique to maximize productivity, and I suggest you to use it to get more stuff done in less time.

Implementing the adding content function

The adding content function is the most complex in the dApp that we're building because we need to complete the following tasks:

1. Check whether the content given by the user is valid
2. Add new content to the right state variables
3. Increase the score of the hashtags included in the content piece
4. Dynamically store contents in a `general` hashtag that people can use to find random content without sorting
5. Add the user to the array of users if they're a new customer

Because of the many functions that we must implement, the function will inevitably be complex. That's why it is important to take your time to get it right, since we could easily create gas traps that consume all the available gas. Before seeing my solution, go to your computer to implement them as best as possible on your own by performing the following steps:

1. Add the `require()` checks to be sure that the content is valid:

```
/// @notice To add new content to the social media dApp. If no
hashtags are sent, the content is added to the #general hashtag
list.
/// @param _content The string of content
/// @param _hashtags The hashtags used for that piece of content
function addContent(string memory _content, bytes32[] memory
_hashtags) public {
    require(bytes(_content).length > 0, 'The content cannot be
```

```
empty');
    Content memory newContent = Content(latestContentId,
msg.sender, now, _content, _hashtags);
    // If the user didn't specify any hashtags add the content to
the #general hashtag
```

2. Depending on whether the user added a hashtag, we'll execute the corresponding functionality to sort and increase the value of those hashtags:

```
if(_hashtags.length == 0) {
    contentByHashtag['general'].push(newContent);
    hashtagScore['general']++;
    if(!doesHashtagExist['general']) {
        hashtags.push('general');
        doesHashtagExist['general'] = true;
    }
} else {
    for(uint256 i = 0; i < _hashtags.length; i++) {
        contentByHashtag[_hashtags[i]].push(newContent);
        hashtagScore[_hashtags[i]]++;
        if(!doesHashtagExist[_hashtags[i]]) {
            hashtags.push(_hashtags[i]);
            doesHashtagExist[_hashtags[i]] = true;
        }
    }
}
```

3. Sort the arrays by score using the function described earlier and we create the user while emitting the right events:

```
hashtags = sortHashtagsByScore();
contentById[latestContentId] = newContent;
contents.push(newContent);
if(!doesUserExist[msg.sender]) {
    users.push(msg.sender);
    doesUserExist[msg.sender] = true;
}
emit ContentAdded(latestContentId, msg.sender, now, _content,
_hashtags);
latestContentId++;
}
```

Here's a breakdown of what I did in that function step by step:

1. I checked that the `_content` variable that contains the message is not empty, by converting it to bytes and checking the length of it. It's one of the ways that you can check whether a string is empty since you can't get the length of a string type.

2. I created the `Content` struct instance with the required parameters and worked on populating the mappings that use that struct, so that we can find that piece of content later.

3. The user is free to not specify any tags, in which case the content will be added to the `#general` hashtag to organize it in some way for those that want to get general information from the application. Remember that we interact via hashtags mainly, so it's imperative to organize each message into one.

4. If the user specified a few hashtags, we add the content to all of those while also creating new hashtags that people can follow. For now, we don't have any limits on how many hashtags people can use, since we are experimenting with how the application will work. We can focus on those details later, if we decide to set up such limitations.

5. Add the user to the array of users and emit the `ContentAdded` event to notify others about new content.

Creating the promotion engine

We need a way to tell users which accounts are performing the best by creating a scoring system that increases hashtags' value. That's why we created the `hashtagScore` mapping, as a measurement of the popularity of the hashtags being used. The promotion engine is simply a way of rating hashtags by popularity. So, the score of the hashtag will increase when someone subscribes to that hashtag or adds new content for that hashtag. It will decrease when someone unsubscribes. This will all be invisible, so that users just see the top hashtags.

Let's continue with the subscribe functions to give people the power to follow particular topics that interest them. To implement the promotion engine, we simply have to update the score of the particular hashtag being used in the subscribe and unsubscribe functions. Again, try to implement it yourself before seeing the solution, to sharpen your skills while learning and gaining experience. The following is the subscribe function, which increases the score of the selected hashtag for that particular user:

```
/// @notice To subscribe to a hashtag if you didn't do so already
/// @param _hashtag The hashtag name
function subscribeToHashtag(bytes32 _hashtag) public {
    if(!checkExistingSubscription(_hashtag)) {
```

```
            subscribedHashtags[msg.sender].push(_hashtag);
            hashtagScore[_hashtag]++;
            hashtags = sortHashtagsByScore();
        }
    }
```

Then we have the unsubscribe function, which reduces the hashtag value because it's becoming less relevant:

```
/// @notice To unsubscribe to a hashtag if you are subscribed otherwise it
won't do nothing
/// @param _hashtag The hashtag name
function unsubscribeToHashtag(bytes32 _hashtag) public {
    if(checkExistingSubscription(_hashtag)) {
        for(uint256 i = 0; i < subscribedHashtags[msg.sender].length; i++)
    {
            if(subscribedHashtags[msg.sender][i] == _hashtag) {
                delete subscribedHashtags[msg.sender][i];
                hashtagScore[_hashtag]--;
                hashtags = sortHashtagsByScore();
                break;
            }
        }
    }
}
```

The subcribeToHashtag function simply checks whether the user is subscribed already to add that new topic to their list of interests, while also sorting the hashtags since the score of that particular one has been increased. In our smart contract, hashtags are valued by use. The more people that subscribe to them and the more content that gets created for that particular tag, the higher its ranking will be.

The unsubscribeToHashtag function loops through all the hashtags for that particular user and removes the selected one from their list. This loop shouldn't cause any gas problems since we don't expect people to follow hundreds of thousands of topics. Regardless, the right thing to do is to limit the number of subscribable tags to avoid gas errors. I'll leave that up to you. Finally, we reduce the score of that hashtag and we sort all of them with the changes.

Implementing the getter functions

Next, let's see the getter functions that we'll use to show data to our users. These functions don't cost any gas because they are reading data from the downloaded and synchronized blockchain, which is always available without depending on an internet connection. Let's take a look at the following steps:

1. Create the `getTopHashtags()` function, which returns a list of names in bytes32 format to the user so that they can see which ones are trending. This is the main discovery system for new content:

```
/// @notice To get the top hashtags
/// @param _amount How many top hashtags to get in order, for
instance the top 20 hashtags
/// @return bytes32[] Returns the names of the hashtags
function getTopHashtags(uint256 _amount) public view
returns(bytes32[] memory) {
    bytes32[] memory result;
    if(hashtags.length < _amount) {
        result = new bytes32[](hashtags.length);
        for(uint256 i = 0; i < hashtags.length; i++) {
            result[i] = hashtags[i];
        }
    } else {
        result = new bytes32[](_amount);
        for(uint256 i = 0; i < _amount; i++) {
            result[i] = hashtags[i];
        }
    }
    return result;
}
```

2. Add the function to get the followed hashtags, which is quite straightforward because it returns the specified list using the `subscribedHashtags[]` mapping:

```
/// @notice To get the followed hashtag names for this msg.sender
/// @return bytes32[] The hashtags followed by this user
function getFollowedHashtags() public view returns(bytes32[]
memory) {
    return subscribedHashtags[msg.sender];
}
```

3. Implement the `getContentIdsByHashtag()` function. This will be responsible for returning an array of IDs that contain all the pieces of content for a particular hashtag that a user may be subscribed to:

```
/// @notice To get the contents for a particular hashtag. It
returns the ids because we can't return arrays of strings and we
can't return structs so the user has to manually make a new request
for each piece of content using the function below.
/// @param _hashtag The hashtag from which get content
/// @param _amount The quantity of contents to get for instance, 50
pieces of content for that hashtag
/// @return uint256[] Returns the ids of the contents so that you
can get each piece independently with a new request since you can't
return arrays of strings
function getContentIdsByHashtag(bytes32 _hashtag, uint256 _amount)
public view returns(uint256[] memory) {
    uint256[] memory ids = new uint256[](_amount);
    for(uint256 i = 0; i < _amount; i++) {
        ids[i] = contentByHashtag[_hashtag][i].id;
    }
    return ids;
}
```

4. Add the simple `getContentById()` function, required to get the struct of IDs broken down into digestible variables, since we can't return structs yet:

```
/// @notice Returns the data for a particular content id
/// @param _id The id of the content
/// @return Returns the id, author, date, content and hashtags for
that piece of content
function getContentById(uint256 _id) public view returns(uint256,
address, uint256, string memory, bytes32[] memory) {
    Content memory c = contentById[_id];
    return (c.id, c.author, c.date, c.content, c.hashtags);
}
```

The preceding functions are pretty straightforward . The `getContentIdsByHashtag` function is a bit tricky since we wouldn't normally need it, but, because Solidity doesn't allow us to return arrays of structs or arrays of strings, we have to get the IDs so that to later we can get each piece of content independently with the `getContentById` function, which does return each variable successfully.

Setting up the smart contract instance

The first thing that must be done when implementing a smart contract inside a React application is the contract instance so that we can start calling methods from that contract all over the decentralized application. We'll use the compiled contract provided by Truffle and the address of it. Let's perform the following steps:

1. Import web3 into your project:

```
import Web3Js from 'web3'
```

Why do you think I've named the variable `Web3Js` instead of just `Web3`? Because MetaMask injects its own version of web3, which is precisely named `Web3`, so when we develop, we may be used the injected version of web3, instead of the one that we are interested in importing. It's important to use a slightly different name to avoid interfering with the injected web3 by MetaMask.

2. Set up web3 with the current provider globally so that you can use it with in your entire application without having to worry about scope problems.

3. Create a function named `setup()` that contains the MetaMask setup logic. This function will be executed in the constructor, right when the page loads:

```
class Main extends React.Component {
    constructor() {
        // Previous code omitted for simplicity

        this.setup()
    }

    async setup() {
        window.web3js = new Web3Js(ethereum)
        try {
            await ethereum.enable();
        } catch (error) {
            alert('You must approve this dApp to interact with it,
reload it to approve it')
        }
    }
}
```

We created a new setup function because we can't use await on the constructor, given that it's not an asynchronous function. Inside it, we created a global `web3js` variable which is not called `web3` (in lowercase), since MetaMask is already using that variable name and we risk using the wrong version. As you can see, the provider in this case is called `ethereum`, a global variable coming from MetaMask that includes all we need to start using web3; it's a new way of initializing a web3 instance that is compatible with older dApps because of some changes the MetaMask team made regarding security. Then we wait for the `enable()` function to get permission from the user to inject web3 because we don't want to expose user keys without the user's consent. If the user doesn't allow it, we show an error to let them know that we need them to grant permission for this dApp in order to work properly.

4. Set up the smart contract instance. Because we have Truffle installed, we can compile our smart contract to generate the JSON file that contains the ABI, which is required to use the application. Then we can deploy our contract to `ropsten`:

```
truffle compile

truffle deploy --network ropsten --reset
```

You might get the following message:

```
"Unknown network "ropsten". See your Truffle configuration file for available networks."
```

5. This means that you didn't set up the Truffle config file properly with the `ropsten` network. Install the wallet provider with `npm i -S truffle-hdwallet-provider`. Then modify `truffle-config.js` with the following code:

```
const HDWalletProvider = require('truffle-hdwallet-provider')
const infuraKey =
"https://ropsten.infura.io/v3/8e12dd4433454738a522d9ea7ffcf2cc"

const fs = require('fs')
const mnemonic = fs.readFileSync(".secret").toString().trim()

module.exports = {
  networks: {
    ropsten: {
      provider: () => new HDWalletProvider(mnemonic, infuraKey),
      network_id: 3, // Ropsten's id
      gas: 5500000, // Ropsten has a lower block limit than mainnet
      confirmations: 2, // # of confs to wait between deployments.
```

```
(default: 0)
      timeoutBlocks: 200, // # of blocks before a deployment times
out (minimum/default: 50)
      skipDryRun: true // Skip dry run before migrations? (default:
false for public nets )
    }
  }
}
```

6. Tell Truffle to deploy your contract by creating
   a `2_deploy_contract.js` filename inside your `migrations/` folder with the
   following code:

```
const SocialMedia = artifacts.require("./SocialMedia.sol")

module.exports = function(deployer) {
  deployer.deploy(SocialMedia);
}
```

7. As you can see, we only have the minimal configuration parameters so keep it
   clean. Create a `.secret` file in your project folder and paste your Ethereum seed
   phrase, which you can get by resetting MetaMask or installing it in another
   browser if you are worried about making your seed public. That seed phrase will
   be used by Truffle to deploy the contracts, so be sure to have enough `ropsten`
   Ether in your first account. Then run `truffle deploy --network ropsten --reset` again.

8. Update your `setup` function with the following to create a contract instance:

```
async setup() {
    window.web3js = new Web3Js(ethereum)
    try {
        await ethereum.enable();
    } catch (error) {
        alert('You must approve this dApp to interact with it,
reload it to approve it')
    }
    const user = (await web3js.eth.getAccounts())[0]
    const contract = new web3js.eth.Contract(ABI.abi,
ABI.networks['3'].address, {
        from: user
    })
    await this.setState({contract, user})
}
```

We've set up the user account in the app's state to have easy access whenever we need it.

Decentralizing your data

To fully implement the smart contract, we have to take a look at each section of the website to update its contents with data from the smart contract. Let's go from top-left to bottom-right. In that order, the first thing we have to decentralize is the top hashtags sections, using the `getTopHashtags()` function:

```
async setup() {
    window.web3js = new Web3Js(ethereum)
    try {
        await ethereum.enable();
    } catch (error) {
        alert('You must approve this dApp to interact with it, reload it to
approve it')
    }
    const user = (await web3js.eth.getAccounts())[0]
    window.contract = new web3js.eth.Contract(ABI.abi,
ABI.networks['3'].address, {
        from: user
    })
    await this.setState({contract, user})
}
```

You'll also have to update your `render()` function for when you don't have any top hashtags, since you just deployed your smart contract. We'll get the content from another function named `getContent()`:

```
render() {
    return (
        <div className="main-container">
            <div className="hashtag-block">
                <h3>Top hashtags</h3>
                <div className="hashtag-
container">{this.state.topHashtagBlock}</div>
                <h3>Followed hashtags</h3>
                <div className="hashtag-
container">{this.state.followedHashtagsBlock}</div>
            </div>
            <div className="content-block">
                <div className="input-container">
                    <textarea ref="content" placeholder="Publish
content..."></textarea>
                    <input ref="hashtags" type="text" placeholder="Hashtags
separated by commas without the # sign..."/>
                    <button onClick={() => {
                        this.publishContent(this.refs.content.value,
this.refs.hashtags.value)
```

```
                    }} type="button">Publish</button>
            </div>

            <div className="content-container">
                {this.state.contentsBlock}
            </div>
        </div>
    </div>
)
}
```

So it looks like this after the changes:

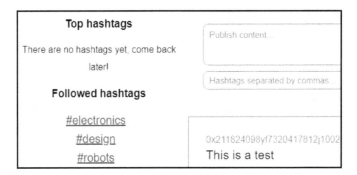

Let's update the get content function to generate data based on whether the user has any active subscriptions:

1. To get all the content the user will be seeing, we need to get `latestContentId`, which is a number of how many pieces of content are available at that moment, in case the user is not subscribed to any hashtags yet:

```
async getContent() {
    const latestContentId = await
this.state.contract.methods.latestContentId().call()
    const amount = 10
    const amountPerHashtag = 3
    let contents = []
    let counter = amount
```

2. Get the content pieces if the user is following hashtags by looping through all the IDs:

```
    // If we have subscriptions, get content for those
subscriptions 3 pieces per hashtag
    if(this.state.followedHashtags.length > 0) {
```

```
                    for(let i = 0; i < this.state.followedHashtags.length; i++)
    {
                // Get 3 contents per hashtag
                let contentIds = await
    this.state.contract.methods.getContentIdsByHashtag(this.bytes32(thi
    s.state.followedHashtags[i]), 3).call()
                let counterTwo = amountPerHashtag
                if(contentIds < amountPerHashtag) counterTwo =
    contentIds
                for(let a = counterTwo - 1; a >= 0; a--) {
                    let content = await
    this.state.contract.methods.getContentById(i).call()
                    content = {
                        id: content[0],
                        author: content[1],
                        time: new Date(parseInt(content[2] +
    '000')).toLocaleDateString(),
                        message: content[3],
                        hashtags: content[4],
                    }
                    content.message =
    web3js.utils.toUtf8(content.message)
                    content.hashtags = content.hashtags.map(hashtag =>
    web3js.utils.toUtf8(hashtag))
                    contents.push(content)
                }
            }
        }
```

3. If the user isn't subscribed to any hashtags yet, update the counter variable to loop inversely so that we get the most recent pieces first:

```
    // If we don't have enough content yet, show whats in there
    if(latestContentId < amount) counter = latestContentId
    for(let i = counter - 1; i >= 0; i--) {
        let content = await
    this.state.contract.methods.getContentById(i).call()
        content = {
            id: content[0],
            author: content[1],
            time: new Date(parseInt(content[2] +
    '000')).toLocaleDateString(),
            message: content[3],
            hashtags: content[4],
        }
        content.message = web3js.utils.toUtf8(content.message)
        content.hashtags = content.hashtags.map(hashtag =>
    web3js.utils.toUtf8(hashtag))
```

```
                    contents.push(content)
        }
```

4. Generate `contentsBlock`, which contains all the elements that create a piece of content, which is similar to a tweet or a Facebook post:

```
    let contentsBlock = await Promise.all(contents.map(async
(element, index) => (
        <div key={index} className="content">
            <div className="content-address">{element.author}</div>
            <div className="content-
message">{element.message}</div>
            <div className="content-
hashtags">{element.hashtags.map((hashtag, i) => (
                <span key={i}>
                    <Hashtag
                        hashtag={hashtag}
                        contract={this.state.contract}
                        subscribe={hashtag =>
this.subscribe(hashtag) }
                        unsubscribe={hashtag =>
this.unsubscribe(hashtag) }
                    />
                </span>
            ))}
            </div>
            <div className="content-time">{element.time}</div>
        </div>
    )))

    this.setState({contentsBlock})
}
```

This `getContent()` function checks whether the user has any active subscriptions so that it can retrieve up to three pieces of content per hashtag. It will also get up to the 10 most recent articles uploaded to the dApp. It is quite large because it generates data based on the number of hashtags that are available on the smart contract. If you follow 100 hashtags, you'll see 300 new pieces of content since we're getting 3 articles per hashtag in the feed. We're also adding 10 random contents that will be taken from the array of `contents` in the smart contract.

Creating the hashtag component

Each hashtag is a little machine that contains lots of logic to detect whether the user is subscribed. It may seem simple, but remember that we need to get the state of each hashtag for each user, which means that we have to execute a lot of requests that could slow our dApp's performance. Be clean when creating the function so that they run smoothly.

We're using a new component named Hashtag, which is an HTML object that returns an interactive hashtag text that can be clicked to subscribe to it, or unsubscribe. This is the cleanest way of creating such functionality to reduce complexity:

1. Create the constructor with a few state variables to display or hide the hashtag depending on the user's behavior:

```
class Hashtag extends React.Component {
    constructor(props) {
        super()
        this.state = {
            displaySubscribe: false,
            displayUnsubscribe: false,
            checkSubscription: false,
            isSubscribed: false,
        }
    }
```

2. Create the `bytes32()` and `checkExistingSubscription()` functions to check whether the current user is already following this particular hashtag:

```
componentDidMount() {
    this.checkExistingSubscription()
}

bytes32(name) {
    let nameHex = web3js.utils.toHex(name)
    for(let i = nameHex.length; i < 66; i++) {
        nameHex = nameHex + '0'
    }
    return nameHex
}

async checkExistingSubscription() {
    const isSubscribed = await
this.props.contract.methods.checkExistingSubscription(this.bytes32(
this.props.hashtag)).call()
    this.setState({isSubscribed})
}
```

3. The `render()` function is quite large, so we'll break it down into two main
   pieces: the functionality to detect whether a user is subscribed and the
   functionality to display the right buttons:

```
render() {
    return (
        <span onMouseEnter={async () => {
            if(this.state.checkSubscription) await
this.checkExistingSubscription()
            if(!this.state.isSubscribed) {
                this.setState({
                    displaySubscribe: true,
                    displayUnsubscribe: false,
                })
            } else {
                this.setState({
                    displaySubscribe: false,
                    displayUnsubscribe: true,
                })
            }
        }} onMouseLeave={() => {
            this.setState({
                displaySubscribe: false,
                displayUnsubscribe: false,
            })
        }}>
```

4. Implement the subscribe or unsubscribe buttons that will be shown when the
   user hovers over the hashtag:

```
            <a className="hashtag"
href="#">#{this.props.hashtag}</a>
            <span className="spacer"></span>
            <button onClick={() => {
                this.props.subscribe(this.props.hashtag)
                this.setState({checkSubscription: true})
            }} className={this.state.displaySubscribe ? '' :
'hidden'} type="button">Subscribe</button>
            <button onClick={() => {
                this.props.unsubscribe(this.props.hashtag)
                this.setState({checkSubscription: true})
            }} className={this.state.displayUnsubscribe ? '' :
'hidden'} type="button">Unsubscribe</button>
            <span className="spacer"></span>
        </span>
    )
}
}
```

The `render()` function displays the hashtag, which shows a subscribe or unsubscribe button when hovered. The `checkExistingSubscription()` function gets the state of a particular hashtag subscription to display the right type of button for the user that wishes to unsubscribe.

Creating the hashtag getter

We can now create a function to get the top hashtags and the followed hashtags from the smart contract when the page loads. We'll do it by retrieving the followed and top hashtags. Those will be shown to the user by looping through all of them until the interface is filled with data.

Try to implement it yourself and see the following result once you're done:

1. Define the variables needed to create the resulting hashtag JSX:

```
async getHashtags() {
    let topHashtagBlock
    let followedHashtagsBlock
    const amount = 10
    const topHashtags = (await
contract.methods.getTopHashtags(amount).call()).map(element =>
web3js.utils.toUtf8(element))
    const followedHashtags = (await
this.state.contract.methods.getFollowedHashtags().call()).map(eleme
nt => web3js.utils.toUtf8(element))
```

2. Start looping through the hashtag blocks until we fill the list of top hashtags:

```
if(topHashtags.length == 0) {
    topHashtagBlock = 'There are no hashtags yet, come back
later!'
} else {
    topHashtagBlock = topHashtags.map((hashtag, index) => (
        <div key={index}>
            <Hashtag
                hashtag={hashtag}
                contract={this.state.contract}
                subscribe={hashtag => this.subscribe(hashtag)}
                unsubscribe={hashtag =>
this.unsubscribe(hashtag)}
            />
        </div>
    ))
}
```

3. If the user isn't following any hashtags, we'll display a message. If they are, we'll loop through all the followed hashtags to generate the Hashtag component with the required data. Update the state with the new blocks that we just created to display them on the `render()` function:

```
    if(followedHashtags.length == 0) {
        followedHashtagsBlock = "You're not following any hashtags
yet"
    } else {
        followedHashtagsBlock = followedHashtags.map((hashtag,
index) => (
            <div key={index}>
                <Hashtag
                    hashtag={hashtag}
                    contract={this.state.contract}
                    subscribe={hashtag => this.subscribe(hashtag)}
                    unsubscribe={hashtag =>
this.unsubscribe(hashtag)}
                />
            </div>
        ))
    }
    this.setState({topHashtagBlock, followedHashtagsBlock,
followedHashtags})
}
```

Creating the publishing functionality

Publishing new pieces of content is a simple task that requires that we verify that all the inputs contain valid strings of text. Since we are storing hashtags in a bytes32 variable, we need to format the hashtags introduced by the user properly so that the smart contract is able to process them securely.

Let's make the publish function work so that we can start generating content by performing the following steps:

1. Create the `bytes32()` function if you haven't done so, because we'll need it soon:

```
bytes32(name) {
    let nameHex = web3js.utils.toHex(name)
    for(let i = nameHex.length; i < 66; i++)
    {
        nameHex = nameHex + '0'
    }
```

```
        return nameHex
    }
```

2. Add the `publishContent()` function to process the message with the hashtags.
   The hashtags will be given in a string format that contains a list of comma-
   separated strings without the hash symbol (#). Make sure that the hashtags are
   properly separated and formatted for the contract:

```
async publishContent(message, hashtags) {
    if(message.length == 0) alert('You must write a message')
    hashtags = hashtags.trim().replace(/#*/g, '').replace(/,+/g,
',').split(',').map(element => this.bytes32(element.trim()))
    message = this.bytes32(message)
    try {
        await this.state.contract.methods.addContent(message,
hashtags).send({
            from: this.state.user,
            gas: 8e6
        })
    } catch (e) {console.log('Error', e)}
    await this.getHashtags()
    await this.getContent()
}
```

Here's the explanation for the two functions we just added:

- `bytes32()`: This function is used to convert normal strings into hexadecimals
  valid for Solidity, since the new update forces web3 users to convert data to
  hexadecimal when dealing with `bytes` types of variables.

- `publishContent()`: This function looks a bit messy because we are using regex
  to convert the hashtag input from the user to a valid array of clear strings per
  hashtag. It's doing things such as removing spaces, removing duplicate commas
  and tag symbols, and then breaking the string into a valid array that can be used
  in our smart contract.

3. Remember to update your `setup()` function so that it gets the latest contents
   when loading:

```
async setup() {
    window.web3js = new Web3Js(ethereum)
    try {
        await ethereum.enable();
    } catch (error) {
        alert('You must approve this dApp to interact with it,
reload it to approve it')
    }
```

```
        const user = (await web3js.eth.getAccounts())[0]
        window.contract = new web3js.eth.Contract(ABI.abi,
    ABI.networks['3'].address, {
            from: user
        })
        await this.setState({contract, user})
        await this.getHashtags()
        await this.getContent()
    }
```

4. It's time to focus on creating the subscription functions. They will be executed when the user clicks on subscribe or unsubscribe, depending on the current state. Try to implement them yourself and come back once you're done to compare your solution with mine. Remember, this is about trying and failing until the code becomes good enough. Here's my solution:

```
async subscribe(hashtag) {
    try {
        await
this.state.contract.methods.subscribeToHashtag(this.bytes32(hashtag
)).send({from: this.state.user})
    } catch(e) { console.log(e) }
    await this.getHashtags()
    await this.getContent()
}

async unsubscribe(hashtag) {
    try {
        await
this.state.contract.methods.unsubscribeToHashtag(this.bytes32(hasht
ag)).send({from: this.state.user})
    } catch(e) { console.log(e) }
    await this.getHashtags()
    await this.getContent()
}
```

Both functions are quite simple. They run the appropriate subscribe or unsubscribe functions when the user presses the button next to the hashtag name. Notice how we're using a try catch to avoid breaking the entire application if something fails when calling the contract; that's also because sometimes it has a weird failing system where it stops executing for no reason. Just add try catch blocks when you feel like you need to.

You can find the updated version in GitHub at `https://github.com/merlox/social-media-dapp` with the complete implementation code for your reference. That's about it! You now have a new project in your blockchain development resume that you can show to employers, or build upon creating a better decentralized social media platform for raising funds.

Summary

That's about it when it comes to creating a fully-decentralized social media platform for users to publish content freely. In this chapter, you learned about the benefits of creating this type of application on the blockchain versus creating it on a centralized system. Then you created the user interface by setting up everything from scratch with Truffle and React. After that, you developed the smart contract and connected it to the dApp to make it interactive. Overall, you gained a big chunk of experience that you can expand upon to create a different type of social media platform with interesting features, such as following users and adding oracles for interacting with different APIs.

In the next chapter, we'll explore the build process behind a decentralized e-commerce marketplace on the blockchain, where you'll create a fully-functioning shop for your business.

Creating a Blockchain-Based E-Commerce Marketplace

12

A decentralized e-commerce marketplace is one of the best cases of blockchain technology for the simple reason that you don't have to pay fees or entrust your data into the hands of powerful corporations that will sell it for profit. Ethereum is an excellent solution for this, is the new ERC-721 token standard has been approved for you to generate digitalized objects on the blockchain. In this chapter, you'll learn how to deal with personal user data so that it's protected for each individual, given that Ethereum is a public system.

In the first section, we'll look at how an e-commerce website should be structured so that users can interact with it as if it were a real store. You'll build the user interface that will display the unique products identified with the ERC-721 convention. Then, you'll implement the React router module to organize your different views in a user-friendly interface. Finally, you'll create the smart contract that implements ERC-721 tokens and creates the functions needed to manage decentralized products.

Also, in this chapter, you'll learn what it takes to create a fully featured e-commerce marketplace for your business on Ethereum by learning about the following topics:

- Creating the user interface
- Understanding ERC-721 tokens
- Developing the e-commerce smart contract
- Finishing the dApp

Creating the user interface

The great thing about these types of guides is that you can take what you learn about decentralize e-commerce here and expand upon those ideas to create a more advanced product that will provide a complex solution in order to raise funds, or so that you can simply build a business out of it.

Planning the marketplace interface

This marketplace has almost unlimited options, given that you won't have to face many blockchain limitations. Each product is an independent instance that can be molded as you need, so you're free to add as many features as you desire, such as the following:

- A carting system to add products to the cart while shopping instead of purchasing them directly for larger, combined purchases
- A dynamic shipping address functionality to add several different addresses so that you can send orders quickly to many locations by saving your preferred locations
- A bidding system to create auctions for user products
- Profile and review functionalities for better user interactions

In this project, we won't implement any of those advanced features because they would take way too much time to develop, although you can add them yourself once the base product is completed. That's why we'll create a simple interface with the following features:

- A buy system to purchase physical and digital products directly with Ethereum
- A sell functionality to publish products to the marketplace as an independent seller
- An order-display functionality to see pending orders as a buyer and as a seller

In general, users will be able to interact as a normal online store with direct payments, using MetaMask instead of a credit card. The marketplace won't charge fees to users, compared to e-commerce stores such as Amazon that charge about 15% of the total payment in fees, which really adds up. Another important point is that there won't be any censoring or rules to follow, meaning users can freely publish products without fearing a ban from a centralized entity, a recurring problem that has affected sellers, causing them to lose thousands of dollars in locked funds and reverted orders.

There won't be several quantities of a single product because we'll use unique, **non fungible tokens** (**NFTs**), which means that each product has to be unique. Since we will be exchanging tokens from one user to another, we won't be able to have multiple copies of the same product. You could, however, implement an ERC-20 token or a system to generate multiple copies of the same token ID for multiple quantities of the same product.

Let's start by setting up the project by cloning the base repository (`https://github.com/merlox/dapp`) or by configuring `npm` and Truffle yourself. You should have the following folders and initial files after setting up Truffle or cloning the repository:

- `contracts/`
- `dist/`
- `migrations/`
- `node_modules/` (remember to use `npm install` after cloning the repository)
- `src/`
    - `index.js`
    - `index.html` or `index.ejs` ,based on your preference
    - `index.css` or `index.styl` ,based on your preference

- `.babelrc`
- `.gitignore`
- `LICENSE`
- `package.json`
- `README.md`
- `truffle-config.js`
- `webpack.config.js` (remember to set up your webpack configuration)

Inside your `src/` folder, create a new folder called `components/` ,which will contain a file for every single JavaScript component, since this is a larger dApp and we will have lots of different components. Because we'll have multiple pages, we want to use the react router to manage the history location and URLs so that the user will be able to navigate between pages. Install the React router and `web3` libraries by running the following command on your terminal:

```
npm i -S web3 react-router-dom
```

Setting up the index page

Open up your `index.js` file, import the required libraries, and set the initial state with some placeholder products using fake data just to see how the final design will look. we do this by going through the following steps:

1. Import the required libraries. We need several components from the `react-router` library, as shown in the following code:

```
import React from 'react'
import ReactDOM from 'react-dom'
import MyWeb3 from 'web3'
import { BrowserRouter, Route, withRouter } from 'react-router-dom'
```

2. Create the constructor with a few products that have the necessary properties to display the greatest amount of information to the user as possible, as shown in the following code. Properties such as `title`, `description`, `id`, and `price` are a must:

```
class Main extends React.Component {
    constructor(props) {
        super(props)

        this.state = {
            products: [{
                id: 1,
                title: 'Clasic trendy shoes',
                description: 'New unique shoes for sale',
                date: Date.now(),
                owner: '',
                price: 12,
                image:
'https://cdn.shopify.com/s/files/1/2494/8702/products/Bjakin-2018-S
ocks-Running-Shoes-for-Men-Lightweight-Sports-Sneakers-Colors-Man-
Sock-Walking-Shoes-Big_17fa0d5b-d9d9-46a0-bdea-
ac2dc17474ce_400x.jpg?v=1537755930'
            }
            productsHtml: [],
            productDetails: [],
            product: {},
        }
    }
```

3. You can add more products by copying the `product` object and changing a few parameters to make it look unique. Then add the `bytes32()` function to convert strings into valid hexadecimal and the `render()` function, as shown in the following code:

```
bytes32(name) {
    return myWeb3.utils.fromAscii(name)
}

render() {
    return (
        <div>
            <Route path="/" exact render={() => (
                <div>The dApp has been setup</div>
            )} />
        </div>
    )
}
}
```

4. Use the `withRouter()` function provided by the React router to provide our `Main` component with the history property, which is necessary to navigate between pages in your dApp. This is shown in the following code:

```
// To be able to access the history in order to redirect users
// programmatically when opening a product
Main = withRouter(Main)
```

5. Add the `BrowserRouter` component from the react router to initialize the router object, as shown in the following code:

```
ReactDOM.render(
    <BrowserRouter>
        <Main />
    </BrowserRouter>,
document.querySelector('#root'))
```

The `BrowserRouter` component is the main component that is used to initialize the router so that they can manage different pages. We're using the `withRouter` import to access the navigational history so that we can change pages programmatically. Basically, we need it to redirect users to different pages in our dApp at specific times whenever we need. Then we set up some basic products with different properties in the `this.state` object. Note how the image is a URL instead of a file. Since we don't have a server that handles files, we need sellers to host their own pictures on some kind of public service, such as Imgur.

The React router library will use several `Route` instances to determine which page has to be loaded at what time. We also have to add the high-level `BrowserRouter` component on top of our `Main` component to activate the router. Note how we're rendering a single route with `exact path="/"`, which shows the setup text to confirm that the application has loaded successfully after the configuration.

Configuring the webpack dev server

After creating the `Main` component, you will want to run the application to see how it looks, however, in this case, we'll use the `webpack-dev-server` extension, which automatically reloads the website as we develop so that we don't have to constantly reload it manually and compiles the files in the backend. So instead of setting up a webpack watcher and a static server, it's all contained in a single command. Install the webpack server locally with the following command:

```
npm i -S webpack-dev-server
```

Then update your `package.json` file with a new script under the `scripts` section(as shown in the following code); otherwise, it won't work, since we need to execute this command from inside the project:

```
{
  "name": "dapp",
  "version": "1.0.0",
  "description": "",
  "main": "truffle-config.js",
  "directories": {
    "test": "test"
  },
  "scripts": {
    "dev": "webpack-dev-server -d"
  }
}
```

This simply runs the `webpack-dev-server` command with the -d flag, which sets the mode to development, allowing you to see complete error messages from uncompressed files. If you wish, you can add the -o flag, which opens a browser when you run the command. Execute it by running the following command line:

```
npm run dev
```

If everything is correct, you'll be able to go to `localhost:8080` and see your page with the router set up.

Creating the Header component

Our application will have several pages for buyers, sellers, and orders. That's why it's important to separate each component as much as possible into unique blocks that can be imported where required by performing the following steps:

1. Create a new component inside the `src/components/` folder to display a header for our website, and create a file named `Header.js` inside your `components` folder, as shown in the following code:

```
import React from 'react'
import { Link } from 'react-router-dom'

function Header() {
    return (
        <div className="header">
            <Link to="/">ECOMMERCE</Link>
            <div>
                <Link to="/">Home</Link>
                <Link to="/sell">Sell</Link>
                <Link to="/orders">Orders</Link>
            </div>
        </div>
    )
}

export default Header
```

2. Export it with `export default Header` so that other files can access your component. Then import it into your `index.js` page as shown in the following code to display it right under your imported libraries to keep them in order:

```
import React from 'react'
import ReactDOM from 'react-dom'
import MyWeb3 from 'web3'
import { BrowserRouter, Route, withRouter } from 'react-router-dom'
import Header from './components/Header'
```

3. Update your `render()` function with the component instance, as shown in the following code:

```
render() {
    return (
        <div>
            <Route path="/" exact render={() => (
                <Header />
```

```
            )} />
      </div>
    )
}
```

You'll see your header loaded automatically without having to refresh your webpack service, as shown in the following screenshot:

4. It doesn't look good yet, so let's improve the design with some `stylus` CSS. If you haven't configured it already, install the `stylus` and `stylus-loader` libraries with the following command:

```
npm i -S stylus stylus-loader
```

5. Update your `webpack` configuration as follows:

```
require('babel-polyfill')
const webpack = require('webpack')
const html = require('html-webpack-plugin')
const path = require('path')

module.exports = {
    entry: ['babel-polyfill', './src/index.js'],
    output: {
        filename: 'bundle.js',
        path: path.join(__dirname, 'dist')
    },
    module: {
        rules: [
            {
                test: /\.js$/,
                exclude: /node_modules/,
                use: {
                    loader: 'babel-loader'
                }
            }, {
                test: /\.styl$/,
                exclude: /node_modules/,
                use: [
                    {loader: 'style-loader'},
                    {loader: 'css-loader'},
```

```
                        {loader: 'stylus-loader'}
                    ]
                }
            ]
        },
        plugins: [
            new webpack.HotModuleReplacementPlugin(),
            new html({
                title: "dApp project",
                template: './src/index.ejs',
                hash: true
            })
        ]
    }
```

Here are the main things that we changed in the webpack file:

- We imported webpack so that we could use webpack.HotModuleReplacementPlugin() to reload the page partially when we make changes. Instead of reloading the entire page, only the changed components will be reloaded.
- Then we set up the stylus loader to load styl files.

6. Create index.styl with the following design, although it's up to you to decide how your e-commerce store will end up looking:

```
productPadding = 20px

body
    background-color: whitesmoke
    font-family: sans-serif
    margin: 0

button
    border: none
    background-color: black
    color: white
    cursor: pointer
    padding: 10px
    width: 200px
    height: 50px

    &:hover
        opacity: 0.9

input, textarea
    padding: 20px
```

```
        border: 1px solid black

    .header
        background-color: black
        color: white
        padding: 15px
        margin-bottom: 20px
        text-align: center
        display: flex
        justify-content: space-around

        a
            color: white
            text-decoration: none
            margin-right: 10px

            &:hover
                color: lightgrey
```

7. Note the `productPadding` variable at the top. Stylus allows us to create variables so that we can configure multiple instances of the same value across the styling file easily; we'll use that variable later on. Then import the stylus file in your `index.js` file like so:

```
import './index.styl'
```

Now check how your app looks in your browser; you may have to reload your webpack server since you updated the webpack configuration:

Creating the Home component

The `Home` component will contain the logic to display the first page that users see when opening the dApp for the first time so that they can begin buying products. This component will be the core component to manage the remaining pages.

Create a `Home` component with the default design for the main page; it will contain the latest products in a clean design. Here's the code for the `Home.js` file inside the components folder:

```
import React from 'react'
import MyWeb3 from 'web3'
import Header from './Header'

class Home extends React.Component {
    constructor() { super() }
    render() {
        return (
            <div>
                <Header />
                <div className="products-
container">{this.props.productsHtml}</div>
                <div className="spacer"></div>
            </div>
        )
    }
}

export default Home
```

You can import it into your `index.js` file, which will be the main source of data and functions. Also remove the `Header` import in the index because it's already included in the `Home` component. The following steps show the changes that you have to make to include the `Home` component in your dApp:

1. Import the component at the beginning of the file while removing the `Header` component, because we have included it in the `Home` component:

    ```
    import React from 'react'
    import ReactDOM from 'react-dom'
    import MyWeb3 from 'web3'
    import { BrowserRouter, Route, withRouter } from 'react-router-dom'
    import Home from './components/Home'
    import './index.styl'
    ```

2. To make things simple, I've created a prototype JavaScript method for the `Array` object. This is an advanced implementation of JavaScript methods that you can use to change how certain functions work. In particular, I've created an asynchronous `for` loop, which can be `awaited`, to make sure that it's completed before continuing with the rest of the code, as shown in the following code fragment. Essentially, it's a clean way of running loops:

```
Array.prototype.asyncForEach = function (callback) {
    return new Promise(resolve => {
        for(let i = 0; i < this.length; i++) {
            callback(this[i], i, this)
        }
        resolve()
    })
}
```

3. Inside your constructor, include a `setup()` function call, as shown in the following code fragment:

```
constructor(props) {
    super(props)
    // State object omitted for simplicity
    this.setup()
}
```

4. Implement the `setup()` function with code to start a web3 instance and to display the products, as shown in the following code fragment:

```
async setup() {
    // Create the contract instance
    window.myWeb3 = new MyWeb3(ethereum)
    try {
        await ethereum.enable();
    } catch (error) {
        console.error('You must approve this dApp to interact with it')
    }
    const user = (await myWeb3.eth.getAccounts())[0]
    let products = []
    for(let i = 0; i < this.state.products.length; i++) {
        products[i] = this.state.products[i]
        products[i].owner = user
    }
    this.setState({products})
    this.displayProducts()
}
```

5. We've included a call to the `displayProducts()` function, which will be used to display products by looping through our array of products inside the `state` object, as shown in the following code fragment:

```
async displayProducts() {
    let productsHtml = []
    await this.state.products.asyncForEach(product => {
        productsHtml.push((
            <div key={product.id} className="product">
                <img className="product-image"
src={product.image} />
                <div className="product-data">
                    <h3 className="product-
title">{product.title}</h3>
                    <div className="product-
description">{product.description.substring(0, 50) +
'...'}</div>
                    <div className="product-
price">{product.price} ETH</div>
                    <button onClick={() => {
                        this.setState({product})
                        this.redirectTo('/product')
                    }} className="product-view"
type="button">View</button>
                </div>
            </div>
        ))
    })
    this.setState({productsHtml})
}
```

6. Modify the `render()` function and include a function named `redirectTo()`, which will allow you to change pages when the user clicks on a button using the React router, as shown in the following code fragment:

```
redirectTo(location) {
    this.props.history.push({
        pathname: location
    })
}

render() {
    return (
        <div>
            <Route path="/" exact render={() => (
                <Home
                    productsHtml={this.state.productsHtml}
```

```
                                          />
                            ) } />
                  </div>
            )
      }
   }
```

We made the following important additions to this index file:

- First, we set up a custom prototype function for the `Array` object, named `asyncForEach`. You may not be familiar with how JavaScript works in depth, but you have to understand that all types of variables are objects with a property called `prototype`, which contains the methods for that type of variable. The default `forEach` method is defined somewhere in JavaScript as `Array.prototype.forEach = function () {...};` the point of this is to create a custom `for` look which we can `await` until it is finished to take full advantage of the `async` functions. So instead of typing `for(let i = 0; i < array.length; i++) {}`, we can type `await array.asyncForEach()`, which is way easier to read and has less confusing code. That's just an implementation that I wanted to use for improving code readability while increasing its usability.

- Then we imported the `Home` component instead of the `Header` component and replaced that in the `render()` function inside `Route`.

- The `redirectTo` function changes the `Route` that we're currently seeing by loading a new page using the `withRouter` history object that we saw previously. This function will be used when the user clicks on the `View` button inside the `displayProducts` function.

- After this, we added a `setup` function that configures MetaMask while adding the owner address to each of those sample products so that you can see who owns those objects.

- Finally, we created a `displayProducts()` function that generates the HTML for each product while pushing it into the array of products and updating the state. The `Home` component then receives those products as `prop` and displays each product.

Now we can add some CSS code to improve the appearance of the home page, as follows:

```
.products-container
    display: grid
    width: 80%
    margin: auto
    grid-template-columns: 1fr 1fr 1fr
    justify-items: center
    margin-top: 50px

    .product
        width: 400px
        border: 1px solid black

        .product-image
            width: 100%
            grid-column: 1 / 3
            box-shadow: 0 3px 0px 0 lightgrey

        .product-data
            display: grid
            grid-template-columns: 1fr 1fr
            grid-template-rows: 50px 20px 40px
            align-items: center
            padding: 10px productPadding
            grid-column-gap: productPadding
            background-color: white

            .product-description
                font-size: 10pt

            .product-price
                font-size: 11pt

            .product-view
                width: 200px
                grid-column: 2 / 3
                margin-top: 50px
                height: 50px

.spacer
    height: 200px
    width: 100%
```

Now the web page looks like the following:

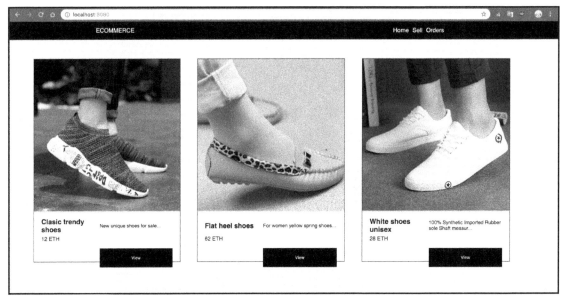

As you can see, we are progressing fast! The initial setup takes a bit of time for these kinds of complex applications, but then it's a wonderful thing to work on because you can update each separate section with ease while guaranteeing a great maintainability factor for future improvements. The theme for the e-commerce shop is similar to many shoe stores: it uses flat designs and black tones while also popping an element, such as buttons, to give it that three-dimensional feeling. It reminds me of a fashion magazine.

Creating the Product component

Now that we have a basic design, we can create the product pages when the user clicks on the **View** button so that the user can see in detail more information about that particular piece. The user will be able to purchase products inside the product page. Let's go through the following steps:

1. Add a new `Product.js` file inside your components with the following code, although I always recommend you to try it yourself before seeing the solution:

```
import React from 'react'
import Header from './Header'

class Product extends React.Component {
```

```
constructor() { super() }
render() {
    return (
        <div>
            <Header />
            <div className="product-details">
                <img className="product-image"
src={this.props.product.image} />
                <div className="product-data">
                    <h3 className="product-
title">{this.props.product.title}</h3>
                    <ul className="product-description">
{this.props.product.description.split('\n').map((line, index) => (
                        <li key={index}>{line}</li>
                    ))}
                    </ul>
                    <div className="product-data-container">
                        <div className="product-
price">{this.props.product.price} ETH</div>
                        <div className="product-
quantity">{this.props.product.quantity} units available</div>
                    </div>
                    <button onClick={() => {
                        this.props.redirectTo('/buy')
                    }} className="product-buy"
type="button">Buy</button>
                </div>
            </div>
        </div>
    )
}
}

export default Product
```

2. We need a new header because when we change pages, a new component will be loaded (in this case, the `Product` component,) so we need to show only the essential information to the `Product` component. Then we can import it into a new `Route` in the index file, as shown in the following code:

```
import React from 'react'
import ReactDOM from 'react-dom'
import MyWeb3 from 'web3'
import { BrowserRouter, Route, withRouter } from 'react-router-dom'
import Home from './components/Home'
import Product from './components/Product'
```

```
import './index.styl'

class Main extends React.Component {
    // Omitted previous code to keep the demonstration short

    render() {
        return (
            <div>
                <Route path="/" exact render={() => (
                    <Home
                        productsHtml={this.state.productsHtml}
                    />
                )} />
                <Route path="/product" render={() => (
                    <Product
                        product={this.state.product}
                    />
                )} />
            </div>
        )
    }
}
```

3. You should be able to access the custom product page when you click on the
   View button, given that we set up the required history functionality. The
   product prop for the Product component is set up when the user clicks on the
   View button as well. Add the following CSS code to fix the design of the product
   page:

```
.product-details
    display: grid
    width: 70%
    margin: auto
    grid-template-columns: 70% 30%
    grid-template-rows: 1fr
    margin-bottom: 50px
    grid-column-gap: 40px

    .product-image
        grid-column: 1 / 2
        justify-self: center

    .product-title, .product-description, .product-price, .product-
buy
        grid-column: 2 / 3

    .product-description
```

```
            white-space: pre-wrap
            line-height: 20pt

        .product-data-container
            display: flex
            justify-content: space-between
            margin-bottom: 20px
```

4. You can open your dApp, click on the **View** button of a product, and see the detailed product page, which shows larger images and the full description, as shown in the following screenshot:

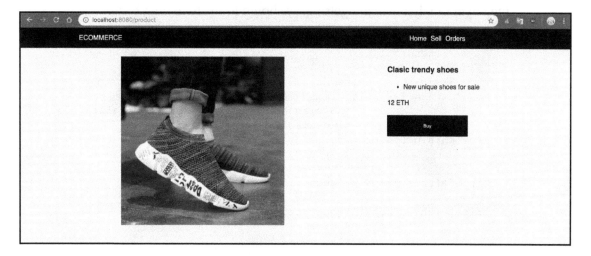

What's left is adding the buy, sell, and orders pages. Here's how we use the `Buy` component, which will be displayed when the user clicks on the `Buy` button located in the **Product** page:

1. Import the required libraries using the following:

```
import React, { Component } from 'react'
import Header from './Header'
```

2. Define the constructor inside the `Buy` component with empty state variables, just so you know which variables will be used across the entire component, you can do this by using the following code:

```
class Buy extends Component {
    constructor() {
        super()
        this.state = {
```

```
                nameSurname: '',
                lineOneDirection: '',
                lineTwoDirection: '',
                city: '',
                stateRegion: '',
                postalCode: '',
                country: '',
                phone: '',
            }
        }
```

3. The `render` page function will display some basic product information to inform the buyer of what they are getting, as shown in the following code:

```
        render() {
            return (
                <div>
                    <Header />
                    <div className="product-buy-page">
                        <h3 className="title">Product details</h3>
                        <img className="product-image"
src={this.props.product.image} />
                        <div className="product-data">
                            <p className="product-
title">{this.props.product.title}</p>
                            <div className="product-
price">{this.props.product.price} ETH</div>
                        </div>
                    </div>
```

4. Include a block with the shipping information for the users to include their address so that they can receive the product with free shipping, as shown in the following code:

```
        <div className="shipping-buy-page">
            <h3>Shipping</h3>
            <input onChange={e => {
                this.setState({nameSurname: e.target.value})
            }} placeholder="Name and surname..." type="text" />
            <input onChange={e => {
                this.setState({lineOneDirection: e.target.value})
            }} placeholder="Line 1 direction..." type="text" />
            <input onChange={e => {
                this.setState({lineTwoDirection: e.target.value})
            }} placeholder="Line 2 direction..." type="text" />
            <input onChange={e => {
                this.setState({city: e.target.value})
            }} placeholder="City..." type="text" />
```

```
                    <input onChange={e => {
                        this.setState({stateRegion: e.target.value})
                    }} placeholder="State or region..." type="text" />
                    <input onChange={e => {
                        this.setState({postalCode: e.target.value})
                    }} placeholder="Postal code..." type="number" />
                    <input onChange={e => {
                        this.setState({country: e.target.value})
                    }} placeholder="Country..." type="text" />
                    <input onChange={e => {
                        this.setState({phone: e.target.value})
                    }} placeholder="Phone..." type="number" />
                    <button>Buy now to this address</button>
                </div>
            </div>
```

5. Export the component so that it can be imported into your router manager, as
   shown in the following code:

```
export default Buy
```

We only need to display a form with the user address parameters, since that's the only
information we'll need. The shipping costs we can assume will all be free, included in the
price. We'll update the state of this `Buy` component with the details so that we can later
submit that data to the smart contract. Then import the `Buy` component at the beginning of
your index file. I've highlighted the new import for you to see where the `Buy` component
should be located, as shown in the following code:

```
import React from 'react'
import ReactDOM from 'react-dom'
import MyWeb3 from 'web3'
import { BrowserRouter, Route, withRouter } from 'react-router-dom'
import Home from './components/Home'
import Product from './components/Product'
import Buy from './components/Buy'
import './index.styl'
```

Then add the new `Route` and `props` parameters to the `Buy` component that you just
imported inside your `render` functions. The changes are highlighted so that you can find
them quicker, as shown in the following code:

```
class Main extends React.Component {
    // Omitted the other functions to keep it short

    render() {
        return (
            <div>
```

```
                    <Route path="/" exact render={() => (
                        <Home
                            productsHtml={this.state.productsHtml}
                        />
                    )} />
                    <Route path="/product" render={() => (
                        <Product
                            product={this.state.product}
                            redirectTo={location => this.redirectTo(location)}
                        />
                    )} />
                    <Route path="/buy" render={() => (
                        <Buy
                            product={this.state.product}
                        />
                    )} />
                </div>
            )
        }
    }
```

We only need to send `state.product` to this component so that we can see which product is being purchased. Add some CSS code to make it look good by performing the following steps:

1. Add the CSS code for the product section of the `Buy` component using the following code:

```
.product-buy-page
    display: grid
    margin: auto
    width: 50%
    padding: 20px
    padding-top: 0
    grid-template-columns: 50% 50%
    grid-template-rows: auto 1fr
    margin-bottom: 50px
    grid-column-gap: 40px
    border: 1px solid black
    background-color: white

    .title
        grid-column: 1 / 3
        justify-self: center

    .product-image
        grid-column: 1 / 2
        height: 150px
```

```
        justify-self: end

    .product-title
        margin-bottom: 25px

    .product-price
        font-size: 15pt
        font-weight: bold
```

2. Add the CSS code of the shipping form of the `Buy` component, as shown in the following code:

```
.shipping-buy-page
    display: grid
    flex-direction: column
    justify-items: center
    width: 50%
    margin: auto
    margin-bottom: 200px

    input
        margin-bottom: 10px
        width: 100%
```

Creating the Sell component

We're building a decentralized marketplace where users all over the world can join with their own products that they will publish for free. No fees will be charged and purchases will be completed in cryptocurrency. Therefore, we need a dedicated page for those sellers, which we'll make by creating a `Sell` component by going through the following steps:

1. Import the essential libraries to create the React component and include `Header`:

```
import React from 'react'
import Header from './Header'
```

2. Create the `Sell` class with an empty constructor that contains the `state` object with the `title`, `description`, `image`, and `price` of the product that the user will sell, as shown in the following code:

```
class Sell extends React.Component {
    constructor() {
        super()
        this.state = {
            title: '',
```

```
                            description: '',
                            price: '',
                            image: '',
                        }
                    }
                }
```

3. Create the `render()` function with a neat form that will allow users to access public products, as shown in the following code. Note how the image is a string, since we'll use external URLs for images instead of hosting the files ourselves:

```
render() {
    return (
        <div>
            <Header />
            <div className="sell-page">
                <h3>Sell product</h3>
                <input onChange={event => {
                    this.setState({title: event.target.value})
                }} type="text" placeholder="Product title..."
/>
                <textarea placeholder="Product description..."
onChange={event => {
                    this.setState({description:
event.target.value})
                }}></textarea>
                <input onChange={event => {
                    this.setState({price: event.target.value})
                }} type="text" placeholder="Product price in
ETH..." />
                <input onChange={event => {
                    this.setState({image: event.target.value})
                }} type="text" placeholder="Product image
URL..." />
                <p>Note that shipping costs are considered free
so add the shipping price to the cost of the product itself</p>
                <button onClick={() => {
                    this.props.publishProduct(this.state)
                }} type="button">Publish product</button>
            </div>
        </div>
    )
}
```

4. Export this new component using the following code so that other files can import it:

```
export default Sell
```

After saving the `Sell` component, import it into your index JavaScript file. We'll have to add a function named `publishProduct` ,which will call the respective smart contract function.

The following steps show the changes that need to be made to the index file (highlighted for clarity) that are needed to import this `Sell` component:

1. Import the `Sell` component right under the `Buy` component import, as shown in the following code:

```
import React from 'react'
import ReactDOM from 'react-dom'
import MyWeb3 from 'web3'
import { BrowserRouter, Route, withRouter } from 'react-router-dom'
import Home from './components/Home'
import Product from './components/Product'
import Buy from './components/Buy'
import Sell from './components/Sell'
import './index.styl'
```

2. Include the `Sell` component in the `render()` function with its own `route` object while also defining a `publishProduct()` function, as shown in the following function:

```
class Main extends React.Component {
    // Omitted the other functions to keep it short

    async publishProduct(data) {}

    render() {
        return (
            <div>
                <Route path="/" exact render={() => (
                    <Home
                        productsHtml={this.state.productsHtml}
                    />
                )} />
                <Route path="/product" render={() => (
                    <Product
                        product={this.state.product}
                        redirectTo={location =>
this.redirectTo(location)}
```

```
                                    />
                            ) } />
                            <Route path="/buy" render={ () => (
                                <Buy
                                    product={this.state.product}
                                />
                            ) } />
                            <Route path="/sell" render={() => (
                                <Sell
                                    publishProduct={data =>
        this.publishProduct(data) }
                                />
                            ) } />
                        </div>
                    )
                }
            }
```

3. Add some CSS code to improve the design of this page, as shown in the function:

```
.sell-page
    display: grid
    flex-direction: column
    justify-items: center
    width: 50%
    margin: auto
    margin-bottom: 200px

    input, textarea
        width: 100%
        margin-bottom: 10px
```

You can see how it looks by clicking on the `Sell` button in the header, which redirects to the `/sell` URL, loading the `Sell` component.

Creating the Orders component

Add the final `Orders.js` component by going through the following steps. Try to do it yourself before seeing the solution so that you practice your skills with some `stylus` CSS to complete the design. You'll find that it takes more time than expected, but it's well worth the effort:

1. Import the required libraries, as shown in the following code:

```
import React, { Component } from 'react'
import Header from './Header'
```

2. Define the constructor with some invented orders so that you can see how it will look, as shown in the following code:

```
class Orders extends Component {
    constructor() {
        super()

        // We'll separate the completed vs the pending based on the
order state
        this.state = {
            sellOrders: [{
                id: 1,
                title: 'Classic trendy shoes',
                description: 'New unique shoes for sale',
                date: Date.now(),
                owner: '',
                price: 12,
                image:
'https://cdn.shopify.com/s/files/1/2494/8702/products/Bjakin-2018-S
ocks-Running-Shoes-for-Men-Lightweight-Sports-Sneakers-Colors-Man-
Sock-Walking-Shoes-Big_17fa0d5b-d9d9-46a0-bdea-
ac2dc17474ce_400x.jpg?v=1537755930',
                purchasedAt: Date.now(),
                state: 'completed',
            }],
            pendingSellOrdersHtml: [],
            pendingBuyOrdersHtml: [],
            completedSellOrdersHtml: [],
            completedBuyOrdersHtml: [],
        }

        this.displayOrders()
    }
```

3. We'll need a function to get users' orders by getting the data from the smart contract while also marking orders as completed. We won't implement those functions yet because we have to create the smart contract first, as shown in the following code:

```
async getUserOrders() {}

async markAsCompleted(product) {}
```

4. Add those empty functions, then create a function named `displayOrders()`, which will take the state data to output the resulting HTML. Define the arrays used inside first, as shown in the following code:

```
async displayOrders() {
    let pendingSellOrdersHtml = []
    let pendingBuyOrdersHtml = []
    let completedSellOrdersHtml = []
    let completedBuyOrdersHtml = []
}
```

5. Read the different order objects to loop through them and generate the resulting valid JSX. Classify the products based on the state of the product, as shown in the following code:

```
await this.state.sellOrders.asyncForEach(product => {
    if(product.state == 'pending') {
        pendingSellOrdersHtml.push(
            <div key={product.id} className="product">
                <img className="product-image"
src={product.image} />
                <div className="product-data">
                    <h3 className="small-product-
title">{product.title}</h3>
                    <div className="product-state">State:
{product.state}</div>
                    <div className="product-
description">{product.description.substring(0, 15) +
'...'}</div>
                    <div className="product-
price">{product.price} ETH</div>
                    <button className="small-view-button"
onClick={() => {
                        this.props.setState({product})
                        this.props.redirectTo('/product')
                    }} type="button">View</button>
                    <button className="small-completed-button"
onClick={() => {
                        this.markAsCompleted(product)
                    }} type="button">Mark as completed</button>
                </div>
            </div>
        )
```

6. If the state of the sell order is completed, push it into the `completedSellOrders` array because we want to classify the orders based on their state, as shown in the following code. Create a new HTML block because it will be slightly different, since we want to use a button to mark products as completed:

```
} else {
        completedSellOrdersHtml.push(
            <div key={product.id} className="product">
                <img className="product-image"
src={product.image} />
                <div className="product-data">
                    <h3 className="product-
title">{product.title}</h3>
                    <div className="product-state">State:
{product.state}</div>
                    <div className="product-
description">{product.description.substring(0, 15) +
'...'}</div>
                    <div className="product-
price">{product.price} ETH</div>
                    <button onClick={() => {
                        this.props.setState({product})
                        this.props.redirectTo('/product')
                    }} className="product-view"
type="button">View</button>
                </div>
            </div>
        )
    }
})
```

7. Use the same process for the `buyOrders` array to design the HTML of each product while looping through the arrays, as shown in the following code:

```
await this.state.buyOrders.asyncForEach(product => {
    let html = (
        <div key={product.id} className="product">
            <img className="product-image" src={product.image}
/>
            <div className="product-data">
                <h3 className="product-
title">{product.title}</h3>
                <div className="product-state">State:
{product.state}</div>
                <div className="product-
description">{product.description.substring(0, 15) +
'...'}</div>
```

```
                              <div className="product-price">{product.price}
            ETH</div>
                              <button onClick={() => {
                                  this.props.setState({product})
                                  this.props.redirectTo('/product')
                              }} className="product-view"
            type="button">View</button>
                      </div>
                  </div>
              )

              if(product.state == 'pending')
            pendingBuyOrdersHtml.push(html)
              else completedBuyOrdersHtml.push(html)
          })
```

8. Update the state of the component with the generated HTML objects, as shown in the following code:

```
    this.setState({pendingSellOrdersHtml, pendingBuyOrdersHtml,
    completedSellOrdersHtml, completedBuyOrdersHtml})
```

9. Create the render() function to display those generated orders, as shown in the following code:

```
 render() {
     return (
         <div>
             <Header />
             <div className="orders-page">
                 <div>
                     <h3 className="order-title">PENDING ORDERS AS A
SELLER</h3>
                     {this.state.pendingSellOrdersHtml}
                 </div>
                 <div>
                     <h3 className="order-title">PENDING ORDERS AS A
BUYER</h3>
                     {this.state.pendingBuyOrdersHtml}
                 </div>
                 <div>
                     <h3 className="order-title">COMPLETED SELL
ORDERS</h3>
                     {this.state.completedSellOrdersHtml}
                 </div>
                 <div>
                     <h3 className="order-title">COMPLETED BUY
ORDERS</h3>
```

```
                    {this.state.completedBuyOrdersHtml}
                </div>
            </div>
        </div>
    )
  }
}
```

10. Export the `Orders` component object, as shown in the following code:

```
export default Orders
```

This one is big piece of code because we added some sample order data in the state object to display a realistic view of the orders page. You can see that we added a `state` property for each product, which shows us whether the order is pending or completed. This will be set up in the smart contract. The `displayOrders` function generates the HTML objects for each type of order because we want to separate the completed and pending and buy and sell orders so that you can see all the important information. The orders will come from the `getUserOrders` function when the smart contract is implemented. Add some CSS to make it look decent. You can check out my design on the official GitHub at `https://github.com/merlox/ecommerce-dapp` inside the `src/` folder.

Finally, you will get a cool-looking orders page, as shown in the following screenshot:

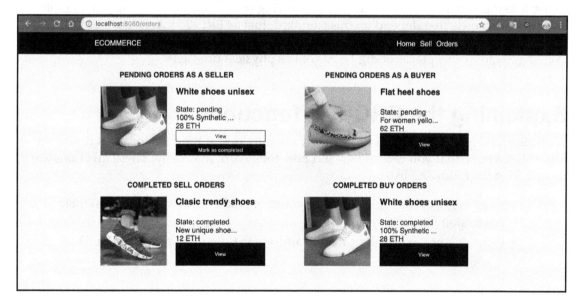

That's about it when it comes to the User Interface in React! Just to make sure, you should have the following files inside your `src/` folder once all the components are created:

- `components/`
    - `Buy.js`
    - `Header.js`
    - `Sell.js`
    - `Product.js`
    - `Home.js`
    - `Orders.js`
- `index.ejs`
- `index.js`
- `index.styl`

Understanding ERC-721 tokens

This new type of tokens is used to generate unique products in our smart contract. The ERC-721 standard has been approved by the official Ethereum team, meaning you'll be able to use it as it is for all sorts of applications, knowing that it will be compatible with tools and smart contracts that depend on this standard. Just as ERC-20 tokens gave birth to decentralized token exchanges, we can expect the creation of decentralized ERC-721 exchanges and marketplaces of digital as well as physical products.

Explaining the ERC-721 functions

To understand how ERC-721 tokens work, it's best to look at the functions that define an ERC-721 token so that you can understand how they work internally. These functions are described in the following list:

- `balanceOf(owner)`: Returns the count of all the tokens a user has in their possession for the given address.
- `ownerOf(tokenId)`: Returns the address that owns a specific token ID.

- safeTransferFrom(from, to, tokenId, data): Sends a token from one address to another after giving an allowance, just as this phrase does with ERC-20 tokens. It's called safe because if the receiver is a contract, it checks that the contract is capable of receiving ERC-721 tokens, meaning that the receiver contract has implemented the onERC721Received function so that you don't lose your tokens to a contract that can't manage these types of tokens. The data parameter can be omitted, and it simply includes additional byte information that you may want to send to the to receiver address. The from address must be the current owner, so you can use this function as a normal transfer function or as a transferFrom function (which you may be familiar with from your use of ERC-20 tokens) with for approved sending tokens to another address.

- transferFrom(from, to, tokenId): This is the same as the previous function, but it does not ensure that the receiver address, is capable of managing these types of tokens if it turns out to be a smart contract.

- approve(to, tokenId): This is used to approve a specific token to another owner so that they can use it however they want.

- setApprovalForAll(operator, approved): This is to create an allowance of all your tokens to another address, known as an operator address that can manage your entire balance. You can revoke access to a specific operator by setting the approved parameter to false.

- getApproved(tokenId): Returns the address that has an allowance for this token.

- isApprovedForAll(owner, operator): Returns true if the operator has access to all the owner's tokens.

Note how they removed the transfer function that we're familiar with from the ERC-20 specification because it simplified the process by allowing the transferFrom and safeTransferFrom functions to be used as a normal transfer or as an approved transfer, removing the need for a standard transfer function.

The _mint(owner, tokenId) and _burn(tokenId) internal functions are used to generate and delete tokens; however, they are not usable in the standard ERC721.sol smart contract because they are internal, meaning they require you to create a new contract that inherits that ERC-721 contract and implements custom mint(owner, tokenId) and burn(tokenId) functions (without the underscore) with any modifications you may need because we want to limit who can create or delete tokens.

Can you imagine everybody being able to generate tokens as they please? That would defeat the purpose of having valuable tokens, so that's why they force you to create your own minting functions with limited access, probably with an `onlyOwner` modifier. In our case, we'll allow sellers to mint new types of ERC-721 tokens for their products.

Each product in our decentralized e-commerce store will represent a unique ERC-721; that's why we don't want to add multiple quantities per product, because we'd have to create several unique instances of ERC-721. On another note, NFT means that each token is unique in its differentiating properties. Compared to ERC-20, where each token is the same, the ERC-721 standard is meant to be used for unique items, such as household products, handmade products, art, or unique digital assets, such as skins for games. What's interesting is that you can combine both standards as you see fit to create unique tokens, while also being able to generate multiple instances of the same one.

The ERC-721 smart contract

Now that you understand how these types of NFTs work, let's take a look at the ERC-721 contract interface. The implementation is available on GitHub at `https://github.com/merlox/ecommerce-dapp/blob/master/contracts/ERC721.sol`, since the full code is too large to display here:

```solidity
pragma solidity ^0.5.0;

contract IERC721{
    event Transfer(address indexed from, address indexed to, uint256 indexed tokenId);
    event Approval(address indexed owner, address indexed approved, uint256 indexed tokenId);
    event ApprovalForAll(address indexed owner, address indexed operator, bool approved);
    function balanceOf(address owner) public view returns (uint256 balance);
    function ownerOf(uint256 tokenId) public view returns (address owner);
    function approve(address to, uint256 tokenId) public;
    function getApproved(uint256 tokenId) public view returns (address operator);
    function setApprovalForAll(address operator, bool _approved) public;
    function isApprovedForAll(address owner, address operator) public view returns (bool);
    function transferFrom(address from, address to, uint256 tokenId) public;
    function safeTransferFrom(address from, address to, uint256 tokenId) public;
    function safeTransferFrom(address from, address to, uint256 tokenId,
```

```
bytes memory data) public;
}
```

This contract is pretty similar to the ERC-20 contract because the basic idea behind them is the same. This contract is used to generate many unique tokens with a mining function that has to be implemented separately, since you want to control who's able to create tokens and who's able to destroy them.

Create a file named `ERC721.sol` inside your `contracts/` folder and add that code, as we'll use it in a moment. We'll create a contract that inherits the ERC-721 smart contract to implement the `mint()` function, since it's not accessible by the default ERC-721 implementation. Create a new file named `Ecommerce.sol` and import the `ERC721.sol` contract there, using the following code:

```
pragma solidity ^0.5.0;

import './ERC721.sol';
```

The Solidity version doesn't matter as long as it's the same functionality. Create a custom implementation of your own ERC-721 smart contract that inherits this one, like so:

```
pragma solidity ^0.5.0;

import './ERC721.sol';

/// @notice The Ecommerce Token that implements the ERC721 token with mint
function
/// @author Merunas Grincalaitis <merunasgrincalaitis@gmail.com>
contract EcommerceToken is ERC721 {
    address public ecommerce;
    bool public isEcommerceSet = false;
    /// @notice To generate a new token for the specified address
    /// @param _to The receiver of this new token
    /// @param _tokenId The new token id, must be unique
    function mint(address _to, uint256 _tokenId) public {
        require(msg.sender == ecommerce, 'Only the ecommerce contract can
mint new tokens');
        _mint(_to, _tokenId);
    }

    /// @notice To set the ecommerce smart contract address
    function setEcommerce(address _ecommerce) public {
        require(!isEcommerceSet, 'The ecommerce address can only be set
once');
        require(_ecommerce != address(0), 'The ecommerce address cannot be
empty');
        isEcommerceSet = true;
```

```
        ecommerce = _ecommerce;
    }
}
```

This token contract will only allow the e-commerce contract to generate new tokens, which will be moved to the buyer after the purchase is completed; the `setEcommerce` function must be set up before you will be able to mint tokens.

Developing the e-commerce smart contract

Developing a smart contract that interacts with ERC-721 tokens is simple, because we only have to make sure that users have a token ID associated with their products. Users will be able to interact with their tokens independently if they wish to do so. For our marketplace, we'll focus on creating the buy and sell functions to create and burn tokens. As usual, we'll also create multiple getters to extract the data from the smart contract for the user interface.

Let's start to create the e-commerce contract, which will have all the market logic in the same file, since it doesn't take up that much space:

1. Define the variables needed for the smart contract, starting with the structs that you'll need, as shown in the following code:

```
/// @notice The main ecommerce contract to buy and sell ERC-721
tokens representing physical or digital products because we are
dealing with non-fungible tokens, there will be only 1 stock per
product
/// @author Merunas Grincalaitis <merunasgrincalaitis@gmail.com>
contract Ecommerce {
    struct Product {
        uint256 id;
        string title;
        string description;
        uint256 date;
        address payable owner;
        uint256 price;
        string image;
    }
    struct Order {
        uint256 id;
        address buyer;
        string nameSurname;
        string lineOneDirection;
        string lineTwoDirection;
        bytes32 city;
        bytes32 stateRegion;
```

```
uint256 postalCode;
bytes32 country;
uint256 phone;
string state; // Either 'pending', 'completed'
}
```

2. Add the mappings, arrays, variables, and constructors, as shown in the following code:

```
// Seller address => products
mapping(address => Order[]) public pendingSellerOrders; // The
products waiting to be fulfilled by the seller, used by sellers to
check which orders have to be filled
// Buyer address => products
mapping(address => Order[]) public pendingBuyerOrders; // The
products that the buyer purchased waiting to be sent
mapping(address => Order[]) public completedOrders;
// Product id => product
mapping(uint256 => Product) public productById;
// Product id => order
mapping(uint256 => Order) public orderById;
Product[] public products;
uint256 public lastId;
address public token;

/// @notice To setup the address of the ERC-721 token to use
for this contract
/// @param _token The token address
constructor(address _token) public {
    token = _token;
}
}
```

We have to set up the variables first by starting with the structs, in this case, Product and Order. Each order will reference a particular product through the ID, which will be the same in both cases, meaning that each product will have a corresponding order with the same ID. There will be mappings for pending orders that have not been fulfilled yet and other mappings for those that have been completed so that we have a reference of completed orders. The constructor will receive the token address so that the e-commerce contract can create new tokens.

Creating the publish function

Create a function to publish new products so that users can sell products by themselves, using the following code. The image URL will be where the image is located:

```
/// @notice To publish a product as a seller
/// @param _title The title of the product
/// @param _description The description of the product
/// @param _price The price of the product in ETH
/// @param _image The image URL of the product
function publishProduct(string memory _title, string memory _description,
uint256 _price, string memory _image) public {
    require(bytes(_title).length > 0, 'The title cannot be empty');
    require(bytes(_description).length > 0, 'The description cannot be
empty');
    require(_price > 0, 'The price cannot be empty');
    require(bytes(_image).length > 0, 'The image cannot be empty');

    Product memory p = Product(lastId, _title, _description, now,
msg.sender, _price, _image);
    products.push(p);
    productById[lastId] = p;
    EcommerceToken(token).mint(address(this), lastId); // Create a new
token for this product which will be owned by this contract until sold
    lastId++;
}
```

This function will check the parameters so that they are set up while also minting a new token.

Creating the buy function

Now that users can publish products to sell, you can work on the buy function to purchase products:

```
/// @notice To buy a new product, note that the seller must authorize this
contract to manage the token
/// @param _id The id of the product to buy
/// @param _nameSurname The name and surname of the buyer
/// @param _lineOneDirection The first line for the user address
/// @param _lineTwoDirection The second, optional user address line
/// @param _city Buyer's city
/// @param _stateRegion The state or region where the buyer lives
/// @param _postalCode The postal code of his location
/// @param _country Buyer's country
/// @param _phone The optional phone number for the shipping company
```

```
function buyProduct(uint256 _id, string memory _nameSurname, string memory
_lineOneDirection, string memory _lineTwoDirection, bytes32 _city, bytes32
_stateRegion, uint256 _postalCode, bytes32 _country, uint256 _phone) public
payable {
    // The line 2 address and phone are optional, the rest are mandatory
    require(bytes(_nameSurname).length > 0, 'The name and surname must be
set');
    require(bytes(_lineOneDirection).length > 0, 'The line one direction
must be set');
    require(_city.length > 0, 'The city must be set');
    require(_stateRegion.length > 0, 'The state or region must be set');
    require(_postalCode > 0, 'The postal code must be set');
    require(_country > 0, 'The country must be set');

    Product memory p = productById[_id];
    require(bytes(p.title).length > 0, 'The product must exist to be
purchased');
    Order memory newOrder = Order(_id, msg.sender, _nameSurname,
_lineOneDirection, _lineTwoDirection, _city, _stateRegion, _postalCode,
_country, _phone, 'pending');
    require(msg.value >= p.price, "The payment must be larger or equal than
the products price");

    // Delete the product from the array of products
    for(uint256 i = 0; i < products.length; i++) {
        if(products[i].id == _id) {
            Product memory lastElement = products[products.length - 1];
            products[i] = lastElement;
            products.length--;
        }
    }

    // Return the excess ETH sent by the buyer
    if(msg.value > p.price) msg.sender.transfer(msg.value - p.price);
    pendingSellerOrders[p.owner].push(newOrder);
    pendingBuyerOrders[msg.sender].push(newOrder);
    orderById[_id] = newOrder;
    EcommerceToken(token).transferFrom(address(this), msg.sender, _id); //
Transfer the product token to the new owner
    p.owner.transfer(p.price);
}
```

First of all, the `buy` function must be payable so that users can send the required price in Ethereum, which will be sent to the seller without any fees besides the gas costs. When purchasing a product, the buyer needs to send all the address details so that the seller can process the shipping; that's why there are so many parameters in the `buy` function where the phone number and the second address line is optional. The `products` array deletes the product so that the user interface displays the most recent ones. A new `order` struct instance will be created and the order will be added to the pending mappings.

Creating the mark orders function

After the orders are created, we need a way to tell the customer that the product has been shipped. We can do so with a new function, called `markOrderCompleted` as shown in the following code:

```
/// @notice To mark an order as completed
/// @param _id The id of the order which is the same for the product id
function markOrderCompleted(uint256 _id) public {
    Order memory order = orderById[_id];
    Product memory product = productById[_id];
    require(product.owner == msg.sender, 'Only the seller can mark the
order as completed');
    order.state = 'completed';

    // Delete the seller order from the array of pending orders
    for(uint256 i = 0; i < pendingSellerOrders[product.owner].length; i++)
{
        if(pendingSellerOrders[product.owner][i].id == _id) {
            Order memory lastElement =
orderById[pendingSellerOrders[product.owner].length - 1];
            pendingSellerOrders[product.owner][i] = lastElement;
            pendingSellerOrders[product.owner].length--;
        }
    }
    // Delete the seller order from the array of pending orders
    for(uint256 i = 0; i < pendingBuyerOrders[order.buyer].length; i++) {
        if(pendingBuyerOrders[order.buyer][i].id == order.id) {
            Order memory lastElement =
orderById[pendingBuyerOrders[order.buyer].length - 1];
            pendingBuyerOrders[order.buyer][i] = lastElement;
            pendingBuyerOrders[order.buyer].length--;
        }
    }
    completedOrders[order.buyer].push(order);
    orderById[_id] = order;
}
```

Then, create a `.secret` file with your seed phrase and create a file named
`2_deploy_contracts.js` in your `migrations/` folder to tell Truffle what needs to be
done when deploying the contracts, mainly for setting up constructor parameters, as shown
in the following code. Truffle will fail without this file when deploying:

```
const Token = artifacts.require("./EcommerceToken.sol")
const Ecommerce = artifacts.require("./Ecommerce.sol")
let token

module.exports = function(deployer, network, accounts) {
    deployer.deploy(
        Token,
        { gas: 8e6 }
    ).then(tokenInstance => {
        token = tokenInstance
        return deployer.deploy(Ecommerce, token.address, {
            gas: 8e6
        })
    }).then(async ecommerce => {
        await token.contract.methods.setEcommerce(ecommerce.address).send({
            from: accounts[0]
        })
        console.log('Is set?', await
token.contract.methods.isEcommerceSet().call())
        console.log('Deployed both!')
    })
}
```

Your migrations folder should have the `1_initial_migrations.js` and
`2_deploy_contracts.js` files. The syntax is a bit confusing, but what's important is that
we're using the `deployer.deploy()` function, which returns a promise to get the token
address and run the `setEcommerce()` function from the token contract so that we can start
using the contracts right away. Note how we have access to the `accounts` by adding that
third parameter to the main function; this is required to run the `setEcommerce()` function
with the first Ethereum address. Finally, I'm checking whether the e-commerce contract has
been properly set up in the token by calling the `isEcommerceSet()` public variable from
the token.

Run the following deployment command:

```
truffle deploy --network ropsten --reset
```

If you want to test that everything runs properly without waiting for `ropsten`, you can spin up a `ganache-cli` private blockchain and deploy it there instantly by running the following command line:

```
truffle deploy --network development --reset
```

After deploying your contract, you'll find the address and the ABI inside the `build/contract/Ecommerce.json` folder.

Finishing the dApp

To complete the dApp, we have to modify the React code to integrate the smart contract changes while also making sense of the way we receive the information from the blockchain using the right methods to display that data properly. Before this, make sure that your contracts are deployed to `ropsten`, as shown in the previous steps.

Setting up the contract instance

Because we are using webpack, we have access to all the files inside the source folder from the React files, which means that we can get the deployed smart contract ABI and the deployed contract address, as well as the required parameters to create a contract instance. This is shown in the following code:

```
import React from 'react'
import ReactDOM from 'react-dom'
import MyWeb3 from 'web3'
import { BrowserRouter, Route, withRouter } from 'react-router-dom'
import Home from './components/Home'
import Product from './components/Product'
import Sell from './components/Sell'
import Header from './components/Header'
import Buy from './components/Buy'
import Orders from './components/Orders'

import './index.styl'
import ABI from '../build/contracts/Ecommerce.json'
```

The `build` folder will be created when you successfully deploy your smart contract with Truffle, and it contains important smart contract parameters that we may need for our dApp. Modify your setup function to have access to the contract object globally, making things easier for the external components. I've highlighted the contract instance in the following code for you to find the changes:

```
async setup() {
    // Create the contract instance
    window.myWeb3 = new MyWeb3(ethereum)
    try {
        await ethereum.enable();
    } catch (error) {
        console.error('You must approve this dApp to interact with it')
    }
    window.user = (await myWeb3.eth.getAccounts())[0]
    window.contract = new myWeb3.eth.Contract(ABI.abi,
ABI.networks['3'].address, {
        from: user
    })
    await this.getLatestProducts(9)
    await this.displayProducts()
}
```

Note how we've reduced the `state` object to a few elements without any dummy data because we'll use the real smart contract data. The contract instance is created by using `abi` and the contract address, which is also contained in the build JSON file. At the end of the setup function, we're calling the `getLatestProducts()` and `displayProducts()` functions, which, as you will see in a moment, are necessary to get the data from the contract while displaying it properly.

Updating the index file

Now that we have a working contract instance, we can work on the required functionality for the index file so that we are keeping the functionality contained inside smaller components as shown in the following code:

1. Implement the `displayProducts()` function to display products sorted by properties:

```
async displayProducts() {
    let productsHtml = []
    if(this.state.products.length == 0) {
        productsHtml = (
            <div key="0" className="center">There are no products
```

```
yet...</div>
        )
    }
    await this.state.products.asyncForEach(product => {
        productsHtml.push((
            <div key={product.id} className="product">
                <img className="product-image" src={product.image}
/>
                <div className="product-data">
                    <h3 className="product-
title">{product.title}</h3>
                    <div className="product-
description">{product.description.substring(0, 50) + '...'}</div>
                    <div className="product-price">{product.price}
ETH</div>
                    <button onClick={() => {
                        this.setState({product})
                        this.redirectTo('/product')
                    }} className="product-view"
type="button">View</button>
                </div>
            </div>
        ))
    })
    this.setState({productsHtml})
}
```

2. Add the updated redirect function, as shown in the following code:

```
redirectTo(location) {
    this.props.history.push({
        pathname: location
    })
}
```

3. Implement the function to get products from the smart contract by taking the length of those products and looping each one of them:

```
async getLatestProducts(amount) {
    // Get the product ids
    const productsLength = parseInt(await
contract.methods.getProductsLength().call())
    let products = []
    let condition = (amount > productsLength) ? 0 : productsLength
- amount

    // Loop through all of them one by one
    for(let i = productsLength; i > condition; i--) {
```

```
        let product = await contract.methods.products(i - 1).call()
        product = {
            id: parseInt(product.id),
            title: product.title,
            date: parseInt(product.date),
            description: product.description,
            image: product.image,
            owner: product.owner,
            price: myWeb3.utils.fromWei(String(product.price)),
        }
        products.push(product)
    }
    this.setState({products})
}
```

In our home page, we'll display the latest products added by other sellers so that you can start buying straight away. For this reason, we'll use `getLatestProducts()`, which receives the number of products to display as the parameter while getting the data from the blockchain. How do we get all the product data without a `getter` function? Well, the process goes like this:

1. We get the length of the array of products. We use the `getProductsLength()` function because we can't get the length of an array without a proper `getter` function.

2. Once we know how many products are available in the smart contract, we loop through that size to run the `products()` function, which is available because our products array is public, meaning that it has a `getter` function automatically created for it. Public arrays have to be accessed one by one; that's why we're using a reverse `for` loop.

3. We need a reverse loop to get the latest products first. How the `for` loop works because it could be the case that we run out of product to display, given that we start with exactly zero products when we want to display 9, indicated at the end of the setup function. That's why we created the `condition` variable – it checks whether the amount of products requested to display is actually available; if not, we simply get all the products available, however few they are.

On the other hand, once the `state` object has been populated with the products contained in our smart contract, we use the `displayProducts()` function, which takes care of generating the proper HTML needed for each product while updating the `productsHtml` state array.

Finally, we have the `render` function, which has been slightly modified for these new updated components, as shown in the following code:

```
render() {
    return (
        <div>
            <Route path="/product" render={() => (
                <Product
                    product={this.state.product}
                    redirectTo={location => this.redirectTo(location)}
                />
            )}/>
            <Route path="/sell" render={() => (
                <Sell
                    publishProduct={data => this.publishProduct(data)}
                />
            )}/>
            <Route path="/buy" render={() => (
                <Buy
                    product={this.state.product}
                />
            )} />
            <Route path="/orders" render={() => (
                <Orders
                    setState={state => this.setState(state)}
                    redirectTo={location => this.redirectTo(location)}
                />
            )} />
            <Route path="/" exact render={() => (
                <Home
                    productsHtml={this.state.productsHtml}
                />
            )} />
        </div>
    )
}
```

After making the implementation changes, take a look at the entire index file, available on GitHub at `https://github.com/merlox/ecommerce-dapp`.

Updating the Buy component

Let's move on to the `Buy.js` file since the `Home.js` and `Product.js` components will stay as they are without any required modifications, considering that the product data will have the same expected format. In the `Buy` component, we need to add a function to purchase products, which will send the transaction to the smart contract, here's that function:

```
async buyProduct() {
    await contract.methods.buyProduct(this.props.product.id,
    this.state.nameSurname, this.state.lineOneDirection,
    this.state.lineTwoDirection, this.bytes32(this.state.city),
    this.bytes32(this.state.stateRegion), this.state.postalCode,
    this.bytes32(this.state.country), this.state.phone).send({
        value: myWeb3.utils.toWei(this.props.product.price)
    })
}

bytes32(name) {
    return myWeb3.utils.fromAscii(name)
}
```

The `buyProduct()` function takes all the state data regarding the user address and sends the transaction with the required product price as the transaction's payment. The `bytes32` function is required to convert some string values to bytes32, saving gas costs. That's the entire change required for this particular component. Check the final implementation of the entire component on the updated GitHub at: `https://github.com/merlox/ecommerce-dapp/blob/master/src/components/Buy.js`.

Updating the Sell component

Let's work on creating the required functionality for the `Sell.js` function so that you can start adding purchasable products to the marketplace. In this case, we need to add a function that will call the `publishProduct()` function from the smart contract. Here's how the updated `publish` function looks:

```
async publishProduct() {
    if(this.state.title.length == 0) return alert('You must set the title
before publishing the product')
    if(this.state.description.length == 0) return alert('You must set the
```

```
description before publishing the product')
    if(this.state.price.length == 0) return alert('You must set the price
before publishing the product')
    if(this.state.image.length == 0) return alert('You must set the image
URL before publishing the product')

    await contract.methods.publishProduct(this.state.title,
this.state.description, myWeb3.utils.toWei(this.state.price),
this.state.image).send()
}
```

Note how we check for all the required parameters to let the user know when something's missing. You could add some additional checks to make sure that the image URL provided is actually a valid picture that can be displayed on the marketplace. I'll leave that up to you. It shouldn't take you more than 10 minutes, and it's a great exercise to practice your JavaScript skills.

The final updated version is available on GitHub at: `https://github.com/merlox/ecommerce-dapp/blob/master/src/components/Sell.js`.

Updating the Orders component

Now let's update the `Orders.js` component, which is the most elaborate component, given that we have to generate multiple products. Let's start by creating a function to get all the orders related to the current user, as shown in the following code:

```
async getOrders(amount) {
    const pendingSellerOrdersLength = parseInt(await
contract.methods.getOrdersLength(this.bytes32('seller'), user).call())
    const pendingBuyerOrdersLength = parseInt(await
contract.methods.getOrdersLength(this.bytes32('buyer'), user).call())
    const completedOrdersLength = parseInt(await
contract.methods.getOrdersLength(this.bytes32('completed'), user).call())

    const conditionSeller = (amount > pendingSellerOrdersLength) ? 0 :
pendingSellerOrdersLength - amount
    const conditionBuyer = (amount > pendingBuyerOrdersLength) ? 0 :
pendingBuyerOrdersLength - amount
    const conditionCompleted = (amount > completedOrdersLength) ? 0 :
completedOrdersLength - amount

    let pendingSellerOrders = []
    let pendingBuyerOrders = []
    let completedOrders = []
```

```
    // In reverse to get the most recent orders first
    for(let i = pendingSellerOrdersLength; i > conditionSeller; i--) {
        let order = await contract.methods.pendingSellerOrders(user, i -
1).call()
        pendingSellerOrders.push(await this.generateOrderObject(order))
    }

    for(let i = pendingBuyerOrdersLength; i > conditionBuyer; i--) {
        let order = await contract.methods.pendingBuyerOrders(user, i -
1).call()
        pendingBuyerOrders.push(await this.generateOrderObject(order))
    }

    for(let i = completedOrdersLength; i > conditionCompleted; i--) {
        let order = await contract.methods.completedOrders(user, i -
1).call()
        completedOrders.push(await this.generateOrderObject(order))
    }

    this.setState({pendingSellerOrders, pendingBuyerOrders,
completedOrders})
}
```

We're generating three different arrays by following the same procedure we used for the products in the index file. We have the same condition operators but for different types of orders. We then run a `for` loop for each of the desired orders in reverse so that we get the most recent ones. Because the data returned by the smart contract is a bit messy, we've created a function named `generateOrderObject()`, which receives an order object and returns a cleaned object with converted hexadecimal values at that have been converted to readable text. Here's how it looks:

```
async generateOrderObject(order) {
    let productAssociated = await
contract.methods.productById(parseInt(order.id)).call()
    order = {
        id: parseInt(order.id),
        buyer: order.buyer,
        nameSurname: order.nameSurname,
        lineOneDirection: order.lineOneDirection,
        lineTwoDirection: order.lineTwoDirection,
        city: myWeb3.utils.toUtf8(order.city),
        stateRegion: myWeb3.utils.toUtf8(order.stateRegion),
        postalCode: String(order.postalCode),
        country: myWeb3.utils.toUtf8(order.country),
        phone: String(order.phone),
        state: order.state,
        date: String(productAssociated.date),
```

```
                description: productAssociated.description,
                image: productAssociated.image,
                owner: productAssociated.owner,
                price: myWeb3.utils.fromWei(String(productAssociated.price)),
                title: productAssociated.title,
            }
        return order
    }
```

It's important to separate repetitive code in external functions to keep your code neat. As you can see, this function converts the byte types of variables to a readable `utf8` string while also converting BigNumbers to integers so that they can be displayed in our user interface properly.

After updating the state object with the recent orders, we can create a function to generate the proper HTML for each element by going through the following steps:

1. Set up the required array variables, which in this case is simpler, since we want to create three blocks for the different types of orders:

```
async displayOrders() {
        let pendingSellerOrdersHtml = []
        let pendingBuyerOrdersHtml = []
        let completedOrdersHtml = []
```

2. In case there aren't orders for each type of order, we want to display a message to let the user know that there aren't orders by using the following code:

```
  if(this.state.pendingSellerOrders.length == 0) {
        pendingSellerOrdersHtml.push((
            <div key="0" className="center">There are no seller orders
yet...</div>
        ))
    }
    if(this.state.pendingBuyerOrders.length == 0) {
        pendingBuyerOrdersHtml.push((
            <div key="0" className="center">There are no buyer orders
yet...</div>
        ))
    }
    if(this.state.completedOrders.length == 0) {
        completedOrdersHtml.push((
            <div key="0" className="center">There are no completed orders
yet...</div>
        ))
    }
```

3. Update the pending orders by adding an address section using the following code:

```
await this.state.pendingSellerOrders.asyncForEach(order => {
    pendingSellerOrdersHtml.push(
        <div key={order.id} className="product">
            <img className="product-image" src={order.image} />
            <div className="product-data">
                <h3 className="small-product-
title">{order.title}</h3>
                <div className="product-state">State:
{order.state}</div>
                <div className="product-
description">{order.description.substring(0, 15) + '...'}</div>
                <div className="product-price">{order.price}
ETH</div>
                <button className="small-view-button"
onClick={() => {
                    this.props.setState({product: order})
                    this.props.redirectTo('/product')
                }} type="button">View</button>
                <button className="small-completed-button"
onClick={() => {
                    this.markAsCompleted(order.id)
                }} type="button">Mark as completed</button>
            </div>
```

4. Right under the product data, add the address information so sellers can fulfill those orders using the following code:

```
<div className="order-address">
    <div>Id</div>
    <div className="second-column"
title={order.id}>{order.id}</div>
    <div>Buyer</div>
    <div className="second-column"
title={order.buyer}>{order.buyer}</div>
    <div>Name and surname</div>
    <div className="second-column"
title={order.nameSurname}>{order.nameSurname}</div>
    <div>Line 1 direction</div>
    <div className="second-column"
title={order.lineOneDirection}>{order.lineOneDirection}</div>
    <div>Line 2 direction</div>
    <div className="second-column"
title={order.lineTwoDirection}>{order.lineTwoDirection}</div>
    <div>City</div>
    <div className="second-column"
```

```
                    title={order.city}>{order.city}</div>
                        <div>State or region</div>
                        <div className="second-column"
         title={order.stateRegion}>{order.stateRegion}</div>
                        <div>Postal code</div>
                        <div className="second-
         column">{order.postalCode}</div>
                        <div>Country</div>
                        <div className="second-column"
         title={order.country}>{order.country}</div>
                        <div>Phone</div>
                        <div className="second-
         column">{order.phone}</div>
                        <div>State</div>
                        <div className="second-column"
         title={order.state}>{order.state}</div>
                    </div>
                </div>
            )
        })
```

5. We do the same thing with the pending buyer orders: we display the product data first, using the following code:

```
await this.state.pendingBuyerOrders.asyncForEach(order => {
        pendingBuyerOrdersHtml.push(
            <div key={order.id} className="product">
                <img className="product-image" src={order.image} />
                <div className="product-data">
                    <h3 className="product-
         title">{order.title}</h3>
                    <div className="product-state">State:
         {order.state}</div>
                    <div className="product-
         description">{order.description.substring(0, 15) + '...'}</div>
                    <div className="product-price">{order.price}
         ETH</div>

                    <button onClick={() => {
                        this.props.setState({product: order})
                        this.props.redirectTo('/product')
                    }} className="product-view"
         type="button">View</button>
                </div>
```

6. The address data will be exactly the same, so copy and paste it into this pending buyer orders loop. We're using the same code because we need to update the appearance of each HTML block, but the class names have to be different. Add the `for` loop to the completed orders array using the following code:

```
await this.state.completedOrders.asyncForEach(order => {
    completedOrdersHtml.push(
        <div key={order.id} className="product">
            <img className="product-image" src={order.image} />
            <div className="product-data">
                <h3 className="product-
title">{order.title}</h3>
                <div className="product-state">State:
{order.state}</div>
                <div className="product-
description">{order.description.substring(0, 15) + '...'}</div>
                <div className="product-price">{order.price}
ETH</div>
                <button onClick={() => {
                    this.props.setState({product: order})
                    this.props.redirectTo('/product')
                }} className="product-view"
type="button">View</button>
            </div>
```

7. Paste the address block right under the product data. Update the state of this component with the `setState()` method:

```
this.setState({pendingSellerOrdersHtml, pendingBuyerOrdersHtml,
completedOrdersHtml})
```

It's a big function because we have repetitive functionality for the sake of keeping it simple. We have three loops for the three order arrays, so that we can put the order information at the user's disposal. Nothing too fancy, just the data in a clean design. We're adding that data to the `state` object so that we can display it easily.

8. Create a `setup()` function to run both functions when the component loads, as shown in the following code:

```
bytes32(name) {
    return myWeb3.utils.fromAscii(name)
}

async setup() {
    await this.getOrders(5)
    await this.displayOrders()
}
```

9. In this case, we're requesting five orders per type, as we don't want to overwhelm the user with information – this is easily changeable to your preferences. You can even add a slider in the UI so that the user changes how many items are displayed. The `render()` function has also been updated to reflect the buyer's address data, as shown in the following code:

```
render() {
    return (
        <div>
            <Header />
            <div className="orders-page">
                <div>
                    <h3 className="order-title">PENDING ORDERS
AS A SELLER</h3>
                        {this.state.pendingSellerOrdersHtml}
                    </div>

                <div>
                    <h3 className="order-title">PENDING ORDERS
AS A BUYER</h3>
                        {this.state.pendingBuyerOrdersHtml}
                    </div>

                <div className="completed-orders-container">
                    <h3 className="order-title">COMPLETED
ORDERS</h3>
                        {this.state.completedOrdersHtml}
                    </div>
                </div>
            </div>
        )
    }
```

That's the complete set of changes for the `Orders` component. Take a look at the updated implementation in the official GitHub link at: `https://github.com/merlox/ecommerce-dapp/blob/master/src/components/Orders.js`.

You can find the updated CSS code at `https://github.com/merlox/ecommerce-dapp/blob/master/src/index.styl`, where you'll get the exact same design.

That's the entire e-commerce dApp for you! Here's how it looks, just so you can see the potential of this simple yet capable application:

Remember to deploy your smart contract to `ropsten` and run `npm run dev` to start the webpack server so that you can interact with it. This is a prototype of what can be done in Ethereum in the e-commerce department; it's up to you to build upon this idea now that you understand how the smart contract interacts with the user interface.

Be sure to check out this chapter's code on GitHub link at: `https://github.com/merlox/ecommerce-dapp`.

Summary

In this chapter, you began by learning about the potential of using ERC-721 tokens to create a marketplace of unique products using decentralized smart contract technology so that you can easily manage NFTs created by users freely. Then you built a clean interface to display the most important data so that users have a comfortable place in which to interact with the underlying smart contract. Next, you built the smart contract by learning how NFT tokens work, including all of their functions. You deployed your own version of the ERC-721 standard to then create the e-commerce smart contract that contained the logic required to publish products for the public so that others can purchase them with real Ethereum. Finally, you put everything together by creating the necessary functions to interact with the smart contract on the React user interface.

In the next chapter, we'll go further by building a decentralized bank and lending platform that implements complex smart-contract systems to guarantee that people have access to a reserve of secure funds, with a user interface for them to interact with it.

Other Books You May Enjoy

If you enjoyed this book, you may be interested in these other books by Packt:

Ethereum Cookbook
Manoj P R

ISBN: 9781789133998

- Efficiently write smart contracts in Ethereum
- Build scalable distributed applications and deploy them
- Use tools and frameworks to develop, deploy, and test your application
- Use block explorers such as Etherscan to find a specific transaction
- Create your own tokens, initial coin offerings (ICOs), and games
- Understand various security flaws in smart contracts in order to avoid them

Ethereum Projects for Beginners
Kenny Vaneetvelde

ISBN: 9781789537406

- Develop your ideas fast and efficiently using the Ethereum blockchain
- Make writing and deploying smart contracts easy and manageable
- Work with private data in blockchain applications
- Handle large files in blockchain applications
- Ensure your decentralized applications are safe
- Explore how Ethereum development frameworks work
- Create your own cryptocurrency or token on the Ethereum blockchain
- Make sure your cryptocurrency is ERC20-compliant to launch an ICO

Leave a review - let other readers know what you think

Please share your thoughts on this book with others by leaving a review on the site that you bought it from. If you purchased the book from Amazon, please leave us an honest review on this book's Amazon page. This is vital so that other potential readers can see and use your unbiased opinion to make purchasing decisions, we can understand what our customers think about our products, and our authors can see your feedback on the title that they have worked with Packt to create. It will only take a few minutes of your time, but is valuable to other potential customers, our authors, and Packt. Thank you!

Index